The Counterinsurgency Era:
U.S. Doctrine and Performance

The Counterinsurgency Era: U.S. Doctrine and Performance

1950 to the Present

★ ★ ★

Douglas S. Blaufarb

THE FREE PRESS
A Division of Macmillan Publishing Co., Inc.
NEW YORK

Collier Macmillan Publishers
LONDON

The Free Press
A Division of Macmillan Publishing Co., Inc.
866 Third Avenue, New York, N.Y. 10022

Collier Macmillan Canada, Ltd.

Library of Congress Catalog Card Number: 77–72692

Printed in the United States of America

printing number
1 2 3 4 5 6 7 8 9 10

Library of Congress Cataloging in Publication Data

Blaufarb, Douglas S
   The counterinsurgency era.

   Bibliography: p.
   Includes index.
   1. Counterinsurgency--Case studies. 2. United
States--Military policy. 3. Asia, Southeastern--Politics
and government. 4. United States--Foreign relations--
Asia, Southeastern. 5. Asia, Southeastern--Foreign
relations--United States. I. Title.
U241.B53   355.02'184   77-72692
ISBN 0-02-903700-X

To the young men who went out knowing
so little . . .
And quickly learned and taught much of
what is written here . . .
And especially to those who did not make
it back . . .
This book is dedicated.

Contents

★ ★ ★

Foreword

★ ★ ★

This is an extraordinarily honest and measured book, drawn from long first-hand experience, on a difficult subject ordinarily discussed in journalistic superficialities, professional abstractions, or polemics. It will stand, I think, as a major contribution to the history of the cold war period that began about 1950, ran till the late 1960s, and had its epilogue in Vietnam in the debacle of 1975.

I first met Douglas Blaufarb in the summer of 1953, at the height of the inquisition being conducted by Senator Joseph McCarthy into the State Department, the U.S. Information Agency, the Army, and even, for a later brief moment, the Central Intelligence Agency, in which Blaufarb and I both worked. What brought us together was that Roy Cohn, McCarthy's infamous minion, had taken after a man in USIA who had worked with Doug in the wartime Office of War Information and was also an old friend of mine. This man had written to each of us separately. Such was the fear then infecting the environment that our meeting was held outside our separate offices, in a car parked near the Lincoln Memorial. There we introduced ourselves, sat together and tried to piece out ways to help. Momentarily (through Senator Mike Mansfield, for whom our friend had worked) the rot was stopped, but in the end the political head of USIA succumbed to McCarthy's pressure and yet another victim walked the plank. Although he found his way in private life, it was always a second best, for he was a man who cared passionately, as we did, about the work of government and the role of the United States in the world.

I mention the episode not merely because it is a poignant memory bespeaking a time of shame, but because it makes clear that the author of this book is not to be confused for a moment with that small minority of

CIA employees typified by the unfortunate Mr. E. Howard Hunt, men of such passion and anti-Communist sentiment that they would stop at very little. Doug Blaufarb was, and remains today, a mainstream 1930s-vintage liberal, who went to war with total conviction against Nazism and after the war saw enough of the same dangers from Communism to enlist in the covert side of the CIA, serving it faithfully until his retirement in 1970. To him, as to a great many others in government service who thought in the same way, the preservation of liberal values, for America and other nations, required the use of the full range of U.S. power, including if necessary its more shady applications. That the balancing of the two might involve ambiguity—as it has throughout history—was nothing strange to him, and the professional in Douglas Blaufarb keeps him from any trace of hand-wringing. But the tension between liberal values and the apparent needs of power in dealing with the enemies of those values is present throughout this book and expressed in a hundred ways and examples.

Nowhere, of course, was that tension more evident than in the area of government action christened, in the early 1960s, "counterinsurgency." Although the term was coined by John and Robert Kennedy (or those close to them), in fact—as Blaufarb makes clear in the two particularly good opening chapters—both the perceptions and the practices announced with such fanfare in 1961–62 had ample precedent in the 1950s. The term "indirect aggression" appears in the Southeast Asian Treaty of 1954, and I can personally recall being the note-taker at several high-level meetings in 1956 that bemoaned the problem, thought of it in worldwide terms, and recognized how little of the American military posture (especially but not only in the days of "massive retaliation") was relevant to it. The experiences of Greece and the Philippines were still very fresh in people's minds, and Malaya an ongoing example. Blaufarb gives excellent summaries of all three, rightly underscoring what seemed at the time their "lesson": that the proper kind of outside help could make an important if not decisive contribution to eventual success in beating back a Communist insurgency—that, in short, the key existed if it could be found and turned. In *The Ugly American,* a best seller of the late 1950s, the twin heroes were a colonel patterned on Edward Lansdale, and an agricultural technician, both good and effective, who gave the book its title. Later, of course, that title was turned on its head.

Yet, for all this 1950s background, Blaufarb is clearly right in stressing the input of the Kennedy years. His third chapter is by all odds the best and most balanced account I have seen of the doctrines that were explicitly developed in the early 1960s—by Walt Rostow and Roger Hilsman especially—their limitations, and the early forebodings felt by some, notably Alexis Johnson, who had lived and worked for long periods within Asian societies. There was indeed an evangelical and overconfident flavor to the period, and it was reflected particularly in the Interdepartmental Seminar, fully described by Blaufarb, a graduate of the first class.

Here and later, though, I miss any real discussion of one point that bulks large in my own reflections on the tragic mistakes and disasters that followed, experiences in which I was deeply involved from senior posts in the Defense and State Departments. Was there not far too much emphasis on doctrine and management, and far too little on the importance of a real grasp of the culture of the country involved? After all, Americans had known quite a lot about Greece and even more about the Philippines, while the British had known Malaya for generations. In the case of Indochina and Thailand, no such residue of experience existed either in the world of scholarship (as John King Fairbank pointed out eloquently some years ago) or in terms of personal exposure. Well into the 1960s it remained the custom to choose men for Indochina service on the basis of ability to speak French rather than knowledge of Sinic cultures or command of Asian languages. And even after the American involvement had come to include major military forces and the leadership role in pacification, only belatedly was there a serious training program in the Vietnamese language and culture. From my limited field exposure, it seemed to me that many of the graduates of that program made extraordinary contributions. Surely a nation that took its Vietnam role (or, as some would claim, its imperium) seriously would have trained tens or even hundreds of such speakers much sooner. Of course, this statement poses a larger question: with such men, would the United States have done a much better job of executing the policy that was followed—or (as many Frenchmen have suggested, both directly and indirectly) would more local grasp have caused policymakers to sense that the task was beyond even American powers, that for better or worse Ho was bound to win over the weak and divided adherents of a non-Communist nationalism? Either way, local knowledge, or the lack of it, seems to me to have made a much greater difference than Blaufarb allows.

This problem, I hasten to add, was not significant in Laos, where the struggle between Communist and non-Communist Lao was a sideshow to that between North Vietnamese, on the one side, and the Lao government and minority tribesmen, especially the Meo, on the other. Blaufarb's masterly chapter on this theater of the war, and especially on the CIA's support of the Meo, rightly makes this distinction, and stresses the marked resemblance of the Meo to World War II resistance movements rather than to classic counterinsurgency. Drawing on his two years (1964–66) as CIA station chief in Laos, Blaufarb gives a uniquely clear description of the complex tribal situation in that country, and recounts the course of the conflict, especially as it affected the Meo, with vivid sketches of the key characters, Pop Buell, General Vang Pao, and the rest. In the process, he explains clearly how the CIA came to have responsibility for the Meo operation and why the charge of a "secret war" was and remains a canard. (Those who still believe that charge should be given two research tasks: to read the newspapers, especially the news magazines, of the period, and to interview the many Senators and Congressmen who got as far as Bangkok at the time. "Secret" it was not, except to the extent desired by the men who governed Laos, in a desperate effort to preserve their neutralist posture.) That the effort was in the end tragic for the Meo and all concerned is a fact Blaufarb faces frankly in a concluding evaluation; Of all the aspects of the Indochina war, this experience may be both the saddest and, in human terms, the most understandable.

There are no such heroes (or tragedies), only frustrations, in Blaufarb's companion account of the long history of American efforts to stimulate effective programs in Thailand, where indeed the struggle continues in an increasingly murky setting. With characteristic bluntness, the author concludes that the massive American effort "has had little measurable effect" in meeting the threat, and that the experience well illustrates two of his central points—the split between an urban-oriented government and a rurally-centered population and the difficulty of inducing fundamental reform in the face of the concern, felt especially in military-dominated governments, that reform can only mean shaking apart the structure on which incumbent power rests. If Blaufarb had chosen to discuss Cambodia—doubtless omitted on the grounds that this imbroglio was largely a conventional conflict—he would surely have found these fundamental defects decisive there.

And so, of course, to Vietnam, which occupies three chapters of the nine and heavily colors the final summary and conclusion. Here my impression is that, for the reader of any significant part of the Vietnam literature, Chapters Four and Seven, dealing with the 1961–64 and 1964–67 periods respectively, pull together what happened with precision and competence, but with few special new insights.

Chapter Eight on the 1967–72 period, however, is a gold mine for professional and layman alike. The author's involvement with Vietnam fell partly in this period (from 1967 to 1969); he provides both a vivid account of major events and the best analytic critique of the conduct of "pacification" that I, at least, have seen anywhere. No short summary could do justice to its highlights, which I found myself underscoring on nearly every page. The treatment of the defects of the American military approach seemed to me particularly convincing, and again and again Blaufarb comes back to the point that unless the threatened government can reform itself, the task of an assisting nation is Augean. In the case of Vietnam, the deep politicization of the Vietnamese military was, in his view, the biggest obstacle to progress. Equally basic was the deficiency in administrative experience and capacity. For example, Blaufarb argues that this defect vitiated and distorted the controversial Phoenix program, which was not in practice (or in intent) a program of "massive assassination"; most of the casualties reported under it were in fact civilians killed or wounded in normal military operations but charged to Phoenix to build up its bureaucratic score and cover up its ineffectiveness. This and other mistakes are never glossed over; he concludes that while a lot of progress was made at times, especially in 1969–70, the various efforts simply did not reach the roots of the problem, inspire the people to positive loyalty to the government (although they did come to reject the Viet Cong), or leave behind the kind of strength that could withstand the final 1975 assault.

Finally, in Chapter Nine, Blaufarb reviews briefly the scattered episodes in Latin America that fall within the subject, showing tersely why Castro succeeded where, through basic errors of strategy or judgment, most of the Communist efforts of the 1960s failed. And so, in the end, the picture of a "monolithic conspiracy" that President Kennedy had seen in 1961 gave way to a far more complex and realistic view of the world: "Rarely," states the author, "has there been so complete a reversal of strategic views and assumptions by a great power within so short a time. [see page 297]" Within the U.S. government, the specific programs that had borne the hallmark of counterinsurgency were wound down or discarded entirely, and the whole experience of 1950–75 seemed consigned to history.

Yet Blaufarb argues that there may still be cases when, even in a different world setting, the United States will find itself coming, in its own national interest, to the aid of a government beset by "insurgency" aided from without. If so, he believes, we should look back over these twenty-five years and draw many lessons from them. The U.S. Army, in particular, must learn that guerrilla warfare is indeed a distinct art and not one that can be delegated to a token (and ever-suspect) force of Green Berets. The political structure of the government to be defended must be one that responds to its people, and its political base must extend well beyond its military elite. Put thus baldly, the lessons of the counterinsurgency era may seem obvious. But if there is one underlying theme to this book, it is the extraordinary difficulty, for the United States in particular, of applying these lessons in practice.

"The fundamental lesson to draw from our misadventures of the 'counterinsurgency era,' " he concludes, "is . . . the lesson of the limits of American power. . . . Too many have fallen back on the easy excuse that we failed in Indochina because our power was constrained and leashed, that more bombs, more destruction, more firepower was the answer. At the end of this account of what we tried to do and why it fell short, it is to be hoped that some will be convinced that the failure was one of understanding, of inability to perceive the underlying realities of both our own system and that of the countries into which we thrust our raw strength." The book's case for this conclusion seems to me unanswerable.

William P. Bundy

Preface

★ ★ ★

The work here presented was produced in the hope that the author's experience both as a participant in some of the events described and later as a professional analyst (at the Rand Corporation) of the same policies and programs would provide a vantage point from which a useful review and a better understanding of our counterinsurgency experience would emerge. Participation in the events described, of course, has disadvantages as well as advantages. I have striven for detachment, but undoubtedly I have not entirely succeeded. The reader should know and make allowances for the fact that I served for twenty years in the Central Intelligence Agency (1950–1970) in Greece, Vietnam, Singapore, and Laos, as well as in Washington, and also that, after retirement from the CIA, I served briefly as a consultant to the National Security Council staff in an abortive study of insurgency in Thailand (1972). Although I make no apologies for that service, I am also aware of errors of omission and commission by the government and agency for which I worked, and where I deemed it necessary I have pointed them out.

That background has made it possible for me to fill some of the gaps in the public knowledge of the events I describe. Since most of what I was involved in was classified and considered sensitive, and since I have not wished to violate my voluntary commitment to respect that secrecy, I have limited my discussion of such matters either to material in the public domain or, where that was not available, to my recollections of the general outlines of policies and programs, avoiding such details as the names of people, amounts of funds and other resources involved, and operational methods. Where possible in discussing sensitive matters I have cited public sources such as press reports or such resources as the *Pentagon Papers.* By doing so, I have in effect confirmed some unofficial reporting, which seemed to me to be a useful rather than a harmful thing to do. Much has been written about secret activities in Laos and Vietnam that was true but also much that was exaggerated or untrue. The reports I have cited are among the accurate ones. Needless to say, none of this means that CIA has responsibility for this work, which is solely my own.

The reader will also note that occasionally I describe events without providing sources for my statements. In such cases, unless a public source is clearly implied, I am basing my account on what I learned from my personal involvement at the time, either on the scene or in Washington, where I was privy to reports sent in from the field or interviewed officers returning from there.

I also wish to call attention to one situation in which I am in the curious position of having to speculate and piece together a picture from limited fragments of information despite the fact that the country and activity were familiar to me from having worked there. I refer to Chapter V, "People's Counterinsurgency," which concerns the Meo resistance effort in Laos. Although much of that activity was intimately known to me from personal involvement from 1963 through 1966, I never became familiar with important aspects of the earliest phase dating from late 1960 and early 1961. Because the account I am able to give is clearly based on fragmentary information together with some inference and deduction, the reader may get the impression that I know more than I am telling. This is not the case. For better or worse, history for its own sake does not play any part in the lives of active operations officers in the CIA, and I never thought to delve into events of the years before I became involved. Clearly, at the time it never occurred to me that one day I would be writing a book on these matters and would regret my lack of curiosity.

It remains to acknowledge the help of many people whom I consulted in the course of writing this book. Certainly the person to whom my debt is greatest and who has helped me the most with his encouragement, his enthusiasm, his vast knowledge, and his impatience with error is Ambassador Robert W. Komer, now of the Rand Corporation, who served as head of CORDS in Vietnam in 1967 and 1968. From beginning to end of this lengthy enterprise he has been unfailingly helpful and willing to share his knowledge. I thank him for this essential help but hasten to add that I alone am responsible for the content of this work.

I also must acknowledge the good advice of Dr. Bernard Brodie of UCLA, Joseph J. Zasloff of the University of Pittsburgh, McAllister Brown of Williams College, Lewis J. Lapham, Stephen T. Hosmer, Jeanette L. Koch, Charles A. Mann, Dr. Patricia McCreedy, Dr. Charles Weldon, James Thomas Ward, George K. Tanham, William P. Bundy, Richard M. Bissell, Jr., and William Moss of the John F. Kennedy Library at Waltham, Massachusetts. All gave generously of their time and knowledge. Again, however, I am solely responsible for what has emerged.

    Part of the work on this study was made possible by several generous grants from the Earhart Foundation of Ann Arbor, Michigan. My grateful thanks are owed to that institution and to its officers, Richard L. Ware and Antony T. Sullivan.

    Typing assistance by Rosalie Fonoroff and the late Suzanne Tourault was both efficient and intelligent and was of a quality to make me permanently in debt to these two gracious ladies.

    Finally, to my busy wife, Marjorie, I am indebted not so much for direct assistance, for she studiously kept out of this enterprise, but for the opportunity to spend several years of unremunerated labor on this book—an opportunity which would not have been possible if she had not at the same time performed her dedicated and remunerated labor in her own field.

Douglas S. Blaufarb

Lehew, W.Va.
Washington, D.C.

Glossary of Abbreviations

★ ★ ★

AID	Agency for International Development (U.S.)
ARD	Accelerated Rural Development (Thailand)
ARVN	Army of the Republic of Vietnam
BCT	Battalion Combat Team
BPP	Border Patrol Police (Thailand)
CAO	Civil Affairs Office (of the Philippine Army)
CAP	Combined Action Platoon
CAT	Civil Air Transport
CCP	Chinese Communist Party
CI	Counterinsurgency
CIA	Central Intelligence Agency (U.S.)
CIDG	Citizens Irregular Defense Group (Vietnam)
CIP	Counterinsurgency Plan
COMUSMACV	Commander, U.S. Military Assistance Command, Vietnam
CORDS	Civil Operations and Revolutionary Development Support (Vietnam)
CPM	Civil, Police, Military Combined Centers (Thailand)
CSOC	Communist Suppression Operations Command (Thailand)
CSOR	Communist Suppression Operations Region (Thailand)
CT	Communist Terrorist
CTT	Counter Terror Team (Vietnam)
DOLA	Department of Local Administration (Thailand)
DRV	Democratic Republic of Vietnam
EDCOR	Economic Development Corps (Philippines)

FAR	Forces Armées Royales; Royal Armed Forces (Lao)
FIDP	Foreign Internal Defense Program (U.S.)
GVN	Government of Vietnam
HES	Hamlet Evaluation Survey (Vietnam)
HMB	People's Liberation Army (Philippines)
Huk	Hukbong Bayan Laban Sa Hapon; People's Army Against Japan (Philippines)
ISOC	Internal Security Operations Center (Thailand)
JCS	Joint Chiefs of Staff (U.S.)
JSC	Joint Security Center (Thailand)
JUSMAAG	Joint U.S. Military Assistance Advisory Group (U.S.)
JUSPAO	Joint U.S. Public Affairs Office (Vietnam)
KKE	Greek Communist Party
MAAG	Military Assistance Advisory Group (U.S.)
MACV	Military Assistance Command, Vietnam
MAP	Military Aid Program (U.S.)
MCP	Malay Communist Party
MDU	Military Development Units (Thailand)
NAMFREL	National Association for Free Elections (Philippines)
NLHS	Neo Lao Hax Sat; Lao People's Front
NLF	National Liberation Front (Vietnam)
NSC	National Security Command (Thailand)
NSC	National Security Council (U.S.)
OCO	Office of Civilian Operations (Vietnam)
OIDP	Overseas Internal Defense Program or Policy (U.S.)
PARU	Police Aerial Resupply Unit (Thailand)
PAT	People's Action Team (Vietnam)
PAVN	People's Army of Vietnam
PF	Popular Forces (Vietnam)
PIC	Prisoner Interrogation Center (Vietnam)
PL	Pathet Lao; Lao State
PRG	Provisional Revolutionary Government (Vietnam)
PRP	People's Revolutionary Party (Vietnam)
PRU	Provincial Reconnaissance Unit (Vietnam)
PSDF	People's Self Defense Force (Vietnam)
RD	Revolutionary Development (Vietnam)
RDP	Revolutionary Development Program (Vietnam)
RF	Regional Forces (Vietnam)
RLG	Royal Lao Government
RTA	Royal Thai Army
RTG	Royal Thai Government
RY	Republican Youth (Vietnam)
SA/CI	Special Assistant/Counterinsurgency (Thailand)
SACSA	Special Assistant (to the Director, Joint Staff) for Counterinsurgency and Special Activities (U.S.)

SGU	Special Guerilla Unit (Laos)
STOL	Short Take-off and Landing (aircraft)
TNPD	Thai National Police Department
USAF	United States Air Force
USAID	United States Agency for International Development
USIA	United States Information Agency
USOM	United States Operations Mission (USAID overseas office)
USSF	United States Special Forces
VC	Viet Cong
VIS	Vietnamese Information Service
VNQDD	Vietnam Quoc Dan Dang (Vietnamese political party)

The Counterinsurgency Era:
U.S. Doctrine and Performance

1

Communist Rural Insurgency: From National Liberation to People's War and Beyond

★ ★ ★

The Term "counterinsurgency" conveys today, in the late 1970s, various impressions mostly having to do with cold war attitudes, now considered outdated, and specifically with U.S. intervention, now considered misguided, to prevent revolutions in distant lands. At one time, however, it had a more precise meaning which underlay an effort to thwart a perceived threat to U.S. interests and to the global balance of power, and which achieved a priority on the foreign affairs agenda of the highest levels of the government. As in the case of other policies of the postwar era, such as "containment" and "détente," its advocates were dismayed, as time went on, to find that it had degenerated into a vague slogan behind which various policy interests contended for their own goals, not all of which were in fact consistent with the intentions of the originators of the ideas and policies involved. Even worse, a tendency developed to formularize into simple and rather simpleminded rules a most complex group of concepts. This was perhaps an inevitable result of the headlong attempt to indoctrinate a large number of soldiers and civilians who approached the subject with little preparation or background and yet were expected to carry out programs initiated in its name in a long list of countries scattered over several continents. Partly in reaction to these tendencies new names were given to the overall policy such as "pacification," "internal defense," and "stability operations." In this work, we will use the original label in most cases because it remains the one which

1

needs the least further explanation and conveys to most people the general character of the subject matter.

As the word implies, counterinsurgency was conceived of as a response to a danger that appeared to threaten U.S. global interests and did so in a guise which made it difficult to detect in timely fashion and, even if detected, to deal with effectively. It was seen as novel and unprecedented and, for these reasons among others, exceedingly dangerous. Somehow, the Communists had devised methods of mobilizing and organizing military and political forces in areas where the materials for such efforts were most unpromising, where political awareness was low, traditional and backward economies poor and unproductive, and familiarity with modern technology limited to a handful. The threat was also perceived to have the quality of staying below the threshold of international concern for the peace; large conventional forces were not involved, much less nuclear weapons. This suggested that something surreptitious was afoot, a worldwide campaign to make major changes in the power balance masquerading as something else. Further study confirmed that, indeed, a sophisticated method was being employed, and from that fact it was not a large step to conclude that the world was witnessing a concerted and clever effort to revise the balance among the major powers by stealth and deception.

This concern progressively evolved into rather alarming conclusions and then into policies which it is our purpose in this work to study both in terms of the doctrines and the results. First, however, we must examine the phenomenon of Communist rural insurgency in backward, rural lands in somewhat more detail, scrutinizing not only what the Communists said publicly about what they were trying to do but their actions as well.

MAO THE INNOVATOR

Communist rural insurgency is one heritage of the Leninist variety of Marxism. The particular form that became a matter of acute concern to the United States in the late 1950s and led to a policy dedicated to countering it wherever it appeared was evolved in China under the leadership of Mao Tse-tung in the years between 1927 and 1937. Lenin and the Communists who base themselves on the orthodoxy as interpreted by the Soviet party have traditionally looked to the urban factory workers as the base upon which a policy aimed at the revolutionary seizure of power must rely. This class—massive, proletarianized, and aroused behind the leadership of its "vanguard party"—would form the troops of the revolution, and power would be seized in its name to produce the "dictatorship of the proletariat." The problem confronted by

Mao in China in 1927 was that of writing *Hamlet* with a midget Prince of Denmark. He was required to organize a proletarian revolution in a country which boasted only a tiny proletariat. As a result of close contact with the peasantry, among whom he had been assigned to work, and of bitter trials and failures as he attempted to proceed according to the line of party leadership sitting in the cities who, in turn, were strongly influenced by the views of Stalin, sitting eight thousand miles away, Mao led a deviation from the official line. Because, although a much-criticized deviationist, he nevertheless produced the only success of the Chinese Communist Party—a Chinese "Soviet" with its own army and government, first in the hinterland of Kiangsi province (South Central China) and later, after the Long March, in Shensi (Northwestern China)—his view prevailed and he became the leader of the Communist Party of China.

That view has been simplified and sloganized into the concept that, in those countries of the world which remain largely rural and agricultural, the people of the countryside can be successfully organized and led in a movement to encircle and eventually to take over the cities. The much-despised peasantry, who in traditional Marxism represent a backward force from whom nothing progressive can develop, were transformed into an honorary proletariat, out of which a devastating revolutionary weapon could be forged.

THE STRATEGY

How did Mao envisage accomplishing this feat? Although he wrote extensively on the subject, he never actually brought all the elements—tactics, strategy, political concepts—into a single coherent formula. From his various writings, augmented by his practice, the essential elements emerge. Different analysts have distilled a varying number of such elements from the sources and what follows is not set forth as a hard and fast codification but a summary based not only on the statements of Mao but on his practice as well—a practice which included some policies not freely discussed in Maoist literature.

We will begin with the first step—what Western analysts came to call Phase I—which is agitation and propaganda among the peasantry. The agitators are armed but the weapons are used largely for the purposes of impressing the audience and intimidating civilian opponents—a technique sometimes called "armed propaganda." The cadres doing this work are Communist Party members sent into the area for this purpose; ideally, they come from the area, but this is not always possible. Their purpose is to recruit supporters to form the beginnings of a political organization and of a guerrilla unit. From part-time guerrillas—

sometimes called self-defense forces—they gradually seek to upgrade the units until they have full-time regular forces, some of which serve locally. The cream of these units are organized into regular "main" forces which come under a national command and are used anywhere.

The second phase (again a Western designation) begins with the outbreak of overt violence, true guerrilla operations. It can last a very long time, for the final phase—Phase III—is the climactic offensive by large, regular military units. Phase II can succeed only if its launching is accompanied by the establishment of base areas, usually in some remote and inaccessible zone. Here, the Communist movement becomes the government, collects taxes, establishes training camps, hospitals, and depots, and builds reserve supplies of food and ammunition. In one of the earthy metaphors he enjoyed, Mao used to say, according to one of his soldiers, "A revolution's need for a base area . . . [is] just like an individual's need for buttocks. If an individual didn't have buttocks, he . . . would have to run around or stand around all the time. . . . His legs would get tired and collapse under him, and he would fall down."[1]

From the outbreak of hostilities, the guerrilla fights according to the principles of guerrilla warfare, the traditional weapon of a movement that has some popular support but is militarily weak. Guerrilla warfare, says Mao, is warfare that places a premium upon flexibility, surprise, quick decision, initiative, and careful planning. These, of course, are also some of the basic principles of success in any form of warfare. To venture a simplification, guerrilla warfare is a style of fighting in which the combatant, because of his inferiority, seeks never to be forced into battle but to fight only at times and places of his own choosing. To follow such a strategy he must be highly mobile but not highly visible, and that means he is lightly armed and equipped—which, in most cases, he is anyway—thus making a virtue of necessity. Control of terrain matters little to him. He cannot afford the risk of being forced into battle to defend it. This principle can come into conflict, of course, with the need for base areas, but in a pinch the guerrilla chieftain must be willing to give those up, too, painful as it may be. This was the origin of Mao's decision to make the Long March in 1934: it was that or total defeat.

Most critical to success is support of a sufficient number of the population to provide advance information about enemy movements and concealment when the insurgent force needs to disperse rapidly. The guerrilla always "runs away to fight another day" and "wins by not losing." Guerrilla warfare in any form is likely to take a long while to have significant impact—and even more so in Mao's version, which relies entirely on this form of combat during a critical phase that may drag on for many years. Indeed, this is one of the unique features of Mao's strategy. No other serious strategist has taken such a position. In Spain and Russia against Napoleon, in South Carolina against the

British, in Arabia against the Turks, guerrillas fought as auxiliaries, supporting a regular army. Mao insisted that it was possible for guerrillas to fight and win on their own, but that the process would inevitably be a lengthy one.

Indeed, he erected this quality into another basic principle, that of protracted war.[2] He was speaking, in his writings on this point, of the particular circumstances of China in 1938 and of the fight against the invading forces of Japan. As some later date, his formulation became a general principle of the new style of revolutionary warfare. The principle held that such a conflict would of necessity be a lengthy one because of the weakness of the insurgents compared to their enemies. This imbalance would take a long time to be corrected, and the correction would take place in three phases. The first phase is defensive, when the enemy penetrates deep into friendly territory and the guerrilla force conducts a strategic defensive. Next comes a period of rough balance when the enemy is forced to give up the goal of expansion and concentrates on consolidation while the insurgents prepare their counteroffensive. Finally, in the third phase, comes the insurgents' victorious offensive which is undertaken in the style of "mobile warfare" rather than guerrilla warfare, i.e., the insurgents are now actively seeking battle at any time and put aside concealment, dispersion, and the other methods of avoiding combat.

Although clearly applied to foreign invasion, Mao's phasing was taken over as part of the Maoist creed and echoed faithfully by the Vietnamese and others. In fact, it is arbitrary and awkward, and in the hands of Vo Nguyen Giap, for instance, it is used selectively and "imaginatively"—in fact, eventually abandoned.[3] To all practitioners and analysts, the process is of necessity a phased one, and the critical phase after the initial launching and gradual growth is the one calling for the abandonment of guerrilla war. Giap made costly mistakes in attempting to solve that problem. His eventual formula is esoteric and owes little to Mao.

The concept of protracted war is important for a different reason: it means that the insurgents never accept defeat as final. They behave on the assumption that they have actuated a historical process rather than an event or a series of events. They expect setbacks in the course of this process and concentrate on learning from them and doing better the next time. The Chinese Communists fought first the Kuomintang, then the Japanese, and finally again took on Chiang Kai-shek for a total of twenty-two years. The Vietnamese Communists fought the French, the South Vietnamese, and the Americans from 1945 to 1975 with an interim truce period of five years (1954–1959). The Malayan Communists are still at war with the government in Kuala Lumpur after twenty-seven years, and the Burmese "White Flag" (Chinese-influenced) Communists have been shooting at the forces of the Rangoon government off and on for twenty-nine years. The record shows few cases in which an insurgency of this type has been abandoned short of success.

Of equal importance to these principles is the political dimension of the insurgency, comprising a type of organization and a strategy which distinguish the Communist-led peasant uprising and give it its special character. The political dominates the military, which is never permitted to pursue military goals for their own sake. This is the true meaning of Mao's famous aphorism, "Political power grows out of the barrel of a gun. Our principle," he goes on to say, "is that the Party controls the gun and the gun must never be allowed to command the Party."[4]

The priority political objective is to build a fully controlled mass base among all important classes save the small ruling groups, but initially and preeminently among the peasantry, who comprise the overwhelming majority and who also populate a rural hinterland with many remote, lightly governed corners where a revolutionary base can develop and survive. Mao discovered the peasantry not by any prescient wisdom or by a brilliant stroke of theorizing. He found them to be the main revolutionary resource of China only after the Communists were bloodily expelled from the cities and had nowhere to go except to the remote countryside, although even before that event, Mao had concluded that the peasantry offered significant revolutionary potential to a movement that understood how to appeal to and organize them. This emerged not only from their overwhelming numbers but from the conditions that prevailed in the Chinese hinterland, where a degenerated system of tenancy unchecked by central authority gave the landlords virtually unlimited power which they did not hesitate to exploit.

The appeal Mao devised made land redistribution and suppression of the landlords a major theme and one which, in those early days, the Communists carried out vigorously wherever they established themselves. This approach worked well enough to help them build a strong but limited base area in Kiangsi and a few other, smaller enclaves elsewhere during the period 1927–1934. But that is by no means the whole, or even the most important part, of the successful Communist appeal. As Chalmers Johnson was the first to point out, Mao and his associates made rather limited progress winning over the peasantry and undermining the Nationalist regime until the Japanese invasion made it possible for them to add nationalism to their appeal.[5] They appeared, in fact, to be caught in a "no-win" situation and were merely surviving against Chiang and the Nationalists who—a fact that is often forgotten—not only controlled greatly superior forces but offered serious competition as a modernizing, reforming, and unifying force. Being a guerrilla army, dependent upon popular support, the Communists found it difficult to expand into the vast, Nationalist-controlled areas where a reasonably effective military and governing apparatus existed, one which the peasants were not prepared to challenge.

The final proof of Chiang's superiority, of course, was his success in forcing the Communists to make the Long March, a hegira of six thousand miles during which the Red Army abandoned its largest base and shrank to about one-third of its earlier size. What rescued the Communists and solved the problem of their limited appeal was the Japanese invasion. Militarily, the Japanese made rapid progress. Their armies moved swiftly to encompass large areas and populations. As they moved on, they left small garrisons behind, and in effect a vacuum into which the Communists rapidly moved. Far more adept in the style of political-military warfare required to deal with these circumstances, the Communists quickly outdistanced the Nationalists who made barely any effort to operate behind Japanese lines. The Communists also showed their usual political flexibility. They abandoned their old themes of land distribution and elimination of the landlords, contenting themselves merely with enforcing fair rents and practices. Their overwhelming theme became nationalism, the summons to the population to rise up and resist the Japanese.

The Japanese obliged the Communists by reacting vigorously and typically, carrying out so-called mopping-up campaigns, which wreaked severe punishment upon the population. Their attitude made it clear that they considered all Chinese to be a lesser breed with no rights. In Chalmers Johnson's words, the trauma of this period

> broke the hold of parochialism on the Chinese peasant. Before the Japanese invasion the Chinese peasant was indifferent to 'Chinese' politics, being wholly absorbed in local affairs. The war totally destroyed the rural social order and sensitized the Chinese peasantry to a new spectrum of possible associations, identities and purposes. Foremost among the new political concepts were those of 'China' and 'Chinese nationality.'[6]

Nationalistic feelings were thus critical to the success of the first of the modern Communist rural insurgencies and remained an essential element in those that followed. Where national feelings could not easily be mobilized, the revolts tended to sputter and develop very slowly, if at all. Where they could, preeminently in such later examples as Indochina and Cuba, they succeeded. This is not to say that genuine nationalist feelings were sufficient to bring success, but they seemed one of several necessary factors.

It further appears to be the case that these nationalist feelings are internal to the Communist movement as well as external to it. It may be pure coincidence, but it is a fact that almost all the successful Communist insurgencies—Yugoslavian, Chinese, and Cuban—were conducted without Soviet help and often in disregard of Soviet wishes. The Indochinese movements had both Soviet and Chinese help and apparently yielded to

Soviet pressures in negotiating the Geneva Accords of 1954, but later became quite skillful at accepting help without succumbing to domination, thanks largely to the split between Moscow and Peking. Perhaps the most critical decision of Mao Tse-tung, the one most responsible for his victory, flouted the known policies of Stalin. This was the decision to fight a guerrilla war against the Japanese rather than joining forces with Chiang's armies to fight a conventional war of clearly drawn battle lines and direct confrontations. The victorious civil war was equally opposed by Moscow. In 1945, Stalin signed a treaty of friendship and alliance with the Nationalist government and later "advised the Chinese Communists that their insurrection 'had no prospect' and that they should join Chiang's government and dissolve their army."[7] The irony of this fact about successful Communist insurgencies lies in its contrast to the American perceptions which lay behind the development of a policy of countering insurgency, perceptions which saw in each insurgency the hand and will of a monolithic movement under Soviet domination.

The various appeals developed by the Communists to attract followers were important ingredients of the approach, but of themselves they are insufficient to achieve the sweeping aims of the movement. A vital additional ingredient is organization, unique in quality and style, which has characterized the Chinese Communists and their imitators. First, of course, the members of the organization were, in the Leninist pattern, professional revolutionaries, committed in every aspect of their lives to the movement. In theory, discipline and obedience to party requirements were complete; in practice of course there were exceptions, but the norm was close enough to the ideal to produce the desired result. In effect, a Chinese Communist (or a Communist in any other society) became a participant in a new culture with entirely novel values. To a large degree, he ceased to be culturally Chinese. He became a puritan in habits and life-style and the supporter of an abstract cause which superseded loyalty to family, clan, and region. Nothing could be more un-Chinese, or perhaps one should say untraditional, for the phenomenon occurred in all underdeveloped lands where the Communists became active, producing the same contrast between ancient and persisting cultural patterns and the values of the new Communist man. It is the explanation of the perennial complaint of the Westerners involved in counterinsurgency or other activities in competition with the Communists. "Why are our friends so much less efficient, more corrupt, less dedicated, and more disorganized than the enemy? After all, they are the same people." In all that concerned organized social activity they were not, in fact, any longer the same people. They now belonged to a different culture with purposes far transcending individual, family, or clan concerns. Thus, they became a formidable modernizing force while their opponents, despite the efforts of some, remained far more traditional, with all that that implies in terms of the quality of performance in large-scale organized activity.

In the approach to the peasants, the style was fatherly and aimed at producing an impression of benevolence. This was particularly true of the Red Army, which was employed as a propaganda as well as a military force. For instance, each Red Army soldier was required to memorize the "Eight Points" governing general conduct, to repeat them daily, and to sing them in a marching song. Point 3 was "be courteous and help when you can"; point 7 was "don't flirt with women"; and point 6, "be honest in all transactions with the peasants."[8] The contrast between this style and that of the Japanese and even the Nationalist forces was entirely in the Red Army's favor, as far as concerned its goal of winning peasant support. The pattern was followed in all other insurgencies modeled after the Chinese.

Indeed, a great deal of the political program was carried out through the army itself which, to the population it dealt with and lived and worked among, was by all odds the most impressive institution of the Communist movement. The Red Army conducted propaganda, recruited and guided the population, and was a proud symbol of what the Communists claimed to stand for. Its political work was far too important to be handled casually: the "gun" had to be totally under Party control. This was accomplished by the system of political commissars, Communist cadres assigned to military service, first created in Russia as a means of assuring the loyalty of Czarist officers and men in Red Army ranks. In China, it assured that the vital political role of the army was properly carried out.

The benevolent image of the Red Army was limited to those regarded as friendly. At the same time, the movement employed an armed fist against those identified as its enemies. In the early days, before the United Front against Japan, landlords were particularly harshly treated, stripped of their belongings, and often tried for crimes and executed. In the anti-Japanese period, the treatment of landlords eased but the same ruthlessness applied to any suspected sympathizers with the enemy or the puppet regime set up by the Japanese. On the other hand, terrorism, although employed on occasion, was not the systematic political tool it became in later versions of the pattern, especially in Vietnam. Mao also claimed that during all the twenty-two years of the war, his forces never executed a single captured enemy soldier.[9] The entire approach was calculated to produce an overwhelming impression of controlled power, benevolent to those it favored and implacable against its enemies. It sought to contrast its certainty, efficiency, and rigid personal standards with the laxness and ineffectiveness of its Chinese opponents and thus convince waverers that it had inherited "the mandate of heaven" and would certainly win.

Finally, there was the enormous appeal inherent in all of this to the ambitious and energetic, the appeal of "upward mobility" under a new political dispensation. The movement emphasized the peasant origins of its cadres and leaders, both civilian and military. It provided education and all that that meant to the villagers of China and other backward rural lands, where literacy was a key to position and power, denied to the great majority. A chance to rise in status, to achieve power in a hierarchy in which poor peasants were made particularly welcome, had an obvious appeal to the ambitious.[10] It also served to increase the confidence of the villagers in the insurgency, where they were substantially represented, and to keep the leadership in touch with village attitudes. All of these factors were of importance to the political substance of the movement and account significantly for its strengths.

A standard political practice in the Chinese pattern was the formation of so-called mass organizations in the communities under Communist control or influence. At the same time, the Communists sought to function behind the screen of a "united front" of various groups who could be claimed to have come together to achieve shared goals. In the Chinese model, the front included genuine non-Communist individuals or groups. In later examples, notably Vietnam and its "National Liberation Front," the front was entirely a Communist creation and had no life of its own. In either case, control was in Communist hands.

A final aspect of this type of warfare to be considered is the relationship to the international political arena and to friendly forces in other countries. Here, there is no particular pattern to be discerned. Although Mao Tse-tung in his writings frequently had reference to the factor of internal Japanese problems as a potential force on the side of the insurgency, and particularly to the possibility of a revolution led by the Japanese Communists, and although he spoke of Stalin and of the USSR as revered mentors and allies, he did not rely upon any of these factors. In fact, neither Russia nor the Japanese Communist Party gave important help to the CCP and, indeed, the Soviet action in removing whole factories from Manchuria at the war's end could be considered less than helpful. On the other hand, at the time the Soviets did not believe the Chinese would prevail in the civil war and they did, in fact, turn over to the renamed People's Liberation Army some of the lighter weapons and ammunition they had taken from the Japanese in Manchuria. In later years, the Chinese version of insurgent warfare emphasized self-reliance as a key quality in the success of a revolutionary movement.

The familiar example of Vietnam, however, shows a radically different pattern. During the first period of that war, when France was the enemy, Chinese help began to flow to the Viet Minh in important amounts after the Communists reached the border of Vietnam. When the arena became South Vietnam, political direction, cadres, and technical equipment flowed south from Hanoi from the beginning. After the involvement of the U.S., whole North Vietnamese divisions and a complete supply of up-to-date weapons and ammunition also moved by various routes from north to south.

The Vietnamese Communists, of course, did not consider this to be foreign intervention, but they also found it necessary to rely entirely on their Communist allies, notably the Soviet Union, for all the sinews of modern warfare. No qualms of principle prevented them from accepting this aid.

AND ITS NAME WAS PEOPLE'S WAR

Such are the main ingredients of the policies that eventually came to be called "people's war" by the Chinese and their emulators. Its cardinal principles were: development of a nucleus of peasant support by focusing on economic and social grievances and also, most importantly, on nationalist feelings built up by a skillful combination of propaganda and terrorism; mastery of the techniques of guerrilla warfare to keep the movement alive and growing and to gradually wear down the strength of the enemy, although final victory would only be achieved by conventional military means; development of base areas and their expansion as made possible by increasing strength, together with a willingness to abandon them, if necessary; commitment to a protracted conflict, which might last indefinitely with many turns of fortune but which must be persisted in until the final victory; direction by a trained and tested Communist cadre organized in the traditional hierarchy and acting with military discipline but also with considerable autonomy at different levels and locations; control of all aspects of the effort, particularly the military, by the party organization; creation of a variety of mass organizations and of a national political front purporting to represent all progressive elements of the population; and, finally, acceptance of foreign help if necessary with the preferred course being to proceed with as much self-reliance as possible. If the policy leads to suffering and setbacks such are considered ultimately a strengthening factor.

The strategy, according to its supporters, was particularly keyed to overturning "imperialism" in the underdeveloped, largely rural lands of Asia, Africa, and Latin America; and indeed, by the late 1950s power had been seized by these means in North Vietnam and apparently in Cuba, and the method appeared to be a serious threat in South Vietnam and Laos and in several countries of Latin America. It had been attempted with less success in Burma, Malaya, and the Philippines. In Algeria an analogous movement, supported but not dominated by the Communists, appeared likely to achieve success.

Of these various insurgencies, those in French Indochina, Malaya, and the Philippines were most closely patterned after the Chinese, and of these the most successful was the Vietnamese. The writings of such Vietnamese leaders as Vo Nguyen Giap and Truong Chinh (whose pseudonymous name translates as "Long March") closely followed the theses of Mao Tse-tung. The phrase, "the people are the water and our army the fish," appears without attribution in one of Truong Chinh's tracts.[11] So do references to protracted war, guerrilla war developing into mobile war, and a war of Mao's three phases. Similar formulations appear in Giap's work. The obvious derivation of the Vietnamese war strategy reinforced the view that a general offensive by movements of this persuasion was under way.

THE VIETNAMESE VARIATION

There were, at the same time, some significant differences between the Vietnamese and the Chinese approaches. A noteworthy one, to which attention has been called by Chalmers Johnson,[12] was Hanoi's strategy of operating upon the domestic political vulnerabilities of the two Western democratic powers it fought in turn. This was indeed an important innovation and brought the Vietnamese a victory which was far more of their own making than that of Mao Tse-tung. The fact that the United States and not the Chinese Communists destroyed Japan's war-making power goes virtually unmentioned in Chinese accounts of their revolution. The Vietnamese faced an even greater imbalance between their power and that of their enemies. Unlike China, their country and their population were small. Ho Chi Minh perceived and made a cardinal target of the fact that, in both France and America, if he could hold out long enough and inflict high enough costs, the war would become unpopular and the public would cease to support it. This was the strategy behind such critical battles as Dien Bien Phu and the Tet offensive: to persuade the public and the politicians successively in France and the U.S. that they could never win at an acceptable cost. Indeed, the Tet offensive had serious internal political consequences for the Communists, but, nevertheless, it must be considered a success because it achieved the external political and psychological results it was intended to. Such a strategy, determining military operations on the basis of presumed effects in the internal politics of a foreign, "imperialist" country, was not part of Mao's thinking. Ho Chi Minh, on the other hand, had lived for years in France and had visited America briefly. We may make the reasonable speculation that this was his contribution to the strategy followed by the movement.

Another Vietnamese variation was an increased reliance upon terrorism, which we will describe in greater detail at a later point. The systematic assassination of GVN officials and sympathizers was a highly organized instrument of both psychological and material effect. Toward the end of the conflict, when many of the restraints on both sides had eroded, the terrorist campaign became far less discriminating. Whole villages and refugee centers were attacked and decimated. Nothing of this broad and systematic character appeared in Mao Tse-tung's formula or practice, but one is hard put to explain the difference. It may have had its origins in the fact that at the beginning of their revolt the Vietnamese lacked armed force, or it may reflect the greater disparity between their forces and those of their enemy. Rather then speculate further, however, we shall simply note the fact and pass on.

THE CUBAN VARIATION

The differences between the Chinese and Vietnamese versions of people's war were not insignificant but they did not affect fundamentals. The Vietnamese thought of themselves as disciples of Mao, and in its main outlines their doctrine and practice was recognizably a somewhat altered derivative of the Chinese. Chronologically, the next major version of people's war, however, was the Cuban, and it incorporated some startling departures from the Maoist prototype. Indeed, Castro's official interpreter and philosopher, Regis Debray, states:

> One may well consider it a stroke of good luck that Fidel had not read the military writings of Mao Tse-tung before disembarking on the coast of Oriente: he could thus invent, on the spot and out of his own experience, principles of a military doctrine in conformity with the terrain. It was only at the end of the war, when their tactics were already defined, that the rebels discovered the writings of Mao.[13]

This pristine state of mind was a "stroke of luck" because it meant that Castro was not constrained to follow patterns devised in quite other conditions but lethally risky in Cuba. The first mistake he avoided, according to Debray (clearly speaking for Castro himself) was that of propagandizing first and shooting afterward, of seeking to establish a political foundation among the population of the area of operations before forming the guerrilla band from local peasants. In the conditions prevailing in Latin America, the argument continues, the only way to impress the cowed and skeptical peasants is by actions which demonstrate the power and seriousness of the rebels. After a period during which the guerrilla band would have to survive by its own devices and at the same time actively harass the forces of authority, it would then be possible to appeal convincingly to the local population to join and support the movement.

> Let us think, writes Che Guevara, of how a guerilla focus could begin.
> Relatively small nuclei of people choose favorable places for guerilla warfare . . . and thus they begin to act. The following must be clearly established: at first, the relative weakness of the guerilla movement is such

that it must work only to settle in the terrain, establishing connections with the populace and reinforcing the places that will possibly become its base of support.

There are three conditions for the survival of a guerilla movement that begins its development under the situation just described: constant mobility, constant vigilance, constant distrust.[14]

This principle of the preeminence of the guerrilla *foco,* as it came to be called, the guerrilla band moving into a remote and rugged area from the outside, is the core of the Castro/Guevara approach to people's war around which the rest is built. In consequence, the theory dispenses with much of the Maoist apparatus. The military force is not a separate arm of the movement under strict party control expressed through the system of political commissars. The military arm and the party are one: the military leaders are also the party leaders and so no need exists for a political directorate penetrating the armed force. Nor is the *foco* responsible to a political center in the capital city or anywhere else. On the contrary, any such political movement, particularly if it is an urban movement—as most political movements were and are in Latin America—is subordinate to the *foco* and must put its needs first.

Castroism is equally skeptical about the creation of fixed bases, at least until the forces in the *foco* have learned how to survive without them, have increased in strength, and have split off into several groups which can provide mutual support. Until that stage has been reached, "the guerilla base is, according to an expression of Fidel, the territory within which the guerilla happens to be moving; it is where he goes. In the initial stage the base of support is in the guerilla's knapsack."[15] It becomes an obvious question, then, how the *foco* survives the vulnerable early stage, deprived of a physical or a political base—without, as Mao might say, a "buttocks" to sit down upon. The answer seems to be that few do or will. "As with infants in poor countries," says Debray, "the mortality rate is very high during the first months, decreasing with each passing month thereafter. To wage a short war, to destroy the *foco* in its embryonic stage, without giving itself time to adapt itself to the terrain or link itself with the local population or acquire a minimum of experience, is thus the golden rule of counterinsurgency."[16] It is also clear that Castro's version makes no particular point of the protracted nature of the war, nor distinguishes precise stages during which tactics and strategy differ. His struggle lasted two years, and the numbers under his command—until the sudden collapse of Batista—never exceeded two thousand.

The Castro version of peoples war was palpably based on a set of exceptional circumstances, among them the qualities of the leadership provided by the Castro brothers and Che Guevara combined with the bottomless incompetence of Batista. What is surprising is that the leadership then began to generalize boldly from this experience and to prescribe for all of Latin America. Debray's writings, as well as Che Guevara's, were part of the effort to put Castro's signature upon a theory of revolutionary action that claimed to be tailored to the special conditions of all of Latin America—conditions which, it was alleged, invalidated much of what Mao and Ho/Giap advocated. Moreover, the Castro regime proceeded to act upon this belief. Training camps were established in Cuba for recruits from other countries who, after being trained and equipped, were secretly sent back to their homelands. The slogan, repeated on billboards and posters and the press throughout Cuba, was from Che Guevara: "Two, three—many Vietnams." Venezuela and Colombia were important targets, and then, in 1967, came Che Guevara's bungled effort to launch a *foco* in Bolivia, which ended in his death. In the event, nowhere it was tried did the *foco* prove to be the potent weapon the theory alleged it to be. In spite of the Cuban view that Castro's feat could serve as a model to all Latin America, the claim remains without any support in experience after more than fifteen years of trying. One factor which Castro and his associates clearly did not appreciate in analyzing and trying to project their own success into other countries is the extent to which they had benefited from surprise and unawareness both in the United States and Cuba where their commitment to socialist revolution was not taken seriously and certainly not understood to mean a victory for the Communist form of totalitarianism.

After a number of Castroist attempts petered out in failure, a turn was taken by leftist extremists toward other forms of violence and revolutionary activity, particularly toward urban terrorism—and sometimes merely toward spectacular terrorist incidents for the sake of the broad psychological impact of such acts, with little of a considered strategy behind them. There is no need to discuss this trend and its spread throughout the world in a work on U.S. counterinsurgency policies. These policies were directed toward dealing with what was perceived as a specific Communist-supported strategy which seriously threatened to upset the existing balance of forces in the world.

THE SOVIET VIEW

The Soviet Union's position toward all of these developments has had no fixed theoretical basis but has changed with the changes in Moscow's view of the world situation and its own interests. One theoretical point is clear, however, and that is that Soviet Communism does not accept Maoism or Castroism, much less urban terrorism, as correct forms of revolutionary activity. The Communist parties under its influence stick to the old formulas of Leninism and most particularly to the necessity of a vanguard party of professional revolutionaries whose establishment is the essential first step toward launching revolution. In this matter, Mao is in agreement. The Soviets and the orthodox parties continue to emphasize the vital role of the proletariat as the main motor force of a socialist revolution, although they admit the peasantry to a role of great importance in predominantly rural countries with the proviso that it be under Communist leadership. Of even greater significance is the fact, also noted by Chalmers Johnson,[17] that old-line, Soviet-influenced parties insist upon the need to await the right combination of events— the classic "revolutionary situation" as defined by Lenin—before launching into a violent attempt to overthrow the existing system. This specific characteristic of Moscow-style Communism is precisely the quality that Castro and his adherents have turned away from, believing that in Latin America it has only led to the formation of alleged revolutionary parties which quickly degenerate into political posing and paper-shuffling in lieu of action. In their view, the need to await the right constellation of events becomes a mere excuse to avoid any action that threatens the party functionaries with risk, change, and new challenges. In answer to the classic reliance upon the eventual arrival of a revolutionary situation, they have replied that to start a revolution it is merely necessary to have men who are ready to start it.

Mao's position is somewhat different, for he does not explicitly repudiate Lenin. Judging from some formulations, however, he seems to believe that all "imperialist-dominated"—or, as we should say, less-developed—nations are in a revolutionary situation today and that a Communist party is duty-bound to assume the historic task of carrying out the revolution according to the principles of people's war. This, at least, is what appeared to be the Maoist view at the height of Peking's advocacy of people's war.

The Soviet Communist Party has steadfastly opposed this view within the Communist movement, and has repeatedly reaffirmed its continuing adherence to Lenin's formulation. The picture is far more complicated than that, however, for Lenin can be interpreted in any way that is convenient, which means in any way that conforms to the current Moscow view of Soviet interests. Thus, in 1948, at the height of the cold war in Europe (which was also a time when Moscow was the unchallenged center of the Communist world), Stalin apparently attempted to increase the pressures bearing upon the Western powers by directing that the Communist movements of the Far East take direct revolutionary action, despite the fact that in most of the countries involved, evolution toward independence was under way or even completed. The instruction is believed to have been delivered and explained at a Conference of Youth and Students of Southeast Asia which met at Calcutta in February 1948.[18] Soon afterward, violent upheavals were launched in Malaya, Indonesia,

India (Hyderabad), and Burma.[19] Even if by some stretch of the dialectic one could identify a revolutionary situation in some of these countries, this was hardly the case in all of them; in fact, in none of them did the uprisings succeed, although, as we know, in several countries they continued for long periods. They were launched in the service of Soviet foreign policy and in support of the new Cominform line, announced in 1947, of a world divided into "two camps" implacably hostile to each other.

During this same period, China was still a member in good standing of the international Communist movement and endorsed the Cominform line without reservation. In 1949, Liu Shao-chi, speaking in Peking to a meeting of the World Federation of Trade Unions, called upon Asia "to create, wherever and whenever possible, people's armies . . . and supporting bases."[20] In 1951, after the Korean War had begun and China was deeply engaged in a military confrontation with the United States, the CCP even called upon the Japanese Communists to launch insurgent operations and an attempt was loyally made with total lack of success.[21] There is thus little doubt that during the period of the Cominform "two camps" line, Stalin, fully supported by Mao, sought to make use of the Communist movements of the Far East to weaken and distract his global adversaries. To interpret this line of action as a serious attempt to change the world balance does not strain credulity, especially since it was accompanied by such major and violent Communist moves as the conquest of mainland China, the invasion of Korea, the continuing Viet Minh war against the French, and the Huk rebellion in the Philippines. In doing so, however, assumptions were made that were later falsified by events or by more complete knowledge. Among them were the belief that fomenting of rural insurgencies was a permanent commitment of the Communist movement, that the specific form of peasant uprising identified with Mao also had Soviet endorsement and, of course, that there was a single worldwide threat orchestrated by Moscow. Even at the time, the impression of a worldwide effort was somewhat belied by the quiescence of the Communists in Latin America, which was apparently due to lack of capability and interest in armed struggle by the parties concerned.

After the death of Stalin, there came the abandonment of the "two camps" line by his successors and the adoption of "peaceful coexistence"—an inherently ambiguous formula which carried little conviction in the West, in an era of many upheavals, particularly when its spokesman was the erratic and strident Khrushchev. "Peaceful coexistence" did not rule out the several crises over the Chinese offshore islands, or over Berlin, nor did it restrain Khrushchev from rattling his rockets and threatening to "bury" his adversaries in the West. (There were, of course, two sides to these issues which we need not explore in this discussion of how exaggerated impressions grew of Soviet policies and intentions.) Amidst all this, although no real or solid evidence could be adduced to suggest that the Soviets were actually fomenting and encouraging the Communist parties of the less-developed world to launch insurgencies, it is not surprising that this subtle change should be overlooked. Where such insurgencies occurred, they had Soviet propaganda support, and Khrushchev assured the world that they would continue to have it. In actual fact, however, the Soviet Union by the late fifties had no voice in determining the policies of the Vietnamese Communists or of Castro and his group, to cite the two insurgencies which caused most concern in Washington. "Peaceful coexistence" may not have had much objective content in terms of amicable behavior, but it did seem to mean that the Soviets no longer indiscriminately called upon Communists everywhere to do violent battle with the "imperialists" in support of Soviet goals; and, in fact, in some Communist countries, they had lost the power to do so. Yet it was precisely during this period—the late 1950s—that a school of thought became prominent in the United States which identified low-profile, "brushfire" wars under Soviet sponsorship as a major new threat to the world balance of power. In 1958, Senator John F. Kennedy identified this threat in a Senate speech as "Sputnik diplomacy, limited brush-fire wars, indirect non-overt aggression, intimidation and subversion, internal revolution."[22] When Khrushchev made a routine speech to a Communist meeting in Moscow which came to Kennedy's attention a few days after his inauguration and which reiterated a by now standard formula concerning Soviet support for "just wars," "wars of national liberation," it made, according to Arthur Schlesinger, Jr., "a conspicuous impression" upon the new president, especially the "bellicose confidence which surged" through it.[23] The president's impression had some major consequences for American policy. The Khrushchev speech was a trigger for a new policy departure reflecting convictions that, in Kennedy's case, however, had been building at least since 1954. Although there was some substance to the fears that lay behind the policy of counterinsurgency, the actual position in the Communist movement on "wars of national liberation" was far more complex and ambiguous than Washington realized.

China and People's War

A complicating factor was the fact that during this period the Chinese were, in actuality, pressing the Russians and Communists everywhere to adopt precisely the policy that the movement was accused in the United States of already following. Up until 1957, the Chinese Communists had gone along with Soviet views on peaceful coexistence and had developed some variations of their own on the theme, e.g., the "spirit of Bandung" and "the five principles of peaceful coexistence." In that year, however, Mao decided that a more aggressive line against the West would exploit what he saw as the growing weakness of the capitalist world in relation to the Communists. From this eventually developed the momentous Sino-Soviet schism and, in the course of the polemics accompanying it, one Chinese accusation regularly made against the Russians was the latter's failure to support "wars of national liberation" or "people's war" as it then began to be called. Some of Khrushchev's rhetoric which so impressed President Kennedy was a Soviet response to this pressure.

The U.S. commitment to counterinsurgency was thus stimulated by a perception which had had some substance ten years earlier but which gradually became detached from reality. Even as the U.S. girded to deal with the threat, it changed significantly and continued to change. The Sino-Soviet split surfaced publicly in bitter polemics and abuse. The Chinese became increasingly insistent upon the necessity of pressing ahead with people's wars everywhere while the Soviets stood pat upon their general assurances that they supported "wars of national liberation."

> The Chinese did believe that it was necessary to keep up Communist pressure on "imperialism," that is, the United States, and that, in order to do so, there were means available short of general war. When the Soviet Union failed to agree, the Chinese struck out on their own. . . . The Chinese answer . . . was "people's war," sponsored, endorsed, supported, and idealized—in short, "exported"—by Peking.[24]

A principal vehicle for this policy was a speech by Lin Piao, then Mao Tse-tung's designated successor, which he entitled "Long Live the Victory of People's War!" Lin's message, delivered in 1965, considerably enlarged the scope and historical role of people's war. It now became the principal means by which "imperialism" was to be destroyed. The speech made a parallel between the situation existing inside rural, less-developed nations and the situation in the world at large. In the former, the mass of the people lived in the countryside and could, if the right policies and action were followed, arm themselves and encircle and take the cities, thereby gaining power despite their rural beginnings. Similarly, in the world at large, the vast mass of population lived in the rural, less-developed countries and could, following the same pattern on a worldwide scale, encircle and defeat the industrialized states, the so-called imperialists.

> History has proved and will go on proving that people's war is the most effective weapon against U.S. imperialism and its lackeys. All revolutionary people will learn to wage people's war against U.S. imperialism and its lackeys. They will take up arms, learn to fight battles and become skilled in

waging people's war, though they have not done so before. U.S. imperialism, like a mad bull dashing from place to place, will finally be burned to ashes in the blazing fires of the people's wars it has provoked with its own actions.[25]

The formula had the sweeping simplicity of many of Mao's formulations dating from his later years. It amounted to prescribing a "Long March" for the whole world. The actual results were trivial compared with the aspirations. At about the same time that the commitment to people's war peaked in Lin's speech, guerrilla activity increased or broke out in Thailand and Burma, Malaysia, and the Philippines. Attempts were made to instigate uprisings in Africa which met with humiliating indifference and resentment. And during the same period, the Indonesian Communist Party met with disaster as it attempted and failed to take power by *coup d'état.* The Chinese role in this episode remains uncertain, but the results were clearly a setback for Peking, which had had an especially close relationship with the Indonesian Communists.

The motives that lay behind the Lin Piao policy line remain obscure, and there is no agreement among analysts on whether it represented a serious attempt to inspire a wave of uprisings which would sweep the Western world into the dustbin of history or was merely a ploy with a variety of Chinese internal and external goals in view, none of which was to overturn the global distribution of power. Some analysts judge the seriousness of the policy by its results, which were trivial. Others find in it the same irrationality about the outside world that characterized the "foreign policy" of the Great Proletarian Cultural Revolution, if one can call the frenzies that were visited upon foreign diplomats in that period a policy. Some would dismiss them as a spasm reflecting the general hysteria and chaos that possessed China in those years.

The period during which Communist China pushed Lin Piao's line lasted only a few years and was followed by the complete reversal of China's stance in the form of the rapprochement with the United States—the Nixon visit and its momentous consequences. Very little has been heard publicly about people's war in recent years, although limited Chinese support for guerrilla movements in Southeast Asia does continue, while, at the same time, Peking develops and expands government-to-government relations with the same countries. One must conclude that the theme of people's war does not meet the current priorities of the Peking regime but that it is kept alive as an alternative card to be played in event of need. In effect, then, Peking's attitude amounts in the end to the same as Moscow's: Maoist insurgencies, or in Moscow's case, wars of national liberation, will be supported and instigated in accordance with the needs and interests of the supporting power. No overriding strategy exists to orchestrate a global threat based on a cunning technique for mastering the obstacles to power in backward countries. On the other hand, if and when a situation develops in a particular country which serves Moscow's or Peking's need, insurgency will be supported and, in Peking's case, the Maoist strategy of people's war will provide the pattern to be followed.

So much is clear now, but it was indeed far from clear at the time that counterinsurgency became an important theme in U.S. foreign and national security policy. Hindsight should not be permitted to obscure the case that could be made in the late 1950s and through more than half of the 1960s that a serious threat was posed by the apparent commitment of the Communist world to a novel and ingenious form of attack against the non-Communist world. We will turn shortly to an account and a criticism of the American response, but at this point it seems appropriate to note that those—Chalmers Johnson most notably, in view of his especially knowledgeable grasp of the background—who criticize the response to people's war as excessive and mistaken are themselves mistaken in assuming that the response was mainly generated by Maoist fulminations and actions of the mid-sixties.[26] The true origins of Washington's counterinsurgency policies trace back to the period from 1948 to 1961, to the now obscure little wars in Malaya, the Philippines, Burma, and even as far back as the Greek civil war of 1947 to 1949. Most important was the renewal of guerrilla activity, first in Laos and then in Vietnam, not long before the Kennedy Administration came into office pledged to confront and master the various threats it perceived to America's global position.

We turn now to two of those "limited brush-fire wars" as then Senator Kennedy called them, episodes that were particularly important in establishing the background against which counterinsurgency theories and practice developed.

2

Prefigurations: Counterinsurgency in the Philippines and Malaya

★ ★ ★

The U.S. experienced its first involvement in countering a Communist insurgency when, in consequence of the Truman Doctrine, it came to the aid of the Greek government in 1947. The Greek civil war, which lasted from approximately 1947 to 1949, was in several ways similar to later insurgencies in the Far East, although it seems unlikely that Mao Tse-tung was read in the Grammos and Vitsi base areas of the Greek Communist Party (KKE). On the other hand, the experience was attended by good fortune which made it atypical of later U.S. involvements of this character. Thus, at about the time of the U.S. entry on the scene, the Yugoslav Communists split away from Moscow's hegemony and ceased to provide the aid and asylum for the insurgents which had made a vital contribution to their effort. Secondly, soon after the U.S. involvement, Field Marshal Alexander Papagos, the authentic hero of Greece's victory over Italy in World War II, emerged from retirement and assumed command of the effort against the guerrillas. He proved to be an exceptional leader who reformed and reorganized the demoralized forces of the government and soon regained the initiative in the war.

The U.S. contribution to victory comprised logistic support, training, equipment, and advisory services. These, together with economic aid, were indispensable in a bankrupt land striving to rebuild its institutions after six years of war of which five years were under enemy occupation. On the other hand, the U.S. involvement dealt largely with the conven-

22

tional aspects of military activity. This sufficed in Greece for the reasons noted above and for one additional and critical reason. In 1948, in search of a quick victory, the insurgents conventionalized their forces and organization and sought to defeat the regular Greek Army in head-on conflict.[1] In Maoist terms, ignoring the concept of protracted war, they abandoned the guerrilla style and did so as the Greek National Army reached the peak of its effectiveness. They were outnumbered and outgunned and quickly went down to defeat in the campaigns of the summer of 1949. Without doubt if they had studied and practiced the precepts of Mao Tse-tung they would have been far more difficult to defeat.

The U.S. involvement in the Greek civil war, which was relatively painless and short, as well as being gratifyingly successful, had little impact on the U.S.'s awareness of Communist rural insurgency as a special or serious new problem. Nothing new had been tried because it had not seemed necessary, thanks to Communist failures and inadequacies. Many years were to pass before the Americans were to be forced to debate and agonize over the dilemmas posed by a skillful insurgent opponent. If anything, the Greek success added an increment of complacency to the outlook of a military command which had helped the Greeks to surmount the challenge of the KKE and had done so with little strain.

THE PHILIPPINE BAPTISM

The involvement in the Philippines, although even smaller in size than that of Greece, can be looked upon as the beginning of active counterinsurgency by the U.S. because the experience was clearly different from conventional combat and because the program undertaken by the Philippine government encompassed, at least embryonically, the wide gamut of activity which became characteristic of American counterinsurgency thinking. It is important to emphasize, however, that the Philippine success was largely the work of Filipinos and, most particularly, of course, of the unique Ramon Magsaysay. The Philippine experience, like the Greek, was characterized by extraordinary good fortune in this critical aspect of the quality of leadership, and tended, along with the Greek experience, to create unrealistic impressions of the costs that counterinsurgency involvement might exact from the participants under a different set of circumstances.

The situation in the Philippines as World War II ended was inauspicious and included factors that spelled serious trouble unless dealt with promptly by the leadership to which power was turned over by the United States. The Japanese occupation had been harsh and the economy was in ruins. Some of the authentic nationalist leadership—notably the group around Jose P. Laurel Senior, who had served as president under Japanese control—had been compromised by association with Japan. The men who assumed power—Manuel Roxas and then, on his death, Elpidio Quirino—led a type of political organization for which issues were secondary and the spoils of power of first importance. Their techniques for gaining and holding power owed something to political bossism as practiced in the United States but included a degree of thuggery and violence endemic in Philippine politics. In effect, beneath the panoply of constitutional principles adopted under American tutelage, the Philippines was politically half-developed in that the constitutional system was manipulated by parties which were little more than cliques competing for the spoils of office by methods which often violated the spirit and law of the constitution.

Although the United States had, during the two generations of its imperial rule, fulfilled what it saw as its obligation to develop political and social institutions to prepare the Philippines for independence in the modern world, it had left the economic structure of the Spaniards virtually unchanged. In consequence, landed wealth in this overwhelmingly agricultural country remained largely in the hands of a small class of plantation owners and latifundists, the latter with many tenants living in semifeudal dependence. The major parties in the political structure responded more often than not to the interests of this class, and the largest group of the population, the landless and poor peasants, were weakly represented in the government. In those areas of central Luzon where the insurgents became most active the situation was particularly acute because the pressure of population on the land had reduced tenant holdings below the point where they produced enough to live on.[2] As usual in this kind of economic condition, private moneylenders charged exorbitant interest for the credit essential to carry farmers from one harvest to the next. The courts which heard cases involving tenant/landlord relations were crowded and slow and the lawyers' fees were high, compounding peasant problems. In other areas of the Philippines economic conditions varied greatly and none reproduced the problems of central Luzon to the same degree.

THE RISE OF THE HUKS

Insurgency in the Philippines, as in many other areas, was in part a product of events during the Second World War. Both the insurgents, the self-styled Hukbong Bayan Laban Sa Hapon (abbreviated first to Hukbalahap and then to Huk), or People's Army Against Japan, and the most notable leaders of the government's antiinsurgency efforts had first learned about guerrilla war during the effort against Japan. The Huks formed one of the larger anti-Japanese guerrilla forces. They were the outgrowth of a Communist-led popular front movement which had already established a substantial political base in central Luzon by the time the Japanese invaded. Ably led by a group of experienced organizers, of whom Luis Taruc was the best known, they moved their combat-worthy followers into remote areas where bases could be established and training carried on. At the same time they converted their political base in the villages into a separate organization, the Barrio United Defense Corps,[3] to provide food, intelligence, recruits, and other essentials to the fighting force. There appears to have been some representation in these camps from the Chinese Communists, although estimates of the numbers vary.

Armed with weapons scavenged from the battlefields of Bataan, they soon launched small-scale harassment operations against the Japanese occupiers, but as the war continued the Huks began to concentrate upon the development and conservation of their own power and fought frequent skirmishes against other anti-Japanese guerrilla groups. When the United States Army returned to the Philippines, its attitude toward the Huks was reserved, and some of the principal leaders, including Luis Taruc, were jailed for having continued to carry out "liquidation" of Filipino enemies in spite of a ban imposed by General MacArthur's headquarters.

The Huk leaders were soon released in preparation for the formal declaration of Philippine independence. Not long after that event, however, the Huks, reacting with vigor against the refusal of the new government to seat their six congressmen (Taruc was one) and accept their local control in areas of central Luzon, went into armed dissidence. In moving thus early in the postwar period they do not seem to have been responding to any external direction but to be reacting to the efforts of the government, as they saw it, to rob them of the fruits of their successes of the preceding four years. Nor was any preparatory effort necessary for agitation and organization. The wartime guerrilla structure, along with the support organization, had not been dismantled and merely needed to be reactivated.

Although the Philippine Communist movement had only limited relationships with the Chinese Communists, the pattern of its activities, particularly in the provinces of central Luzon where its main strength lay, was remarkably similar to the pattern of people's war elsewhere. Because of Huk domination the area came to be called "Huklandia." The guerrillas fought according to the principle of protracted war, relying on ambush, concealment, and mobility. They reestablished their base areas and their support organization in the villages. Through terrorism and superior organization, they became the de facto government in wide areas of Huklandia and maintained schools and provided other, if limited, government services in return for the taxes they collected. Although their armed forces were estimated to number only twelve thousand, this was almost the same number of men in the entire Philippine Army at the time. Government forces, however, also included the Constabulary, a rural police, which actually outnumbered the army, totaling twenty-four thousand.[4] The total Communist organization is estimated to have been about one hundred thousand.[5] During the first phase of the Huk insurgency—1946 to 1950—the central direction remained in Manila while the military headquarters was situated in central Luzon. There were, in fact, two parallel politburos, one in Manila and one in the combat zone, until 1950 when the entire Manila organization was apprehended by the police in a notable intelligence coup.

THE INITIAL RESPONSE

The initial reaction of the Philippine government to this assault upon its existence was the instinctive response of a democratic and constitutional regime run by elected officeholders. The threat was minimized and the task of managing the situation was left to the normal functioning of the appropriate services. The insurgency was treated as a series of criminal acts. The usual attempts were made to apprehend and bring the criminals to justice but no important changes were made in the organization of the security services or in the laws or legal processes. For political reasons the available armed force was scattered about the threatened area providing static protection to local officials and installations, thereby yielding the initiative to the guerrillas. The government described its policy as "the mailed fist," by which it intended to convey an impression of vigor and firmness. In fact, as usually happens in such situations, the army and the police, lacking effective tactics, good intelligence, or adequate training, struck out at the nearest available target, the population of the villages in the affected areas.

> Soon many Filipino farmers and civilians feared the constabulary troops as much or more than the Huks. This destroyed the respect and confidence in many of the people, not only in their armed forces, but in the central government. In many areas of Luzon, the people now openly supported the Communist troops.[6]

Bribery and extortion were common practices of the soldiers, treatment of civilians was often abusive, and villages were sometimes shelled. The police and army of the Philippines, in short, made most of the mistakes an ill-prepared, poorly led conventional force is likely to make when dealing with well-organized Communist guerrillas whose tactics and strategy are aimed precisely at those weaknesses to which conventional armies are prone. The situation was compounded by the confused transition of the Philippine Republic and its institutions from enemy occupation to complete independence and by the very processes of democracy. Politicians concerned to win the next election were inclined to seek special favors for influential constituents and to decry vigorous operations if they upset the even tenor of life in their home areas. The boisterously free press vigilantly surveilled the enforcement of habeas corpus and other democratic rights, which was no doubt their duty. On the other hand, the situation was not normal, the new republic was already in danger, and emergency measures were called for.

After the death by heart attack of President Roxas in 1948, his successor, President Quirino, attempted a new tack based on amnesty and negotiations which, after the insurgents had exploited the respite to rest, train, and refurbish, failed entirely. There followed a resumption of the policy of suppression by police action with no greater success than before. Matters reached their lowest point after the presidential election of 1949. The balloting was widely reputed to have been outrageously rigged by the incumbent administration, which exploited its control of the police and army to alter returns, stuff ballot boxes, and the like.

According to information obtained after the arrest of the Manila Politburo in late 1950, the Communist leadership viewed the deteriorating situation as offering the possibility of complete victory by 1951.[7] The Huks increased their harassment of officialdom and actively sought to spread their organizing and guerrilla operations farther afield, to the other principal islands of the archipelago. The wartime name of the insurgent force was changed to something thought to be more appealing, "People's Liberation Army" (HMB). The ineffectual reactions of government and the armed forces to this offensive and the occasional brutality of the military led to widespread criticism which was embittered by the recollection of how the government had secured its reelection. In the face of this crisis President Quirino came to appreciate that far-reaching changes would have to be made in the government's approach. Although the product of a political system based to a considerable extent on cronyism, nepotism, and corruption, Quirino nevertheless appears to have grasped the basic point that eluded leaders in other countries faced with similar threats: the system would have to be reformed in the critical areas of government that bore on the insurgency despite the possible risks of such a course to the administration. It was a perceptive decision and a risky one which in the end did result in the loss of power by Quirino and his Liberal Party. At the same time, however, it saved the Philippine Republic.

ENTER MAGSAYSAY

Quirino's solution focused on the armed forces. For example, the Philippine Constabulary, the rural police which had traditionally been civilian, was merged into the army to form a single service which had the responsibility for suppression of the insurgency. Provisions were made to increase this force even further and to reorganize it into battalion combat teams (BCTs), an enlarged infantry battalion with artillery, heavy weapons, and service units (engineers, signals, etc.) attached. It was a self-sufficient miniature division numbering about a thousand men and was well suited to ferreting out guerrillas, a task which is poorly done by large, heavily equipped conventional units. Ten such battalions were formed at first, a number gradually increased until it reached twenty-six. The BCTs bore the brunt of counterguerrilla operations throughout the remainder of the war against the Huks. They were supplemented by various other arms of which the most useful to them was a variety of "hunter-killer" unit called the Scout Rangers—five-man squads of highly trained volunteers whose job was to find the enemy in his remote hideouts and either attack on the spot or report back to the parent BCT which would take appropriate action.[8]

On deployment each BCT was assigned a geographical area in which it was responsible for eliminating the insurgency. It usually took the initiative in bringing under their control all the law-enforcement capability in the area, including municipal police and especially the so-called civil guard, usually rag-tag groups of armed civilians. Where the BCT commander saw the need, he would strengthen these units, assigning one of his noncommissioned officers to command them, and when they were capable, using them for static guard duties. The civil guard groups were provided radio communications to summon help from the regulars on short notice. Gradually, the packets of regulars stationed about the countryside guarding local notables and buildings who were easy prey to the enemy became available again for offensive operations with their parent units.[9]

These details of the gradually evolving Filipino approach to counter-guerrilla operations are of interest because they illustrate themes that recur throughout two decades of counterinsurgency. The superior effectiveness of light infantry units, the use of specialized scout squads to reach into and strike at enemy base areas, the reliance on armed civilians under military supervision to defend their own homes, and other unconventional devices were all "discovered" and demonstrated in the Philippines, arrived at after trial and error and repeated failure of more conventional approaches. So was the inadvisability of reliance on either artillery or air bombardment which, according to the commander of one BCT (Colonel Valeriano) "too often . . . inflicts casualties and damages only upon presumably innocent civilians."[10] The Filipinos had no models to base themselves upon and most of their American advisers were equally inexperienced. They arrived at these courses of action by reflecting upon their experience which, in the early years, was mostly one of failure, and seeking to apply its lessons.

One of the sharpest critics of the performance of the armed forces in the late 1940s was the congressman from Zambales province who had access to most government military information as chairman of the Committee on National Defense of the Philippine House of Representatives. Ramon Magsaysay had been a wartime guerrilla himself in his native province and had commanded a force of ten thousand at the time of the Japanese defeat. Instead of returning to private business (he had managed a large bus company in the prewar years after graduating from college), he entered politics. By 1950, when Quirino was seeking a new secretary of national defense to manage the reorganization and buildup of the military forces, Magsaysay had acquired some reputation as a specialist in the military field and as a critic of the military's performance. He also had an unblemished political reputation to go along with his impressive war record and Quirino turned to him, offering the post of secretary of national defense. Magsaysay promptly accepted.

It was a stroke of good fortune for the cause of the Philippine Republic, though not necessarily for Quirino. Magsaysay was a man of rigid honesty, sharp intelligence, and abundant energy. He was also a colorful, unpretentious, and earthy human being, and his few years of immersion in Manila politics had not dulled his instinctive understanding of the needs and problems of the people in the barrios and sitios—the villages and hamlets—of the rural hinterland. He not only sympathized with their difficulties, he also understood the connections between popular grievances and the support gathered by the insurgency, while not forgetting that military effectiveness was also an essential ingredient of success. In addition to these and the other qualities that he brought to the task, he was also a born leader, an instinctive democrat, and a firm anti-Communist. In short, he combined the essential qualities required to meet the crisis of the Philippine Republic. His arrival on the scene rapidly changed the dismal prospects we have described.

On the military side of the conflict, he moved rapidly to carry out the reorganization and reform of the armed forces, setting as his goal their conversion from a politically dominated adjunct of the spoils system to a competent, aggressive combat force. This objective he accomplished in time by personal involvement and intervention at every level. The armed forces of the Philippines were not large and the secretary of national defense was endowed with great energy. Magsaysay followed a policy of surprise inspections and where possible of correcting on the spot the deficiencies he found. He obtained presidential authority to promote or relieve military personnel without reference to the military command and to order courts-martial where he considered it necessary. These were extraordinary powers for a civilian cabinet officer and the fact that he obtained them demonstrated another quality: he was prepared to use the leverage he had built up within the Philippine government even if to do so involved considerable political risk and made him the target of those

he shunted aside.[11] The secretary of national defense went to the lengths
of rejecting an entire promotion list presented for his approval on the
grounds that not a single officer on it had a combat record.

The effects of such an approach by the civilian head of the armed
forces was quickly felt throughout the system.

> No commander, even in the most isolated outpost, could go to bed at night
> sure that he would not be awakened before dawn by an irate Secretary of
> National Defense. . . . He would want to know how much the commander
> knew about the situation in his area; about the state of his command; when
> the troops had last been paid; what they ate for supper that night; how many
> Huk they had killed in the last week; why they hadn't killed more; what was
> the state of motor transport; what were the needs of the civilians in the area;
> what was the attitude of the civilians. And the commander could also be sure
> of a personally administered "shampoo," a sort of verbal but violent Dutch
> rub, if he didn't know the answers.[62]

Improved troop behavior toward civilians was another major facet of
the reform Magsaysay was seeking. He issued a directive "declaring that
every soldier had two duties: first, to act as an ambassador of good will
from the government to the people; second to kill or capture Huk."[13] He
directed that troops entering a settlement do so in a friendly manner and
saw to it that a supply of chewing gum and candy was made available to
pass around to children. Troops were required to carry more food than
they would need themselves and to dispense it to civilians when they saw
the need. Ultimately this "program of attraction" was reinforced by a
new organization established within the army, the Civil Affairs Office of
the Secretary of National Defense. It had units assigned down to
battalion level, where they functioned as advisers to commanders as well
as being responsible for operations in the fields of troop information,
psychological warfare, public information, and civic action.

This was a peculiar amalgam of duties whose common denominator
was political effect, either on the enemy, the population, or the Filipino
soldier. Civic action was, in particular, a novel concept for an army in
combat. In his memoirs, Magsaysay's American adviser General Lansdale states that both the Civil Affairs Office (CAO) and the concept of
civic action—soldiers using the facilities of the military to assist civilians
in a wide variety of ways—were suggestions he made which were
enthusiastically adopted and supported by the secretary. In any event,
the CAO, a small group of about two hundred men, gave the secretary
and the armed forces a capability to shape the political impact of military
operations which was critical to success in the kind of war they were
fighting. Lansdale also points out the similarity between the CAO and
the political commissariat that is a feature of every Communist army—
and with the same purpose, i.e., to assure that the all-important political
dimension of military operations is kept constantly in view. On the other

hand, the CAO was advisory and was not linked to a political party, so the similarity was limited.

The CAO's work in psychological warfare stressed imagination rather than technology and equipment. Leaflets, rumor campaigns, black propaganda (issuance of material purporting to come from the enemy), exploitation of superstitions (an example was the painting of a huge eye—"the eye of God"—opposite the home of an identified Huk informer), and loudspeaker broadcasts directed at enemy units from low-flying airplanes were a few of the many techniques used. The total effect is difficult to assess with any precision, but individual operations are known to have had impact. The institution of a system of rewards for information leading to the capture or killing of insurgents brought direct results but was also important for the psychological impact, the buildup of mistrust within enemy units both for fellow guerrillas and for villagers on whom they ultimately depended for their supplies and other support. For this and other reasons many guerrilla units became divided, as time went on, by internal suspicions, and for fear of betrayal went to the extreme of cutting off all contact with the outside world.

THE MANY-SIDED DEPARTMENT OF DEFENSE

Having a lively awareness of the political needs of the counterinsurgency campaign, Magsaysay before long began expanding the activity of the Department of National Defense into fields well removed from purely military activity. Where he saw a need and a related capability, he would move to fill it regardless of whether it was part of his formal area of responsibility. In effect, his department became a general-purpose agency for combating the Huks either directly, in the military mode, or indirectly, by dealing with the problems of the population which the enemy exploited to build its political base. In the process, the effort became truly multifaceted, a characteristic of successful counterinsurgency which could be realized in the Philippines only in this manner because of the lack of interest displayed by the other arms of government.

Among Magsaysay's innovations, one in particular kept him abreast of civilian/military problems in the combat area as well as providing a direct response to Huk claims that the government was indifferent to the sufferings of the people. He let it be known that any citizen with a grievance against the army or information about the Huks had merely to send a telegram to his office for which the charge would be the equivalent of five cents. A special staff responded to these messages, checked them out, and attempted to get at least a preliminary answer back to the sender within twenty-four hours. The service was lightly used at first, but in time the flow of telegrams became a flood and the program grew to have a substantial effect on public attitudes.

The Huk claims that government justice was biased against the poor and helpless—which had some substance to it—led the secretary of national defense to extend the assistance of the army's Judge Advocate General's Corps to those who needed legal help but could not afford it. These interventions were mostly in land-court matters where tenants without resources were confronted by lawyers employed by landlords and often were helpless to deal with process. By this means, Magsaysay sought to take the edge off the Huk demand for "equal justice for all." It was an imaginative expansion of the military's role to put lawyers in uniform at the side of ragged peasants and one which clearly established the point that the government was attempting to be a friend to the poor.

The army also found itself building schoolhouses—four thousand of them prefabricated by the Corps of Engineers[14]—and providing teachers where no civilians were available. It dug wells, gave medical assistance, and repaired and built bridges and roads. But the most ambitious scheme of all in this expansion of the department's reach was EDCOR (Economic Development Corps), the program to resettle ex-Huks on newly cleared land which became one of the best known of Magsaysay's programs and impacted significantly on insurgent morale and motivation.

EDCOR grew out of the effort to eliminate the basis for the successful Huk appeal to the land-hungry people of Huklandia, building upon an earlier but dormant program to resettle former Philippine soldiers on undeveloped public land. The communities were created on virgin lands; a simple infrastructure was provided—roads, wells, power, community facilities, and housing—and roughly ten-hectare farms were assigned to participants who had the responsibility of clearing them and putting them under cultivation. Until they could bring in a crop the settlers were also provided with food, work animals, and tools—all charged to an account which was to be gradually paid off as the settler began to be self-supporting.

Each community was made up largely of ex-Huks with a stabilizer group of former soldiers who also became administrators of the new village. About one hundred families formed the first settlement at Kapatangan on Mindanao Island. Later, four more settlements were established, two on Mindanao and two on Luzon. Eligibility was extended to all Huks who had no criminal charges against them, and one source claims that no former Huks who met the minimal eligibility standards were turned away by EDCOR.[15] Financial support, according to one source, was initially provided by Magsaysay from a "peace fund" built by popular contribution.[16] According to another, it derived from an appropriation for the new BCTs which authorized that any surplus be used for the rehabilitation of ex-Huks.[17] In any event, the project was conducted by the Department of National Defense throughout its history. Military engineers did the clearing and construction and administered all aspects. Although no cost figures are available, EDCOR was undoubtedly a most economical use of available resources because its impact, magnified by widespread dissemination by government propaganda outlets, reached the remote hiding places of the Huk units. Combined with the increased military pressures of the BCTs, it had an undermining effect on the dedication and commitment of the guerrilla fighters, many of whom had been drawn into the insurgency by the slogan "land for the landless." One source estimates that about fifteen hundred insurgents surrendered or dropped out because of EDCOR and further guesses that it would have taken some thirty thousand troops to eliminate that many of the enemy.[18] All of this was accomplished by a program which in all resettled some fifty-two hundred persons. We may estimate some twelve hundred families were involved, of whom probably something under a thousand were headed by ex-Huks.

If EDCOR was an unusual military activity, equally unusual was the role that Magsaysay assumed in assuring that the midterm congressional and regional elections of 1951 were an accurate reflection of the electorate. As noted earlier, the Huk cause had gained exceptionally in credibility and support as a result of the general view that the presidential election of 1949 had been outrageously rigged. The resultant outcry had convinced the Huks that a "revolutionary situation" existed and that they could hope for victory in a matter of a few years. The secretary of national defense concluded that it was of critical importance to the anti-Huk campaign that the public perceive the 1951 election to have been honest. Only in this way could the government wipe out the effects of 1949 and make it clear that a thorough reform had cleansed the electoral process.

Although nominally a member of the administration that had been elected as a result of the 1949 frauds—which administration was planning to assure victory by the same means in 1951—Magsaysay had already become an independent power who could not either be controlled or dispensed with by Quirino. As we proceed with our description of the development of counterinsurgency theory and practice we will see that this precise matter of reform in the midst of crisis became the most problematic matter confronting government forces attempting to deal with Communist insurgency. Most of them have had a rather precarious hold on power based upon the careful balancing of power nuclei—police, army, and government services—all of which had to be rewarded to assure continued loyalty. The rewards most often took the form of issuing a "license" to exploit a given situation by one form of corruption or another. Hence the sensitivity of reform which would be likely to reduce or eliminate corruption, emphasize performance rather than prestige or status, and thus undermine the motives for continued loyalty. Yet without reform to improve the functioning of key arms of the government, little could be done to upgrade the performance of the services which were essential to gaining public support in competition with the insurgents and to confronting and defeating the insurgency.

In the Philippines, the administration's ability to retain the loyalty of its important political supporters depended on its continued control of Congress and of provincial governorships; hence the significance of the 1951 elections to Quirino. To the president of the Philippines an honest election would mean risking a political destruction by his electoral opponents far more immediate than the threat of destruction by the Huks. If matters had been left in his hands, another rigged election would have been inevitable.

As events turned out, the decision was preempted by Magsaysay, taking advantage of a peculiarity of Philippine law which placed the control of balloting in the hands of an independent Commission on Elections. The commission had the right to call on any Philippine group or institution to help it assure a fair electoral process. In mid-1951 Magsaysay was officially requested to provide the assistance of the military forces for that purpose. The implications of one account of this request are that it was solicited.[19] In any event, with this invitation Magsaysay was able to assign troops to public meetings to guard against intimidation of opposition speakers by armed gangs. The army also stood guard in the neighborhood of polling places and took custody of ballot boxes after the polls closed, transporting them to provincial capitals.

Several private organizations were formed at the same time, apparently with the secretary of national defense's quiet support, to supplement the army's effort. They were called the National Association for Free Elections (Namfrel) and the Philippine News Service, a combine of newspaper publishers. They also assisted the Commission on Elections at its own request and in a variety of ways. Namfrel members, for example, brought people to the polls and also kept watch at polling places for any signs of manipulation. The Philippine News Service assured that as soon as ballot counts were completed they were made public. Backing up his officers and men assigned to election duty stood Magsaysay, prepared to see that they were not penalized—as was threatened—for upholding the law.

A TURNING POINT

The upshot of these preparations was not only an honest election but an upsurge of public support for the government's cause, for the army, and particularly for Magsaysay. Most observers agree that the 1951 elections were a turning point of the war and from that point onward the trend for the Huk movement was sharply downward. Surrenders steadily increased and the guerrilla bands grew smaller and ever more harassed. The reward system of the government, together with numerous psychological-warfare tricks targeted upon individual guerrilla units, built up serious strains within the remaining bands where mutual suspicion and fear paralyzed initiative. In a major move to find respite, the Huks abandoned the densely settled areas of central Luzon and moved to the rugged, sparsely populated Sierra Madre range of mountains in eastern and southern Luzon. Despite the difficulties, government forces pursued them closely and the insurgents gained no respite. Although the final roundup of the hard core remaining on the enemy side was still some years off, the pursuit did not slacken and the declining trend was unmistakable.

At the same time, Magsaysay emerged as a popular leader with an unprecedented hold on the public mind and imagination. The Philippine people attributed the new responsiveness of the government and the honesty of the elections to him personally. His unique style of leadership, which seemed to result in his appearing wherever there was trouble and improvising a satisfactory response, had made him known widely among the common people as well as the educated. At his home in Manila petitioners lined up in the early morning to see him with their problems and grievances against the government, and while eating his breakfast he tried and usually was able to see them all.[20] One observer wrote:

> When the troops campaigned, Magsaysay was there. When a soldier was killed in action, Magsaysay was there to express his . . . concern. When acts of bravery were performed, Magsaysay was there to promote the officers and men. When the troops were in need, Magsaysay was there with supplies. . . . And when the Huks surrendered or were captured, Magsaysay was there to listen to their stories and to see that they received fair treatment.[21]

Almost inevitably, Magsaysay was nominated by the opposition Nationalist Party and ran for president in 1953; he defeated Quirino in an election which was a repeat on a larger scale of the 1951 campaign. Some of the same techniques were used to assure an honest result and, although no longer in control of the army—since he had, of course, to leave the Quirino cabinet—Magsaysay had built up a degree of personal influence which, together with the prospect that he might well soon be president, substituted in some degree for the loss of direct authority. In addition, the Joint U.S. Military Aid Group (JUSMAG) involved itself to the extent of conducting U.S. "advisory" visits to Philippine units active in areas where electoral trouble threatened.[22]

Magsaysay won a sweeping victory and returned to the government in full command of the entire machinery. He used his increased powers to broaden the "program of attraction" and continued the pursuit of the guerrillas along the lines already perfected. In 1954, Luis Taruc, the magnetic "supremo" of the Huk forces, surrendered, and eventually all the principal leaders were rounded up and brought in. By the last year of Magsaysay's term, the end was at hand. In effect, when he died in an airplane crash in March 1957, he had won his war, and, in truth, it had been *his* war in the sense that he had shaped the strategy and dominated the day-to-day implementation of the numerous separate programs that made up the whole.

How Did It Happen?

Twenty years after Magsaysay's death the feat still seems remarkable, especially in view of the difficulties encountered elsewhere in Southeast Asia in the years that followed. Somehow, Magsaysay and his associates managed to solve the precise conundrums which proved so difficult for the United States to master in other countries, notably Vietnam. Their program was well balanced between military pursuit of the insurgents and aid and assistance directed to the needs of the peasant population who formed the base of the insurgency. Military operations were subordinated to the goal of attracting the support of the people. Not only troop behavior but military tactics were dominated by this political objective, something which in later years proved exceedingly difficult for American military commanders to understand and carry out. The Philippine military, fortunately, as it turned out, had not yet been able to reconstruct the Philippine Army in the full image of the U.S. Army and so no combat divisions existed. The substitute devised for the purpose of dealing with the Huks, the Battalion Combat Team, was far better suited to the purpose of chasing guerrillas than a conventional combat division. The Filipinos had some artillery and air power but used it sparingly because of its destructive power, preferring to pursue the enemy with his own tactics, nighttime patrols and ambushes, long-range commando squads and the rest, combined with carefully targeted psychological warfare based on good intelligence effectively exploited.

The intelligence was good and became better because the population was gradually persuaded of the good will of the government and also—equally important—of its competence. In this critical area of public support, Magsaysay's leadership was particularly telling. His ability to understand the needs of the population and to maintain a two-way communication with it avoided the pitfalls of "do-goodism" as practiced elsewhere by the U.S. Largesse handed down from above without the participation of the supposed beneficiaries in the decision-making is not likely to create confidence or support. Magsaysay avoided the trap. The type of leadership he brought to bear spoke directly and impressively, more by actions than words, to popular aspirations.

Somewhat by accident, it would seem, Magsaysay succeeded in unifying the multitude of programs directed at the insurgency under his own leadership. The small size of the Philippine government and of the effort as a whole no doubt assisted him in accomplishing a goal which other governments in similar situations had great difficulty in achieving. Since most of the counterinsurgency effort was initiated by him and carried on by the Department of National Defense, the task was relatively simple in the Philippines. The complications that result when many established agencies with large staffs become involved, pursuing different aspects of a single program, were largely avoided. When he became president, of course, the problem was simplified even further. Other governments, particularly the U.S., were not so fortunate in dealing with the same problem in later years.

Magsaysay also enjoyed certain advantages which, in similar episodes elsewhere, did not exist on the side fighting the insurgency. For example, the issue of nationalism, despite the attempts of the Philippine Communists to focus popular resentment against the United States, was not an important factor. Filipinos did not accept the charge that the Americans were responsible for their problems or that Magsaysay was an American puppet. Another difference was the isolation of the Philippine Islands and the consequent absence of foreign sanctuary from which the Huks could receive help or repair to in times of difficulty.

One other advantage can be suggested but not proved. This is the apparent fact that the Philippine population accepted and grasped the principles on which the government was founded sufficiently well to wish to have them work and, when given the chance, to make them work. They were one of the few peoples in that part of the world to have had both experience and education in democracy, a fact which gave Magsaysay a supportive and approving public response for his attempt to restore democratic practice. With the principles and practice of democracy well understood, the people were aware of what was missing from the system as it existed and understood what the new leadership was trying to do to correct the obvious flaws. The political context was far different in countries where the people at large had no concept or experience of a system which would respond to their needs through democratic processes.

THE AMERICAN ROLE

If this view has any validity, then the indirect role of the United States in establishing a democratic regime and creating an educational system which successfully explained and justified it was a major factor in the successful Philippine experience in defeating Communist insurgency. Beyond this, the U.S. role was important but secondary to that of Magsaysay and the Philippine leadership. The U.S. military and economic presence in this former colony was very substantial, but influence was exercised largely through the economic and military aid missions and the embassy. Such assistance, given the lack of any U.S. policy specifically focused on counterinsurgency, was largely technical. The Philippine Army, which numbered all of twelve thousand men at the start of the insurgency and boasted of a combat strength of precisely two battalions, was not expected to fill the shoes of the departing Americans in conventional firepower or combat capability but to perform internal security duties. The modest size and role of the army was one reason why a capable civilian was able to establish his ascendancy over it and force it to reform its relations with the population as well as its internal organization and methods.

This background did not mean, on the other hand, that the JUSMAG, when consulted, was able to overcome its ingrained training and indoctrination and encourage the Philippine armed forces to follow an unconventional mode of operations in dealing with the insurgency. On the contrary, the evidence suggests the opposite. "Indeed," we are told by two students of the subject,

> many MAAG officers felt that [unconventional] techniques violated the military managerial and tactical principles that had won World War II in the forties and were surely applicable to revolutionary conflicts in the fifties. Filipino officers considered these MAAG views so inappropriate and unacceptable that many of them refused to associate with their MAAG counterparts or communicate to them the true conditions in the countryside or in the Philippine Armed Forces.[23]

Nevertheless, unconventionality was the keynote of that part of the U.S. mission which had the greatest share of influence upon the Philippine approach. Within the JUSMAG was a small, separate mission headed by then Lieutenant Colonel (later Major General) Edward G. Lansdale, an Air Force intelligence specialist with considerable previous experience in the Philippines. In September 1950, Lansdale had arrived back in the Philippines after an absence of two years for a temporary assignment which in his memoirs he describes as follows:

> The United States government wanted me to give all help feasible to the Philippine government in stopping the attempt by the Communist-led Huks to overthrow that government by force. My help was to consist mainly of advice where needed and desired. It was up to me to figure out how best to do this. If funds or equipment was (sic) needed, I was to remember that the United States was straining its resources to meet the war needs in Korea and that any requests from me would have to compete against higher priority demands.[24]

The assignment was the beginning of Lansdale's career as a specialist in unconventional advice to governments threatened by Communist insurgency and to the United States government. In his various overseas assignments (once in the Philippines and twice, with a nine-year interval between, in Vietnam) it appears that at times he functioned under CIA auspices and at times he did not.[25] He does not discuss this aspect of his work in the account of his assignment to the Philippines in 1950 to 1953 and so we are left to speculate. The vague description of his authorization given above together with the fact that, as he describes in his memoirs, he became deeply involved in assisting Magsaysay in both elections that were of critical importance in the defeat of the Huks, as well as dispensing advice on all aspects of the conflict, suggest that during this tour he was wearing a CIA hat. No other government agency would have permitted its representative to have become involved in quite the same way with a foreign government leader as Lansdale became involved with Magsaysay across such a wide range of activities. The two men became close personal friends, shared quarters at various times, and were constantly together on inspection trips. They saw each other at least once a day and often sat up until the early hours discussing the problems and solutions that Magsaysay was preoccupied with. It is clear from Lansdale's account that the two shared basic values and saw most matters in the same light. They both preferred a direct, personal, and often unconventional approach, and both were informal in their dealings. Early in his tour Lansdale gained Magsaysay's trust and was invited to speak his mind, to suggest and criticize on matters related to his mission. There is no reason to doubt his account that his suggestions were often adopted and that he was able to make important contributions to the Philippine success against the Huks. Such departures as the Civil Affairs Office, EDCOR, and the proliferation of devious psychological warfare schemes and even Magsaysay's techniques of surprise inspections owed much to the latter's imaginative friend, the harmonica-playing American Air Force colonel.

On the other hand, none of this diminishes Magsaysay's indispensable personal role in leading the Philippine government and people out of the morass in which they were sunk to a clear-cut victory. Lansdale was especially useful to him as a foreign adviser with no personal stake in Philippine society, whose premises and priorities were the same as the secretary's, and who was gifted with a fertile imagination. The major initiatives and strategies were Magsaysay's, and various myths that made of Lansdale a puppet-master and Magsaysay his puppet were wide of the mark.

The critical contribution of Lansdale which went beyond his personal impact upon the Philippine leader was his role in the two elections of 1951 and 1953. Reading between the lines of his account it appears likely that he designed the strategy and was instrumental in developing the organizations—Namfrel and the Philippine News Service—which were indispensable to assuring an honest poll and hence victory. If funds were involved, and they probably were, in all likelihood they came from the CIA, which, therefore, has some responsibility for intervening in Philippine affairs to assist Philippine democratic processes to function as their constitution called for them to function.

The example of the Philippine success had considerable influence in later years as the United States became more concerned with and involved in counterinsurgency. It explains some of the emphases and preconceptions of U.S. interventions. Most specifically, it explains the confidence that a modicum of advice, of technical assistance, and of economic and military aid could suffice to put a threatened nation back on its feet and on the way to success in counterinsurgency. The element of good luck in finding a Magsaysay was not always understood as what it was—sheer good luck. Nor was it fully appreciated that the Huk movement was still relatively small in size and limited in area and that this accounted in part for the fairly rapid success of a small army and a government of limited capability in reducing it to helplessness. It is also apparent that in later involvements the U.S. disregarded many of the principles that had underlain the Philippine experience, notably the overriding importance of political as against military goals and objectives. It would also seem that the significance of Magsaysay's ability to cope with the problem of self-reform of government institutions in a time of crisis was poorly grasped. His presence on the scene and his remarkable skills made the victory seem far easier than it actually was and perhaps obscured as much as it revealed.

★   ★   ★

MALAYA AND THE BRITISH EXPERIENCE

During the same years that saw the emergence of the Hukbalahaps in the Philippines, a separate but similar episode took form and became a threat to the British position so recently restored after the wartime defeat and occupation in Singapore and the Malay Peninsula. There were many similarities between the two episodes and between the methods developed in both countries to cope with the threat, although there appears to have been very little exchange of experience and ideas among the four friendly governments involved. That fact suggests the existence of underlying realities common to rural Communist insurgencies and to the programs which have successfully thwarted them.

The British experience in confronting and mastering the insurgency of the Malay Communist Party (MCP) has been studied and described by a number of participants and analysts,[26] and a detailed account is not necessary in this history of U.S. counterinsurgency policies and activities. To summarize briefly the main events, the episode in Malaya was also the outgrowth of wartime guerrilla operations against the Japanese. The MCP acquired weapons from the allies and by capture from the Japanese occupying forces. A portion of these weapons was turned in after the British authorities reestablished their rule but many were retained and cached. Although the guerrilla groups under Communist control were nominally disbanded, an organization remained in being in the disguise of a veterans' association. In 1948 the Communists decided that the time had come to make a bid for power. There is considerable evidence suggesting that the decision was influenced by the call issued at the All-Asian Youth Congress in Calcutta in February of that year which was mentioned in the previous chapter. It also coincided with the views of an ascendant faction of the party led by the newly selected secretary general, Chin Peng.

Terrorism against Europeans, but also against simple peasants; attacks on police posts; and intensive propaganda and organization work among the Chinese community, particularly the so-called squatters who lived in shantytowns on the fringes of the jungle; these were the main thrust of the guerrilla effort. Although strongly influenced by study of Mao Tse-tung, the MCP leaders put their own interpretation on his prescriptions, and as a result they relied heavily on terrorism both to force the British out and to cow the population. They also established a timetable which, in the early years at least, made little concession to the concept of protracted war. They were in a hurry and began immediately to operate with company-sized units before their troops were adequately trained and experienced. Another and truly crippling weakness was the fact that the Communist movement was almost entirely Chinese in its ethnic makeup in a country where the Chinese comprised a little less than half the population and were bitterly resented by the original population, the Malays. The Communists also relied heavily for food, recruits, and other support on the squatter population of Chinese who scratched out a living on the edge of the jungle. As it turned out, this was also a major vulnerability.

As in the Philippines, the original reaction of the government was sluggish and inadequate. An emergency was declared and emergency regulations put into effect which made it possible to control the population and to deal summarily with the Communist organization and its supporters, once identified. But neither sufficient resources nor an adequate organization was developed in the early years—a common feature of the reaction of a democratic government to attack by a movement which violates all the accepted norms and thus requires the setting aside of legal restrictions and standard operating procedures if it is to be mastered.

In 1950, after about two years of groping, the British appointed a new senior official who, under the high commissioner, obtained authority to coordinate all "emergency" activity, civilian and military. This was Lieutenant-General Sir Harold Briggs, the author of the plan which eventually subdued the insurgents. The "Briggs Plan" was the beginning of the successful counterinsurgency effort in Malaya. It focused on guerrilla suppression and on the organization of a government apparatus to manage the effort at all levels. Avoiding the temptation to operate everywhere at once, the plan called for clearing the country of guerrillas from south to north. Most important was the decision to concentrate upon creating a physical separation between the guerrillas and the population they depended upon for essential support, particularly food, intelligence, and recruits, i.e., the squatters and the villages inhabited by workers in the two main industries of the country, tin mines and rubber plantations, both often found close to the edges of the jungle. The plan called for the resettlement of a large portion of these people—comprising a population of four hundred thousand—in "New Villages," specially built for the purpose. They were compact, surrounded with wire, and fully under police control. Between 1950 and 1952, 410 New Villages were created with a population of 423,000.[27] It was a major blow to the insurgents who from then on were sorely pressed.

General Briggs also reorganized the government's machinery to manage all phases of the complex program. His prescription was to establish committees at which all relevant branches were represented and which met daily in many cases, making on-the-spot decisions for the prosecution of the war. Such War Executive Committees existed at district, state, and national level, uniting the three main elements—civil government, police, and military—in a single command structure. Each committee at each level had a war room and operations center where all information relating to the course of the conflict was maintained and displayed or stored.

While the British thus evolved a plan and reorganized their effort to deal with the unusual challenges of the insurgency, the MCP also found it necessary to adjust its strategy and tactics to the realities, particularly to the refusal of the government and population to yield, as had been expected, to terrorism. Apparently reacting to criticism from representatives of the Chinese Communists, the MCP made a sharp turn away from miscellaneous terrorism which impacted upon ordinary people and sought instead to court popular support. The insurgents decided at the same time to abandon company-sized operations and to limit themselves to operating in smaller groups more suited to their capabilities.

Although Briggs's plan and organizational changes had decisive long-term results, the effects were slow in manifesting themselves. At the end of 1951, the high commissioner of Malaya, Sir Henry Gurney, was killed in ambush and Briggs himself was forced to resign for reasons of health. It was the low point of the war for the British. Then, early in 1952, Sir Gerald Templer arrived on the scene. Selected by Prime Minister Winston Churchill and placed in charge of both the military and civilian sides of the war, he was in effect a proconsul with full powers to deploy and manage all of the government's resources and organization. Templer concentrated upon vigorous implementation of the plans and programs already on the books, spending most of his time in the field—an interesting parallel with what Magsaysay was doing in the Philippines at about the same time. He gave emphasis to a program of food-denial to the insurgents and at the same time directed resources into rural development to improve living conditions in both Malay and Chinese villages. Also at this time, the British began the exceedingly delicate process of evolving a permanent solution to Malaya's political problems, aiming toward the gradual construction of an independent democratic regime which would unite Malaya's many ethnic groups, its nine sultanates, and its three city-states (the former Straits Settlements of Penang, Malacca, and Singapore) into a stable federal structure.

Food-denial became a devastating weapon against the guerrillas who were almost entirely dependent upon their support organization in the Chinese villages to collect food and deliver it to the edges of the jungle. The government controlled all food stocks and distribution and made certain that no one possessed supplies in excess of current need. In a relatively short time the insurgents were suffering from hunger and malnutrition, and, as a result, more and more of them began to surrender.

Templer established a Rural Industrial Development Authority to carry out small-scale development projects in the countryside. The effort did not overlook the needs of the New Villages. They were assisted in the building of amenities such as electricity, water supply and roads, which the population had never before enjoyed. Local elections began to be held in rural communities, Chinese and Malay alike, and elected village councils assumed responsibility for managing local affairs.

Another of Templer's priorities was the improvement of the police, which, under the system followed in Malaya from the beginning of the emergency, bore much of the responsibility for protecting the population and pursuing the guerrillas. The police force was reorganized under a senior officer borrowed from the London police. Training and retraining were intensified with attention to the "Special Constables," the corps of temporary policemen who had been recruited early in the emergency to relieve the armed forces of static guard duties and routine security. Intelligence work had always been the responsibility of the Special

Branch of the police's Criminal Investigation Division, and this elite unit of covert intelligence collectors was strengthened throughout the peninsula, especially by the recruitment of ethnic Chinese who, until this time, had been poorly represented in the force.

All of this activity—and much more—had its effect. Before Templer completed his tour and left Malaya in 1954 the tide had turned. In 1953 it became apparent that the strength of the guerrillas was declining sharply. About thirteen hundred casualties were recorded, a large loss for a total force which never exceeded six thousand. Toward the end of that year Templer declared the first "White Area," where no enemy existed and where all emergency regulations were lifted. In the immediately ensuing years, more and more of the country was declared "white" and normality returned to the lives of most of the population.

In the meantime the gradual replacement of British by Malayan rule progressed steadily. In 1957, Malaya was formally declared independent with a democratically elected parliament and a cabinet headed by Prime Minister Tunku (Prince) Abdul Rahman. The transfer of power went smoothly, assisted by the fact that many British civil servants stayed on as contract employees of the new government. In subsequent years, of course, they too gradually withdrew. The counterinsurgency programs and organizational systems of the British period were retained and the steady erosion of insurgent strength continued until only a few hundred persisted in their now forlorn effort. Most of them spent most of their time in the border areas of Thailand where the leadership had established itself as early as 1953. In 1966, the emergency, which had been declared in effect in 1948, was formally brought to an end; but by then the war to all intents and purposes had long been over.

THE MAIN PRINCIPLES OF BRITISH STRATEGY

The British achievement in Malaya was a noteworthy one. London accepted responsibility for restoring order and launching the processes whereby Malaya would become a self-governing, independent, and democratic state and did this in the midst of serious internal crisis brought on by the insurgency. Nevertheless, both goals were met at the same time. It is difficult to cite a parallel in this period of the dismantling of the British Empire.

A number of the unique qualities of British operating style were evident. Of great importance was the emphasis on legality and the rule of law, binding on both powerful and weak, governors and governed. The civil service functioned in this mode and was never seriously tainted with corruption or the charge of playing politics. In fact, it became a feature of the "British school" of counterinsurgency to emphasize the vital importance to successful counterinsurgency of an honest and competent civil service functioning under a rule of law.[28] At the same time, we may add, men who had been professionally formed in the British colonial system seemed unable to grasp fully the difficulty of duplicating the qualities of the various British colonial services in a country such as Vietnam, where the major government institutions, including civil service, were not outside the political system but were very much part of it and thus were one means through which political rewards were distributed.

Another feature of the British style evident in Malaya was simplicity of organization—the ability to operate effectively without the burden of an elaborate and cumbersome staff structure. Government by committee was one aspect of this quality and is a type of management style which does not have a good name, at least in the United States. The British in Malaya, however, showed the ability to make it work. The War Executive Committees took rapid and decisive action on a daily basis with a minimum of fanfare and red tape. They successfully unified the operation without the complex reorganizations and many attendant delays that afflicted similar American programs in later years. An unusual degree of flexibility was also evident in the manner in which the various services—civilian, police, and military—set aside normal patterns for the duration of the emergency and (not always happily, but nevertheless loyally) merged their efforts and submerged their separate ambitions and organizational goals.

In addition to these qualities of operating style, certain principles emerged and were followed which stemmed from the special nature of the war and of the British authorities' understanding that it could not be fought in the manner normal to conventional armed conflict. All of these principles revolved around the fact that the central issue in counterinsurgency is the loyalty and commitment of the population at large to the government's cause. From this it follows that counterinsurgency operations should create among the population as few additional or gratuitous reasons as possible for supporting the insurgents. To assure that adequate importance is given to this rule, civilian control over the military and over military operations is an absolute requirement and was so considered in Malaya. When allowed to follow their own inclinations and institutional repertoires, military leaders will naturally give precedence to military considerations, will concentrate their forces and their firepower to strike the most devastating blows of which they are capable. Precisely at that point, of course, the guerrillas will melt away and the blow will land harmlessly except for any civilians who happen to be in the way. Effective military operations against guerrillas, on the other hand, violate many of the principles that are drilled into professional soldiers from their first day in uniform.

In Malaya, civilian domination was maintained from the beginning.

Curiously enough it was largely the doing of two veteran soldiers, Generals Briggs and Templer, a fact which may have had something to do with the willingness of the military command to accept this unusual way of fighting a war. Indeed, it is worth noting that the conflict was officially called an "emergency" rather than a war, a euphemism with some point. Throughout the "emergency" the military forces deployed in Malaya tailored their operations to the kind of war they faced rather than to the kind of fighting they had been trained and organized to carry out. It was a primitive war of long, wearisome foot patrols, small engagements, and light weapons. Artillery and air bombardment were seldom employed. Instead of the traditional and virtually sacred principle of concentration of force, troops were employed in small packets. Divisions were never deployed as such, to the extent that one British commander new to the scene made this oft-quoted comment: "The only thing a divisional commander has to do in this sort of war is to go around seeing that the troops have got their beer."[29] Military operations were controlled through the War Executive Committees on which the military had representation, while the command structure was limited to assuring supply, training, replacements, and similar needs.

In line with the same underlying principle, the task of protecting the population was not assigned to the military but to the police, on the grounds that the latter were trained for and accustomed to dealing with the public at large while the latter were not. The regular police as augmented by the Special Constables outnumbered the soldiers and other military services. In fact, at their peak figure of sixty thousand they almost doubled the peak military figure of 31,400.[30] It was usually the police rather than the army which enforced the emergency laws, the food-denial program, the identification system, and the other control measures that eventually had such a devastating effect. With the police playing a major role, the counterinsurgency program had the character of a large-scale criminal investigation and roundup rather than a war. Operations were meticulously targeted, dossiers were collected and kept up to date on all members of the insurgent organization, and when an insurgent was killed, his body had to be brought to the nearest police post so that he could be properly identified and his name crossed off the list of wanted men. The effect of all this was to increase greatly the precision of the counterinsurgency war, thus minimizing the damage and loss visited upon the civilian population.

Essential to the effective prosecution of war in this style is a high quality of intelligence on the enemy to make possible the degree of precision required. Intelligence was also largely a police responsibility. Through the committee system and the common war-room operations center it became immediately available to the army at the appropriate level. The police forces were made responsible for intelligence because the most important source was the civilian population with which they had the most intimate dealings and also because the police, who had long been following the Communist organization and personnel, boasted the greatest expertise in the subject.

In line with the goal of damaging civilian noncombatants as little as possible, emphasis was placed upon information and psychological warfare operations—another aspect in which the Malayan counterinsurgency resembled that in the Philippines. Intelligence was exploited to target on particular units and even individual enemy soldiers or cadres with leaflets and airborne loudspeakers. Safe-conduct passes were strewn through the jungle by aircraft, inviting the guerrillas to surrender and promising good treatment. Surrendered enemy personnel were exploited to send messages back to their former comrades, reinforcing the government's assurances. Supplementing the propaganda was an elaborate rewards program which allotted graduated financial payments to persons who captured or contributed information leading to the capture of individual insurgents. The rewards ranged from $875 (US) for a common soldier or party member to $28,000 for the chairman of the Central Committee. As the government gained the initiative and showed its ability to protect informers, disaffected associates of the insurgency increasingly took advantage of the rewards program. Many a Chinese laborer was able to set himself up in business with the proceeds of his betrayal of former comrades.

The significance of the reliance on psychological warfare to replace firepower in counterinsurgency is that it reduces the need for combat operations, thus minimizing the destruction of life and property which so often impacts upon the population. It is also much cheaper, a factor not to be ignored.

Finally, we must note the progressive unification of the multifarious activities of the counterinsurgency effort into a single organizational structure which was finally completed when General Templer took charge of both the civilian and military sides. In any large bureaucracy the surrender of organizational independence and the merging of institutional authorities and prerogatives into a single structure is a painful and even a repellent course to have to take. It was taken in Malaya because it was seen as essential if all sides of the effort were to be brought into effective coordination. Otherwise the tendency of each separate service or agency to follow its normal and traditional priorities and practices would have prevailed, to the great detriment of the attempt to deal with the insurgency.

WAS THE EXPERIENCE TRANSFERABLE?

Operating consistently on these principles, the British achieved a notable victory in Malaya and promptly left. In the years that followed, as the U.S. became deeply involved in counterinsurgency in Southeast Asia, there was much discussion back and forth as to the applicability to other countries of the Malayan experience and the principles upon which it was based. Much of what was done in Malaya responded to the underlying realities of Communist rural insurgency and was undoubtedly transferable elsewhere. The principles of civilian control and of combined and unified organization, the stress on honest, impartial, and competent administration, the focus on political rather than military objectives, all of these in time proved to be valid principles for any counterinsurgency operation. There were other aspects, however, that were unique to Malaya and greatly simplified the British task. First, of course, was the restriction of the insurgent movement to the Chinese, who comprised 38 percent of the population, a fact which considerably limited the threat and eased the task of the authorities but did not change the nature of the challenge or the underlying strategies required to meet it. A second uniquely favorable aspect was the concentration of the population on whom the guerrillas depended for support in villages clustered along the edge of the jungle. That circumstance greatly eased the task of bringing this population under tight control and may have misled some into underestimating the difficulty of such a program where more normal population distribution existed.

But the most important advantage of the British in Malaya lay in the fact that they were in charge and that consequently the main instruments—police, civil service, military services—were either their own or under their exclusive management during the critical years. The first and most obvious benefit of this situation was that it obviated the cumbersome, wasteful, and confused management of strategy and programs that resulted when the principal party was forced into the role of adviser or ally, legally a mere guest on foreign soil. The whole question of "leverage"—whether and how to use it to obtain better performance from a host government which the U.S. was helping but did not control—never came up in Malaya. In most matters, the British had only themselves to consult and to direct—a priceless advantage.

A second dividend of exclusive British control was that the question we have described as "self-reform in crisis" never arose in the particularly difficult form in which it arose elsewhere. Civil service, police, and armed services were not part of the political system nor employed to stabilize the regime by balancing powerful satraps. Corruption as a political cement was not a feature of the Malayan political structure. Consequently, the need to reform the police, the military, and the civil service did not exist and did not pose the bitter choice which faced the U.S. on several occasions: the choice between a corrupt, inefficient, but relatively stable system on the one hand and a putatively reformed, hopefully more efficient, but probably unstable system on the other. In most cases, as it turned out, the second choice was not a practical one for the U.S. in the role of ally and adviser where the host regime kept itself in power by the shrewd and cynical balancing of political rewards involving the use and misuse of the government's services. Such a regime naturally shied away from self-reform as an invitation to disaster.

CHOOSING EXAMPLES TO FOLLOW

In both the Philippines and Malaya, operational models existed by the end of the decade of successful strategies against Maoist people's war, models that were rich in lessons and illustrations for those confronted with similar problems elsewhere. They were examples well enough known in the United States to the specialists who concerned themselves with "small wars" and similar matters. As concern and interest grew to the point where the White House was itself deeply immersed in the problems of counterinsurgency, they came under more general study and were accepted as evidence entirely justifying an optimistic outlook upon the challenge posed by people's war.

One other experience, that of the French in both Vietnam and Algeria, was also looked at carefully for lessons and insights. But here the conclusion was reached that the French experience resembled more a series of cautionary tales than examples to be followed. As early as 1951, Senator John F. Kennedy visited Vietnam and returned with an unfavorable impression of the French approach there. "In Indochina," he said,

> we have allied ourselves to the desperate effort of a French regime to hang on to the remnants of empire. There is no broad general support of the native Vietnam government among the people of that area. To check the southern drive of Communism makes sense but not only through reliance on the force of arms. The task rather is to build strong native non-Communist sentiment within these areas and rely on that as a spearhead of defense rather than the legions of General de Lattre. To do this apart from and in defiance of innately nationalistic aims spells foredoomed failure.[31]

The future president expressed similar sentiments about French policies in Algeria six years later. In both areas what was seen as the French failure to deal realistically with the underlying political appeal of the insurgency was believed to vitiate the usefulness of French experience in either Vietnam or Algeria. Their ultimate failure thus limited French influence in these matters to the purview of specialists who studied the output of the French school calling itself "la guerre révolutionnaire." It was a somewhat frantic and intense Gallic effort to generalize from French experience to justify a world wide approach which duplicated the mechanics of the Mao/Giap system while ignoring its political substance.[32] "La guerre révolutionnaire" also received an impressive fictionalized treatment in the writings of Jean de Larteguy, of which *The Centurions* achieved best-seller status in the United States. The basic message of all this was that ruthless control of the details of village life by an occupying army would effectively separate the population from the insurgents and destroy the latter's hold. This, however, was as far as the approach was able to go. It had no answer to the problem of institutionalizing the gains achieved at a high cost or of how the occupying army would be able to let go its hold in the villages. "La guerre révolutionnaire" also became the creed of the right-wing French officers who eventually challenged the French government over Algeria and were firmly suppressed by General de Gaulle. In sum, there was little in these notions, save some tactical innovations, which recommended them as a model to the Americans concerned with the same problem.

The U.S. interest in such matters was hardly intense or general during much of the 1950s, but there was nevertheless a steadily growing concern among some influential academics and policy-level officials related to the larger question of the United States's role vis-a-vis the underdeveloped world. The period of the mid-fifties, when the process of decolonization was changing the political complexion of vast areas which then became an arena for the competing sides in the cold war, saw the beginnings of the view which identified the "third world" as an area sharing common problems and posing common policy issues to the U.S. on three continents. The Center for International Studies at MIT was one principal source of studies and of appeals to the concerned public for a more vigorous American program to confront the problem posed, initially by a more vigorous and better-funded foreign aid program[33] aimed at the developing countries. Increasingly, one thread of this concern was the perceived threat of Communist exploitation of the problems besetting the so-called emerging nations by the use of various techniques, among them guerrilla war. As early as 1955, in *An American Policy in Asia,* W. W. Rostow of MIT wrote:

> What we face in Asia . . . is the possibility that new territories will fall to the enemy by a combination of subversion and guerilla warfare. They do not demand that Soviet or Chinese Communist troops cross borders and create . . . targets for major American military strength. In Vietnam, Laos, Cambodia, Thailand, and possibly Indonesia as well, the enemy is now conducting targetless warfare in which he is a professional and we are amateurs.[34]

The concern was shared by senior officials of the Eisenhower Administration. In an address in 1958, John Foster Dulles called attention to the threat of indirect aggression whereby,

> through use of inflammatory radio broadcasts; through infiltration of weapons, agents and of bribe money; through incitement to murder and assassination; and through threats of personal violence it becomes possible for one nation to destroy the genuine independence of another.[35]

He saw this as a threat which could have disastrous consequences and expressed the view that the United Nations should assume the responsibility of dealing with it. In the following year, a prestigious committee appointed by President Eisenhower to study the U.S. military aid program also noted the challenge of a new variety of threat. The report of the Draper Committee detected "a shift of emphasis of the Communist tactics—for the time being at least—from direct military challenges to subversion, propaganda and economic offenses," and made some limited suggestion for coping with the challenge.[36]

The issue of the proper methods and policies for dealing with this perceived challenge was, however, not confronted by the Eisenhower Administration, which was more seriously concerned with the need to maintain a balanced budget and a policy of fiscal conservatism.[37] The advocates of a policy of greater concern for events in the less-developed world and for the threat of guerrilla warfare turned to the senator from Massachusetts, whose interest was considerable and who was emerging as the standard-bearer for a more aggressive and innovative posture in confronting worldwide challenges. During the election of 1960, the victorious candidate had made the need for a capability to deal with low-level violence one of the minor themes of his campaign. His victory made it possible for him to convert these views into public policy and he did not delay in doing so.

3

The Kennedy Crucible

★ ★ ★

President Kennedy's first few months in office were the crucible for the policies that came to be called counterinsurgency. Moreover, the president personally took the lead in formulating the programs, pushing both his own staff and the government establishment to give the matter priority attention. According to Roger Hilsman, one of the first questions he put to his associates after his inauguration was, "What are we doing about guerrilla warfare?"[1] The immediate stimulus for the question appears to have been the January 6, 1961, speech by Chairman Khrushchev declaring in categorical style that Communists support "wars of national liberation."[2] This speech struck Kennedy so forcefully that he read excerpts from it to the first meeting of his National Security Council and instructed the assembled agency heads to study it and circulate it among their staffs, who were also to digest its contents.[3] From the same meeting emerged the first formal action to translate the president's preoccupation into government policy. It took the form of *National Security Action Memorandum (NSAM) No. 2,* instructing the secretary of defense to look into the matter of "increasing counter-guerrilla resources."[4] It was but the first in a series of actions prodding and guiding the national security system into responding to the president's perceptions in counterinsurgency.

Must we then attribute the president's decisions on guerrilla warfare to his reactions to a Khrushchev speech? Only so far as timing was concerned. The president's insistence on moving ahead on the issue amid distractions of his first days in office does seem to have been prompted by Khrushchev, whose sweeping language caused him some alarm. But that language reverberated against a series of events that appeared related: the trouble in Laos, about which President Eisenhower had given his successor a careful briefing;[5] the dawning of awareness that South Vietnam was encountering a serious guerrilla problem; the problem of Cuba, which had become a major U.S. concern through a successful guerrilla-style revolution; the appearance of Communist guerrilla threats in Colombia and Venezuela; and the continuing agonies of France in Algeria. Although the president was aware that the Algerian revolt was not Communist-controlled, it was not difficult to see a pattern in these events and to relate the Khrushchev speech to it. Indeed, the Soviet premier himself made the point, citing Cuba, Vietnam, and Algeria as current examples of just wars and talking of the opening of a new front in Latin America.

What gave the question added gravity was Kennedy's familiarity with the history of guerrilla involvements—and Communist support of them—in the past decade. As already noted, he had visited Vietnam in 1951, coming away with the conviction that guerrilla-style warfare posed major difficulties which, he concluded then, could only be dealt with politically.[6] He commented similarly about the French predicament in Vietnam in 1954, arguing against American intervention without strict conditions relating to Vietnamese independence.[7] His later critique of the French position in Algeria developed the same ideas. Another kind of reaction to guerrilla warfare emerges consistently in his comments from 1954 until his election. It related to the unreadiness of the U.S. to deal with any sort of military threat except nuclear war. "So in practice," said Senator Kennedy in 1959, "our nuclear retaliatory power is not enough. It cannot deter Communist aggression which is too limited to justify atomic war. It cannot protect uncommitted nations against a Communist takeover using local or guerrilla forces. It cannot be used in so-called brush-fire wars. . . . In short, it cannot prevent the Communists from nibbling away at the fringe of the free world's territory or strength.[8] Arguments of this sort appeared frequently during Kennedy's 1960 campaign, most often in support of the case for a more balanced U.S. military posture, a capability for a "flexible response" to a variety of threats without bringing on nuclear devastation. The theme related directly to the perceived threat of Communist-sponsored guerrilla outbreaks in the less-developed world.

Other factors influenced Kennedy. Most important of these were his own reading of the history of his times and the grounds on which he had appealed to the country to elect him. The Khrushchevian rhetoric was of a nature to arouse the concern of a man of the generation which believed it had learned from intimate and painful experience to attend carefully to the apparent rantings of such a leader. "Is there likelihood of such wars recurring?" asked Khrushchev. "Yes, there is. . . . The Communists support just wars of this kind wholeheartedly and they march in the van of the peoples fighting for liberation."[9] It must have had echoes for this president, who attracted public attention with a book documenting that England had allowed Hitler to become a threat through laziness and inattention. Moreover, he had just won the presidency on the claim that he could rejuvenate a lethargic democracy to deal with a threatening world. Such convictions were fundamental to his view of the world and he responded to Khrushchev in a variety of ways, of which one was to focus on American capabilities to parry the guerrilla threat. Kennedy's strong reaction to Khrushchev's words thus stemmed from long and firmly held views which were fundamental to his political philosophy and to his sense of his mission. He would probably have acted similarly without the stimulus of Khrushchev, although possibly neither so soon nor so urgently.

Experts in Soviet foreign policy have long since dissected Khrushchev's words in his January 6 speech and concluded that they actually represented nothing new in terms of Soviet worldwide policies and that, as we noted in Chapter I, the emphasis placed upon the theme of "wars of national liberation" was probably a response to criticisms voiced within the Communist movement by the Chinese.[10] The few paragraphs concerned were, at any rate, buried in an immensely long review of Soviet domestic and foreign policies and were uttered more or less in passing. On the other hand, they came to Kennedy's attention at a particularly sensitive time and echoed against a long series of verbal provocations by the Soviet leader and against concrete events in the underdeveloped world which combined to produce their strong effect in Kennedy's mind. In Laos and Vietnam, Communist guerrilla techniques were proving as baffling to independent governments as they had been to the French. Cuba was in the forefront of the president's attention and was a symbol of the kind of troubles that could result from successful Communist guerrilla movements. To ignore these factors, not to mention the history recounted in previous chapters, and to suggest that Kennedy overreacted is to apply hindsight unjustifiably to a complex group of phenomena. The reasons for his concern were serious ones and that concern was shared by most of the community qualified and informed in foreign affairs.

Events in the early months of the administration tended to reinforce the initial reaction to the threat of "wars of national liberation." Most particularly, those early months witnessed the failure of the attempt at the Bay of Pigs to reverse the roles with the U.S. striking through a controlled indigenous force. Kennedy's comments immediately after the Bay of Pigs show how that experience had reinforced his concern: "For we are opposed around the world," he said on April 27, 1961, "by a monolithic and ruthless conspiracy that relies primarily on covert means for expanding its sphere of influence—on infiltration instead of invasion, on subversion instead of elections, on intimidation instead of free choice, on guerrillas by night instead of armies by day. It is a system which has conscripted vast human and material resources into the building of a tightly knit, highly efficient machine."

He then called upon the country to support him in resisting the threat by the means appropriate to its peculiar nature. "We intend to profit from this lesson. We intend to re-examine and re-orient our forces of all kinds—our tactics and our institutions here in this community. We intend to intensify our efforts for a struggle in many ways more difficult than war."[11]

ACTIONS TO SUIT THE WORDS

There is no mistaking the strength of the resolve behind these words, and the promised actions followed. The president presided over a sustained effort to reconstruct the fabric of the armed forces and particularly of the army, which was in fact already well begun. After promising, in his first State of the Union message, to submit proposals for change as soon as he could complete a review, he had on March 28 delivered the first of his Special Messages on the Defense Budget.

The message dealt with a good deal more than guerrilla wars, but it gave special emphasis to that subject. It prescribed a "strengthened capability to meet limited and guerrilla warfare. . . . We must be ready now to deal with any size of force, including small externally supported bands of men and we must help train local forces to be equally effective.[12] This message was followed in a few months by a second on "Urgent National Needs" which went beyond purely military responses to include expanded operations in the fields of economic aid, information, and intelligence. The threat was defined somewhat more broadly this time as a concealed form of aggression "exploiting the desire for change in the southern half of the globe" for ends that were subversive of freedom. "Their revolution is the greatest in human history" and the U.S. should support them regardless of the cold war. Although the adversary did not create the revolution, he is seeking to capture it for himself. "And in the contest we cannot stand aside."[13]

Such public appeals were merely the visible tip of the president's campaign. From the White House he personally reached out into the government establishment to deliver the message that he was serious about a new approach to meet the novel threat that he saw hanging over the country. In the early weeks of his term he had started at the top by seeking to educate himself in the writings of Che Guevara and Mao Tse-tung on guerrilla war. He asked to be shown the special equipment provided to U.S. antiguerrilla forces and to read the military training manuals on the subject. On both counts he was dissatisfied; the equipment was antiquated and the manuals scanty. According to Theodore Sorenson, he pressed for better personal equipment, more helicopters, improved firepower. He did this before the Joint Chiefs of Staff at a meeting specially called for the purpose.[14]

Indeed, over the objections of military traditionalists, he singled out the Army Special Forces for attention, authorizing its troopers to wear the green beret as a symbol of its distinctive mission. He followed the progress of his favored unit with interest and, later in the year, spent a day at Fort Bragg, viewing a demonstration of weapons and skills of the Special Forces and the airborne divisions of the sort the U.S. military stages with a certain flair. The high point of the day was an exhibition of a tiny rocket which, strapped to the back of a soldier, enabled him to fly over obstacles and across streams in the style of a comic-book hero.[15]

There is no record of President Kennedy's private thoughts at this exhibition. We must assume that he approved, possibly making allowances for the tendency of the military to overdo its public relations sales appeals. His goal was to break through the resistance of the command to a revision of its priorities and its commitment to unwieldy conventional units, weighed down with heavy equipment. The exhibition at Fort Bragg showed that his message had been noted, although the emphasis was clearly on gadgetry rather than on the far more complex questions of tactical doctrine which go to the heart of the proper use of military force against guerrillas.

The president's interest in Special Forces was the most public of his personal initiatives in counterinsurgency. Later we will discuss some of its effects on the public understanding of that novel term. But in less publicized—and less personal—form, he pursued the effort to achieve a balanced program, one which grappled with political essences as well as military techniques. He was very aware that many agencies of government were called upon to play a role in counterinsurgency warfare and that the president could not himself oversee the detailed elaboration of doctrine and interlocking programs. In March 1961 he named an interagency group under Richard Bissell, a deputy director of the CIA, to study the question of organizing the government for the task. The Joint Chiefs of Staff put a group of its own to work on a similar study. Decisions did not emerge from these efforts until early 1962, but in the meantime the White House pressed ahead with various pieces of the structure, pursuing not only the improvement of the military capability but also new departures in such related subjects as military civic action.

The president also brought onto his staff former Army Chief of Staff General Maxwell Taylor and assigned to him, among other duties, that of monitoring ongoing counterinsurgency efforts. General Taylor had retired in 1959 after four frustrating years as head of the army during the ascendancy of the "massive retaliation doctrine" which reduced the funds and role of the army to a level he found disturbingly low. Now returned to uniform, in June 1961, as the president's special military representative, he seemed to the president well qualified to represent his views to the military on the urgency of a more flexible posture.

The Elaboration of Doctrine

By mid-1961 the Kennedy Administration was thus in high gear in elaborating and ramifying the president's views on counterinsurgency. Before recounting its further actions, however, we will digress and ask what was the doctrine on which the administration based its efforts and established its goals. Was there, in fact, a doctrine that assured a common understanding throughout the foreign affairs and national security apparatus of each participant's role as well as of the general and broad purposes of the concept?

There was, indeed, no lack of effort at public articulation and, within the government, of staff studies, task force reports, and formal policy documents. Regrettably, the latter remain at this time largely in the classified archives, unavailable for study. We must therefore rely on the public statements of men who were close to the president on this issue and spoke with the assurance that they represented his thinking. Among the best-known of such statements was a speech cleared in advance by Kennedy and delivered by Walt W. Rostow at Fort Bragg, in June 1961, on the subject of "Guerrilla Warfare in the Underdeveloped Areas."[16]

Rostow at that time was deputy to Special Presidential Assistant McGeorge Bundy. Formerly a professor at MIT, he had been involved throughout the 1950s in studies of the developing countries, or "emerging nations," as they were called in one influential MIT book of that title. His own *Stages of Economic Growth* had won international attention for an analysis of economic growth which concluded that non-Communist democratic methods were superior to forced-draft command economies of the Russian and Chinese pattern in moving underdeveloped countries from stagnation to economic "take-off." As noted in the last chapter, Rostow was one of the first academics to call attention to the problem posed by Communist-supported guerrilla warfare in the underdeveloped world. He thus had credentials to be considered something of an authority on aspects of insurgency, particularly its relationship to underdevelopment. On the White House staff he was assigned to follow the problems of Vietnam, Laos, and the rest of Southeast Asia where insurgency seemed to be the most critical question.[17] He was a natural choice for public spokesman on a subject to which he had devoted more thought than other Kennedy advisers.

The Fort Bragg speech was necessarily brief and simple, and was therefore anything but a refined analysis. Nevertheless, it contained most of the governing ideas that created the administration's concern and guided its reaction. It first noted that the varied foreign crises confronting the United States had similar origins in "Communist efforts to exploit the instabilities of the underdeveloped areas" by the technique of guerrilla warfare. These instabilities, in turn, could be traced to modernization. "Like all revolutions, the revolution of modernization is disturbing," reducing the power of traditional social elites and leading the ordinary people in the villages and the cities to feel that new possibilities are open to them. The Communists seek to exploit these opportunities, relying upon their techniques of organization to attack the vulnerabilities of the transitional governments usually found in such circumstances. The Communists concentrate on the weakest governments and are in effect "the scavengers of the modernization process." Rostow summed up this phase of his comments with, "Communism is best understood as a disease of the transition to modernization."

Turning to the U.S. attitude toward these phenomena, he asserted that in contrast to the Communists, the United States wished the revolutionary process of modernization to go forward in independence and freedom, adopting the goal of protecting the independence of the revolution of modernization as a way of assuring the kind of world environment "which will permit our open society to survive and flourish."

He described that effort as proceeding on numerous fronts: the nuclear deterrent, the ability to intervene with conventional arms where necessary, the readiness to provide economic aid and thus to assist nations through the difficulties of the modernization process. "Finally," said Rostow, "the United States has a role to play in learning to deter the outbreak of guerrilla warfare, if possible, and to deal with it if necessary." Here the speaker entered a major caveat which has some ironic overtones over a decade later. He stated that, although the United States was prepared to offer considerable help, the main burden of fighting would have to be borne by those "on the spot," the indigenous forces of the threatened country. "An outsider cannot, by himself, win a guerrilla war."

Then, raising what became for him a continuing preoccupation during his years of service to both Presidents Kennedy and Johnson, Rostow noted the distortion that takes place in the balance of internal forces of a threatened country as a result of external intervention by Communist governments in favor of the guerrillas. He found this to be "a crude act of international vandalism." We may note that his strong views on this problem later led him to become a consistent advocate of the bombing of North Vietnam, and to favor other forms of intervention, including the dispatch of American troops to Vietnam. There was thus an incipient dilemma even in this earliest of doctrinal statements, at least as applied to Vietnam, between keeping the burden of the fighting upon the indigenous forces and meeting the threat of external Communist intervention.

The occasion, however, was not one for wrestling with such difficulties, nor was it particularly in the spirit of the administration to perceive murky waters and twisting currents ahead. As a spokesman, Rostow saw the issue as a straightforward problem in the application of the right kind of American resources to the right foreign areas and needs. "We can learn to prevent the emergence of the famous sea in which Mao Tse-tung taught his men to swim. This requires, of course, not merely a proper military program of deterrence but programs of village development, communications, and indoctrination. The best way to fight a guerrilla war is to prevent it from happening. And this can be done." He then concluded his remarks by pledging that the administration would devote "every resource of mind and spirit" at its command to dealing with this major threat.

The salient points of the doctrine at this early stage thus boiled down to a very few general propositions: that insurgency was a major global threat, that it derived from the exploitation by the Communists of certain powerful worldwide social forces summed up in the term "modernization," and that the United States was both able and determined to meet this threat by the proper application of its resources. Although admitting that a learning process was involved for America, he saw no fundamental obstacles nor any need to envision the use of American troops. The statement was thus a confident and optimistic reflection of the mood of the new administration, and it is entirely understandable that it should have been so. It was not the role of an official spokesman to question the optimism and oversimplification of his principals. One can reasonably ask questions about the sources of this optimism, however, and analyze the underlying assumptions, a task we will undertake shortly.

Rostow's statement was a clarion call and remained a basic text in the growing sheaf of doctrinal writing on the subject, referred to and assigned as reading in the various specialized courses that sprang up in response to presidential urging. It was, however, merely the bare bones of a doctrine. The first public effort to elaborate upon it to any degree was the work of another recognized government expert in the field, Roger Hilsman, at that time head of the Bureau of Intelligence and Research at the Department of State. Hilsman was a West Point graduate who had turned to an academic career in international studies after serving in Burma in World War II as a guerrilla organizer and leader in operations of the Office of Strategic Services. By virtue of this experience he was both interested in and accepted as an administration spokesman on counterinsurgency matters. In August 1961, he delivered a speech entitled "Internal War: The New Communist Doctrine" later published in a gathering of such articles by the *Marine Corps Gazette.* It then appeared in book form with a foreword by the president himself.[18] The speech therefore has some claim to official status.

NEW COMPLEXITIES

Hilsman's effort took Rostow's analysis as a starting point but opened new terrain and in the process introduced new complexities. In his hands, the issues acquired more depth. Here and there hints of further problems appeared which, however, were left vague. A major theme was the special and unique character of guerrilla and counterguerrilla military operations. Citing his own experience in Burma and the U.S. Army's counterguerrilla exposure in the Philippines in 1901–1902, he declared that for "effective counterguerrilla operations, we need radical changes in organization, combat doctrine and equipment. Our key units might be decentralized groups of fifty men, self-reliant and able to operate autonomously, fanned out into the countryside."[19] These units were to be employed according to a classic counterguerrilla technique (called *quadrillage* by the French who developed it), which called for dividing the disputed area into equal sections and cleaning it out section by section. A backup force was to assist in eliminating the enemy units, bringing in reinforcements as required by helicopter and airdrop. The process would be repeated until the area was secured, and the defending force would then move on to other sections. In prescribing such tactics, Hilsman implied that in counterinsurgency warfare, heavy weapons and equipment, regimental, divisional, and corps organizations, headquarters staffs, and support elements are superfluous, or nearly so.

> Regular forces [he wrote] are essential for regular military tasks. But guerrilla warfare is something special. Conventional forces with heavy equipment in field formation tend to cluster together, centralizing their power in terrain that allows rapid movement. They rely on roads, consider strong points and cities as vital targets to defend, and so, when they do disperse, it is only to get tied down in static operations. In combat, rigid adherence to the principle of concentration keeps units at unwieldy battalion or even regimental levels, usually with erroneous stress on holding land rather than destroying enemy forces.[20]

This prescription for a new style of warfare was a rather large order which, not surprisingly, Hilsman found the command rather "slow to learn." He blamed the traditionalists who believed that "well trained regulars can do anything," a point which undoubtedly echoed the president, who, during this same period, was attempting by personal intervention and by stressing the buildup of the U.S. Special Forces to turn the military from its accustomed ways. But changing a large, routine-bound institution like the U.S. Army from its most fundamental beliefs is a more difficult task than the president or his advisers appeared to recognize. Certainly, Hilsman gave no indication of appreciating the difficulties in his speech of August 1961. Nevertheless, the speech did make clear the important point which became imbedded in the developing doctrine, that the administration saw the need for a thorough military transformation to meet the challenge of insurgency.

A second theme of Hilsman's which achieved a permanent place in the doctrine was the somewhat portentous question of popular support for counterguerrilla operations, soon to become a subject of endless debate. Even at this early stage, the writer saw pitfalls and attempted to avoid some of the simplicities. He did assert the need for reforms to gain popular acceptance for the threatened regime. But he perceived the question as more complex than the simple equation: popular betterment (reform, development, modernization) equals popular support, equals counterinsurgency success. He introduced the idea of administrative underdevelopment which leaves a vacuum in most of the countryside of an underdeveloped country, the government being looked upon as a distant and occasionally a heavy-handed force. In such an environment, the indifferent mass may permit a guerrilla movement to thrive simply because the government has no means to establish an effective presence.[21] Thus the simple ability to administer its territories can be critical to the success of a threatened regime. Similarly, Hilsman noted that modernization can create instability and thus fuel an insurgency.

Such crosscurrents in the scene he surveyed led him to conclude that effective counterinsurgency was not merely a matter of introducing reforms, development, and modernization, but called for the threatened regimes to develop capabilities to provide security which was not "simply a function of good government or economic growth but a specific problem in its own right."[22] The gaining of popularity by an underdeveloped government was thus, in Hilsman's view, a worthy aim, but not always readily achieved or sufficient in the absence of administrative and technical competence in security activities.

In such fields, the author saw a considerable role for the United States to assist friendly and troubled countries—not only in counterguerrilla and police work, but far more ambitiously in "encouraging reformers to organize mass parties," to help "create citizens militia forces," and generally in "broadening the will and capacity of friendly governments to augment social and political reform programs as a basis for modernization."[23] This was indeed a rather daring prescription and, in truth, one which appeared very seldom in later doctrinal discussion. Clearly it was a prescription for intervention in depth in the intimate internal affairs of such governments. The prospect of the United States actively helping "reformers" to achieve far-reaching change while at the same time maintaining close relations with the government whose ways were to be thoroughly changed suggests that the author had not thought his propositions completely through. But it also indicates that he was aware of some of the dilemmas of counterinsurgency and was seeking to cut a direct—in fact a too-direct—path through them. That such suggestions quickly disappeared from public discussions of the problem is not surprising.

The value of the Hilsman essay for our discussion lies in its dawning recognition of the difficulties to be faced, not yet, however, accompanied by a realization of the stubbornness and complexity of those difficulties. Although a considerable advance over the Rostow statement, it signally lacked any suggestion or implication that the U.S. government might be hard put to innovate and coordinate this novel range of activity or that more was involved than merely recognizing the necessity of such activity, and that, in fact, doing the right amount of the right thing might prove quite elusive in any specific insurgency situation. Nevertheless, the speech augmented the developing doctrine by explicitly declaring counterguerrilla operations to be a special skill requiring a special approach, by urging the importance of administrative capability in the field of internal security, while not neglecting the importance of popular support which, in turn, is seen as a far from simple matter.

GUIDANCE FOR THE BUREAUCRACY

In all these areas, a role is proposed for the United States in the form of appropriate assistance, but the U.S. contribution is merely touched on in a highly generalized form, without any specifics to guide a willing but puzzled participant. Matters did not of course rest in this interim stage. Several study groups were at work during the summer and early fall of 1961 on the development of a more comprehensive doctrine and on improving the organization of the government to deal with the emerging threat.[24] At the same time, the political aspects of the problem were subjected to further analysis. Various classified documents are known to exist in which the results of these efforts were recorded, but none is yet available to scholars. An excellent substitute, however, is accessible, an article written for the *Foreign Service Journal,* the monthly publication of the Foreign Service Association, by U. Alexis Johnson, then deputy under-secretary of state for political affairs and a frequent State Department representative at White House discussions of counterinsurgency. The article is entitled "Internal Defense and the Foreign Service"[25] and, as the author explains, was written to clarify the subject for the civilian services who were assigned a large role in the new area of activity but did not yet understand how to go about it.

To appreciate the authority of the article, we should note that the basic administration statement of counterinsurgency doctrine and procedures, promulgated in August 1962 as NSAM-182,[26] was in the final drafting process as Johnson's went to press. We can safely assume that he based himself on this and related official documentation, it not being the practice of senior career officers to depart in public statements from the official position.

What stands out over a decade later in Johnson's presentation is its all-inclusive sweep. At the outset, he defines the program as the employment of all available resources for assisting new nations "in building the kind of society and government that can maintain itself . . . and above all remain free from domination and control by Communist forces." This he sees as involving the "totality of political, military, economic, social, and psychological responses . . . to all forms of Communist-inspired aggression. . . . It includes the fundamental element of anticipation—the measures we can take to assist in strengthening . . . the weak spots in vulnerable societies not yet under attack, as well as those where violence has actually erupted."

To explain the broad nature of the prescription, the author points—as had the other spokesmen before him—to the revolutionary wave sweeping through the less-developed world and the effort of the Communists to "confiscate" it. But the nature of the response, in his view, is determined by the ability of the Communists to gain the support of the population. "Our strategy must therefore be all-inclusive in scope and directed as much towards the roots of subversion and insurgency as toward its overt manifestations."

He then sketches a strategy for the United States which quite probably follows the doctrine paper being completed at the White House at the time.[27] The main elements of the strategy were: first, a searching political and economic appraisal of the situation in a threatened country; second, development of measures designed to strengthen vulnerable points "and at least ameliorate those grievances and causes of discontent which the Communists exploit"; third, development of effective police and military capabilities in friendly countries to maintain internal security; and fourth, "mobilization of the local government's resources, effectively employed through political, economic, and psychological measures to support the military and internal security capabilities."

Having thus laid out the skeletal strategy, the article focuses on the demands placed upon the foreign affairs and military bureaucracy by this "all-inclusive" approach. He says it requires careful "orchestration" to combine properly the civilian and military contributions, with the civilian agencies being pointed toward the "causes of unrest" and the military toward its military manifestations. Coordination of these roles is the responsibility of the State Department and the ambassador, who are also required to "develop a proper understanding of the factors behind any dissidence." (Although he stresses that coordination is equally important in Washington and the field, he fails to mention the existence of the new White House committee, the Special Group (Counterinsurgency), which was created specifically to guarantee the desired coordination.)

What then are these roles that are to be coordinated? Johnson is careful to leave no doubt, since he was writing for the civilian foreign-affairs bureaucracy. He summarizes each operating agency's special contribution—the military services, AID (including police training and advice), and USIS (the CIA is omitted, for in those more reticent days official spokesmen ignored that agency's role overseas). In this section, we should note (although the author does not) the prescribed mission of each agency is beyond and aside from the functions considered normal and standard for that agency. Thus, the army is called on to assist in a style of warfare it did not normally practice; AID—the development agency—is pointed toward police work and rural assistance; and USIS—which was chartered to project the American image and point of view—is required to assist beleaguered governments to improve their image among their own people. These deviations should be noted at this early point for they became a source of later difficulties in maintaining direction and focus.

In a number of ways the Johnson article contributes further specificity to the work to be done under the new policy, and particularly in distributing responsibilities. It stressed the civilian tasks and, in the process, gives a more accurate picture of what was actually in the minds of the president and his advisers than most of the public statements and actions of the administration throughout this period. From his analysis and description there emerges into view a multifaceted effort far wider in scope than the business of fighting guerrillas with their own tools and tricks. The prescription, in fact, called for the U.S. government to move boldly into the most intimate areas of politics of foreign peoples and advise, instruct, and assist them in placing their affairs in order, to "strengthen" their weak spots, render their efforts at internal defense "effective," and, above all, eliminate the causes of popular discontent. Throughout the article, the view of the problem and the solution as predominently political stands out clearly, correcting, for those who were exposed to it, the view of counterinsurgency as predominantly a military effort. Unfortunately, the administration was its own chief obstacle in projecting an accurate picture to the public of what it had in mind. The more spectacular interventions of the president, such as his visit to Fort Bragg noted earlier, and the preeminent roles of Secretary McNamara and General Taylor, both frequent spokesmen on the subject, not to mention a glamorizing process which heightened and exaggerated the role and effect of the Special Forces, all these tended to put in the shade the critical functions assigned to the civilian agencies and the fact that the military facet of counterinsurgency was subordinate in theory and doctrine to the civilian facets. Yet the record confirms the defenders of the administration—for example Arthur Schlesinger and Roger Hilsman—in their claims that President Kennedy and his advisers saw counterinsurgency as first and last a political task to be carried out under civilian management.[28]

But setting aside that criticism, it is still true that on the face of it the doctrine was somewhat overblown in both its global scope and the demands it placed on the U.S. government machinery. The commitment was open-ended in geographic range, and covered the gamut of challenges that weak and faltering governments might have to meet anywhere in the world. Further, the approach made almost no demands of these governments. The responsibility is placed on the U.S. representative on the spot to bear the burden.

It is suggestive that in the article by U. Alexis Johnson, a very senior and thoroughly experienced foreign service officer, a note of caution briefly appears. In a passing comment he suggests that the problem of insurgency in some circumstances might be beyond solution. Although it is not emphasized, this is a noteworthy exception because of its rarity in the rhetoric of the administration. It is also of interest because it puts a precise finger on the essence of the political problem.

> To bring about some degree of social, economic, and political justice [he wrote] or at the very least to ameliorate the worst causes of discontent and redress the most flagrant inequities, will invariably require positive action by the local government. In some cases only radical reforms will obtain the necessary results. Yet the measures we advocate may strike at the very foundations of those aspects of a country's social structure and domestic economy on which rests the basis of a government's control.[29]

After raising the point, Johnson then placed the burden on the Foreign Service, whose duty he says it is to persuade the threatened government to take the necessary measures. Since he has already noted that such measures may undermine the government's hold on power, he concludes by saying that the job "calls for the utmost skill of our profession, for it is always a difficult task and sometimes an impossible one."

Despite the note of caution, the Johnson article conveys to the reader—and probably was deliberately intended to convey to the foreign affairs professionals to whom it was addressed—the feeling that the administration was putting them on their mettle, that under the Kennedy dispensation, daring, drive, and imagination were the qualities that would advance their careers. We may also speculate that Johnson was seeking to demonstrate to the White House that he, and through him, his department had received the message of the new breed. Thus, in fairness, we must allow for some deliberate exaggeration for these purposes and discount some of the sweep of the article.

Beyond that, the record of the administration in foreign affairs suggests that the rhetoric was not always taken literally by the president and his advisers. Certain it is that the administration exercised discrimination in choosing how and when to intervene and was not unrealistic in assessing—for example in Laos—the risks of ignoring the obvious inadequacies of a given government despite intense U.S. efforts to build a viable regime. When such considerations were brushed aside, as they came to be in Vietnam, it was not for lack of perception of the problem but for reasons primarily related to domestic politics.[30]

Nevertheless, after allowing for these factors, we are still entitled to ask whether the doctrine did not rest on a questionable institutional foundation. It is certain, of course, that the president and his advisers were also aware that deficiencies existed in the apparatus at their disposal and that the new demands would put additional strains on this apparatus. The question to keep in mind is whether the solutions they devised for these problems actually reached deep enough into the system to bring about the profound changes, notably in organizational tightening and centralizing of direction and in a massive shaking-up of the army, which would appear necessary to carry out the doctrines they had developed and approved.

THE DOCTRINE SUMMARIZED

Returning now to the development of the doctrine as it emerges in the first year and a half of the new administration, it comprised a few basic elements of analysis and prescription in a highly generalized form which can be summed up briefly.

First, a global threat was believed to exist in the form of a strategy adopted by the unified Communist apparatus to advance its cause without risking either nuclear or conventional war. The attempt exploited the strains of the modernization process throughout the Third World using the proven techniques of guerrilla warfare.

Second, the United States had the duty and the power to confront and defeat this challenge without, however, the necessity of intervening directly with American forces. Further, it was held that intervention early in the process rather than late would reduce the involvement and prevent serious crises from arising.

Third, that in order to accomplish the task that was set before it, the U.S. government had to adopt a novel approach which included a military strategy of combating guerrilla groups with a set of techniques tailored to the specific challenges of that style of warfare; that this military strategy was merely a limited aspect of a general approach involving all arms of the U.S. government overseas; that the central objective of the effort was the combined goal of improving the ability of the threatened government to govern effectively and to help it to generate sufficient popular support to thwart the Communist strategy of popular participation in a people's war; that this effort required a shift in emphasis and direction affecting the entire foreign affairs apparatus, both military and civilian; that coordination and unification of the multifaceted American effort both in the field and in Washington were critical to its success.

Such, in condensed form, are the principal themes of the counterinsurgency doctrine which formed the basis of a major foreign policy preoccupation of the U.S. government during much of the 1960s. Not surprisingly, given the urgency with which the president viewed the problem, action did not await the formal completion of the doctrinal process. Various specific actions were undertaken to develop programs well in advance of the finished doctrine. But the administration placed most importance on the creation of some sort of umbrella organization to oversee the entire gamut of counterinsurgency activity on behalf of the president.

Reverting back to mid-1961, we have noted that several study groups were considering just this problem of organizing the U.S. response and providing it with a doctrine. Of these, the most influential was the one referred to in the White House as the "Bissell committee," formally chaired by Richard E. Bissell, Jr., Deputy Director for Plans (actually Operations) of the Central Intelligence Agency. In fact, Walt W. Rostow was the moving force behind the group and, when it issued its report, he successfully urged the approval of its recommendations by the president.[31]

A New High-Level Group

The actual text of the Bissell committee report is not available. We know, however, that its key recommendation called for the creation of a high-level interagency committee to monitor and guide the foreign affairs community in its counterinsurgency efforts and to provide a forum for the development of doctrine. The president not only approved, but to demonstrate the importance he attached to this committee's work, he assigned his brother, the attorney general, to act as his representative. To chair the group he designated his military representative, General Maxwell E. Taylor. These decisions were promulgated on January 18, 1962, in National Security Action Memorandum No. 124, a key document in defining the approach chosen by the president as well as the priority he accorded the effort.[32]

The document named by title the members of this new entity, which it designated the Special Group (Counterinsurgency)—abbreviated to Special Group (C.I.). Besides the two named above, these were the deputy under-secretary of state, U. Alexis Johnson; the deputy secretary of defense, Roswell Gilpatric; the chairman of the Joint Chiefs of Staff, General Lyman L. Lemnitzer; the director of Central Intelligence, John McCone; the special assistant to the president for National Security Affairs, McGeorge Bundy; the administrator of the Agency for International Development, Fowler Hamilton; and the director of the United States Information Agency, Edward R. Murrow.

Four functions were itemized in NSAM 124, to wit:

a. To insure proper recognition throughout the U.S. government that subversive insurgency ("war of liberation") is a major form of politico-military conflict equal in importance to conventional warfare.

b. To insure that such recognition is reflected in the organization, training, equipment, and doctrine of the U.S. armed forces and other U.S. agencies abroad and in the political, economic, intelligence, military aid, and informational programs conducted abroad by State, Defense, AID, USIA, and CIA. Particular attention will be paid the special training of personnel prior to assignment to MAAGs and to embassy staffs in countries where counterinsurgency problems exist or may arise.

c. To keep under review the adequacy of U.S. resources to deal with actual or potential situations of insurgency or indirect aggression, making timely recommendations of measures to apply, increase, or adjust these resources to meet anticipated requirements.

d. To insure the development of adequate interdepartmental programs aimed at preventing or defeating subversive insurgency and indirect aggression in countries and regions specifically assigned to the Special Group (C.I.) by the president, and to resolve any interdepartmental problems which might impede their implementation.

A further paragraph made clear that the new group was not a decision-making body nor a new operating agency, but was limited to developing policies (subject to presidential approval), to monitoring and coordinating, except where interdepartmental issues arose, in which event it could make decisions resolving them.

Three countries were assigned to the cognizance of the Special Group (C.I.) at the same time. These were Laos, South Vietnam, and Thailand.

The establishment of the Special Group (C.I.) opened a new phase in the administration's campaign to organize the government to deal with

Communist guerrilla insurgencies. It provided a structure to accomplish the tasks which until then had been left to those—mostly found in the NSC staff—who interested themselves in the problem. It signaled unmistakably to the foreign affairs community that the president was serious in calling for a new approach. If there were any doubt, the presence of the attorney general on a committee far removed from his normal responsibilities would be likely to dispel it. Robert Kennedy was certainly assigned to this duty to act as the president's eyes and ears, and to remind participants, where necessary, of the high importance his brother attached to the work of the Special Group (C.I.). He reported directly to the president after each meeting, a fact which was also known to the members.[33]

According to observers, Robert Kennedy was an aggressive prober and a sharp critic.[34] Occasionally he succeeded in terrifying low-ranking officials who were called before the committee to report on their specialties. But he frequently was able to break through the bureaucratic obstacles which crop up to prevent rapid action in a complex, interdepartmental effort. Although the Special Group (C.I.) had no formal decision-making authority except in cases of disagreement, the attorney general's urging served as a prod to produce action, for example to obtain agreement to release resources or to process specific actions on an expedited basis. He was not above threatening to report what he considered lack of cooperation to the president or to the appropriate cabinet secretary. Usually he was able to gain the compliance he thought necessary.

A New Infrastructure

The first concern of the new group was to build an interdepartmental infrastructure which would reach into the separate agencies and services to generate action, but not merely action for its own sake. What was desired was persistent, coordinated response to the challenge on a day-to-day basis according to a common plan and understanding of the problem and of the preferred solutions. That at least is the implication of the actions taken in the course of the months immediately following the creation of the new committee. On March 13, 1972, another NSAM (No. 131) laid down a comprehensive instruction on the matter of training, civilian and military, in subjects relevant to insurgency and counterinsurgency.[35] The Special Group (C.I.) was apparently responsible for shepherding this paper through the drafting and approval process.[36] The instruction specified four types of training for officer grades with "a role to play on counterinsurgency programs as well as in the entire range of problems involved in the modernization of developing countries."

Thus, officers of all grades were required to study the history of subversive insurgency movements in courses to be introduced into the existing schools of all departments and services. Junior- and middle-grade officers were to study tactics and techniques of the particular departments having a bearing on the subject, and spaces were to be made available in these schools for cross-training between agencies. Middle- and senior-grade officials were to receive special training to prepare them for positions of responsibility in the planning and conduct of counterinsurgency programs. "At this level," the instruction added, "the students will be made aware of the possible contribution of all departments."

Finally, an unfulfilled need was identified to instruct middle- and senior-grade officers about to assume duties in underdeveloped countries "on the entire range of problems faced by the United States in dealing with developing countries, including special area counterinsurgency studies." The memorandum then directed that a national-level school be established to teach counterinsurgency policy and doctrine to such officers, to offer studies on problems of the underdeveloped world, and to conduct research "to improve the U.S. capability for guiding underdeveloped countries through the modernization barrier and for countering subversive insurgency." The Special Group (C.I.) was directed to explore the problem of organizing such a school and to make recommendations on an urgent basis. In addition to this comprehensive program for U.S. government officers, the paper also directed that counterinsurgency training be provided to selected foreign nationals whose countries had actual or potential insurgency problems.

The training directive had an immediate impact. It proved a very specific guideline and called for visible action which could easily be verified and reported. Throughout the armed services, and affected civilian departments, its weight was felt in short order. By July 1962, the Joint Chiefs reported with some pride to the NSC that "during the past 18 months nine special counterinsurgency courses for officers have been created," with 2,099 graduates.[37]

> The curricula of all war colleges have been modified to include freshly prepared counterinsurgency instruction. The average increase is about 53 hours, in a one-year resident course.
>
> Lower level officers' schools have likewise undergone a reorientation, with the addition of an average of 38 hours in a ten-month resident course.
>
> Beyond this, there are now over 1000 officers undergoing language training as a direct reflection of the emphasis on counterinsurgency, and 83 senior officers have been dispatched on orientation tours to areas of incipient or active insurgency.

The same report stated that during the eighteen-month period over a half million U.S. enlisted men had received basic counterinsurgency instruction and that, beyond the basic level, twenty-five courses had been launched for enlisted ranks, ranging "from training in guerrilla warfare, psychological warfare, underwater demolitions and air rescue operations to language training, military assistance training and civil affairs. Over 510,000 enlisted men have completed these courses."

Standard military practice also called for unit training to perfect the knowledge derived from courses where the men were trained as individuals. "It is now obligatory throughout the armed forces, to conduct field exercises addressed specifically to counterinsurgency. These have varied from small unit exercises to major efforts . . . including four joint air/ground exercises and four major amphibious exercises."

In fact, counterinsurgency became something of a fashion in the armed forces and almost all branches sought to participate. Training was a concrete activity which made it possible for a unit to report compliance with directives to become active in the field; some units went to absurd lengths to establish a connection and train their men in it. One civilian skeptic in a position to observe the military's compliance reported that "word went out from the Chief of Staff of the Army that every school in the Army would devote a minimum of 20 percent of its time to counterinsurgency. Well, this reached the Finance School and the Cooks and Bakers School, so they were talking about how to make typewriters explode . . . or how to make apple pies with hand grenades inside them."[38]

Much of the military training, however, was more relevant. Some schools, for example, built facsimiles of Asian villages and conducted training exercises in them to increase the realism of the courses. There is no doubt that considerable thought and resources were directed to the problem of meeting the demand for counterinsurgency training which came to the armed forces from the highest levels of the government. If there is some doubt that it had a deep and lasting impact, that is not necessarily the fault of the training. More plausibly, it reflects the very great difficulty of the task of—as one anonymous officer put it—trying to turn the military "from sophistication to simplicity, from total attention upon great weapons to serious consideration of humble ones, from an environment where technology is preeminent to one where improvisation plays a key part."[39] It proved, in fact, to be a more stubborn problem than the White House anticipated.

The "Counterinsurgency Course"

In compliance with the NSAM on training, the civilian agencies also hastened to establish courses to satisfy that directive. The burden was carried largely by the Foreign Service Institute of the State Department, which has the responsibility for the training of AID, USIA, and Foreign Service personnel. CIA, which maintains its own training department, also of course complied with the White House directive. But it fell to the FSI to carry out the fourth instruction of the NSAM calling for the creation of a new school to instruct middle- and senior-grade officers about to depart for important posts in foreign countries.

This school was designed to be the capstone of the educational pyramid designed in NSAM 131, the highest in level—both in student body and instructional staff—and the most concentrated. The "National Interdepartmental Seminar" opened its doors in June 1962 for the first running of its six-week course. Among the students enrolled for full-time participation were several ambassadors. Such administration notables as Robert F. Kennedy, General Maxwell Taylor, and Edward R. Murrow audited various lectures. Speakers included Walt W. Rostow, U. Alexis Johnson, Brigadier General Edward F. Lansdale from the government, and a number of highly qualified academics.

The first portion of the course, describing the problems of underdevelopment and the Communist effort to preempt the West, was largely in the hands of a group of distinguished specialists from the Center of International Studies at MIT, of which Rostow, until he joined the administration, had been a leading light. A second portion dealt with the government's newly reorganized effort to meet the challenge. The final instructional bloc saw the students broken up into separate "country teams" which were required to produce a report analyzing one country's problems and to propose solutions. At the end of their six weeks, the entire student body was transported to the White House for a meeting with the president and General Taylor. On that occasion, the president said:

> I was anxious to have you come to the White House because we want to emphasize the necessity for the experience which you are going through, that it be shared by all the people in the National Government who have anything to do with international relations. Every senior officer in all key departments must have a comparable experience to yours, have the knowledge that you have, have their attention focused on it. . . . They all must concentrate their energy on what is going to be one of the great factors in the struggle of the Sixties.[41]

On the same occasion, General Taylor seized the opportunity to tell the group that the coordination of America's economic, diplomatic, and military efforts against guerrillas was "indeed a wave of the future that this group represents." He said it meant "a balancing of our assets in working together as a team."

The critical importance of meeting the challenge and of doing so by a carefully combined and unified effort—these cardinal points of the doctrine were thus highlighted at the highest level of the government. The course itself and the finale at the White House were but two further examples of the depth of conviction of the president and his advisers.

Throughout the Kennedy Administration, and indeed for many years afterward, the seminar continued to process between forty and seventy middle- and senior-rank officers eight or ten times a year.[42] Prospective ambassadors were frequently enrolled. For example, Henry Cabot Lodge's arrival in Vietnam in 1963, at a time of deepening crisis, was nevertheless delayed for some weeks to permit him to attend the course.[43] After the Kennedys disappeared from the scene, the high-level interest declined; the length of the course was reduced to four and then to three weeks, and fewer senior officers attended.

As for its usefulness, it is difficult to argue that more knowledge is not useful; undoubtedly it was. On the other hand, the school never produced the research on the problems of underdevelopment called for in the NSAM—nor could it. Neither the faculty nor the student body at the FSI or the seminar was so constituted as to make research possible. One undoubted benefit in the Kennedy years, however, lay in the fact that the course brought home emphatically to the enrollees that the highest level of the government was directly responsible for their presence there and was deeply concerned with underdevelopment and insurgency. In the government bureaucracy such facts have impact, and regardless of whether the students came away convinced of the vital import of the subject matter (and some did not) they were left in no doubt of the president's views. Beyond this, the weaknesses of the course reflected the deficiencies of the doctrine. It was highly generalized and often left the officers at a loss as to how to translate the generalities into policies and, even more difficult, into practical actions. The crux of the problem was the same one that U. Alexis Johnson had put his finger on: how to induce self-reform by an uncertain and unstable regime which saw its control threatened by the very measures urged upon it by the United States.

The "Interdepartmental Seminar" was only one of numerous initiatives of the Special Group (C.I.) to establish the foundation of a unified government counterinsurgency effort. Another of considerable importance has already been noted and discussed: the preparation of a formal doctrine which would be common to all participants. The *Pentagon Papers* includes the text of a NSAM (No. 182) issued August 24, 1962, which announced presidential approval of a document entitled "U.S. Overseas Internal Defense Policy," described as a national counterinsurgency doctrine which was to serve as "basic policy guidance to diplomatic missions . . . and military commands abroad; to Government departments and agencies at home, and to the Government educational system."[44] Agencies were instructed to base their activities on this policy guidance, to develop their own internal doctrine based upon the national policy, and to submit their efforts to the Special Group (C.I.). The State Department was designated to keep the paper (referred to as the OIDP) up to date.

Although the text of the doctrine paper is unavailable to the public, we have already discussed what we believe, on good evidence, to be its substance. It remains to note some of the mechanics included in the document, which went beyond theoretical analysis and prescription to establish a general governmental process. Such evidence as exists suggests that the foreign affairs community was instructed to scan the world scene to note early developments which raised the possibility of divided into various categories considered threatened; it is likely that a requirement was levied upon the country team to provide an analysis and an operational plan to deal with the threat. These were called Country Internal Defense Plans and one instruction stated that they

> will include the military, police, intelligence and psychological measures comprising a well rounded internal defense plan and will be consistent with the military, economic, political and social measures constituting the overall country plan.[46]

The highest categories were probably placed under the cognizance of the Special Group (C.I.), which then reviewed the operational program and monitored its implementation.[47] The system had the merit of simplicity. Its effectiveness would depend upon the alertness of the echelons below the field installations and, of course, upon the validity of the doctrine.

As can be seen, much of the Special Group (C.I.)'s work in its first months involved what may be described as "housekeeping," a matter of considerable importance in a large bureaucracy where prescribed procedures are essential to generate detectable movement. Among other such concerns, it called upon the participating agencies to organize themselves in a manner to reflect the importance of the counterinsurgency effort.

THE MILITARY RESPONDS

The impact of this pressure was felt most obviously in the Pentagon, which had a major role and a large and cumbersome apparatus to force into the new shapes demanded of the secretary of defense and the high command. There exists in the Special Group (C.I.)'s files a report from the chairman of the JCS dated July 17, 1962, and entitled "Counterinsurgency Organization."[48] In forty-nine pages it details the structure that had been created in the Joint Staff and the armed forces to deal with counterinsurgency matters. At the top of the pyramid was the newly established office of the Special Assistant to the Director of the Joint Staff for Counterinsurgency and Special Activities (abbreviated to SACSA). Its chief was Marine Major General Victor B. Krulak. The army had also established several special offices, including a Special Warfare Directorate, which had responsibility for the U.S. Special Forces.

The navy, on the other hand, and with considerable implied irony, stated that it appreciated "fully the importance and growing need for the Armed Forces to improve their capabilities to train and assist friendly countries in combatting subversive insurgency. Over the years Navy/ Marines have directly and routinely participated in similar operations, in response to National Policy and as roving American Ambassadors and are considered equipped to perform counterinsurgency operations now." Between the lines of this quiet dismissal of the fanfare generated by the White House emerges the feeling that the navy and particularly the marines were, upon the grounds of long experience and tradition, the service within the armed forces best suited to handle the military responsibility for counterinsurgency. The air force, on the other hand, found it advisable to react to the new demands by forming two offices, one concerned with operations and the other with research and development.

On the civilian side of the government, the State Department reflected the fact that it had acquired substantial new duties as a result of the administration's preoccupations. A major new staff called the Political-Military Directorate had been created to meet a variety of problems of which counterinsurgency was but one. The staff was a response to the increasing involvement of the military in foreign relations and the consequent need for the department to deal on a systematic basis with the political aspects of this involvement. In the other agencies, reorganizations were less far-reaching, but all placed themselves in a position to respond rapidly to the White House when counterinsurgency questions arose. In a brief span, the Special Group (C.I.) became the pinnacle of a counterinsurgency apparatus linking it to all the operating and policy arms of the foreign affairs community.

The purpose of constructing this apparatus was of course to produce a consistent, precise, and energetic operational response by means of long-term counterinsurgency programs. We now turn to those programs, some of which antedated the Special Group (C.I.), but all of which came under its scrutiny.

THE PENTAGON'S PROGRAMS

The largest in terms of resources and scope were those of the military. Within the armed forces, the army's role was preeminent, but the navy and air force also developed special capabilities (this despite the navy's cool response to the organizational question). In addition, a program of civic action involved all of the services. All also conducted research and development in new weapons and equipment specifically designed for counterinsurgency use.

With respect to the army, the president, as we have seen, viewed the Special Forces with favor, somewhat to the dismay of the Chiefs of Staff. The symbol of the president's favor was the green beret, which he had insisted be restored to the unit after the army command, enforcing a general policy against highly visible insignia, had taken it away.[49] The Special Forces headquarters at Fort Bragg was upgraded to a Special Warfare Center[50] under a brigadier general. Additional Special Forces units were organized and the functions and mission of this elite cadre were expanded. The Special Forces were originally conceived as a permanent version of the improvised guerrilla units of the OSS during World War II. That is, their role was the generation of resistance forces behind the lines of an enemy, and they sought men with special language and other useful talents—particularly a liking for personal combat. In the new version, their role was broadened to include advice, training, and leadership for friendly counterguerrilla forces—somewhat the reverse of the original mission but not, in fact, inconsistent with the requirement that guerrillas be fought with guerrilla-style tactics.

Despite its rapid growth, Special Forces failed a third of its enrollees—all volunteers—and emphasized toughness, self-sufficiency, and ability to improvise to meet unforeseen field situations. "They know," their commander said in 1962, "how to live off the land . . . how to give first aid, how to set up communications, how to patrol and fight an ambush."[51] These qualities attracted wide public attention, fostered by the Pentagon and the White House, and led to something of a cult of the men of the green beret, which reached its peak when a popular song written around them became a leading hit. The effect was to distort considerably in the public mind both the role of the Special Forces and the nature of the counterinsurgency program.

The Special Forces comprised, in fact, only one limited aspect of the military's counterinsurgency response and remained, in spite of increases in size, a small, elite unit. Thus, the air force developed its own version of a "special force" with a counterinsurgency mission. These were the Air Commandos, a unit trained and equipped to fly a variety of unconventional aircraft—fixed and rotary wing—many of which were obsolete in the conventional air firce. These World War II and Korean War airplanes, a large proportion propeller-driven, were slow, durable, and much simpler to fly than high-performance jets. They thus had advantages in a primitive environment and an unconventional situation. Additionally, the men of the unit were trained in skills not required elsewhere in the air force, particularly those thought to be useful in working with villagers and peasants in the underdeveloped world. A similar special unit was also established by the navy. Called Sea, Air, Land Teams (abbreviated to SEALs), these small, special-section units could be launched from any of the three elements to perform missions on, under, or around the water.

Among the military programs viewed at the White House as a major counterinsurgency tool was military civic action, a rather unrevealing label which referred to an effort to exploit the armed forces' considerable resources and skills in civilian spheres—engineering, medicine, schooling, and the like—to affect directly and beneficially the quality of life of ordinary people in the underdeveloped world. A NSAM on this subject (No. 119) had been signed by the president as early as October 1961.[52] It was enthusiastically endorsed by Secretary MacNamara and promptly implemented by the Joint Chiefs.[53] The JCS July 1962 memorandum cited earlier said of this program: "While the military nation-building role is not foreign to the United States—it having been a major task of our military forces in the latter half of the nineteenth century—it has certainly fallen into disuse. Its revival now, largely as a part of our military assistance program, represents a major change in practical orientation."[54]

The report then cited programs in Colombia, Ecuador, Guatemala, Haiti, Turkey, Iran, and various African countries. Of these, the largest was Ecuador, where 1.5 million dollars had been committed for the improvement of roads, water supply, public health, and education. Although some of the effort represented direct assistance by U.S. forces, the larger part was indirect, its purpose being to generate civic action capabilities and programs in the native armed forces of the countries being aided.

Military civic action performed directly by the United States would seem to be a questionable counterinsurgency tool, except as a means to improve relationships with the surrounding population where American armed forces are committed in combat. On the other hand, it has some *prima facie* merit when the objective is to train and equip the armed forces of a threatened regime to perform needful public services. Again, it helps to improve the relations of the military with the communities among which they have to move in order to master an insurgency. For this purpose, however, good troop behavior is equally as if not more important than improvement projects. Moreover, the small, local projects which were within the capability of the military were not a substitute for a national development program. Far too much emphasis during these years was placed on military civic action as a kind of panacea and all-purpose preventative to insurgency.

Civic action does have one merit, on the other hand, which should not be overlooked, although it has little bearing on the effectiveness of a counterinsurgency program. It is quite noncontroversial, and, indeed, it enhances the military's public image for it to appear as a friend to the poor and humble. Some of the enthusiasm in the U.S. armed forces for military civic action may be explained by these qualities.

Much of the civic action program was carried on through the medium of the Military Aid Program—an existing and well-established activity which underwent some enlargement and change of direction in response to the emphasis upon counterinsurgency. The substantial military aid transmitted to South Vietnam, Laos, and Thailand, and to several of the Latin American countries in the early sixties, was increasingly counterinsurgency-oriented. According to the JCS report already frequently cited, MAP assistance to seventeen underdeveloped countries in Asia and Latin America rose in one year (from 1961 to 1962) from a total of 197 million dollars to 309 million.[55] About 11 percent of the latter (33 million) was specifically counterinsurgency-related, according to the military's interpretation of that term.

Such figures tell a good deal less than they appear to, since some of the weapons and ammunition used for counterinsurgency are identical to conventional weaponry. Far more critical is the nature of the advice and training provided, something which does not appear in the dollar figures of aid granted. This advice was patterned, not unnaturally, after the armed forces' own doctrine and practice, about which we will have more to say shortly.

Finally, in this brief summary of the military's programmatic response to counterinsurgency, we must note that a portion of the Pentagon's immense research and development resources was also focused on the counterinsurgency problem—a most natural development in a military system as technologically oriented as ours. Research was carried on both within the armed forces and in civilian institutions such as the Rand Corporation and the Special Operations Research Office of American University—to mention only two of many. Some of this civilian research effort concerned social problems in the threatened areas, a research target which seemed natural enough within the government in view of the universally held view that insurgency grows out of social tensions and frustrations. Nevertheless, such research later came to be seen by critics in the press and the academic world as a dubious use of social science methods, and much of it was terminated.

The bulk of the research effort, however, was technical and concerned itself with improving equipment, weaponry, and the like. The JCS memorandum on counterinsurgency accomplishments as of July 1962 announced that "332 items directly identified with counterinsurgency have been placed under research and development in the past eighteen months."[56] Among those listed were an "Infra-red Target Detector," a "Silent Semi-automatic Rifle, Silent Ammunition," and a

"Hand-Held Air Gun Firing Pellets With Lethal and Paralizing Effects on Human Targets." The same program also developed defoliation chemicals.

The use of sophisticated, high-technology equipment and weapons for combating a militarily primitive threat was to some extent controversial. The guerrilla specialists in the armed forces were not uniformly impressed by the research and development program. Thus, Brigadier General William P. Yarborough, head of the Special Warfare Center, commented that "Special Forces probably relies less on equipment than other troops. They are trained to improvise and scrounge. . . . They don't need sophisticated weapons."[57] He was prouder of the equipment—nylon hats and new jungle boots, for example—which had been developed in response to President Kennedy's urging. Presumably he was not responsible—or if so, it was with some cynicism—for the exotic weapons display produced for the visiting president in October of 1961.

A Key Dilemma

The military response to the demand for an entirely revised approach to meet a novel challenge was therefore quite extensive. It included all of the services and numerous programs and special activities. An effort was made to acquaint all members of the armed forces with the fact that a new challenge was to be confronted and that it placed special demands on them for an effective response. It is too early in our account to ask whether this array of programs answered the need, for, to a degree, that question anticipates later events and experience. Nevertheless, it is important to identify at this early moment the key military dilemma raised by the counterinsurgency doctrine and note how solutions adopted at the start of the long road determined subsequent events.

An early decision concerned the role of such elite units as Special Forces, Air Commandos, and the like. These, it was clear, were not full combat units, being few in numbers and designed to train, advise, and, if necessary, fight with foreign forces or to carry out special limited missions. Thus, they would have a primary role only if the U.S. involvement did not require the deployment of regular combat units. In the event that our involvement did extend to full participation in combat, the regular units would have to assume the responsibility.

It is also clear, of course, that the administration's doctrine sought precisely to avoid the direct involvement of American forces in counterinsurgency combat. The president had more than once made his view known that such wars should not be fought by foreign forces.[58] Nevertheless, he had also insisted that the U.S. be prepared to fight in this mode, if necessary—most notably in his speech to the graduating class at West Point, in June 1962. There he told the future commanders of the army that the challenge of insurgency wars "requires in those situations where we must counter it, and these are the kinds of challenges that will be before us in the next decade if freedom is to be saved, a whole new kind of strategy, a wholly different kind of force, and therefore a new and wholly different kind of military training."[59] The possibility of counterinsurgency combat was thus quite evidently part of the administration's concept—and the question for the military command became: How would this responsibility be distributed? Would certain units be singled out for specialization in counterinsurgency warfare, or would all be required to add this to their other conventional missions?

It was probably the most critical question faced by the high command in view of its long-term effects upon the character and quality of the armed forces' performance in counterinsurgency. However, its answer was more or less predetermined by the reluctance of the Joint Chiefs to accept at face value the president's commitment to a radical revision of its combat style, weaponry, and tactics. Acceptance of such a posture would have required either that all infantry forces be prepared to fight in two entirely different modes—with different weapons, organization, and goals; or, to avoid this manifestly cumbersome and dubious solution, certain units would have had to be designated as counterinsurgency forces, reducing their competence and availability for "general purpose" forces. It was, in effect, this solution that supporters of the marines advocated, and it had some merit in view of the marines' past history, their greater flexibility, and their tradition of specialization in limited warfare roles.[60]

The high command's "solution" to the dilemma was not to see it as such, but rather to dismiss the contrast between conventional and counterinsurgency combat as an exaggerated premise. This view occasionally surfaced at high levels. Thus, on one occasion, Army Chief of Staff Decker "stoutly stood up to the President with the assurance that 'any good soldier can handle guerrillas.' " To which the president retorted with some briskness that guerrilla fighting was a "special art."[61] The Chiefs of Staff, however, proceeded to make a fundamental decision which, in effect, endorsed General Decker's view as against that of the president. All infantry units, marines and army both, were to be made proficient in counterinsurgency combat *as an added duty*. Although far-reaching in its effects, it is not clear that this decision was ever actually committed to paper as such. It simply followed as a matter of course upon certain assumptions and as far as the available record goes was not made explicit.

It is important to understand why this decision not only was critical but in the long run proved harmful to the objective of preparing the infantry to fight guerrillas effectively. The counterguerrilla doctrine adopted by the government was *reductive* in a military sense. It required a reversion to a simpler form of combat, a stripping down of combat units to the weapons they could carry with them and abandonment of the doctrine of concentration of force in favor of the deployment of numerous platoon-sized units on constant patrol. It did allow for somewhat larger backup forces equipped with helicopters—but nothing as sizeable as a division or even a brigade concentrated at one time and place.

This was the doctrine. The military's program, on the other hand, was *additive.* It left the combat division unchanged in organization and equipment but required it to fight in the counterinsurgency mode, when required, *in addition* to its other missions. The question of what a fully equipped division would do with its immense firepower in a counterinsurgency situation was answered by ordaining that this firepower be used "discriminatingly." Clearly, the alternative of leaving behind most of a division's equipment was never seriously contemplated—and one can see why. It appeared to defy common sense to reduce a sophisticated and immensely potent war-making force to something far less potent and fearsome and then deploy it in combat.

The consequences of this pattern of thought are best demonstrated by anticipating somewhat and examining a military manual on "Counterguerrilla Operations" developed after several years of combat in Vietnam. Department of Army Field Manual FM 31–16 is dated March 1967. It prescribes the combat organization and tactics for a regular army brigade of five battalions in a counterguerrilla situation.

Some verbal emphasis is placed upon the necessity of conducting operations so as "to disrupt, as little as possible, the customs, social activities, relationships between ethnic and tribal groups, and the physical well-being of the population . . . the application of fire-power must be selective and restrained to prevent injury or death to the civilian population."[62] Nevertheless, the brigade is instructed to make appropriate use of all its weapons and equipment, which may, depending upon the type of unit, include tanks, heavy artillery (harassment and interdiction fire is approved), armored personnel carriers, heavy transport, radar, military dogs, chemical, biological, and radiological operations, and aircraft, either attached or supporting, for "troop lift, re-supply, reconnaissance and fire support."[63] The only unit of the regular infantry brigade acknowledged to be without a function in counterguerrilla operations is the antitank platoon. The manual suggests that "consideration should be given to organizing this element to accomplish other more pressing missions."[64]

The counterinsurgency forces of the United States were thus ordained, when committed to combat, to be dependent upon roads, to use weapons which would of necessity harm civilians caught in their fire while causing little harm to the nimble guerrillas, and to impact massively upon the host society in a way which could not but arouse nationalistic feelings. It was therefore a decision which appeared to come as a matter of course and with little challenge that ultimately frustrated the president's call for "a wholly different kind of force."

If one asks what President Kennedy might have done to force the military to a serious and radical transformation in the direction called for by the doctrine, one must concede that it presented an exceedingly difficult problem to a civilian chief executive. The wrenching changes would have had to be forced upon the military hierarchy, perhaps at the cost of resignations and dismissals which would have brought on a resounding public confrontation. In the event, the president shrank from even such a relatively minor clash as would have resulted if, as certain advisers urged, he had rejected the Joint Chiefs' nomination of General Paul D. Harkins to command the greatly enlarged advisory command in Vietnam in 1962. Harkins represented a thoroughly conventional approach to military problems in Vietnam and the president was well aware of it.[65] Yet he rejected advice that he reach down into the lower ranks for a counterinsurgency-oriented officer (Brig. General William P. Yarborough was one name mentioned) to command in Vietnam because of the shock this would have administered to the army's career expectations and the unfavorable public comment that would have ensued. If he had intervened to impose specific tactical doctrines resisted by the army, the outcry would certainly have been far greater, and so, if he had considered it, he might have been excused for deciding to abstain.

The fact is that we have no evidence that he considered it or that he or his advisers saw the problem in the light we have described. For this failure there is less excuse. By not seeing the true depth of the revolution they were calling for and not analyzing its impact—if carried out—on the conventional military capabilities of the same army they were relying upon to uphold the U.S.'s position in Europe, they were guilty of a serious oversight. Moreover, if they had delved into these aspects of the problem they might then have arrived at a solution more likely to have satisfied both the army's objections and the demands of their own doctrine. A possible answer to the "reductive/additive" dichotomy we have described is to abandon the notion of adding counterinsurgency to the other responsibilities of a conventional unit. We then arrive at the alternative, which is to establish units that have that type of combat as a principal, if not exclusive, responsibility. Whether these were marines, or airborne, or rangers matters less than the decision to make counterinsurgency the principal mission of a restricted group of units, leaving the bulk of the infantry to perform its conventional functions in the accustomed manner. Some such solution might have given the military the true counterinsurgency capability which it never actually developed.

★ ★ ★

THE CIVILIAN CONTRIBUTION

We must now return to our account of the programs developed in the Kennedy years in answer to the president's clarion call. As we have seen, the doctrine called for a multifaceted set of civilian and military programs under civilian control. The civilian aspects of the effort were therefore at least equal in importance to the military, and frequently they were greater. For the most part, however, the demands made upon the civilian agencies were for changes of emphasis and priority rather than for major restructuring, as was the military case. Thus, CIA—as a lineal descendant of the OSS—had always maintained a paramilitary capability in terms of a trained cadre, a weapons stockpile, and the like. It had also long worked closely with the police forces in friendly underdeveloped countries to improve their performance in countersubversive operations. The new emphasis coming from the White House meant that such activities would be increased. It also meant that high-level support would be forthcoming for initiatives that gave promise of establishing improved capabilities in various threatened countries to cope with an insurgent threat.

In an unplanned and improvised fashion, therefore, CIA developed a pattern of operations with similar results in several Southeast Asian countries. The common theme was an attempt at popular mobilization of directly threatened groups within the larger community—whether tribal, religious, or political minorities. Although very little theorizing accompanied this process, it largely stemmed from the intelligence agency's professional familiarity with Communist styles and particularly its conclusion that the decisive answer to peoples' war was a similar strategy on the government's side. Support was therefore provided to host government efforts toward this goal; or, lacking government interest in creating a movement of popular engagement, the CIA sought and found opportunities to mobilize, train, and arm minorities with a natural antipathy toward the Communists. This was the origin of the intelligence agency's involvement with hill tribes in Laos and Vietnam and other programs with the underlying purpose of direct paramilitary support for communities or for host government programs with the same purpose. In due course, we will discuss this aspect of counterinsurgency in more detail.

In the case of AID, the demands created by counterinsurgency doctrine and policy were, with one exception, consistent with the agency's general mission but called for a considerable shift in emphasis. From its early days, AID had provided technical assistance in agricultural development, administration, public health, education, and the like. Counterinsurgency required a greater emphasis on such matters than would be called for in a balanced program of economic development and modernization. More problematic for the agency, however, was the need which became apparent with experience of taking unusual measures to focus such programs directly into the troubled rural areas of threatened countries. We will be discussing later the approaches that were developed in an attempt to meet this need.

Similarly, in USIA, little substantive change was required to redirect propaganda and informational resources from the task of projecting the United States's image to that of assisting threatened countries to project an improved image to their own people. It was a matter of providing resources, if needed, and advice to host government informational institutions—and, in fact, of helping to create them if necessary. On occasion, the help provided by USIA came to amount to actually doing the job, for it felt under the same kind of pressure as CIA to move in where opportunity beckoned.

Finally, of course, the State Department was also heavily involved. Although it was not responsible for many programs, it had a larger responsibility under the new doctrine to provide leadership and management overseas for the entire gamut of counterinsurgency activity. This duty was an aspect of the president's insistence from the early days of his administration that responsibility for firm leadership of overseas missions be clearly fixed on the ambassador and that his authority be confirmed and strengthened to assure that he was able to perform that task.[66] By his choice of ambassadors and senior departmental officials, he also signaled that he desired decisive leadership to characterize the functioning of the foreign service overseas, and grasp of counterinsurgency realities was explicitly stated to be one aspect of this new-style diplomacy. In his article on "internal defense" cited earlier, U. Alexis Johnson made the point with considerable emphasis.

One particular civilian program was singled out for White House attention. During most of the Eisenhower Administration there had existed in the economic aid agency a small technical assistance program to assist police forces in underdeveloped countries to improve their skills and capabilities in law enforcement. The Kennedy Administration came into office determined to reorganize foreign assistance to achieve better focus on economic development, which was to be its principal objective.[67] As the Kennedy appointees took over the renamed Agency for International Development, they decided that a police program had no place in the new scheme of things and declared their intention to abolish it.[68] At this point, the NSC staff, concerned that a useful counterinsurgency tool might be lost, intervened and persuaded the president to address a memorandum to the AID administrator (NSAM 132, February 19, 1962) asking that a careful study be made of the police program from the point of view of its usefulness in insurgency-threatened countries. A task force was established to consider the best arrangement for continuing and strengthening the program. Its solution provided for the creation of an Office of Public Safety in AID, reporting directly to the administrator.

Activities conducted by the Office of Public Safety and its field office overseas included training and assistance in all forms of law enforcement, from traffic control to paramilitary combat police. Two academies for training foreign police officers were established, one using Spanish as the language of instruction. At the time, the decision seemed unexceptionable on all grounds, but with the later change of climate on counterinsurgency and similar matters, the program became heavily criticized as an effort to strengthen the police arm of authoritarian regimes. That, of course, was not its purpose; but the view that police work is merely a technical matter involving improved administration, training, and the like, does not successfully refute all criticism.

★   ★   ★

By August 1962 the administration thus had in place the main outlines of an organized national approach to the insurgency threat. Detailed and urgent instructions had gone out—and there had been persistent follow-up to insure compliance—to revise the foreign affairs and military educational system, to develop a doctrine, and to establish responsive programs. High-level supervisory machinery had been put in place, and the agencies had been reorganized to assure a satisfactory response. An excellent illustration of the determined pursuit by the White House of its counterinsurgency goals exists in NSAM 162, issued on June 19, 1961.[69] It is a roundup of nine separate counterinsurgency matters bundled into a single memorandum. The first instruction concerns the preparation of Country Internal Defense Plans by country teams assigned in threatened areas. The last calls upon the Department of Defense and CIA to establish separate sections in their R&D programs "devoted to the requirements of counterinsurgency." In between are instructions on personnel development, the deployment of paramilitary trained specialists, the exploitation of specialists from third countries, the exploitation of minorities, and the improvement of indigenous intelligence organizations. The agencies are advised in several cases to report their progress to the Special Group (C.I.) and in one case it is stated that "the President will be given periodic reports on the progress" of a particular instruction. The memorandum is a stop-action photograph of the White House machinery in full operation—detailed, comprehensive, and utterly serious.

Far more was underway, of course, than the organization of Washington's control and support apparatus. U.S. field representatives were in full engagement with actual insurgency in several countries, and it was in the field that the ultimate outcome would be determined. Before we turn, however, to recount the complex story of U.S. counterinsurgency policies and performance in the field, we must call attention to certain factors implicit in the doctrine and the approach. They are factors which will continually surface as the field operations unfold; in most of the experiences we shall be describing they caused profound difficulty and were responsible for much of the ambiguity that attended the government's counterinsurgency effort.

To put it as simply as possible, the apparatus we have just described and the programs it generated did not, in fact, come to serious grips with the problems they were intended to solve. Some of the reasons were organizational. Senior men with heavy responsibilities were involved and were not able to devote the time required to make the Special Group (C.I.) live up to the broad language of its charter. Nor did it have a permanent staff of a size large enough to provide the continuity and persistent monitoring required to make up for the preoccupation of the principals with other matters. But the problem went deeper. The record of the Special Group (C.I.) shows a good deal of activity dealing with organizational and programmatic detail but relatively little with the profounder and more significant problems of concept and doctrine. For example, there was an assumption implicit in the approach as it related to the realities of politics within the threatened countries. Much reliance was placed on the ability of U.S. representatives to persuade indigenous governments to do two things: first, to improve and strengthen their administration of government, notably in security and counterguerrilla military operations, but also in other relevant fields; and secondly, to carry out reforms to satisfy popular needs and undercut Communist appeals. The assumption was that these were primarily technical matters of improving administration and identifying more popular policies, and that technically skilled and persuasive American representatives would readily succeed in such a task.

The truth, however, is more complicated. Improved administration as well as—more obviously—social reform are thoroughly entangled with the distribution of power and rewards in most societies, and this seems to be especially true of regimes which are undeveloped not only economically but, as is usually the case, politically as well. Such regimes, and particularly military dictatorships—which rely heavily on the leadership of the armed forces and the police for their political base—usually survive by purchasing the loyalty of their subordinates with patronage and by balancing powerful satraps off against each other to prevent collusion. As a result, the quality of performance has little to do with continuance in office and is often low. When, in response to counterinsurgency doctrine, the U.S. called upon a threatened government to carry out a program of self-reform in the midst of crisis, it seemed to be insisting that the regime jeopardize its hold on power in order to defeat the Communists. To the ruling group this was no mere technical question but one of survival, for, not unnaturally, the members placed their continued hold on power ahead of defeating the Communists, whereas, in the U.S. view, the priorities were reversed. As U. Alexis Johnson pointed out in the article already cited, "the measures we advocate may strike at the very foundations of those aspects of a government's social structure and domestic economy on which rests the basis of a government's control."[70]

This problem of self-reform in the midst of crisis is one of the factors which lay, like a concealed mine, in the path of the counterinsurgency program in many of the countries. Another troublesome factor related to the U.S. government itself and its ability to meet the demands of the program for innovation, flexibility, and, above all, for actions that were both unified and firmly managed. Much would depend on the State Department's ability to provide ambassadors who were managers as well as skilled negotiators. Also critical was the spirit of the participating agencies and their leaders, and whether they could muster the necessary degree of closeness and intimate cooperation in the field. Finally, this factor would also depend in part on organization, for complicated programs require more than goodwill and committees to run them. The administration made an implicit assumption that it could rapidly bring about the profound changes in the U.S. foreign affairs community that would turn it into the kind of instrument needed for the counterinsurgency task. The problems in this sphere proved a good deal more stubborn than anticipated.

With the perspective of the last decade it is clear that the president, his brother, and his other advisers made assumptions in regard to these and other problematical factors with more optimism than realism. The campaign for a new approach to deal with insurgency was bold, determined, and energetic; but it was also superficial and, responding to the perceived urgencies of the threat, too hasty. A most serious flaw was the failure to grapple seriously with dilemmas the program posed for the military and to arrive at a sensible solution which met the new challenge effectively without sacrificing the ability to cope with the traditional challenge of conventional war. In its haste, the administration also inadvertently spawned a system which left most of the men at the operating end of the apparatus confused about what was expected of them and unable to apply the simplistic slogans of their indoctrination to the real situations they confronted.[71] As a result, they too often resorted to new hardware or to gimmickry as "a quick fix." What never failed to astonish and appall the practitioners was to discover that the very governments they were trying to help often became the most serious obstacles to progress in the effort to gain the support of the population. Their training had not prepared them for this. In many cases, therefore, counterinsurgency concepts were out of touch with reality; there was, as Henry Kissinger was to point out years later, a very grave failure of "conceptualization."[72] Moreover, due to the sometimes brash "new breed" style of the administration, counterinsurgency acquired the trappings of a fad, a subject about which some discoursed knowingly to demonstrate their closeness and sympathy with the new powers in the land—but with little understanding of the hard choices involved.

In part this can be attributed to the fact that the impulse and inspiration for the new policies came from the very top of the pyramid, from men who had little time to focus on day-to-day implementation. Despite the flurry of statements, reorganizations, and reeducation programs, the subject, as we have noted, could only occupy a fraction of the time of the president and the attorney general and their immediate staffs. Reliance had to be placed on such men as General Taylor, Secretary McNamara, Secretary Rusk, and the Joint Chiefs. These men were also busy, and none of them was prepared to deal with or even aware of the grave flaws in the concepts—and so the apparatus carried on with the approach and its innumerable ramifications throughout the national security community, unthinkingly perpetuating the original errors.

None of this, on the other hand, can be taken to support the accusation that counterinsurgency, as conceived and carried out by the Kennedy Administration, was simply another name for counterrevolution, a conspiracy of some sort to suppress popular revolutions around the world. It is clear that the original concept was at the opposite pole. It was intended as a means of encouraging the inevitable and sometimes violent changes taking place in the underdeveloped world to take a democratic and libertarian direction. The motives were therefore consistent with American principles, and the program was indeed thought of as a further development and extension of those principles to deal with new challenges in a tumultuously changing world. In the minds of its originators they were blazing new and worthy paths in the tradition of such recent triumphs as the Marshall Plan.

Not only had they the conviction that what they were doing was principled and right, but they also had reason to assume that the task was far from an impossible one. They were confident that their new team represented or had access to the best talent and brains in the country. They also saw the problem as one where the trail had already been successfully marked. The two previous experiences that carried the most weight were those of the Philippines in the early fifties and of the British in Malaya, only recently terminated. The president was familiar with both cases and also, of course, with the French misadventures in Vietnam and Algeria which he believed were due to wrongheaded policy. These experiences seemed to demonstrate conclusively that the task was well within the reach of a far more powerful America.

In short, America's leaders saw every reason for optimism, since they believed they understood both the problem and the solution. The purpose was far from ignoble; how well and why it succeeded or failed will engage our attention in the pages that follow.

4

Vietnam and Strategic Hamlets

★ ★ ★

As the White House and the national security agencies proceeded in a systematic effort to develop a new style of military and civilian operations, they also confronted an immediate and painful example of the precise problem their new doctrines were designed to solve. At the time of his inauguration, President Kennedy—cued by his briefings—did not view Vietnam as a crisis comparable to Laos or Cuba. In January, he routinely endorsed a modest increase in U.S. military assistance in Vietnam keyed to certain improvements in President Ngo Dinh Diem's government and military organizations.[1] By April, however, several things had occurred to raise the level of concern, notably the setback of the Bay of Pigs and growing uncertainty that Lao policy—then midway in an effort to neutralize the Lao arena—would succeed in preserving anything from Communist control. It began to seem important to improve our posture in neighboring Vietnam lest the administration be accused of infirmity. Nor was the South Vietnamese government making noticeable progress in eliminating the insurgency. The first of many interagency reviews of the Vietnam situation was therefore demanded by the president.

As the administration perceived Vietnam, it was a classic picture of a successful insurgency in the pattern of a "war of national liberation." For more than a year Communist guerrillas had been pursuing a course of violent harassment of the Diem government's facilities and forces in the countryside, causing a rising curve of assassinations, ambushes, propaganda episodes, and terrorism. A "National Liberation Front" had been formed and had set up a competing government authority in remote areas as well. This NLF was widely perceived to be a stalking horse for the Vietnamese Communist movement, i.e., for Hanoi, where that movement had its headquarters. Direction of the movement was believed to come from there, and evidence accumulated that personnel and equipment were dispatched from North Vietnam by various routes of which the most important was a series of jungle paths and way stations through Laos—the so-called Ho Chi Minh Trail. The NFL claimed to be a wholly independent and nationalist South Vietnamese movement. Its leadership included non-Communist figures and it couched its appeals in largely nationalist terms.

Against this well-orchestrated attack, the South Vietnamese regime of President Ngo Dinh Diem was enjoying little success. Its army was small and had been organized and trained by the U.S. Military Assistance and Advisory Group (MAAG) to meet what had been seen as the most likely military challenge, a conventional attack by the North Vietnamese across the seventeenth parallel. The militia, which in theory should have provided the initial local protection against guerrilla attack, was a primitive and largely untrained force. Diem's efforts were also seriously hampered in American eyes by his insistence upon dividing responsibility for security between the military command and the provincial governments, which reported directly to him. This, it was understood, was intended to forestall his enemies in any possible coup attempt. He had no national plan or command to deal with the insurgents and scattered his forces piecemeal around the countryside, standing guard over facilities and outposts, where they were an easy prey to guerrilla strikes.

The regime was obviously floundering, and the official community, which had once looked upon it with respect, was becoming disillusioned. Diem relied more and more on his family to hold positions of trust, narrowing the base of his support. Of those he trusted, his brother Ngo Dinh Nhu—who bore the title of political counselor—seemed to many to be a negative and even sinister influence, sitting at the center of a network of intelligence and semicovert political organizations which he attempted to manipulate to maintain the regime against its enemies. Accusations of arbitrary rule, of the persecution of dissidents, and of corruption were becoming more frequent, but there seemed little alternative to the policy of supporting Diem, who was firmly anti-Communist, personally honest, and dedicated.

Before describing in detail the policies and programs undertaken by both the U.S. and the government of Vietnam (GVN) to confront and master this threat, we must set the stage somewhat more precisely. The course and form of this complex effort and its tragic results can be understood only against the background of the particular circumstances of Vietnam in the late 1950s.

A Fractured Society

South Vietnam was an artificial creation of the Geneva Accords of 1954 consisting of a few provinces of the former French protectorate of Annam (Central Vietnam) and all of the directly ruled French colony of Cochin China. It was but the rump of a nation, and that nation in fact had had no formal existence for several generations, the former Vietnamese Empire having been split into three parts by the French (Tonkin, Annam, and Cochin China) and then submerged in an artificial entity, French Indochina, composed along with many minorities of three main peoples: the Vietnamese, Cambodians, and Lao. The French, to make their imperial chore easier, had done their best to erase the sense of identity binding the three parts of Vietnam (they actually banned the use of the terms "Vietnam" and "Vietnamese") and had also recognized and protected various privileged minorities, such as the Chinese living in the cities and a small native elite which was awarded a French education and a special status that went with assimilation. The experience was a shattering one to the old Vietnamese elite's sense of cultural identity, to its self-confidence, and to its unity. When South Vietnam emerged as an independent republic, the educated stratum was quite unprepared for the leadership role that was proffered to it. It had no experience in open politics or self-government, no unifying commitment to national goals or ethos, and few of the skills needed to manage the institutions of a modern society. As for the traditional institutions persisting through the years of French rule, few were left except in vestigial form. The mandarinate had become a civil service in which key posts were monopolized by Frenchmen; the Imperial Court was a shadow of its former power, and it quickly disappeared. The religion of the majority, Hinayana Buddhism, was never a strongly organized church. Certain religious sects, including the Catholic, showed persistent vitality but involved only small minorities. Only two nationwide institutions persisted with approximately their former vitality: the family and the village. Although these demonstrated remarkable strength and continuity, they were not adequate to the need for a unifying ethos that would provide a common underpinning to the fractured elements of society—indeed, they tended to undermine rather than strengthen the development of a national purpose and individual commitment to it.

The political life of Vietnam quickly degenerated into a turbulent competition of separate groupings, small conspiratorial parties, and religious, ethnic, and regional factions which were unable to cooperate for a common purpose. Briefly, Ngo Dinh Diem was given an opportunity to create a polity based on common goals and aspirations.

What made the situation desperate, of course, was the fact of war and war of a kind that exploited the most basic cleavage of all in Vietnamese society: that between the educated elite of the cities and towns (to which the leadership belonged) and the masses of the peasantry in their conical hats and black pajamas, laboriously cultivating their rice fields. The cleavage was not actually new but had traditionally been contained by the shared values of rulers and ruled in the Confucian pattern that assigned a place with associated rights and responsibilities to all, by the unmobilized state of society which resulted in few demands pressing on the villages from the center, and by an explicit understanding that the villages would manage their own affairs while giving the emperor his due in the form of taxes, allegiance, and military service when required. The French had permitted village autonomy to continue in altered form, and it was only after independence was restored that Diem saw this tradition-al autonomy of the village as an obstacle to his ambition for a unitary state managed in all significant matters from the Presidential Palace. He abolished it by decree. The result was to bring into direct contact the two cultures of modern, educated elite and traditional peasant life which had grown worlds apart, and to charge the elite with managing a new type of society for which the peasants were entirely unprepared, one which provided services but also placed new and stricter demands on the villages.[2] The urban elite, in the form of the civil service, became responsible for communities they did not know or understand, which regarded them as foreigners, and which they could not deal with in an evenhanded fashion. An extension of power was granted to them which—true to the strong persisting loyalty to family—they exploited for the benefit of those closest to them, working in concert with the local elite of landowners and Chinese traders whose outlook was similar and whose access to them was superior to that of the peasants. Although there were numerous exceptions and local differences, in general the peasants were tenant farmers or farm laborers who were forced to pay illegally high rents where the government's writ ran and who often found that the local officials appointed by the central authority collected such rents *for* the landlords, sometimes moving into disputed territory behind the protection of government troops to do so. Indeed, the allegation was sometimes made and confirmed by independent sources that the government's military units actually collected the rents.[3] Like all peasants everywhere, land tenure and ownership were of overwhelming importance to Vietnamese rice farmers. Because, in part at least, the government elites had little understanding or interest in the peasant's point of view, the GVN's efforts to deal with the problems were usually beside the point and ultimately defeated the alleged objective of gaining the peasant's support.

The gaping political vulnerability created by this situation is only apparent if we turn to the other side of the coin and examine the appeal of the Viet Cong and the fashion in which it organized to exploit the gap between the peasant and those who ruled him.

HO CHI MINH'S PARTY

The Lao Dong, or Workers' Party of Vietnam, early accepted Mao Tse-tung's version of Marxism-Leninism and based its strategy on the peasantry. Its approach, however, was not simply a carbon copy of Mao's theories. It was adapted with considerable sensitivity to the needs and opportunities of the special circumstances existing in Vietnam. This was the particular contribution of Ho Chi Minh, a toughened Far East cadre of the Comintern who nevertheless—and despite over a decade spent in Europe and China—retained a refined understanding of his own people. He was also a man of superb organizational talent. The party he and his colleagues created has survived and emerged victorious from over thirty years of war against immensely superior forces. For most of that time, the techniques used were those of people's war, but carefully modified and adapted to the unique Vietnamese environment.

How to account for the persistent strength of the Communists in South Vietnam in the face of all the power of their adversaries? There is no simple answer, for the nature of the war changed drastically, particularly in response to the American intervention and subsequent withdrawal. But the period of most interest in this analysis is that preceding the evolution to more or less conventional war and invasion from the North, the period up to the Tet offensive of early 1968 when the might of over half a million Americans, two divisions of Koreans, and nine divisions of Vietnamese, not to mention the air forces and paramilitary ground forces arrayed against them, did not suffice to suppress or even to take the strategic initiative away from the Viet Cong and NVA.

The usual answer given by the U.S. and GVN was to cite three factors: outside (i.e., North Vietnamese) aid, good organization, and selective terrorism. All these have played a part, but as more has become known about the realities of village life and of Viet Cong tactics as a result of research in captured documents, and interviews with defectors,[4] the point made many years ago by the famous French scholar Paul Mus and expounded more recently for an American public by John T. McAllister, Jr.,[5] and (with considerable exaggeration) by Frances FitzGerald,[6] has become more convincing. The Lao Dong Party under Ho Chi Minh was able to appeal to the peasant population in terms that answered a deep cultural craving for the restoration of the lost unity of the peasant's world with the larger world outside the village and, beyond that, with the mystical forces governing the universe. It was able to convince many that it had inherited the "mandate of heaven" which conferred legitimacy in the traditional polity. Moreover, those features of Communist practice which were most offensive to Western values—its "monism" expressed in totalitarian control—were quite consistent with Vietnamese and indeed Confucian principles of society which saw the nation as a simulacrum of the patriarchal family, a unity mystically presided over by the emperor and his mandarins and which by definition, therefore, ruled out pluralism and the toleration of opposition and dissent.

Some such theory of the Communist appeal—difficult as it is for Americans to grasp—seems required to explain the durability and effectiveness of the movement in the countryside, its ability to recruit and motivate and train simple peasants in large numbers to fight bravely, to persist against great odds, and to remain loyal despite years of struggle. Especially is this true in view of the contrast between the Communist success in these efforts and the bleak record of the French and then the American-sponsored regimes that attempted similar goals but failed to arouse genuine support in the real Vietnam of the countryside.

But how was this impression created and perpetuated—that heaven had transferred its mandate, that the Viet Cong, a secular, irreligious (though not actively atheist) movement, poorly endowed with material goods, had seized the prize of legitimate succession to the Confucian state? Paul Mus, as interpreted by McAllister, saw the critical moment to have been August 1945, when the Japanese, satisfied to have ruled during most of the war years through a colonial regime tied to Vichy France, suddenly cast the French aside and established an indigenous regime under the Emperor Bao Dai. This, in turn, was rapidly replaced by the Viet Minh regime under Ho Chi Minh's leadership, which ruled most of Vietnam from Hanoi for a period of over a year, after which the French commenced the war to regain their empire. According to Mus, the sudden replacement of the French by a Vietnamese authority that could speak effectively to the peasants in terms they understood and produce meaningful decisions, authority, and discipline in the prevailing chaos was a sign to the people that "heaven" had spoken and this was decisive for the remaining years of Vietnam's travail.[7]

We may be pardoned some skepticism that this explanation fully accounts for the phenomenon of Viet Cong persistence and growth throughout the long, bitter conflict that followed, especially in the South. The war that recommenced in South Vietnam in 1960 was far more complex than the war against the French. The so-called mandate of heaven was tested as it had not been before, and one must seek further explanations that compliment Mus's historical and cultural analysis.

Underlying the achievements of the Viet Cong was the party organization which became an instrument of great sensitivity and strength. On this fact, agreement is general. In the Leninist tradition, the party was composed of full-time cadres, acting with military discipline and in secrecy. The party of Ho Chi Minh, however, added some qualities of its own which responded to certain cultural peculiarities of the Vietnamese. Of great importance was the policy of leaving cadres in place in their home areas to work among their own people, moving them up as they earned promotion to greater responsibility, but still dealing with their home communities at higher levels. Besides the obvious advantage of the familiarity of the cadre with his target area, this system drew additional strength from the familiarity of the cadre to the people he sought to influence. He was a relative or a fellow villager, a fact which made it easier to gain a hearing and win the trust of his target community. As the exceptional cadre rose in rank and moved to district level or higher, he was still a local man from the same or a neighboring village. The villager was still dealing with a familiar quantity.[8] This condition was in strong contrast to the situation in areas ruled by Saigon where the village was ruled by officials appointed by district and province level and thus controlled by virtually "foreign" elements. Even after village elections were restored by President Thieu, the chain still led to the same distant and forbidding structure at district and province.

But perhaps the greatest strength of the Communist approach was the fact that it opened the way for the villager to a life and a career that could lift him from the confines of village life, offering him greater status, authority, and importance than had ever been possible before. The offer of upward mobility and a share in the power that controlled their lives had enormous appeal. It spoke to the villager's sense of isolation and helplessness in his relations with the larger world from which the familiar traditional forces and powers had long since disappeared.

THE PARTY AS "THE PEOPLE'S FRIEND"

There is no doubt that the Communist apparatus sought deliberately to cultivate these effects. The style of the cadre in dealing with the villagers, for example, was carefully calculated to reinforce their sense of being in touch with a responsive and benevolent power. The interviews and reports on relations between cadres and people are full of references to the kindly, fatherly approach of the Communist representatives and the contrast between the cadres' attitude and that of Saigon's representatives. To cite just one, a peasant interviewed in 1967 said, "The Viet Cong collect higher taxes but they know how to please the people; they behave politely so the people feel that they are more favored. . . . They do not thunder at the people like the government soldiers."[9] This approach was a calculated reinforcement to the fundamental posture of the Communists that their movement was directed to the liberation of the people by their own efforts. In time, however, the losses inflicted upon the Viet Cong, combined with their own mistakes—particularly in launching the Tet offensive into the teeth of their enemy's immense superiority of firepower—forced a change in approach and a harsher relationship with the villagers. Much of the mystique of Viet Cong cadre as the "people's friend" was lost, but by then the character of the war had changed to the point where the quality of that relationship mattered far less than it had in earlier years.

Of major importance to the success of the system of locally recruited cadre was the decentralization of authority within the organization. Although policies were set at higher echelons and review of policy and performance was constant—generating an enormous amount of documentation and frequent meetings at all levels—the village party committee had a great deal of autonomy in the execution of policy. As Race points out, many of the kinds of decisions that, on the government side, were made at province level or even in Saigon were, on the Communist side, left to the village party secretary.[10] This practice meant that the villager, in his relationship with the Communist apparatus, could often see that his views and his problems had a direct effect on the decisions that concerned his life. In contrast, the government had great difficulty in achieving a similar impact in its decision-making process. The entire approach of both the Americans and the Vietnamese—although some exceptions must be acknowledged and will be noted later—reflected the sense that higher authority knew best what must be done in the villages.

These factors—demonstrating the conscious decision of the party of Ho Chi Minh to fit its approach closely to the special perspectives of village Vietnam—are the most important of the reasons for the continuing strength of the movement and its ability to sustain the belief that it had won the "mandate of heaven." There were, in addition, other reasons, among them the specific issues that were overtly agitated by the Communists. These issues were the familiar ones of nationalism, land reform, government corruption, and "mandarinism" (i.e., rule by a class of bureaucrats who placed themselves on a plane above the people and demanded special privileges). The Communists, of course, did not make overt appeals in the name of Communism or Marxism or Maoism. They spoke in terms of liberation from oppression by foreigners and corrupt puppet rulers and of a new life of prosperity and justice. These generalities were made specific in the daily appeals of the cadres and their propaganda, and the specifics reflected careful study of villager psychology as well as the realities of village life. Where possible, the pledges were carried out, a major example being land reform in areas where the Viet Cong established sufficient control to do so. This not only illustrated the seriousness of the party's pledges but had the additional advantage of placing the government in an invidious position if it regained control in an area where such a reform had been carried out.

Normally, it undid the land distributions of the Communists, thus confirming the accusations brought against it.

There is no doubt that the movement made effective use of the issues, but such issues were by no means the principal reason, as some have maintained, for the continued hold of the Communists. It is probably impossible to determine what share they represented as against the importance of Communist style, organization, and sensitivity to powerful cultural values; but quite certainly it is a gross oversimplification to assume, as many have, that the whole story of Viet Cong capability reflects the power of the issues they were able to seize and exploit. This view overlooks the fact that in Vietnam many political groups sought to arouse the people against the same grievances but only the Viet Cong succeeded. Without genuine grievances there would have been no insurgency, but neither would there have been one without superb organization, effective strategy and tactics, and great sensitivity to the cultural values involved. Nationalism, for instance, has been cited by some as the single most powerful issue underlying the Communist success in Vietnam. Yet, when the guerrilla war was resumed in 1960, it was directed against Ngo Dinh Diem, who was as nationalistic as the Communists. At the time, there were about a thousand Americans in the country and most Vietnamese never saw any. The issue was manufactured for the purposes of the insurgency which eventually accomplished the heavy-handed American intervention that made the grievance a reality to many Vietnamese.

THE ROLE OF TERROR

We have yet to mention an aspect of the Communist approach which also played a significant if indeterminable role in building their strength. This was the use of terrorism as a deliberate and carefully managed weapon in their arsenal. As in every other aspect of VC strategy and tactics, terrorism, or what the Viet Cong called "suppression," was systematized, assigned to a specific organizational arm, and surrounded with an elaborate rationale and routines for assuring precision and control. The section assigned the task was the Security Service of the People's Revolutionary Party, which, in turn, was a department of the Ministry of Public Security of the DRV, the Hanoi government.[11] The purpose of repression, according to Stephen Hosmer, who has made the most thorough investigation of the subject, was primarily to undermine and bring down the GVN by eliminating its personnel. It also served to enhance the prestige of the VC by demonstrating its capability and its superiority to the GVN and was used as a "persuader" in the inducement of defection and recruitment into the VC movement of government personnel.

Although it never reached its goal, which was no less than the elimination of all key government officials, from 1957 onward it caused a serious drain on the government's strength and was a major constraint on the performance of their duties by civil servants, particularly in the countryside. Thus, in 1968, a particularly costly year because of the Tet offensive, the government lost over twelve hundred officials and employees by assassination and abductions, and another seventeen thousand persons in the general population suffered similar fates.[12]

The use of terror on this scale does not actually contradict the "soft" approach to the village population described earlier. The terror, until the years after the Tet offensive, was not indiscriminate but was carried out as "punishment" for what the VC held to be crimes and was sometimes preceded by public trials. By such devices, the VC enacted a portion of its program for educational and propaganda purposes as well as for the more general goal of helping to bring the government down. Terrorism thus assisted the VC in maintaining its domination in the villages by intimidating enemies, by the impression of fear or respect it made on the uncommitted, and by confirming the wisdom of their decision among the committed. It was no doubt an effective tool but one which could backfire if it replaced the other appeals already described. If fear became the main reliance of the VC for control, that control would weaken when the government became able to bring its strength and its appeals to bear. The persistence of loyalty to the VC despite strong and long-lasting government presence in many areas confirms that terrorism was not the VC's main reliance in building its hold upon the rural population. On the other hand, in the years after the Tet offensive and the commencement of the American withdrawal, the harshness of VC rule increased and the use of terrorism and abduction became less discriminating. By this time, however, the contest was becoming rapidly one of rival firepower and the finer distinctions of the earlier years were less important.

THE VC MACHINERY

We have already pointed out that a complex and elaborate organization underlay the Viet Cong's hold on a large part of the rural population of Vietnam. It was not merely an insurgent force but also a political movement and a government with all the essential arms, often on a reduced scale, but nevertheless remarkably complete. It was, in fact, a fully developed competing sovereignty, vying with the GVN for the loyalty and resources of its population. In putting it together, the Vietnamese Communists were faithful to the familiar pattern they had adopted from the Chinese and the Russians—that of a National Liberation Front, purporting to unite all patriotic forces. Within and around that Front, which had no independent source of strength, was a framework composed in part of the southern branch of the Lao Dong Party (separately organized as the People's Revolutionary Party in 1962) and the state apparatus of the DRV, particularly the army (PAVN—the People's Army of Vietnam) and the Ministry of Public Security. This apparatus worked as a unit under the management of the PRP except for the broadest policy decisions and the insertion of resources from outside the borders of South Vietnam. The first of these exceptions was the prerogative of the politburo of the Lao Dong Party (into which the PRP no doubt had significant input); of the second we know little, but it was probably a duty of the PAVN, supported as required by other departments of the DRV and monitored by appropriate arms of the Lao Dong.

The organizational forms of the PRP/NLF (or as it later came to be called, the Provisional Revolutionary Government—PRG) were complex (for there were three parallel elements, the army, the NLF, and the PRP proper). The NLF, however, was essentially a dependency of the PRP element at each level with no independent command line of its own. At the village, district, and province level, the local PRP unit also controlled certain armed forces, but the so-called main force units, the regulars, had an independent command channel. In addition to this organizational skeleton, the NLF, in each village, district, and province, established "mass" organizations of farmers, women, students, and the like, which had an important role in involving the population in the movement and giving an outlet for the ambitions of the more active. But the critical element of the political apparatus was the party secretariat at each level. It usually set up and directed units responsible for finance, communications, security, proselytizing, and lesser functions. It also controlled guerrilla forces and determined their uses in accordance with policies and objectives reached at a higher level.[13]

To draw up a scheme for such an organizational structure is one thing, to staff it with sufficiently trained, able, and dedicated cadres is another. One secret of the VC's success is the fact that it was able to start from a tested base built during the long years of the first Indochina war. Many of the Southern cadres were brought out in 1954 to North Vietnam for further education and training and subsequently reinfiltrated. As the need for additional cadres grew, the organization recruited from the ranks of the guerrilla units and the mass organizations without lowering selection standards. Training and indoctrination remained thorough. Each candidate for membership in the party and subsequently for advancement had to prove himself in action. Membership in the party, in the Leninist tradition, was a commitment of one's entire life and resources. For the cadre, the party became his family, his government, his school, and his church. The psychology and the apparatus of control and domination of this system are well known. What is not well understood is why the approach has worked so effectively in certain

Asian countries—Vietnam, China, and Korea, all of Confucian cultural heritage—and failed signally in most of the others. It seems possible that in some way the Confucian cultural background in a society in confusion and disarray prepares individuals to accept the party's appeal and surmount the hurdles to membership, as it undoubtedly helped Ho Chi Minh's party to make its impact upon the village consciousness.

However that may be, the party organization was a fundamental aspect of the VC's strength and a sine qua non for its continued success. It was this so-called infrastructure that lay behind its persistence, its remarkable unity and consistency despite the distances separating the various elements, behind the ability of the organization to survive heavy blows, to continue to rebuild and repair and recruit, and to motivate the village populations against the evidence of enormous U.S. strength and resources. And lying behind the mechanical aspects of the organizational structure, about which too much can be made, was the true secret of success—the quality of its leadership and cadres, and their understanding of the workings of the village mind which made the party of Ho Chi Minh such a remarkable phenomenon.

Although in 1961 the pattern of the Viet Cong's campaign against the Diem regime seemed a familiar one, following on such recent episodes as the Viet Minh war against the French and the Malayan and Philippine insurgencies, the administration did not have at first a ready response geared to such a conflict. It was too early in the process of evolving a counterinsurgency doctrine. In the event, almost a year elapsed before a strategy was found which the White House saw as meeting the peculiar needs of counterinsurgency war. What filled the gap was a largely military response which paid obeisance to such "people-oriented" concepts as military civic action and improved propaganda, but in strategic and tactical terms focused largely upon measures to transform the Vietnamese armed forces into an effective military apparatus, mobile and professionally managed, able to concentrate its forces effectively when required to strike a massive blow. It was believed that such a force—if properly supported by a competent intelligence effort—could easily meet and disperse the poorly armed insurgents as a "lesser included capability" of its newfound proficiency. Indeed, that view is the only fully endorsed official doctrine of counterinsurgency the United States Army has ever accepted, although it has sometimes felt forced to agree to other approaches, and although other schools of thought have existed within the army at levels below the top.

With this underlying doctrine implicit in their thinking, U.S. officials devised a series of expedients to improve the performance of the Vietnamese military as rapidly as possible. The first such increase was part of the plan approved by the president, as noted earlier, in the earliest days of the administration. It was called the Counter Insurgency Plan

(CIP) and we will return to it shortly. The next increase came in May after the first Kennedy review of the situation and represented an initial effort to meet what was now seen as an alarming problem. It was promulgated in NSAM 52.[14] The third increase resulted from a visit to Vietnam by General Maxwell Taylor (then still the president's military adviser) and Walt W. Rostow in October 1961—a visit prompted by the continuing worsening of the situation. All of these decisions increased the size of the Vietnamese armed forces to be supported by the U.S., both regular and militia, and committed the U.S. to providing larger quantities of equipment and more training and advice.

The climax of the process came in the decisions following the Taylor-Rostow trip. The commitments undertaken in subsequent negotiations and decisions brought the U.S. involvement to its highest peak under Kennedy auspices. A very large increase in military advisers to about three thousand, plus additional military personnel to fly and maintain aircraft and provide logistic support eventually brought the total of American military personnel in Vietnam by the end of 1963 to twenty-three thousand. A major feature of the program was the provision of large numbers of helicopters flown by Americans to airlift Vietnamese forces into battle. Fixed-wing aircraft were also provided with Americans flying alongside Vietnamese as "instructors."

Military assistance was not the entirety of this early counterinsurgency effort. Both the first and the third programs of that first year included requirements for changes in Vietnam command arrangements and demands for political reorganization and reform. Civic action was proposed as an important role for the Vietnamese army. But these were secondary issues, a fact which became clear when the political changes such as broadening the base of the regime and even the consolidation of command under the Vietnamese General Staff, initially demanded as conditions for increased military aid, were resisted by President Diem. Although the conditions were allowed to slide, the aid was provided anyway.

The doctrine under which this assistance was advanced—the only developed doctrine for fighting such a war which existed in official circles at the time—is spelled out in two documents described (although not provided in full) in the *Pentagon Papers:* the CIP and a related paper of September 1961, the Geographically Phased National Plan. The CIP encompassed a good deal more than military matters, for it went into some detail on the necessity for Diem to broaden his regime, to cleanse it of corruption, and to reorganize it for greater efficiency. These latter points, however, were all added by the embassy's insistence onto a military proposal for enlarging the ARVN and assuming U.S. responsibility for supply and training of the militia and the local paramilitary force.[15] They were not the heart of the plan, as we have noted, and were ultimately abandoned as conditions in order "to get on with the war."[16]

The military aspects were central and represented the attempt of a new chief of MAAG and his superiors to put the Vietnamese armed forces on a footing which, in their view, would make them capable of eliminating the VC threat. The greatest obstacles to success were seen to be not the matters of size and equipment but the deficiencies of the GVN's military system, particularly the lack of a unified command and of a national plan and the consequent scattering of the ARVN in static duties across the countryside. If the GVN would reform its military apparatus in these respects, it proposed that the U.S. then proceed to support additional forces and also take over responsibility for assisting the militia with training, advice, and weapons.

The doctrine which underlay the CIP was simply the basic principle of concentration of force, dubbed by General McGarr, the chief of MAAG, the strategy of "the net and the spear." The concept called for a regular pattern of patrolling to find VC concentrations which would then be struck by strong units held in reserve for this purpose.[17] The reforms, which were in fact the substance of the CIP, were thus intended to relieve the ARVN of static duties. These were to be taken over by the Civil Guard (a paramilitary force organized in battalions and controlled at province level) and the Self Defense Corps (organized in companies and controlled at district level), while the regulars stayed in reserve for serious fighting. The proper distribution and combining of the roles of regulars and paramilitary forces required that they be placed under the same centralized command, hence the insistence upon a reorganization of the existing command structure (preferred by Diem for his own reasons) and the elaboration of a national plan encompassing the entire effort.

A more elaborate exposition of MAAG's strategy emerged in the Geographically Phased National Plan of September 1961:

> In the first "preparatory phase," the intelligence effort was to be concentrated in the priority target areas, surveys were to be made to pinpoint needed economic and political reforms, plans were to be drawn up, and military and political cadres were to be trained for the specific objective area. The second, or "military phase," would be devoted to clearing the objective area with regular forces, then handling local security responsibility over to the Civil Guard (CG) and to establishing GVN presence. In the final, "security phase," the Self Defense Corps (SDC) would assume the civil action-local security mission, the populace was to be "reoriented," political control was to pass to civilian hands, and economic and social programs were to be initiated to consolidate government control. Military units would be withdrawn as security was achieved and the target area would be "secured" by the loyalty of its inhabitants.[18]

The plan was to be carried out methodically, according to geographical priorities, a process which would clear the bulk of the country over a three-year period. In an introductory phase the plan prescribed a large ARVN sweep through a major VC stronghold northeast of Saigon to improve its readiness and raise its confidence.

Thus, the U.S. military's plan, although in a rather abstract way for the helter-skelter real world of Vietnam, did seek to incorporate the necessary nonmilitary elements into a complex combined effort and in that respect was in line with the developing doctrine of the counterinsurgency theorists in Washington. Nevertheless, it also called for conventional forces to be used conventionally in the military phase, and this was the keystone of the proposed strategy. The ARVN, operating in its normal formations of battalions and regiments under divisional and corps commands, and fully employing its conventional weaponry, was to clear and hold large areas under VC threat in one year's campaign, after which the security responsibility would be turned over to the militia and the regulars would move on to other areas. There is no hint that the ARVN, which had been formed by six years of U.S. tutelage aimed at protecting the country from external enemies, would need to modify its strategy and tactics to meet an internal guerrilla threat. Indeed, the danger of conventional invasion was still seen as real. "The problem is twofold," said General McGarr, "although at present the counterinsurgency phase is the more dangerous and immediate.[19]

But even if the U.S. command had always viewed the VC internal threat as the main problem, there is reason to doubt that its approach would have been different. The same tendencies were at work upon military thinking in the field as in the Pentagon, where, as we have seen, the preference was to regard counterinsurgency as an added responsibility well within the capability of conventional units without major changes in their training or organization or even their tactics.

"Strategic Hamlets"

As matters turned out, neither the CIP nor the Geographically Phased Plan was ever carried out. The GVN attempted to conciliate and made some limited gestures but never accepted the reforms demanded, and although the additional assistance was nevertheless provided by the U.S., American strategy was not adopted. Instead, the regime moved in the direction of a novel and quite bold attempt to solve the insurgency crisis with a focus not upon the military aspect but upon the village population. It was called the strategic hamlet program.

U.S. policy quickly shifted its major concern from military matters to such questions as village attitudes and local defense—although it would be wrong to suggest that questions of weapons and command organization were neglected. In effect, a second front of U.S. attention and involvement was opened, and it was in this area that the counterinsurgency specialists were given some resources and capability to act. On the other hand, the military side absorbed the greater amount of resources and continued to be managed as a separate and virtually independent front—both on the U.S. and the Vietnamese sides. And in that area, as we shall see, U.S. military predilections, while sometimes challenged, were never successfully altered.

The strategic hamlet program emerged from a complex process of experimentation and interaction in which the participants were the GVN, various arms of the U.S. mission, and a third contributor, the small but influential British Advisory Mission of some six persons, most of them with previous experience in the Malaya counterinsurgency. Their head was R. K. G. Thompson (later Sir Robert) who had played a senior role in Malaya.

The underlying concept of the program was an abrupt break with the actual strategy of the GVN as well as with the proposals of the MAAG. Instead of emphasizing elimination of the armed bands of the VC by military means, the program attempted to go directly to the heart of the insurgency's strength, its ability to gain the willing or unwilling support of the rural population, which it was then able to organize to provide intelligence, food, money, and recruits for armed units. As was repeated endlessly in public explanations of the plan, the purpose was to dry up the sea of friendly peasantry in which swam the VC "fish."

The means by which this was to be done was the cutting off of the village population from contact with the VC by reorganizing and strengthening village government and defense, by bringing the villagers the benefits of better government, and by constructing defenses around each hamlet[20] behind which the population would retire at night. The physical defenses were intended to fend off overt attack and the reorganization and surveillance procedures were to eliminate the covert penetration of communities. In order to accomplish the necessary concentration of population, some villages would have to be resettled and compensated for their losses, but it was expected that the great majority would be able to stay in their existing homes.

Another fact of importance about the plan was that, notwithstanding British influence and U.S. support, it was preeminently a Vietnamese program and specifically the personal project of the president's brother and "counselor," the convoluted and perverse Ngo Dinh Nhu. A result of that fact is that the actual origins and motives of the program are somewhat obscure, for the inner workings of the Diem regime were never spread before the public. Yet most observers at the time and since have viewed the strategic hamlet program as a transfer of Malayan experience to Vietnam through the persuasion of the British Advisory Mission and particularly R. K. G. Thompson. There is no doubt that Thompson's recommendations had some influence, but they may simply have been adopted as a convenient facade for rather different purposes. Such at least is the view of one distinguished member of the British Advisory Mission,[21] and the fact that implementation of the plan departed radically from British proposals would seem to bear him out.

The record is clear, at any rate, that well before the arrival of the British mission the regime had been experimenting with the establishment of hamlets that could defend themselves. These experiments followed upon the clear failure of an ambitious earlier scheme for the resettlement of rural populations in large new communities called agrovilles.[22] The agroville phase had lasted about two years, starting in 1959 and petering out in 1961. It was far too ambitious for the limited resources of the regime, and it placed heavy demands on the peasants with little pretense of consultation. But the motives which had animated Saigon in this venture remained strong and the search for a means to carry them out continued. They were to enable the government to exercise control of peasant life adequate to its ambitions to move Vietnam repidly toward new values, new social discipline, and a new unity behind the leadership of Diem. In seeking this revolution, the regime set itself the awesome goal of eliminating the ancient isolation and virtual autarky of the village. It was toward the end of the agroville phase that the insurgency became a major threat and the preexisting preoccupation of the Ngo family regime became combined and overlaid with a related concern to thwart the VC.

This problem of establishing control in the countryside was the province of Ngo Dinh Nhu, who encouraged various experiments by trusted persons in several locations.[23] In some of these experiments with special hamlet defenses he had the support of the elements of the U.S. mission, which provided arms and other supplies. In contrast, the agroville program had had no help from the U.S., the mission being skeptical of its potential and not yet seriously concerned with the insurgent threat. The new departures included the efforts of a few energetic Catholic priests who had led their flocks into exile from North Vietnam after the 1954 partition and resettled in the South. Of the several such communities to become involved, most attention was attracted by a village of Chinese Catholics led by their priest, Father Hoa, who, beginning in 1950, had conducted a trek from China via North Vietnam, ending in Camau, the southernmost province of Vietnam, in the midst of VC-controlled territory. With the regime's approval, Hoa was able to arm the able-bodied men of his community and maintain it against persistent Communist attacks. Another Father Hoa, a Vietnamese, carried on a similar effort in Phu Yen province, Central Vietnam, and there were other such projects, generally successful but extremely limited in scope.

In all these cases, we may note the existence of a strong community leadership and an already committed village population which required merely the provision of weapons and some rudimentary training to create a firm anti-VC nucleus and a successful counterinsurgency effort, albeit on a tiny scale. But these qualities were preexisting and owed nothing to the Vietnamese government which provided the opportunity and (with American help) the means but not the motivation or the organization. These Catholic communities were "fellow travelers" of the government's cause. In dealing with the vast bulk of the South Vietnamese population the regime faced the necessity of developing from within its own resources the motivation and loyalties already present in the Catholic refugee villages.

As for the American role, there is little in the public record to clarify it. We are safe in assuming, however, that the CIA undertook to support these efforts. That organization is known both to have been functioning in cooperation with Ngo Dinh Nhu at the time and to have been arming and training local groups with strong anti-VC attitudes.[24]

THE BEGINNINGS OF CIDG

A similar but far larger experiment in which the CIA was also involved took place among the tribal populations of the highlands. In November 1961, with the approval of President Diem, organizing activity was undertaken by CIA together with GVN counterparts in two main areas of the Vietnamese highlands.[25] Although limited to a few of the larger tribes, notably the Rhadé located around Banmethuot in Darlac province and others around Kontum, the program moved ahead with amazing rapidity. In a little more than thirteen months, some thirty-eight thousand tribesmen were armed and over two hundred villages were incorporated into the scheme with a population of about three hundred thousand.[26] The inducement for the tribespeople was self-protection against the Viet Cong together with such programs as training for medical aides, dispensaries, education, and similar small-scale improvements in their lives. AID cooperated with CIA in supplying this aspect of the program. The armed villages were supported by strike forces of a few hundred of their own men whose assignment was to come to the aid of a community that was attacked by the VC.

The presence of the Americans was an important factor in the success of the program, for the tribesmen had an abiding suspicion of all Vietnamese. The feeling was reciprocated and, indeed, after more than a year of uninterrupted success, Ngo Dinh Nhu nevertheless became convinced that the program threatened Vietnamese control of the tribal areas. He began a program of disarming many of the purely village defense units. Others remained, and at approximately the same time a decision was made to transfer responsibility for the American side of it from CIA to the Special Forces.[27] After that decision, a subtle change came over it. The armed tribal irregulars—the so-called Citizens Irregular Defense Groups, or CIDG—were no longer a hamlet militia. Given improved training, weapons, and uniforms, and organized in companies, they became military units. As Strike Forces they were used for attack and defense against enemy units rather than as village defenders. In this role they were close to being mercenaries, something rather different from their original role and, from the viewpoint of counterinsurgency, not as useful.

The underlying pattern of CIA recruitment and direct support for a minority group which had motives to resist Communist organizing efforts, but which could not be mobilized by the indigenous government on its own behalf, was one which we will encounter elsewhere, notably in Laos. It has advantages in that the minorities often had strong motivations and were aggressive fighters. It also had some serious disadvantages, among them the strains it placed on an already dubious sense of national unity and the commitment of the tribes to a fight to the death against a more powerful enemy who would not give up easily.

Another thread of the skein leading to the strategic hamlet was a program in the delta province of Vinh Long, where the regime had a somewhat stronger organizational base than elsewhere. Here the term "strategic hamlet" first came into use in the summer of 1961. Similar scattered efforts took place in other provinces. Details varied, but common features were the construction of stockades, the involvement of the hamlet in its own defense, and an organization politically acceptable or actually controlled by the regime to manage the effort. The provincial government's role varied; often it directed the effort but sometimes it played almost no role at all.

Thus, when Thompson and the British Advisory Mission came forward with an analysis and a counterinsurgency plan that adapted the Malayan experience to the situation they found in Vietnam, their proposals coincided superficially at least with the regime's own developing concepts. Thompson's proposals, submitted to President Diem in November 1961, selected one critical area of the country, the Mekong Delta, and advanced a plan for securing and defending the population of the area in strategic hamlets together with a reorganization of the counterinsurgency apparatus to unify and coordinate it.[28]

THOMPSON'S DELTA PLAN

Thompson prefaced his proposal by asserting the proposition that winning the people was the essence of successful counterinsurgency. He assigned the principal security task to the local militia, the Self Defense

Corps, supported by the paramilitary Civil Guard and in the final resort by the army. His proposal actually said little about physical defenses but did prescribe some limited "regrouping" of villagers to make the hamlets more defensible. He emphasized an improved intelligence effort with a pooling of information by all units and a combining of intelligence activity (a constant theme of all British observers in Vietnam based on one of the main strengths of the Malayan effort). Mention was also made of improved information services and of increased social services, particularly medical care and education. Control was a pervading concern of the Thompson plan; he prescribed ID cards, establishment of free-fire zones, curfews, and checkpoints. He clearly believed that security and control were essential to any program for winning the people.

Of equal importance in the British plan was a complete reorganization of the command structure to unify, at least in the delta area, the carefully separated military and civilian security machinery. He proposed that the Self Defense Corps headquarters for the delta take over responsibility for "all anti-terrorist operations; all civilian emergency measures; all security intelligence; information and propaganda; and as a follow-up, social improvements." Notwithstanding the general view that the strategic hamlet program stemmed from British proposals, this key recommendation never obtained even the lip service of the regime. At most, in fact, the Thompson proposals may be seen as a catalyst for certain ideas the regime already had in mind. It is also possible that Diem and Nhu merely appeared to adopt them as a means of creating some acceptability for notions which otherwise might have been rejected.

Be that as it may, the Thompson initiative did forcefully call to the attention of the U.S. the possibility of a new strategy which owed little to the concepts of the CIP and the Phased Geographical Plan. Reaction in the embassy was not unfavorable, although the MAAG at first disapproved vigorously, seeing the Thompson plan as competitive with its own and as diverting attention from what it considered to be the essentials.[29] In Washington, however, and notably in the White House, attitudes were more receptive. General Taylor made a point of talking with Thompson during his Saigon visit and kept in touch with his developing ideas. These, in turn, as the papers circulated in Washington, gathered strong support, particularly among the handful of men who had made counterinsurgency their particular interest. To them it seemed that Thompson's plan provided a specific strategy for counterinsurgency war which until then had been lacking in Vietnam.

Roger Hilsman seems to have been the catalyst in precipitating a definitive reaction supported by Michael Forrestal of the NSC staff. After a visit to Vietnam he returned to Washington with the outlines of a strategy that leaned heavily on the British approach. At Kennedy's request, he prepared a written statement entitled "A Stretagic Concept for Vietnam" which the president approved orally, but not, as far as the record goes, in any formal document. Hilsman was then instructed to brief concerned officials on the strategy, including General Harkins.

The available information on Hilsman's plan indicates that it also took as its starting point the objective of depriving the VC of village support, to be accomplished by making villages defensible, by arming villagers, and by seeking to meet the economic and social needs of the rural population. He also emphasized that on the military side, "the way to fight the guerrilla is to adopt the tactics of the guerrilla," that is, to set aside the doctrine of concentration of force and to eschew heavily armed large-scale sweeps in favor of small units operating frequent patrols, setting ambushes, and the like. He also endorsed Thompson's view that "civil, police, social and military measures had to be combined and carefully co-ordinated in an overall counter-guerrilla program and that there had to be a unified civilian, police and military system of command and control."[30]

The proposed strategy gave much importance to the concept of building security outward from existing areas of strength. This was envisaged in three phases: first, the least-infested areas; second, the heavily infested areas; and finally the areas at the outer periphery. Although he had not incorporated it in the original delta plan, this concept was similar to Thompson's "oil-spot" strategy which he considered a major guideline for an effective program. By this term he meant a process of spreading security gradually outward from already secure areas.

We thus see by early 1962 two of the three principal players—the British and the Americans—developing converging strategies keyed to the notion that counterinsurgency warfare required carefully tailored approaches, diverging significantly from standard procedures, and that the focus of the effort must be the village population. The convergence was accelerated as MACV's original opposition to the concept disappeared when Thompson revised parts of his proposals to which exception had been taken.

The Regime's Goals: Personalism Plus

What of the third principal player, the Vietnamese? On the surface, here too, was harmony. In private and public utterances, the Ngo brothers indicated that their ideas of a new strategy were similar to the notions being discussed by the British and Americans and a number of the activities just described seemed to bear them out. In fact, however, the Vietnamese approached the strategic hamlet program with rather different objectives, time scale, and methods from either the British or the Americans. Earlier, we noted that the Ngo family regime had long been searching for means to establish an effective control of village life, something which had eluded all Vietnamese governments in the past, except the Communists. A well-known symbol of that ambition had been the decision in 1956 to eliminate the elected village councils which had governed the countryside under the French and replace them with appointed officials.[31] There had followed various small-scale resettlement programs, then the abortive agroville program, and finally the campaign for strategic hamlets—which in Vietnamese eyes was clearly in the succession of earlier government programs launched before the insurgency had become a major problem. The obvious difference was the far greater ambition and sweep of the latter, demonstrating a sense of urgency which was no doubt attributable to the VC. Another difference was the support of the United States, support which had been withheld from the agrovilles when the principal justification was that of control.

A second and quite unprecedented objective emerged as the strategic hamlet program moved into high gear. It became a vehicle for the dream of President Diem and his brother to nourish a strong and novel popular culture to replace the traditional, amorphous Confucianism—cum—ancester-worship which formed the underlying values of peasant life. This culture—or ideology—was, however, an exceedingly cloudy body of philosophic and political thought called personalism (Nhan Vi in Vietnamese) related to a French Catholic philosophic school of the same name. In brief terms, Diem and Nhu's personalism saw the highest value of society to be the human personality, which for its proper development required a social setting between Western individualism and the collectivism of the Marxists.[32] The proper development of the human personality was seen as taking place in a communal context in which all elements of the community participated in a "collective advancement" in economic, social, and cultural life. It also required an economic basis of land ownership for each unit within the community. It was vaguely democratic and collectivist in intent, with much emphasis on personal morality, strong family life, and the merging of individual goals into a common, communal purpose.

Despite a copious flow of official explication, the most clear-cut attribute of the creed in terms of governmental policies is that it could be used to clothe in verbal benevolence virtually any line the government chose to follow. More significant than the particular tenets of the personalist creed is that, in seeking to realize its goals, Nhu consciously emulated Communist organizational and control techniques.[33] Also like the Communists, he no doubt pursued worthy ideals but saw the maintenance and strengthening of power as primary, with little scruple as to the means. Thus, in the strategic hamlet program he found a formula which could serve to realize the broad propositions of personalism while at the same time providing increased control over the everyday life of the villages. This was intended to be a benevolent as well as a protective presence; it was also, of course, intended to break the hold of the Communists in the countryside, and in this respect it coincided with American objectives.

Another theme Nhu stressed was peasant "self-sufficiency," an attribute he saw as befitting a people who were to become aware of their dignity and worth in the new setting and thus motivated to contribute the necessary resources by their own labor and readiness to serve. In practical terms, this suggested that the hamlets would get little help but would be expected to build their defenses themselves and man them through the Combat Youth, a "volunteer" militia. According to Nhu, "self-sufficiency" meant, among other things, that the hamlet militia would be loaned their weapons for a period of six months, after which they were to have captured enough arms for their needs and would be obliged to return the captured weapons.[34] Nhu also had no sympathy for the regular military forces' approach to the war, which he saw as dominated by conventional methods. "Since we did not know where the enemy was," he once said, "ten times we launched a military operation, nine times we missed the Viet Cong, and the tenth time we struck right on the head of the population."[35] Hamlet defense, in his scheme, was to be the duty of the village militia supported by the paramilitary forces. Aggressive operations would be the responsibility of "Special Ranger Forces" (sometimes called Special Forces, these were also directly controlled by Nhu), leaving, it would seem, no role for the regular military.[36]

"Self-sufficiency" also meant for Nhu somewhat less emphasis than the British or Americans placed on government action to improve village life. His philosophy here coincided with his suspicion of American intentions in becoming involved in the countryside. His comment to one questioner on the subject was, "You do not understand these villagers. Satisfy one demand and they would return with ten more."[37] As in the case of his military ideas, however, this was an area of activity that Nhu did not control, nor did it appear that President Diem agreed with him.

Nhu's concept did not depend entirely on either the government's cadres or the appeal of personalism. The creation and exploitation of mass organizations in the Communist (and Fascist) pattern was one of Nhu's tools. To achieve the regime's objectives in the hamlets he called upon the Republican Youth, which, after an obscure beginning, had emerged in 1960 as the regime's principal mass organization. With its blue uniforms and its prominence at public demonstrations, it had some resemblance to the Young Pioneers of Communist countries or the Hitler Youth of prewar Germany. But, unlike them, it was not a mass organization of youth who joined voluntarily to realize the principles of personalism or of the Vietnamese Republic. It was a horde of low-ranking civil servants who had joined for fear of reprisals or to advance their careers.[38] Its indoctrination processes were rudimentary and its members were reluctant fodder, doing a job they hardly understood. They were in fact the government apparatus in somewhat altered form. Nevertheless, the RY was entrusted with a limited assortment of weapons and called on to supplement the Self Defense Corps in manning local defenses. It established alarm systems, helped to construct defenses, and one of its major duties was to report on the loyalty and performance of local personalities to the political machine of Counselor Nhu.

As the commitment of the GVN to strategic hamlets became more evident, a further purpose began to emerge: the building up of Nhu himself as a public leader and presumably as a worthy eventual successor to Diem.[39] Until 1961, Nhu had been content to function behind the scenes, in the shadow of the president. By mid-1962 he had stepped into the spotlight at the head of the strategic hamlet effort, traveling the countryside, inspecting, exhorting, and attempting to inspire the government's rural apparatus. Government publications openly described Nhu as "the architect and prime mover" of the program. Duncanson also states, with some plausibility, that Nhu looked upon strategic hamlets and his own role in the effort as a means of bypassing the normal ministries and taking direct control of the rural apparatus.[41] Certain it was that his public position as head of the program (formally announced in March 1962) brought him considerable new powers as well as great visibility. "I was forced," he told one American official, "to take charge of many new areas of government myself."[42]

NGO DINH CAN'S "FORCE POPULAIRE"

An exception of more than minor interest to this public emergence of Ngo Dinh Nhu was the curious situation in the provinces of Central Vietnam, where his power never spread, being blocked by his younger brother, Ngo Dinh Can. Without official position and living reclusively at the family home in Hue, Can nevertheless had established effective control of the government's apparatus in the region. To do this, he used a combination of guile and brutality tempered by a far better understanding of popular attitudes and of the everyday realities of peasant life than either of his older brothers possessed. Can controlled his own intelligence service and, it was rumored, gave short shrift to the agents of Nhu's various intelligence networks. He dominated the local branches of the various Diemist political organizations and devised his own unique approach to securing the countryside against the VC—an approach which he preferred to the strategic hamlet program. This was the *Force*

Populaire, in the opinion of some observers the most successful of the many Vietnamese "cadre" programs that sprang up over the years in response to the VC challenge.

A "cadre organization" in the usage common in Vietnam is a government unit specifically assigned to perform certain tasks in direct contact with the population. It is in theory formed of highly trained and motivated men, with a special dedication to the cause. The form was an effort to imitate and capitalize on Communist organizational techniques, for the "cadre" organization of the Communist party appeared to many to underlie the amazing success of the movement in maintaining its hold on its peasant supporters. The Diem regime had ventured into the cadre field as early as 1955, forming the General Directorate of Civic Action to field teams of trained volunteers from the civil service. Clad in black pajamas, Civic Action cadres were sent to work in the villages, attempting to improve the lot of the peasants and, in the process, to establish a special rapport between governors and governed. After a while, the resistance of the regular civil service to an organization which robbed it of its personnel and cut across normal jurisdictions forced a cutback in the program. Then, as the insurgency challenge became more serious, the Directorate of Civic Action was refurbished and strengthened and assigned duties in the formation of strategic hamlets.

To return to Ngo Dinh Can, his *Force Populaire* was not a formal arm of the government and thus had no need to meet the artificial standards of the civil service or follow its rigid procedures. All members were volunteers and came from peasant backgrounds. They were armed for defense only, and once in their assigned villages they lived with the peasants and helped them with their tasks, paying for their board.[43] The effort was low-key and highly pragmatic; it was not burdened with high-flown rhetoric or noisy slogans. As the *Force Populaire* expanded from its original small nucleus, it attracted the favorable attention of Diem and even of Nhu, and its expansion into the delta was approved. On the other hand, Can's resistance to strategic hamlets was not tolerated and he was forced to get behind the program in Central Vietnam. The question of whether his concepts would have had more success than his brother's is a moot one, but the *Force Populaire* needed a Can or someone like him to function effectively. It probably would have failed in the areas controlled by Nhu, for the latter's deviousness and fundamental contempt for the peasants would have caused it to lose its special touch and to wither.

AN ABORTIVE START: "OPERATION SUNRISE"

From these varied sources, then, the effort sprang that was to preoccupy both the U.S. and Vietnamese governments throughout 1962 and until the final collapse of the regime in November 1963. The first large public program combining inputs of the two governments in this new enterprise was an ill-conceived and ill-fated "spectacular" in Binh Duong province which stamped the program in the U.S. press and public mind as a brutal form of forced resettlement. This was "Operation Sunrise," focusing on a cluster of villages in Binh Duong province, a heavily infested area that was also of strategic value, a crossroads of VC lines of communication northeast of Saigon. The area was picked by the Vietnamese and somewhat reluctantly accepted by the Americans to provide a test of the new concepts in one limited area and because they wished to encourage a Vietnamese initiative.[44] The Vietnamese on their side hoped to induce a highly visible U.S. involvement where, in their view, the circumstances were favorable. Neither appeared to be concerned that a start in a largely VC-controlled location would violate some fundamental principles of the new strategy and encounter problems it was not designed to solve.

The five hamlets moved and rebuilt in Operation Sunrise turned out to have few able-bodied male inhabitants; they were all with the VC. The people were sullen and uncooperative, and most had to be moved forcibly while their homes and belongings were deliberately burned. It was highly inauspicious and not, in fact, typical of the program. But first impressions are lasting ones. The U.S. press found the spectacle repellant and said so; it questioned whether a movement to "win the people" could succeed on such a foundation.

In fact, however, operations like Sunrise were but a minor feature of the program. They were set-piece combined operations, carefully prepared and preceded by sweeps; supplies were prepositioned and support efforts mobilized ahead of time. They represented the U.S. military's style and contribution. They did not, however, suit the style or goals of the GVN, which had little patience or capability for careful national planning. Well before Operation Sunrise was conceived, the GVN, speaking through Ngo Dinh Nhu, announced that it intended to include the entire population within the strategic hamlet program. This announcement was made on January 3, 1962, the occasion being the sixty-first birthday of Ngo Dinh Diem.[45] There followed a series of announcements and decisions which formally established the government's organization and commitments to carry out this plan. An Inter-Ministerial Committee was formed with a charter calling for it to establish plans, set standards and a timetable, and to check compliance.[46] The government announced it had accepted the delta plan first proposed by the British Advisory Mission. Training courses for civil servants were set up, and as early as February 1962 some fifteen hundred students had passed through them.

This flurry of activity at the national level was itself well behind the march of events, and one has the impression that orderly process was something of an afterthought. In April, before any national plan emerged or national standards had been promulgated, the GVN reported to the U.S. that thirteen hundred hamlets had been completed.[47] Observers were to learn that such statistics had little meaning, but coming at this time the claim was interesting in that it represented nearly a tenth of the total number of hamlets in the country, and when it was made no one could say precisely what a "completed hamlet" was.

Finally, in August 1962, a national plan emerged which divided all of South Vietnam into four areas, assigning first priority to a portion of the country comprising the delta and the provinces around Saigon. The goal of the program was set at 11,316 hamlets, and by summer's end 1962 it was claimed that no fewer than 3,225 of these had been constructed.[48] In the meantime, the training course had been extended and a six-point set of criteria established the standards the hamlets were to meet. According to these criteria, a "completed hamlet" had cleared the VC from the area, indoctrinated and organized the population, established a work and a disaster plan which assigned duties to all inhabitants, completed defenses, organized special guerrilla cells, and held an election of an advisory council.[49]

Everywhere in the countryside stockades and ditches appeared, some merely a row of sharpened bamboo stakes, others far more elaborate. Counselor Nhu traveled widely, seeking to publicize and to energize the campaign, stressing over and over the theme of "self-sufficiency," the necessity for Vietnam and Vietnamese to rely largely on their own efforts and resources. "Self-sufficiency" for Vietnam at this stage was of course entirely out of reach. To progress, the program required large amounts of such mundane items as barbed wire, metal pickets, cement, corrugated roofing, and funds for transport, for cadre pay, and for reimbursement to those who had been forced to give up their homes. Nhu preferred to think it possible for the Vietnamese peasant to make do with available resources and his own labor. The Americans, however, persisted with their concept of a program in which government response to village needs was a critical necessity. AID programs dealing with village problems and rural life were increased in size. More important, in view of the lead time for such programs, which could stretch to three years, steps were taken to speed up the process by making local currency available for local procurement. A commitment of $10 million was initially approved and President Diem concurred in September 1962 in a special procedure for focusing these resources directly into the program. The procedure involved "joint sign-off" by province representatives of the U.S. and GVN, after which previously budgeted funds became immediately available for support of the program. The device was a substantial step toward speeding up a system which had been subject to interminable bureaucratic delays within both governments.

CHANGES ON THE AMERICAN SIDE

Other changes on the civilian side of the American organization in Vietnam became necessary to equip it for the challenge of a crash program moving forward rapidly in over forty provinces. Until then the AID organization in Vietnam (called the United States Operations Mission—USOM) had had no permanent representatives in the provinces and conceived its mission to be that of working with Saigon ministries. In effect, the AID management reflected the lofty attitudes toward the provinces of the Vietnamese elite with whom it worked.[50] But now a process set in which has been characteristic of every counterinsurgency program: the decentralization of operations and the movement of personnel to the field to work on the immediate scene—the front line—of the effort. An assistant director for rural affairs was appointed and province representatives were recruited and eventually assigned to each province. This entailed a major shift in focus for the USOM in Saigon, a change which had its advocates and opponents but which was inevitable in the circumstances.

As these men moved out into their areas of duty, a simple U.S.-Vietnamese committee structure was put in place, a Province Rehabilitation Committee, chaired by the province chief and including a U.S. military representative who at this time came to be called the "sector adviser." The instrument they used as a basis for their planning and for feeding U.S. resources rapidly into the program was the Province Rehabilitation Agreement which could go into immediate effect with the signatures of the province chief and the USOM representative.

The expansion of the U.S. government into the provinces was not of course limited to USOM. As noted, a quantum jump took place in the number of military advisers, who were now assigned to province headquarters (sector) and to combat units down to battalion. The other U.S. agencies did not lag behind. Soon CIA and USIA also had representatives in most provinces, while their headquarters in Saigon also grew rapidly. In fact, the multifaceted military and civilian effort prescribed by the doctrines became a reality in a rather short time.

What failed to materialize throughout this period was the fully unified and centralized management also called for by the same doctrines. This lack of unity and of effective central direction characterized both the American and Vietnamese organizations. On the American side, for a brief moment early in the administration, the White House had considered a radical departure for the organization of its Vietnamese programs. It had been proposed in early 1961 by the same Brigadier General Edward Lansdale whose report had impressed the president with the seriousness of the Vietnamese problem in his first days in office. Lansdale briefly became an influential figure in the interagency consideration of solutions and was able to insert into an early study the suggestion for a centralized type of management both in Washington and Saigon.[51] He himself was proposed as head of the Saigon apparatus with authority challenging that of the ambassador.

As pointed out by the anonymous author of the relevant section of the *Pentagon Papers,* this formula "charged directly against the mainstream of current thought as it related to the question of integrating operations abroad. The 'Country Team' concept of the late 1950s . . . assigned clear primacy to the Ambassador. . . . Indeed, it was during the same month (May 1961) that President Kennedy sent his oft-quoted letter to each American Ambassador, reminding him of his co-ordinating duties even while reaffirming that these did not extent [sic] to supervising operational military forces."[52] The proposal for a commander to direct the American side of the counterinsurgency therefore quietly expired in favor of the doctrine, strongly endorsed by Kennedy, that the ambassador, as the president's representative, was fully in charge of U.S. operations in his mission.

The problem with that principle, never fully acknowledged by its advocates, is that each agency overseas is also responsible to its own headquarters in Washington and has a statutory obligation, as well as a practical necessity, to heed the expressed will of Congress. The relationship between an ambassador and the heads of the agencies on his "Country Team" will therefore reflect the character and style of the ambassador, who is free to interpret his powers to "coordinate" in accordance with whether he wishes to command—and risk discontent and opposition possibly leading to serious public controversy—or to bargain, conciliate, and negotiate in normal bureaucratic fashion. Kennedy made it clear that he wished his ambassadors to be commanders, and he attempted to staff his embassies with men of the requisite qualities but did not always succeed. In the case of Vietnam an added complication was the existence of an overseas command, MACV, which was exempted from ambassadorial control, though not from the necessity to "coordinate."

The new ambassador to Vietnam, Frederick E. Nolting, appreciated the need for full control of his mission but also saw it as a goal to be accomplished by the traditional methods which concede the participating agencies full authority over their operations within agreed programs and policies—in effect, management by committee. He appointed such a committee under his deputy chief of mission, William C. Trueheart. It negotiated agreed positions, maintained contact with Ngo Dinh Nhu's Strategic Hamlet Committee, and attempted to resolve disagreements within the American group. Nolting also tried to gain equivalent authority over the military but, according to Hilsman, was rebuffed by both his own chief, Secretary Rusk, and by the secretary of defense.[53] Hilsman adds, "He and Harkins did manage to maintain excellent personal relations, but the cost was a mutual forbearance that probably foredoomed the two halves of the American effort to proceed independently of each other."

Even if Nolting had obtained the added authority there is some doubt whether he could have wielded it effectively. True command is a rather different matter than "coordination" by committee. To manage a large and complex operation the commander must have an adequate permanent staff and control of personnel and resources that belong, typically, to a variety of established agencies. Indeed, the end result is the creation of a new ad hoc agency in the field with rather wrenching effect on traditional lines of authority and bureaucratic convention. Only exceptional circumstances will permit so startling a deviation from accepted norms. Most important is the recognition of the need at the highest levels, especially by the ambassador, who must, in turn, have the knowledge that the president either actively supports him or at least does not object.

Such circumstances did not yet exist in Vietnam, nor did they become apparent there for four more years. Yet, on the civilian side, most testimony suggests that at this early stage lack of effective centralized management was not yet a crippling problem. A reasonable speculation based on some firsthand experience suggests that cooperation among the representatives of different agencies working on different parts of the same program varies directly with their distance from field headquarters and from Washington. The greater the distance, the greater the cooperation. Americans (and this includes military men assigned to work side by side with civilians) thrown together in a crisis situation in a remote Vietnamese province center will usually cooperate closely, sharing resources and tasks in a way that would be unlikely in a formal setting. Such was predominantly the pattern in this phase of counterinsurgency in Vietnam.[54]

THE ABSENCE OF COMMON APPROACH AND DIRECTION

More serious at this time—and for future years as well—was the lack of common approach and direction between American civilian and military *organizations* in Vietnam. The civilian side was committed to a concept of counterinsurgency which focused on the population as the heart of the matter. Necessarily, this meant that priority would go to the shaping of favorable attitudes to be accomplished first by providing security, followed up by improved and responsive government services, until finally the people were committed and fully engaged in their own defense. The military, despite concessions—no doubt sincere—to the importance of winning the population, was quite unshakably wedded to the idea that priority must go to destroying the enemy's armed force, and doing it by the familiar means of concentrating manpower and firepower at the right time and place.

Translating these doctrinal differences into the realities of the day, they meant that instead of one program to defeat the insurgency there were in fact two: strategic hamlets and all that went with them on the one hand, and the military effort to corner and destroy the VC main forces on the other. Except in such set-piece operations as Sunrise, which were preceded by military sweeps, seldom was there any real coordination and common planning between the two efforts. Nevertheless, the military persisted, devising and obtaining GVN approval in November 1962 to a National Campaign Plan which called for the intensification of aggressive military operations in all corps areas.[55]

Among the effects of this dichotomy was the gradual expansion of firepower in ways hardly suited to the nature of the war being fought. Available air power was increasing rapidly. Theoretically under careful control, it actually began to be used against any suspicious target and sometimes against none. Bombing and artillery barrages were a standard preliminary to large-scale operations and inevitably alerted the enemy, who was usually able to slip away in ample time. Pressures on the president to allow the use of napalm and of defoliants became so strong that he yielded and they became a common feature of the war.[56] Inevitably, the bombing and the increased use of artillery involved destruction of property and death and injury of the very civilian population whose loyalty was being sought as the key to victory.

Large-scale sweeps and set-piece military operations were the standard employment for regular forces. These plans were concurred in and supported by MACV, which objected not to the concept but to the consistently poor implementation, to the lack of ARVN aggressiveness and follow-through. To the dismay of U.S. advisers, ARVN was not often prompt in its response to hamlets or paramilitary units when they came under attack and called for help. Nor was the advisory apparatus able very often to influence its clients in this critical aspect of the program.

Turning again to Hilsman, a report he made to the president after another visit to Vietnam in late 1962 described some of the problems noted above and commented, "The American military mission must share some of the blame for the excessive emphasis on large-scale operations and air interdiction which have had the bad political and useless military effect described in our report." Then, at a later point, he summed up: "The real trouble, however, is that the rather large U.S. effort . . . is managed by a multitude of independent U.S. agencies and people with little or no overall direction. No one man is in charge. What co-ordination there is results from the kind of treaty arrangements worked out in the country team meetings. . . . What is needed ideally is to give authority to a single strong executive."[57]

Among the unhappy results of the lack of unified direction on the American side was the loss of capability to correct the disarray on the Vietnamese side, where the burdens were heavier and the negative effects more serious. Although Ngo Dinh Nhu had achieved substantial control of the governmental apparatus in the countryside, he had hardly any ability to influence the military command. ARVN therefore had little resistance from its civilian superiors to overcome in following the inclinations bred into it by its years of U.S. training in conventional strategy and tactics. Indeed, the influence of the Presidential Palace on Military affairs was all in the direction of caution to avoid the political costs of taking casualties or losing essentially meaningless military outposts. But Nhu apparently believed that the strategic hamlet program was adequate to defeat the insurgency with little effective support from the regular military forces. With fanatical intensity he drove for completion of the program in the shortest possible time, exerting pressure everywhere, without regard to priority and with no real plan.

By means of statistics the effort was made to project a picture of surging success. Official sources claimed over three thousand completed hamlets in October 1961, rising to 5,900 in April 1963, and to 7,200 in July 1963. The population protected by these means rose from a claimed 4,322,000 in October 1962 to 8,737,000 in the following year.[58] In April 1963, *Vietnam Press,* the government news agency, boasted that "this movement has upset all the subversive maneuvers of the enemies of the nation, and it has, in addition, strongly shaken the foundations of their very organizations."[59]

Before long, events exposed the emptiness of such claims, but in the second half of 1962 and in early 1963 sober and skeptical observers perceived distinct improvement in the situation. The incidence of VC attacks and defections took a favorable turn, and the propaganda of the enemy began to focus shrilly on the program, suggesting that the VC found it to be an increasing problem. Amid many episodes that suggested halfheartedness, inefficiency, and failure on the government side, there were also frequent examples of effective hamlets, well defended by their inhabitants against heavy attack. Such observers as Duncanson and Osborne, not inclined to overlook the failings of the Ngo regime, accept the evidence that in 1962 the overall situation improved enough to give hope that the right formula had now been found.[60]

On the military side, the influx of American weapons, and particularly the deployment of hundreds of helicopters, added capabilities to the ARVN which had an obvious impact on the enemy. One official observer,

Michael V. Forrestal of the NSC staff, wrote a detached survey of the situation at the end of 1962 in which he said, "The Viet Cong, in sum, are being hurt—they have somewhat less freedom of movement than they had a year ago, they apparently suffer acutely from lack of medicines, and in some very isolated areas they seem to have trouble getting food."[61] This same report also stated that serious difficulties and problems remained and was reserved about the total picture. Nevertheless, at the end of 1962 the net of the various indicators was considered favorable, and U.S. spokesmen made frequent public assertions of an improved outlook, including one by the president himself in his State of the Union message of January 1963. Instructions were given to the JCS by Secretary McNamara to develop detailed plans for the withdrawal of the American military presence from Vietnam.[62]

Very soon, however, the optimism—although officially unchanged—began to be challenged as evidence accumulated that progress had halted or reversed and that in numerous cases it had been illusory to begin with. Public controversy focused particularly on the performance of ARVN, notably after the battle of AP Bac on January 3, 1963, when heavily armed Vietnamese units cornered a large VC force and then, through failure to move in aggressively, allowed it to escape. The American press in Vietnam became progressively more skeptical and began a drumfire of criticism directed at all aspects of the Ngo regime. The strategic hamlet program, of course, did not escape. Despite public claims of confidence in continued progress, divisions sprang up within the mission, and many civilians who were close to the program began to express private uneasiness and even dismay. While the military maintained an optimism which persuaded the visiting secretary of defense, accompanied by General Taylor, to announce in October that one thousand advisers would be home by Christmas, the head of USOM's Rural Affairs Division made a personal report to President Kennedy in September stating that the delta was "falling under Viet-Cong control in areas where pacification was supposedly complete."[63]

Sir Robert Thompson reported to President Diem that the program had now gone too fast. "I told him that . . . we were in a situation where the available provincial forces were overextended, the Viet-Cong had been presented with a number of soft and vulnerable targets and the government had been unable to secure any base areas."[64] Within the American mission a special committee was appointed to review the progress and problems of the strategic hamlet program. In October it concluded that the time had arrived for a reevaluation.[65]

These developments took place at a time when public and official attention had shifted to the political status of the regime, which had rapidly deteriorated through the summer and fall of 1963 and collapsed in the coup that abruptly ended the power and the lives of the Ngo brothers.

The entire edifice they had constructed in their nine years in office disintegrated overnight, and the strategic hamlet program was no exception. Despite lip service to its goals, the successor regime in fact turned its back on the program, most of it disappearing from a combination of neglect and VC action. In the provinces, the American apparatus of civilian and military advisers remained in place, administering the assistance which continued to flow through the pipelines. But for some time no concerted nationwide program existed, merely a rural aid effort administered separately in each province.

AN APPRAISAL

Among Americans and Vietnamese alike, the strategic hamlet program suffered some of the same obloquy directed at all the works of the Ngo regime. Nevertheless, with the perspective of fourteen years, the picture of the program emerges as more complex than many of the critics have acknowledged then or since. About one aspect, however, there is general agreement: the program moved much too quickly under the whip of Ngo Dinh Nhu, leading to gross failures of implementation. Among the results were falsified statistics and claims that the criteria for a completed hamlet had been met when, in fact, all that had been done was to throw up a fence or dig a moat. "Basically," writes Sir Robert Thompson, "the Vietnamese seemed unable to understand that the establishment of strategic hamlets would accomplish nothing unless the other necessary measures were taken to achieve their three objectives of protection, of uniting and involving the people, and of development. . . . The Vietnamese tended to confuse the means with the end. . . . In under two years in Vietnam 8,000 strategic hamlets were created. . . . No attention was paid to their purpose; their creation became the purpose in itself."[66]

What happened in hamlet after hamlet was that the population was hastily organized to construct defenses and man them, and promises of reimbursement were made for support of all the varied types required, but all too often these promises went unfulfilled, sometimes because of outright embezzlement, more often for reasons of disorganization. The pressure for results was interpreted by province chiefs as justifying a show of compliance of which the evidence was the construction of defenses far beyond their capacity to support the effort after the fences were built. To be carried out as planned, the program made heavy demands on the government apparatus for logistic support, supervisory officials, cadres to work directly with the peasants in explaining and guiding the effort, and then, in the follow-up stages of development, for engineers, teachers, medical teams, agricultural specialists, and other technicians. Ideally, the various parts of this complex machine would be meshed together to operate with considerable precision, for all agreed that the elusive ingredient of popular loyalty depended on commitments being fulfilled promptly.

The actuality was the reverse of this ideal. Far too often peasants contributed their labor and paid for necessary materials out of their pockets on the promise of reimbursement which never came. Ditches were dug by the mile, and stakes implanted, but the barbed wire failed to arrive. Young men and women agreed to serve as Combat Youth to defend their villages, but the promised arms came late or were too few or never arrived at all. In many cases the preparations for establishing a hamlet were so slapdash that the secret VC cell organization remained intact within the defenses, able to plot and assist surprise attacks at will.

Some improvement was noted by early 1963 in the supply of equipment, for by then the American pipeline began to deliver the materials necessary; the deployment of advisers into the provinces and the arrival of trained cadres also brought some much-needed strength to the process. But the frantic pace of the program meant that the U.S. and Vietnamese administrative and support structure, despite these improvements, could not keep up with the need. In many of the hamlets the peasants never seriously attempted to resist the VC; they gave them what they wanted and kept the matter quiet. Where they resisted, attacks were launched, aided from within, and the defenses were destroyed with severe casualties among the hapless militia.

Compounding these failures of program administration was the even more critical lack of an overall, well-integrated plan following the principle of building outward gradually from areas of strength. Instead, groups of hamlets were located wherever a province chief or a division commander felt, for whatever reason, it might be desirable to put them. Province chiefs were, in effect, free to fight their own separate wars, and military commanders were largely free to support them or not, as they wished. As a result, large gaps were left behind areas of hamlet development, with a serious danger from the VC embedded in the heart of the territory supposedly secured. In other cases, clusters of hamlets sprang up completely surrounded by hostile areas, requiring heavy military support for their continued existence. This, for instance, was the case of the villages in Operation Sunrise, which remained under government control only so long as the ARVN continued to stand guard in the immediate area.

Such gross inadequacies in implementation created ambiguity in the assessment of the program and particularly of the doctrine on which it was based. Critics who were convinced that the plan was unsound could point to its collapse as confirmation. Those who supported the basic concept were able to say that their ideas were never properly implemented and remained valid. There was in fact something to be said on both sides. As an abstract prescription to counter people's war, the American doctrine had merit. The problem was that its realization in the Vietnam of the early sixties in the form of the strategic hamlet program posed difficulties that were never acknowledged or seriously attacked.

First, some criticisms which are easily answered. Thus, opponents have pointed out that a very large number of South Vietnamese live in the delta in hamlets that literally string out for miles along the canal. For such communities, the building of defenses was impractical unless most inhabitants moved to a central point, in which case they were far removed from their fields and faced the problem of finding or making enough ground above the flood level to build homes, plant orchards, and the like. The program was, in fact, too rigidly committed to the building of defenses in every hamlet. Defenses were useful, but their value depended on local conditions; a flexibility in designing them to account for local problems could have resolved that difficulty.

Again, other critics point to Ngo Dinh Nhu's slighting of the development aspects of the program and maintain that his true objective was nothing more than fastening the shackles of the government on the relatively free peasants of the Vietnamese countryside. In fact, Nhu was quite inconsistent on this subject; he did sometimes emphasize government responsiveness as an important ingredient of his plan while at other times he slighted it. More important is the fact that President Diem and the American mission were both committed to improving the quality of life in the hamlets, as witnessed by the "joint sign-off" approach and the buildup of numerous rural programs devoted to health, education, improved water supply, communications, fertilizer, improved strains of animals, and the like. Whatever Nhu's preference, in reality considerable progress was achieved in the program phase of the effort, with the promise of much more if time had permitted.

More difficult to answer is the question of whether the essential principles of building outward from strength and of carefully meshed phases eventually covering the whole country was not far beyond the capability of the civil and military apparatus of the GVN to carry out even under a delayed timetable. Of all the problems facing South Vietnam in those years, the "lack of cadres," of trained and experienced manpower, was the one least susceptible of quick solutions. In 1960 the entire civil service had only three thousand high-school graduates,[67] and most of its senior levels were French-oriented holdovers from the colonial regime with no interest in the countryside or understanding of the peasants. This bureaucracy was overstaffed, rigid, and obsessed with procedural routine. Although it was gradually changing, the process had only begun. The question is not whether it could eventually have improved sufficiently but whether it could have done so in time to overcome the head start of the VC. In the final analysis that is of course an unanswerable question. Still, a strong doubt must remain that the highly demanding task of implementing such an intricate program was within the halting grasp of the military and civilian services of South Vietnam in the early sixties, at least in the time available and under the leadership of the Ngo family. Indeed, the mandarin proclivities of Diem and the philosophic aberrations of Nhu—not to mention his clumsy deviousness—made matters so much worse that a final question remains as to whether, no matter what its human and material resources may have become in time, the Ngo family leadership could have achieved anything constructive against the enormously more skilled and sophisticated challenge of Ho Chi Minh, Vo Nguyen Giap, and Le Duan.

For these reasons—and enjoying the considerable benefit of hindsight—it would seem inescapable that the strategic hamlet program was foredoomed. Nevertheless, despite the shambles of their hopes, there remained among the interested Americans a conviction that they had been on the right track. Their ideas had been reshaped on the anvil of experience; some lasting conclusions emerged. Among them was the importance, in crises of this nature, of focusing personnel and resources directly into the provinces. The experience had also reinforced the opinion that central direction was an essential ingredient. Most important, enough had been accomplished to validate the conviction that it was possible to affect the motivations of remote villages by bringing them responsive and effective government and providing them with the means and support to defend their own homes and property. This had happened in a sufficient number of cases to persuade interested persons in AID, CIA, USIA, and the State Department that their initial and more or less instinctive preference for an approach centering on meeting village needs was sound.

Later, this came to be described as the "hearts and mind" approach from the recurring use of the phrase "winning the hearts and minds of the people" to describe the goal. Eventually the phrase came to be used somewhat scornfully, and it is not in any case a particularly accurate label. Counterinsurgency doctrine continued to insist on an effective combination of measures of which security was a sine qua non, and that, in turn, was the product of coordinated intelligence and of local defense linked by good communications to paramilitary and military formations. Responsive government then could perform its necessary function of improving conditions of village life in ways that answered felt needs. From this combination would come the commitment of the villagers to the cause of the government, for it would then be their own cause. To make all of this possible on a countrywide scale, the essential ingredient was a marked improvement in the quality and effectiveness of government services—police, administrative, and technical. Without such improvement any success would be the accidental result of a few exceptional personalities working in a few limited areas.

Such were the outlines of the viewpoint which emerged from this first major experience of the U.S. in counterinsurgency. Unfortunately, no authoritative public statement of this view is available, although the unofficial writings of such thoughtful participants as William Nighswonger and George K. Tanham expound it effectively. Most revealing is the absence of any authoritative military critique of the experience. Under extremely heavy criticism from the press, the military stuck to their stance that their approach in Vietnam had been succeeding until the political collapse of the regime. This meant in effect that the dichotomy between the civilian approach focusing on the village population and the military approach focusing upon the concentration of firepower against enemy units would be perpetuated.

As between the two approaches, the first would clearly seem to reflect an appreciation of the nature of people's war. Nevertheless, one seeks in vain in the work of the most responsible and thoughtful advocates of counterinsurgency for discussion of the problem we have already noted as a most difficult one, and also one which the experience with strategic hamlets illustrated with considerable clarity. Throughout the two years during which the U.S. wrestled with the Diem regime to induce an effective program against the VC, a key issue had been reform. The military insisted upon the urgency of reforming the command structure, all participants insisted on a reformed intelligence structure, the civilians insisted upon the importance of reformed administrative practices, a broadened political base, an attack on corruption, and the serious pursuit of land reform. All of these demands had purposes related to counterinsurgency. In none of these areas was any significant progress made, and yet the U.S. continued to press forward with programs whose success depended upon their implementation. Finally, of course, the Buddhist crisis and Nhu's attack on the pagodas made the situation seem hopeless and the regime was allowed to collapse, if not actively pushed.

Was it simply stubbornness and wrongheadedness that caused Ngo Dinh Diem—who had fought off at least four military coup attempts in nine years—to resist turning all military assets over to the military command and to abstain from sharing power with quarrelsome splinter-group leaders to whom politics was merely a form of conspiracy? Or did he have some reason to fear that the proposed changes would shake his insecure hold on the government? In November 1961, J. Kenneth Galbraith, asked by the president to visit Saigon and comment on the situation, sent a message in which he said, among many other things: "In my completely considered view . . . Diem will not reform either administratively or politically in any effective way. That is because he cannot. It is politically naive to expect it. He senses that he cannot let power go because he will be thrown out."[68] After more than a decade, these words have a distinctly prescient ring, despite the harsh light they focused on the leader of a highly unstable, tragically divided, and politically underdeveloped country. Diem's dilemma was not entirely of his own making, and experience would show that it was one that seemed built into the fabric of many countries which came under Communist insurgent threat.

The U.S. was asking the GVN to reform itself in a situation of crisis, and the invitation looked something like a demand to commit political suicide. Yet, without such fundamental reforms the counterinsurgency effort of necessity was forced to deal in terms of separate programs, for the weakness of the central authority meant there was no other means of affecting the situation favorably. The result was an effort that was less than the sum of its parts, a scattering of resources in the countryside where much devoted and expensive activity achieved no general effect. There were many dilemmas confronting the protagonists of counterinsurgency. The Vietnam experience suggested that at the very outset of such an effort it might be wise to deal with the one we might call the dilemma of "self-reform in crisis," for it could negate the effort or else, as happened in Vietnam, bring about a painful and grievously burdensome attempt to substitute American will and resources for Vietnamese, to make up for the deficiencies of the threatened government and its inability to reform itself to deal with them.

At the same time, of course, no two situations are exactly alike. On the other side of the Annamite range from Vietnam another country was undergoing an ordeal related and in some ways similar to that in Vietnam—and in other ways very different. One of the important differences between counterinsurgency in Laos and the experience we have just described in Vietnam was the quite novel approach and involvement of the United States. We turn then to this unprecedented scene where, however, the underlying realities and dilemmas will not be entirely unfamiliar.

5

People's Counterinsurgency

★ ★ ★

The Indochinese country of Laos was the unlikely arena for an unprecedented ramification of counterinsurgency activity with effects unlike those experienced anywhere else. We are in fact stretching the concept to consider the Lao example as being in the same category as the experiences in Vietnam, the Philippines, and Malaya. It was closer in pattern to classic guerrilla war against a foreign occupier such as occurred throughout Axis-occupied Europe and Asia in World War II. The "occupier" in this case was the Lao Communist movement formally known as the *Neo Lao Hax Sat* (Lao Peoples' Front) but generally called by its earlier name of Pathet Lao (Lao State). It was foreign in the eyes of a significant portion of the indigenous population not only because it was Lao and they were tribal minorities but because it was associated with—and in fact was popularly perceived as indistinguishable from—the North Vietnamese.[1] Besides seeing it as foreign, a large portion of the population identified the presence of the Pathet Lao and the Democratic Republic of Vietnam as oppressive. Despite the propaganda addressed to them which told them they had been liberated, despite increased opportunities for education and for minorities to rise to positions of authority, the tribesmen chafed under the close observation kept on them by Communist cadres, under the taxation, and particularly under the heavy demands for corvée labor to build roads and serve as porters for the Communist troops.

Those at least were the negative motivations for the guerrilla resistance of the Meo and some other hill tribes of north central and northeast Laos to the PL/DRV. There were, as we shall see, important positive motivations as well, which related the movement to counterinsurgency strategies described earlier, that is, an engagement of people in defend-

128

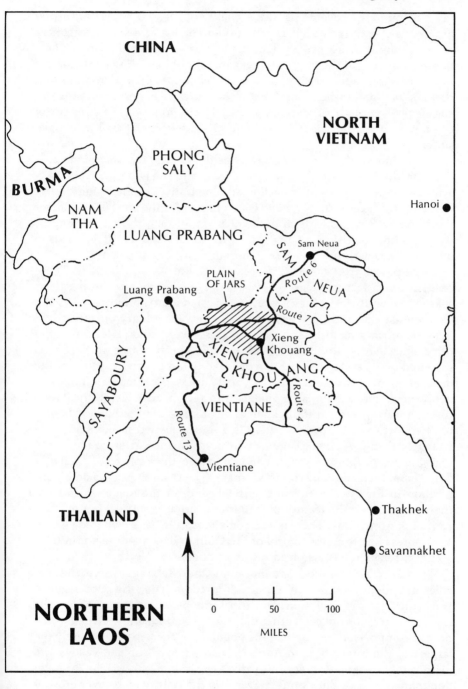

CHINA

PHONG
SALY

NORTH
VIETNAM

BURMA

NAM
THA

LUANG PRABANG

Hanoi ●

SAM

Sam Neua

PLAIN
OF JARS

NEUA

Luang Prabang ●

Route 6

Route 7

Xieng
Khouang

XIENG

KHOU

ANG

SAYABOURY

Route 4

VIENTIANE

Route 13

THAILAND   N

Vientiane ●

Thakhek ●

Savannakhet ●

NORTHERN
LAOS

0   50   100

MILES

ing newfound improvements in the quality of life and hopes for further progress along the same lines. As time went on—and we are talking here of a movement which persisted for fifteen years—the gradual intensification of combat and the tragic and repeated flight of entire populations of large areas reduced or eliminated many elements of the program that partook of "nation-building." Yet they were of major importance in earlier phases of the undertaking and explain some of the strength of commitment of the tribal population in spite of great and prolonged suffering.

The scene of this lengthy drama was the heavily forested mountains between the Lao–North Vietnamese border and the two principal northern Lao cities of Vientiane, the administrative capital, and Luang Prabang, the seat of the king and court. Except for the level flood plain of the Mekong River, on which both cities are located, the area is rugged, with mountains rising as high as nine thousand feet. It is virtually undeveloped, with but a few French-built roads bearing names suggesting well-paved arteries—e.g., Route 13, Route 7, and Route 6. These roads were in fact mere gravel tracks, not always passable in the rainy season. Nevertheless, they were of critical military importance to the Communist side and have been major targets of military operations.

A significant feature of the area is a grassy, upland plateau, roughly forty miles across, the Plain of Jars, so-called for the large, ancient urns scattered on its surface, which are believed to have been used to bury the dead of some early community. The Plain is a center of ethnic Lao population, dotted with large villages and several airfields. Route 7 runs through it in an east-west direction and connects the Vietnamese border to the north-south road (Route 13) running between Vientiane and Luang Prabang. At the village of Ban Ban, on the eastern edge of the Plain, it meets Route 6 which winds north to the Pathet Lao capital of Sam Neua, then continues on to Vietnam. The Plain thus has a dominant position in the area, both for its airfields and for the roads which meet there. It is a terrain feature of importance to anyone seeking military control of north Laos. There is also some reason to believe that the North Vietnamese see friendly control of the Plain to be a major factor in their security, for its roads also lead to the back door of North Vietnam.

If one excepts the low ground along the Mekong, where all large cities are found and where ethnic Lao predominate, the population of Laos consists mostly of numerous tribal groups, quite different from the lowland Lao and from each other in language and customs. Overall, such groups comprise more than half the population, the Lao being merely the largest of the minorities. In northern Laos, narrow upland valleys and district towns—areas where "wet rice" cultivation is possible—are still dominated by Lao. But as one moves into the hills, which cover most of the landscape, the Lao are left behind along with wet rice. Between fifteen hundred and three thousand feet above sea level the predominant group is called Lao Theung, also known as Kha (a Lao word meaning slave) and who actually divide into numerous distinct tribes. Climbing higher, from three thousand to five thousand feet, we find the Meo (or Miao),[2] of whom a large number, but by no means all, became involved in the guerrilla war against the PL/DRV. This layered pattern predominates in the critical areas between the two Lao capitals and Vietnam. Elsewhere in the north there are many other groups beside the Lao Theung at the intermediate levels, but they played little role in the events we will be discussing. At the higher levels, in addition to the Meo, only one other tribe thrives, the Yao or Man, a group similar to the Meo in many ways but much fewer in number.

THE MEO CHARACTER AND CULTURE

The Meo have not been thoroughly studied by ethnologists, and much of their story is obscure. For example, almost nothing is known of their past before they emerged from China into Laos in the mid-nineteenth century. There is agreement that they are relative newcomers in Southeast Asia and that the bulk of the people still live in China and many others in North Vietnam. But estimates of the Meo population in Laos today vary widely. Before the early 1960s most authorities estimated the total at about fifty thousand. Today, estimates are sometimes put as high as five hundred thousand and usually range between three and five hundred thousand. This ten-fold growth in spite of heavy war-caused losses reflects an increase in our knowledge of the Meo rather than a unique population explosion.

The Meo had no written language until recent years. The Lao government, in fact, had actively discouraged efforts to create one.[3] Traditionally, a few members of each village have been literate in Chinese. Usually, these were the shamans, who used Chinese for arcane religious purposes. The religion is basically animist and involves placating the malign and benign spirits that inhabit the natural world, some of them being ancestors or famous leaders of the past. The religion also involves very strong taboos to avoid offense to such spirits, including, for example, a bathing taboo in certain times of the year, which may explain the fastidious emphasis in some of the French literature on the filthiness of the Meo. The Meo attach religious importance to certain sites, of which the outstanding one is Phou Pha Thi, a nine-thousand- foot mesa a few miles northwest of the town of Sam Neua.

Key qualities of Meo culture and social structure explain, in part at least, the role they have played in recent Lao history and the peculiar forms it took, notably the association with the United States. Although not nomadic, as sometimes claimed, the Meo, in common with other tribes of the region, practice shifting or slash-and-burn agriculture. This means that every ten or fifteen years, when the fields it cultivates have worn out, a whole village will abandon its homes and move to another site, where the villagers construct new homes of wood and woven palm leaf, clear new fields by slash-and-burn methods, and plant their crops.

On their fields they grow upland (dry) rice, corn, vegetables, and the opium poppy. Of these, the most fateful for the Meo is the poppy, for it has brought them notoriety and some criticism, particularly after Southeast Asian opium became a source of heroin flowing to American forces in Vietnam and to addicts in the U.S. Nevertheless, opium was a simple economic necessity to many tribal groups in Southeast Asia, the Meo among them. For survival in the mountains they required certain products of the lowlands, particularly iron, steel, and salt. To pay for such necessities they were obliged to produce some commodity which was suited to their environment, would not spoil during the long trip to market, and was valuable enough so that the small amounts they could move by the limited available means would earn the money they required. The result of a village's work for a year had to be transportable on the backs of men or horses.

Under these circumstances, some tribes produced beeswax. Others gathered and processed valuable forest products such as stick-lack (for varnish) or benzoin (a perfume base). In some areas on the edge of the Plain of Jars, Meo raised cattle and drove them to market. But for the vast majority of Meo, opium was the most profitable cash crop, and they knew of no reason not to take advantage of its relatively high price and ready salability, for it was illegal neither to produce nor to sell it. In time of peace, some villages became relatively prosperous on this trade, but, in actual fact, the Meo received a pittance compared to the traders, smugglers, and dealers farther down the chain of distribution.

As for their own consumption of the drug, under certain circumstances no stigma attaches to smoking opium for what are considered good reasons, that is, for older people or sick people suffering pain. It does appear, however, that regular opium smoking by breadwinners on whom a family depends is frowned upon. A young man loses the respect of his community if he becomes an addict. Survival is an arduous matter in the mountains of Laos, and a man sodden on opium is of little use to his family or his clan. At a later point we will have more say on further ramifications of the tribesmen's economic dependence on opium.

A Meo village is an authoritarian hierarchy based on age and position in the family. Villages often consist of one extended household, headed by the eldest male, who is traditionally the village headman. Decisions are made after consultation among family heads and are binding once made.[4] It is possible for the headman to be persuaded in council to take a position he might otherwise have preferred not to take—in fact, to be overborne and forced to go along with the strong views of younger men. Something like this happened in numerous villages during the Meo resistance, which in some ways was a political revolt against conservative elders by younger men pressing a bold course of action which seemed hazardous to the traditional leadership.

The Meo, therefore, have a simple but strong internal organization although not an extensive one. Villages of the same clan were often linked, but only in the province of Xieng Khouang did they have a province-wide polity, and this was the creation of the French who decided to recognize one respected elder as a paramount chief, bearing the title of *chao moung* (actually a district chief in the administrative system), with responsibilities involving all the Meo of Xieng Khouang. Although their traditions speak of epochs when some at least of the large Meo groupings were united under "kings," no such unity exists today, and, aside from Xieng Khouang, the formal organization rises no higher than the *tasseng,* or canton, comprising a group of villages.

Among the other characteristics of the Meo bearing on their role in the war is their traditional independence allied with historic animosity toward the lowlanders of the area, the Lao and the Vietnamese. Precisely what reason the Meo originally had for preferring the highest ground is anything but clear, but it hardly stretches credulity to speculate that it reflected a determination to live according to their own lights, out of reach of the more powerful lowland peoples. Historic suspicions were compounded by the governing methods of the French empire in Laos and Vietnam, where the impositions of the government—the opium and other taxes, corvée labor to build and maintain the network or roads, "borrowing" of draft animals—were enforced by Lao and Vietnamese lesser officials, there often being under the French system no more than a handful of French officials in an entire province.[5] Thus, the Meo not only cherished independence but saw the lowlanders as a threat. Also, as they became more evolved and subject to outside influences under the French, they saw that they were regarded with contempt by the authorities and discriminated against, particularly in education. In 1919–1921, a bitter Meo revolt took place which was directed as much against the Lao and Vietnamese as against the French. It was suppressed with bloody reprisals and the French installed new leadership.[6] After that experience, the Meo avoided direct confrontation with the powerful lowlander but sought accommodation with the least hostile of the various lowland groups. In Xieng Khouang province, descendants of the former royal family of the area (it had once been an independent kingdom) were retained in a favored position by the French, and it was with them that the Meo established a *modus vivendi.*[7] Throughout the period of the Meo resistance, the province chief of Xieng Khouang, Chao (Prince) Say

Kham, head of the former royal family, remained the Lao civilian official in closest touch with the Meo, although for long periods he was forced to live and work in Vientiane.

Accommodation with groups within the Lao elite, however, was simply a concession to harsh reality. The goal was an end to interference by lowlanders and freedom from their exactions. Although this attitude has given the Meo a reputation for "fierce independence," one may question whether it was not simply a normal reaction to being forced to pay heavily while receiving very little in return. For it is clear that virtually no government services were ever provided the Meo or the other Lao tribes by either the French or their successors, the Royal Lao Government—until the United States became involved.

The Meo reputation for ferocity comes also from the fact that when engaged in combat they are not inhibited by the religious and cultural constraints of the Lao, whose Buddhist beliefs condemn the deliberate taking of life and whose concurrent animist beliefs hold that to kill another human is to invite the vengeance of his restless spirit. In this regard, the Meo resemble Westerners: when their lives are at stake, they will seek to kill to avoid being killed. Although they do not maintain a warrior class or cult like the American Indian, they are accustomed to weapons and use them routinely in hunting game and shooting tigers. They long since adopted a homemade firearm, a muzzle-loading flintlock that looks like a toy but is deadly enough at short range. They are physically extremely durable and accustomed to long treks on foot, ambling along on their short bandy-legs for immense distances.

A fact of importance in understanding the commitment of the Meo in the war against the PL/DRV is the existence of an ambition among a growing number to emerge from their immemorial isolation and the limitations it imposed to partake of modernization. Students of their development note the stirrings of such desires resulting from increasing contact with the lowlands, with the French, and with the missionaries. In the last twenty-five or thirty years an increasing number of young men moved to lowland towns to work for wages. In some areas conversions to Christianity were also common, and with such conversions came a new openness to change and modernization.[8] A growing desire for schooling was evidenced; some communities started their own schools and hired Lao teachers out of community funds. Barney sums it up: "The Meo appear to be competing consciously in the Lao national society for recognition in many phases of life—political, economic, occupational, educational, and religious."[9]

The movement to take up arms against the PL/DRV was in one of its aspects an expression of the desire among younger, "modernizing" elements of the community to share in the benefits of a modern way of life. With such aspirations they were naturally drawn to the leadership of the first Meo to rise to high rank in the army of the royal government, General Vang Pao, and also of the first Meo to achieve a university degree and became a minister in the Vientiane government, Touby Lyfong, who some (but no Meo) called "the King of the Meo." (He was actually the Meo *chao muong* of Xieng Khouang province.) The appeal of these leaders was reinforced when, through their direct access to the Americans, they began to secure benefits which the Meo had never known before. There were also more cautious and hesitant elements who had no well-known leaders but often included the village chiefs, men who had earned their positions through seniority and tended to prefer familiar ways and shrink from high-risk enterprises. In later years, Touby Lyfong also became more cautious and looked for support to the traditionalists.

THE POLITICAL CONTEXT

To understand how the Meo became involved in an unequal contest to drive the PL/DRV from their homeland we must now turn to the political and military situation in Laos in 1960 and to the search of the U.S. for an answer to the dilemmas posed by that situation. That year was a watershed in the brief history of independent Laos. Four different governments succeeded each other in Vientiane as a disputed national election was set aside by a *coup d'état,* followed in turn by a civil war. In the accompanying turmoil, the U.S. strove to master events and to achieve what with hindsight seems to have been a futile goal of establishing an anti-Communist regime capable of responding effectively to the attack mounted by the Pathet Lao. That task as complicated by an American presidential election leading to a change of administration with the arrival of the new year.

From its founding, three principal political tendencies had competed for power in independent Laos. The Pathet Lao, led by the able aristocrat Prince Souphannouvong, comprised one grouping. It was considered by the U.S., and was in fact, Communist dominated. Despite its claim to speak for a broad front of political and ethnic groups, the Pathet Lao had in truth been assisted from its beginnings by the Lao Dong Party of Vietnam, the party of Ho Chi Minh, and carefully nursed into reality. While by Lao standards a strong and determined political and military force, it nevertheless continued to be heavily dependent on the Vietnamese Communists for vital skills and resources in all fields, but most especially the military.[10] The PL had been in and out of the Vientiane government during the years of independence, but since 1954 it had also maintained a separate regime in two provinces close to North Vietnam and China, Phong Saly and Sam Neua. Both were heavily populated with hill tribes and in Sam Neua the ethnic mix included many Meo. By 1960 then, members of the tribe had had experience of the PL. Although low-key and concealed where possible, the presence of North Vietnamese advisers, cadres, and military units was well known to the inhabitants of the area. The governing system enforced by the PL/DRV was also more efficient than that of the RLG. Thus, taxes, forced labor for road building, and annual drafts of men to serve as porters were enforced and difficult to evade.

On the other hand, the PL made much of the fact that they advocated the equality of all Lao peoples and that tribesmen served in positions of responsibility in their government.[11] Indeed, a Meo clan leader, Fay Dang, was a member of the NLHS Central Committee, along with two other Meo. The PL had also opened schools where Meo were welcome. There were thus some reasons for Meo to support the PL/DRV cause and a considerable number did, although the exact figures are not known nor is the proportion of those who did so by choice possible to establish. Some of the pro-PL Meo were influenced by the fact that Fay Dang headed a leading Meo clan, one which was involved in a rivalry with Touby Lyfong and his clan.[12] Very possibly, if the choice for the Meo had lain between the PL and Fay Dang on the one hand, and the RLG and Touby Lyfong on the other—as it had until 1960—the overwhelming majority would have seen no choice, for the RLG had been pushed out of much of the area and was shortly to be threatened in the rest. At this point, however, a choice again became possible, a result of the initiative of Touby Lyfong in alliance with Vang Pao and proceeding in concert with the right-wing government of General Phoumi Nosavan and, most importantly, with the United States.

To understand how this combination of forces came about, we must return to our description of the contending Lao groupings. Occupying the center of the political spectrum were the neutralist factions whose leader was the veteran Lao politician Prince Souvanna Phouma, French educated and trained, head of an important semiroyal family from Luang Prabang, and older half-brother of the "Red Prince," Souphannouvong. Souvanna Phouma's military strength came from General Kong Le, about whom more in a moment. Beginning with the aftermath of the first Geneva accords which in 1954 ended the war between the PL and the French, Souvanna Phouma had believed in and worked toward a coalition government which would include the Pathet Lao with his half-brother in the cabinet. In this objective he had been consistently opposed by the U.S., which, under the leadership of Eisenhower and Dulles, had become active in military and economic support of the RLG, insisting as the price for its aid that Laos assume a firmly anti-Communist stance. The U.S. maneuvered and intervened in Lao politics both overtly and covertly during the years 1957 to 1960, always with the same purpose, which came to seem an ever-receding will-o'-the-wisp. The U.S. did succeed in excluding Souvanna from the successive cabinets after 1958, but none of them survived long. Nor did they accomplish much in the way of establishing government control throughout the land or in dealing with the Pathet Lao threat. Using the same hit-and-run guerrilla tactics combined with skilled political organization perfected by the Viet Minh in the war against the French, the PL deepened its hold in areas it already controlled and expanded into new areas.

The problem of perennial instability and weakness stemmed in good part from the factionalism and disunity of the right which, despite American efforts to promote unity, remained divided and quarrelsome. A national election conducted in April was the precipitating cause of the upheavals of 1960. The election was grossly rigged to secure an over-whelming victory for the right wing. According to competent observers, this was done with covert American support, a fact which became widely known.[13] Tired of the division of the country between Communist and anti-Communist, of the increasing toll of spreading guerrilla warfare, and of the corruption and ineffectiveness of succeeding right-wing governments, many Lao were ready for a change. The coup staged in September by the commander of the most effective unit of the Royal Armed Forces (FAR), the Second Parachute Battalion, responded to the mood. The leader, Captain Kong Le (he soon jumped all the intervening ranks to become a general and commander of all the neutralist forces) took over control of Vientiane, repudiated the policies of the right-wing regime, and invited Souvanna Phouma to form a government.

The ensuing months were a period of enormous confusion in Laos and also in the councils of the U.S. government, which for a time seemed to be supporting both the government of Souvanna Phouma and of his right-wing opponents led by General Phoumi Nosavan and Prince Boun Oum, both conservative, anti-Communist southerners with close ties to the government of Thailand. In the end, the American aid given to the right-wing group proved conclusive. Phoumi used the aid to set up a rival government headquartered in the southern city of Savannakhet, pro-ceeded to rally most of the FAR and much of the political establishment to his banner, and eventually began a march on Vientiane, which he took on December 16, after a head-on clash with Kong Le's forces.

The rightist victory in the battle of Vientiane, however, did not end the civil war. Kong Le withdrew in good order northward. With amazing rapidity, the Soviet Union improvised an airlift to resupply his columns as they followed the road into the mountains and toward the Plain of Jars. At the same time, an agreement was reached between the neutral-ists and the Pathet Lao to fight as allies against the regime of Prince Boun Oum and General Phoumi.

THE MEO FIND ALLIES

It was some time during these turbulent months that the concept took shape of an irregular armed force of Meo tribesmen fighting for its own and the rightist government's cause and enjoying, with the RLG's consent, the direct support of the United States. The origins of the program, however, are by no means entirely known, the U.S. not having made its records available to the public. A few versions have been published but, although reliable as far as they go, they obviously only tell part of the story and contain inaccuracies.[14] It is nevertheless possible to be certain about a few key points. First, it is known that the involvement of some Meo groups in guerrilla operations goes back to the Viet Minh/French war when the French army organized many tribal units to operate in both Laos and North Vietnam. (It was in this activity that Vang Pao got his first combat experience. He also attended several French military training courses.) Later, after the Geneva Accords of 1954, when the heavily Meo-populated province of Sam Neua was, along with Phong Saly, assigned "temporarily" to Pathet Lao control, apparently spontaneous anti-PL guerrilla activity sprang up again in the vicinity of the province capital of Sam Neua. These groups managed to obtain some help from FAR officers stationed in adjoining areas controlled by the Vientiane government and continued a sporadic resistance for several years. In the meantime, through these same FAR officers, both U.S. military intelligence and CIA not only learned of the resistance but began to obtain intelligence from it about conditions and military activity in the Communist-controlled province. It was as a result of these contacts that the U.S. became aware of Vang Pao and obtained some initial familiarity with the Meo. (The period concerned is approximately 1956–1958.) No support was authorized for the resistance which, at any rate, ceased during the period 1957–1960 when the PL was formally part of the Vientiane government.

In 1960, however, the PL, which had earlier broken with the Vientiane government once again, resumed operations with North Vietnamese help and retook Phong Saly and Sam Neua. Again a spontaneous Meo resistance broke out in the vicinity of Sam Neua town. This time, emissaries were sent south to obtain help. Their arrival more or less coincided with the growth of a threat that all of Xieng Khouang, the province which included the largest part of the Meo population of Laos, would follow Sam Neua into PL/DRV control. Touby Lyfong and his associates, including Vang Pao, were aroused about this threat for both had long been opposed to the PL domination in Meo tribal areas. They turned to General Phoumi, whose interest in resisting the PL coincided with theirs. Finally, the U.S. was also interested in building

Phoumi's strength (or, at least, according to most accounts, the U.S. military and the CIA were committed to the general; the State Department wavered between Phoumi and Souvanna Phouma).[15] To this known background we must add several reasonable assumptions. It is probable that the U.S., through the CIA, was in covert contact with Touby and Vang Pao and, of course, with Phoumi. All three elements had reason to fear the consequences of a joining of PL forces with the neutralists in the critical Plain of Jars area, a threat which began to appear a serious possibility as the beleaguered Souvanna regime moved to carry out its pledges of negotiations with the Pathet Lao and also invited a Soviet Embassy into Vientiane for the first time.

The result of the commonality of interest among Americans, Lao, and Thai was, we can presume, an understanding, but no details are available, and its nature must be deduced from ensuing events. One such event, which has been variously interpreted, is reported by G. Linwood Barney, a reliable social scientist who has made a special study of the Meo. He states that during the confused period of the civil war, in the fall of 1960, Touby Lyfong, at that moment a minister of the Vientiane government of Souvanna Phouma, traveled to Xieng Khouang in the company of Chao Say Kham, the province chief. At a meeting of local officials, Say Kham declared that "he was breaking away from the central government and asked all his district chiefs to join with him in resisting all enemies."[16] Barney sees this as a bid to regain Xieng Khouang's ancient autonomy. Nevertheless, he adds that Say Kham made an alliance with General Phoumi in Savannakhet who supplied the dissidents' requirements for arms. When Phoumi took Vientiane, Xieng Khouang gave up its short-lived claim of autonomy and pledged allegiance to Phoumi and Boun Oum.

The source of this account appears to have been Touby himself.[17] Its mention of arms supplied by Phoumi from Savannakhet immediately suggests U.S. involvement, since Phoumi had no means to deliver weapons to Xieng Khouang. To the Americans, on the other hand, such deliveries presented no problem for they were already supplying Phoumi by CIA-controlled commercial aircraft.[18] In other words, Barney's account confirms a tripartite understanding between Phoumi, the U.S., and the Meo. The reference to autonomy for Xieng Khouang is a puzzler and difficult to take at face value since it had no sequel. If true, it appears to have been a device by Touby and Say Kham to straddle the issues of the civil war until they could see the outcome.

This political step was preparatory to the execution of a plan which in actuality was the first in a long series of improvisations. It was a bold move but also an improvident one, and it almost ended in disaster. Vang Pao and Touby agreed that the Meo population living on the edges of the Plain of Jars would be organized in advance to abandon their villages en masse in the event that the neutralists threatened to take over the Plain. The tribespeople would move on signal to seven base areas selected in advance and located on high ground overlooking the Plain. From these vantage points Meo scouts would keep the enemy under observation and raiding parties would harass him.

Such are the outlines of the plan, described in some detail by Schanche and confirmed in general by Woodruff.[19] Obviously, these versions leave out certain essentials, such as the provision of weapons and ammunition, training, and communications for the irregular units. Nor do they examine the implications of the understanding which induced Phoumi to agree to the highly unusual arrangement whereby a foreign power (in fact, as we shall see, two foreign powers) directly supported a separate armed force on Lao territory. As for the first point, it is quite evident that CIA was the principal U.S. sponsor of the Meo guerrilla resistance. This is made explicit in a memorandum of General Lansdale's included in the *Pentagon Papers* and apparently written in July 1961:

> Political leadership of the Meo is in the hands of Touby Lyfong, who now operates mostly out of Vientiane. The military leader is Lt. Col. Vang Pao, who is field commander. Command control of Meo operations is exercised by the Chief of CIA, Vientiane, with the advice of Chief Maag, Laos. The same CIA paramilitary and U.S. military teamwork is in existence for advisory activities (9 CIA operations officer, 9 LTAG/Army Special forces personnel, in addition to 99 Thai PARU under CIA control), and aerial resupply.[20]

Thus, the provision of the essential military wherewithal was a combined CIA/U.S. Army operation under CIA management and assisted by a Thai contingent, of which more in a moment. The Lansdale memo notes in passing the critical factor of aerial resupply, which later in the memo he credits to Civil Air Transport or CAT. Actually, the firm active in Laos was a corporate offspring of CAT called Air America, which presumably, in common with the parent firm, was a CIA instrument—or "proprietary" in Lansdale's term. Operating under contract to various U.S. government agencies, Air America was active in supplying Phoumi's forces, and support for the Meo was originally an extension of that work. From this early period dates the remarkable network of mountain landing strips used by a fleet of tiny short-takeoff-and-landing (STOL) aircraft supplementing a variety of larger transports which dropped their cargoes by parachute. The aircraft were flown by a few dozen adventurous (and reputedly well-paid) pilots with none of the navigational aids of normal commercial flying. They provided the indispensable transport and communication facility of the Meo guerrilla movement and a unique feature of a strange war.

On the second major point left undiscussed in existing accounts, the understanding with General Phoumi, we have no specifics and can only speculate. No doubt the important consideration to Phoumi and to Prince Boun Oum with respect to direct involvement by the U.S. with an irregular armed force was that they be kept informed of major developments, be consulted on important policy questions, and have some residue of control. To some extent the latter was achieved through Vang Pao's status as a FAR officer, subordinated to the FAR commander of the Second Military Region. The Meo irregulars were described as "auto-defense" forces, a designation for part-time village militia dating from French rule, giving them a semblance of official status. Of some additional reassurance to Phoumi, we may guess, was the existence of a Thai role in Meo operations. In the above quotation from Lansdale's memo, reference is made to ninety-nine Thai working with the Meo. They are described as PARU, an acronym for Police Aerial Resupply Unit, a special force which, as Lansdale states elsewhere in the same memo, "had a mission of undertaking clandestine operations in denied areas."[21] He also states that PARU is supported by the U.S. In Laos, the ninety-nine Thai augmented the eighteen CIA men and Special Forces in training, advisory, and technical tasks, and thus made it possible for a rather large program to be handled by a very few Americans.

Such a Thai involvement would certainly have required the assent of the head of the Thai government, Field Marshall Sarit Thanarat, who was also a relative and ally of General Phoumi. The arrangement gave Phoumi an additional safeguard that he would be kept informed and his interests protected. There was therefore a rather intricate network of understandings involving three governments as well as the Meo leadership preceding the bold stroke of January 1961. Although all had differing purposes, their interests coincided with respect to maintaining the Plain of Jars in friendly hands. Of all those involved, the Meo had the most at stake; they were offering the lives of their fighting men and the well-being of their people. They, least of all, foresaw the consequences.

The Operation Is Launched

As feared, Kong Le and his few men continued their successful march from Vientiane to the Plain of Jars while the Pathet Lao brought pressure from their forward lines on the eastern side of the Plain. At the end of December, Kong Le took the PDJ airfield. To the south, the Pathet Lao closed in on Xiengkhouangville. Its garrison was commanded by Vang Pao who withdrew to the mountains in good order. At the same time, he gave the signal for the Meo to abandon their villages and to move toward the seven rendezvous points. He himself established his headquarters at the Meo village of Padong, southwest of the Plain. According to

Schanche, seventy thousand Meo left two hundred villages in accordance with the prearranged plan and trekked on foot to their new destinations.[22] They left with the harvest ungathered, their only food supply what they could carry. It is not known whether any supplies had been prepositioned at the gathering points. If so, not enough could have been transported by available means to last until the next harvest, presuming there was enough land at the new locations for this host to farm.

We face an obvious question. The purposes of the operation were to establish a force of irregulars to collect intelligence and harass the PL/DRV and their allies, the neutralists. Why was it necessary for an entire population to launch itself into the unknown but certainly hazardous future, abandoning their homes and fields and trusting to providence for survival?

There seem to have been several interlocking reasons for this apparently reckless behavior. First, the movement was not based on the recruitment of individual fighting men. The decision to join, to follow Touby and Vang Pao, was a community decision taken by village family heads. Once made, all able-bodied men who were needed were sent forward to Vang Pao for training by his American and Thai allies and deployment in operations. But neither soldiers nor families were prepared to accept a condition of permanent separation, with the village under enemy control while the fighting men stayed on the other side of the line and fought. To avoid such a painful and, in fact, crippling advantage for the enemy, the decision was made to move the families out of harm's way—a course made easier by the roving habits of the population.

This pattern, in the years that followed, remained a persistent feature of the Meo resistance which sometimes gave it the character of a mass migration. If the Meo irregulars were forced to give up ground, the population of the lost area would flee to avoid both Pathet Lao control and forced separation from their fighting men. By the same token, Vang Pao and his allies soon found that the irregular troops became undependable in a situation where their families were threatened and were forced to fend for themselves. On more than one occasion, soldiers and population fled from attack together, making orderly withdrawal impossible and leading to scenes of mass panic.

It was in anticipation of such possibilities that the decision was taken at the very outset of the resistance to extricate the entire population base from the enemy's reach. Probably a second factor underlying the decision is the likelihood that Touby, Vang Pao, and the Americans anticipated the early return of the FAR to the Plain of Jars and its reconquest by the Vientiane government, thus permitting the Meo villagers to return to their homes and resume their normal lives. We deduce this simply from the fact that no provision was made for the permanent support of the resisting population; on the other hand, a considerable effort was put into strengthening the FAR for its offensive to retake the Plain.[23]

Whatever the reasons, the striking fact is that an estimated 70,000 men, women, and children were launched into the mountains to find within months that they were face to face with starvation. How the problem was dealt with will be described in due course. For the moment, we wish to note again the improvised nature of the program and its very short-term goal, which was merely to assist the regular forces to retake the Plain of Jars. None of those involved, least of all the Meo villagers, saw this step as the first skirmish of a thirteen-year war of the Meo (and other tribal groups) of Xieng Khouang and Sam Neua against the North Vietnamese and the Pathet Lao. Two events conspired to make it such: first, the strong reaction of the PL/DRV to a center of resistance on North Vietnam's doorstep; secondly, the fighting capabilities of Meo soldiers when led by their own officers, with a reliable system of supply and transport, and when the cause seemed vital. In time, the Meo stood out in contrast to the woeful performance of Lao regulars and attracted increasing U.S. support and reliance.

To set the stage for the transformation of this initial, short-range effort into the full-blown resistance and counterinsurgency program it ultimately became, we must return to events elsewhere. The campaign of Phoumi and his regulars to retake the Plain was a serious U.S. commitment taken over by the new administration in toto from the old, with, however, some reduction of objective. The notion of completely retaking the Plain of Jars was replaced by the more modest goal of defending the Mekong Valley, considered a critical strategic buffer for Thailand, by confronting the enemy on the Plain and holding him there.[24] For the first time, combat aircraft were deployed by the FAR, and a four-hundred-man U.S. Army contingent was dispatched to provide training and advice to the Lao forces. These were the White Star Mobile Training Teams, composed of Special Forces. The larger number were assigned to work with regular units, particularly those attempting to reach the Plain. (Some worked with tribal groups, including the Meo. As made clear in the Lansdale memo, quoted earlier, direction of U.S. support for the Meo remained with CIA.)

Despite these increases in U.S. support, the FAR campaign made almost no progress and stalled well short of its objective. Then, in March, the PL and neutralists counterattacked, easily driving the FAR toward Vientiane. It was a humiliating failure that entirely collapsed the U.S.'s hopes of achieving a military standoff and triggered the painful shift of American policy toward the neutralization of Laos under a coalition government. During that period only the Meo irregulars achieved any military success, fulfilling their limited mission of intelligence reporting and harassment by ambush, despite hardship and the greater strength of the enemy.

The PL/DRV awoke suddenly to the fact that a large area all around the Plain of Jars, which they claimed to be theirs by virtue of the people's support, had, in fact, risen up against them. They rapidly organized countermeasures, directing the main thrust of their attack against Vang Pao's headquarters at Padong. Gradually the attacking forces were built up into a sizeable concentration, some artillery was laboriously dragged into range, and a siege began. Although in the meantime negotiations between the three factions began and led to a cease-fire, the savage little war at Padong continued for weeks, until finally Vang Pao was forced to abandon it in the first of many pell-mell retreats complicated by a panic-stricken horde of villagers. Several other Meo strongholds fell in the same period. Despite these setbacks and the discouragement they brought, the Meo did not abandon the fight. A new headquarters was selected in an upland valley separated from Padong by several high ridges. Harassment and intelligence activities were maintained and the movement continued to grow. According to Lansdale's memo of July 1961, there were as of that date nine thousand armed tribesmen in Vang Pao's irregular forces.[25]

RELIEF FOR THE WANDERING MEO

During this phase, the seriousness of the miscalculation that had separated the Meo villagers from their homes and crops became apparent. At the same time, thanks to some effective improvisation, a solution was found. Urged on by the only American in the organization who was familiar with the situation, AID in Vientiane commenced air-dropping supplies to the seven sites at which the Meo were concentrated. The person responsible was a remarkable International Voluntary Service volunteer of whom much has been written, Edgar M. "Pop" Buell, a retired farmer from Indiana. Supplies were purchased in Thailand and elsewhere, air transport was contracted for from Air America, and AID undertook a program of "blind" airdrops—that is, the cargoes were delivered without prearrangement with the people who received them, truly a haphazard process. According to Schanche,[26] for lack of coordination among American agencies, this was nevertheless the approach followed for three months until Buell, determined to find out more, parachuted into Padong to see Vang Pao. He landed there in the midst of the siege, to find not only the Meo leader, but some CIA and White Star officers who traveled in and out regularly by helicopter.

After this inauspicious beginning, cooperation between agencies improved rapidly. The Meo program became a notable example of what has already been cited to be the normal cooperativeness among Americans working in remote areas under critical conditions, which is to share resources without formality and concentrate on the common goals. In the meantime, Buell and his Vientiane headquarters were able to organize a more responsive and precise assistance program, based on coordinated information regularly provided.

The need for relief continued to increase. Buell discovered in the course of several walking tours of the involved areas that the numbers of Meo families fleeing the fighting was steadily rising, apparently a result of PL/DRV countermeasures as they moved against the center of Meo resistance. The figures at this early stage rapidly went over one hundred thousand.[27] In addition to food, the refugee program distributed salt, blankets, and medicines provided by CIA and the military.

THE DECISION TO CONTINUE

It is clear that at some point in the months immediately following the cease-fire of May 3, 1961, a decision was made jointly by the United States government and the Meo (and presumably by the Thai as well) to continue the resistance movement. On the other hand, it is not clear whether this was a formal decision or the result of short-term reactions to developments in the field and at the conference table. On the Meo side, we must assume that Touby and Vang Pao saw the fight as a desperate necessity and were able to persuade their people that with continued American and Thai help they could regain and hold their original homes. On the American side, we have little documentary evidence and can only speculate that the conclusive factor was the strategy adopted by the administration in the protracted negotiations at Geneva and elsewhere to neutralize Laos and establish a coalition government including the Pathet Lao. President Kennedy and his negotiators were engaged in an exceedingly delicate maneuver, modifying their policy of support for the right, while attempting at the same time to avoid an impression of weakness which would tempt the Communists to press their attack in hope of a complete victory.[28] The strategy called for a double-track approach to maintain a belief on the part of the opposite side that the U.S. retained a military option to which it would resort if the negotiating terms offered were not acceptable. The impressive fighting performance of the Meo as compared with the futility of the other anti-Communist groups gave them some value in the hand the president was trying to play at a time when the outlook was most uncertain, when the U.S. had alerted its own forces and was reluctantly contemplating the possibility of direct intervention.

We note also that this was the period of intense administration interest in guerrilla warfare, a fact which made it all the more difficult to withdraw support for the most effective guerrilla movement in the area.

Also of some weight must have been the fact that withdrawal of support would have meant abandoning a population to Communist rule. Without direct evidence, these are the best reasons we can reconstruct for the continuation of the program through the first year after the cease-fire, a year of maneuver, uncertainty, and sometimes hectic bargaining. The program not only continued, but as additional villages threw in their lot with Touby and Vang Pao the numbers of armed men increased as well. Sporadic fighting recurred and new refugees continued to be generated and taken care of, but the new headquarters was remote from Communist military centers and was never seriously threatened. The experience confirmed the usefulness of the Meo during a highly delicate passage of U.S. diplomacy.

Yet the very success of the policy—in which the Meo resistance could have played only a small role—created new dangers and dilemmas for the resistance and for the administration. Much of the delay in the negotiations stemmed from the refusal of General Phoumi and Prince Boun Oum to accept the posts allotted to them in the proposed coalition. Strenuous pressures finally brought them around. In June 1962 agreement on the makeup of the coalition was reached, and in July the nations gathered at Geneva finally signed the neutralization agreement and decreed that its terms were to be enforced within no more than seventy days. During the months leading up to this denouement the position of the U.S. in relation to the Meo resistance began to involve internal contradictions. On the one hand, the arguments already cited made continued support advisable in event the neutralization effort failed. On the other hand, the proposed terms of the Geneva Accords made it difficult for the U.S. to continue support for the resistance. As the various obstacles to neutralization were overcome, some at the policy level questioned the wisdom of ever having undertaken so far-reaching a commitment and one so difficult to dissolve. "Arming the tribesmen," wrote Roger Hilsman some years later, "engendered an obligation not only to feed them when they were driven from their traditional homeland but also to protect them from vengeance. This was an obligation . . . that might come to be a hindrance to implementing the Geneva accords and achieving a truly neutral Laos."[29] It was a critical moment for the resistance and a time when a decision to extricate the U.S. was probably considered.

With the benefit of hindsight, some may argue that the Meo would have suffered less in the long run if support had been withdrawn at this point and they had been forced to make their peace as best they could with the more powerful forces arrayed against them. A realistic assessment of the factors shaping U.S. policy at the time, particularly the strong conservative opposition to the neutralization policy, not to mention the obvious risks of failure recognized on every side, make it understandable that the administration chose to foreclose the fewest options. Support for the Meo was continued; but gradually, as neutralization approached, recruiting was terminated, ammunition stockpiles were reduced, and most American advisers were withdrawn. By the time the accords went into effect, tribal units were limited to the ammunition needed to repel attack for a few days. Succor, however, was not far off. A base existed in Thailand. In case of need, advisers and supplies were no more than an hour away.

From this decision also dates the long-term commitment of the CIA to the management of a large military operation which, although secondary to the major conflict in Vietnam, became thoroughly entangled with aspects of that part of the Indochina war. The role was thrust upon the CIA because of the desire of the U.S. to minimize any violations of the Geneva Accords and later because of the State Department's conviction that U.S. military management of the resistance support effort would bring increasing difficulties of political control and very possibly would inevitably lead to pressures to commit American combat forces. The later growth of public knowledge about the CIA's role and of criticism of a "secret," allegedly unauthorized war put the matter in an unfavorable light which is not borne out by the facts, at least as far as concerns the CIA. The task was not asked for nor particularly welcome, nor was it kept a secret from key members of Congress.

This was the answer worked out by the administration to its conflicting obligations. Souvanna Phouma, prime minister again in the coalition regime he had worked so hard to achieve, was told the essentials of all this during a visit he paid to Washington in August 1961. The U.S. government entered the agreements seriously hoping they would succeed, but not depending upon it. As far as concerned the Meo, if the accords were carried out, they would eventually be able to disband their forces and return to their homes in peace. If not, the fighting would resume. The foresight which might have suggested that, regardless of the extent of U.S. aid, Meo forces could not be equalized with those of North Vietnam, did not exist. Also lacking was an appreciation of the importance attached by the Vietnamese to keeping Xieng Khouang province out of the hands of a powerful enemy. Seeing the Meo as surrogates for the U.S., they appear—judging by their actions over the next ten years—to have concluded that it was a matter of vital national importance to defeat the Meo resistance. No other reasoning justifies the price they eventually paid to seize and hold the depopulated Plain of Jars and the hills around it.

MEO "NATION-BUILDING"

As agreement between the contending parties grew closer, fighting dropped off, and life among the Meo and the Americans involved with them became less preoccupied with simple survival. Refugees were able to sow and harvest crops, and something like normality prevailed. During this period, which lasted less than a year, the resistance evolved the programs which came to represent the positive portion of its appeal.

A factor in the launching of some of the programs was the coincidence that Touby Lyfong was at the time minister of health and was able to wield some influence in Vientiane, while Vang Pao perceived the importance of placing his movement at the head of Meo aspirations for bettering their lives. Edgar M. Buell took much of the initiative and displayed his particular talents for improvisation and for bridging the cultural gap between the hill-tribe villages in Xieng Khouang and the U.S. government establishment in Vientiane.

The first steps came even before the temporary lull in the fighting. As Schanche recounts it, Buell was able to get a one-room school started in one refugee village even before the fall of Padong in May 1961.[30] In its earliest phase, the program to bring schooling to the Meo was not officially sponsored. USAID in Vientiane found little enthusiasm for it in the RLG and appears to have tried to discourage Buell from proceeding. He persisted, however, using whatever materials he could find, borrow, or buy with funds he contributed himself or solicited from others. Books were found in the warehouse of USIS in Vientiane; funds for pencils and notebooks and other needs were contributed by Air America pilots, by Buell's friends and relatives in the United States, by American dependents in Vientiane, and by CIA. Teachers proved to be the most critical shortage, and in those early days any literate villager could become a part-time teacher.

From these beginnings the school program moved ahead rapidly, and soon every refugee village had one, usually built out of fuel drums hammered flat. The villagers willingly performed the work required to build and maintain the schools. Indeed, the driving force behind the movement was the Meo thirst for education as a first step toward moving into the modern world. In a few years, AID and the Lao Ministry of Education withdrew their objections. They accorded the effort official status and regular funds from the AID program and the Lao budget. In 1965 a junior high school was founded, and by 1969 there were nine of them, two high schools, and a teacher-training school. By then, some two dozen Meo students had gone on to universities in Australia, France, and the United States.[31]

Of particular importance in persuading the Lao government to support Meo education was the fact that from the beginning Lao was the language of instruction and a Lao flag was displayed in each school along with the picture of the king. More than any other fact, this practice refutes the suspicion that Touby and Vang Pao launched and conducted their movement with the secret motive of achieving Meo independence or some form of political autonomy. The evidence suggests that what they sought could best be described as "Meo power," that is, the right to communal self-rule in local matters within a Lao state that accorded all groups equal status.

Of equal importance with schooling was the beginning of a public health program which had its start with the appearance of Special Forces advisers working with Vang Pao's units. Buell recruited a Lao paramedic to assist at a tent hospital run by Special Forces and to train Meo medics. From this start a ramified program developed, guided by Buell's two closest American associates, Drs. Charles Weldon and Patricia Mc-Creedy (Mrs. Weldon). The heart of it was a hospital at the headquarters of the refugee program, Sam Thong, in the mountains between Vientiane and the Plain of Jars. The Sam Thong facility eventually grew to be a two hundred-bed hospital with several doctors on duty—American, Filipino, and Lao—and a full-time American nurse supervising a corps of tribal women trained as nurses at a school at the same location.

As each new group of refugees was relocated, a trained Meo paramedic supervised the construction and stocking of a dispensary. He also selected a candidate for training, dispatching him to Sam Thong for a four-month course. On completion of training, the new recruit returned to his home area and operated the dispensary.[32] By 1970 over one thousand medical corps men and practical nurses had been trained; 450 of them were located in over 125 refugee centers.[33] In a report to Senator Kennedy's Sub-Committee on Refugees in 1970, Dr. McCreedy said:

> In any refugee move the resident Lao medic is responsible for the care of the people on the march. Base supply areas are contacted through the nearest radio net and medical resupply points are arranged. Medicines are delivered by air, landed or dropped in combination with other commodities. . . . Patients flow from outlying dispensaries and front-line medics to receiving stations manned by more qualified medical auxiliaries. These in turn refer those cases outside their competence to base hospitals manned by the most qualified personnel available at the professional level: Lao doctors . . . with (USAID) American and Filipino . . . advisers.[34]

The program had been developed in seven years from a base point of zero. Until the resistance of the Meo, the hill people of Laos had had virtually no medical care, while the Lao themselves were hardly better off. This system, primitive as it had perforce to be, significantly reduced the physical toll of the resistance.

The basic purpose of USAID's effort, including the public health program, was the emergency care of refugees and their resettlement and rehabilitation until they had produced a crop and could look after themselves. Edgar Buell remained in charge, with the title of refugee coordinator for northeast Laos. During the brief lull following the

Geneva Accords, he established a permanent base at Sam Thong, and constructed a few modest buildings to serve as living quarters, offices, and warehouses. At about the same time, Vang Pao set up his headquarters in a long, narrow upland valley near a tiny village called Long Tieng. It was separated by a single ridge from Sam Thong and in a straight line was only six kilometers away.

Buell attempted personally to visit every new refugee group as it came out to ascertain needs and establish the size of the group. In time, however, he developed an able corps of American assistants who filled in for him when necessary. The essential requirements were usually for blankets, pots, medicines, clothing, and tools. To provide the latter two items, steel bars and black cloth were delivered out of which the refugees were able to meet their own needs.[35] As for food, rice was the basic need but it was supplemented by other grains from U.S. Public Law 480 (Food for Peace) supplies, and in later years canned meats were added to make up for protein deficiency. Refugees were told that "rice from the sky" would be provided only until they could grow their own. During the period of need, a village was placed on a regular schedule of rice drops, assigned a signal marker, and instructed in the technique of setting up a drop zone.

Buell was able to routinize these arrangements and quickly trained tribesmen and Lao to handle the routines. Whenever he contacted a new group, he traveled if possible with a Lao official from the office of the province chief, Chao Say Kham. In effect, he maintained a program to delegate responsibility to RLG officials and to tribesmen. The refugee program thus redressed to some extent the long-standing tribal grievance regarding their lack of voice in managing important affairs that concerned them directly.

Another theme of Buell's effort was the improvement of agriculture. Although plows were an impossibility because of the lack of draft animals, he attempted to spread knowledge about such matters as the row-cropping of vegetables and the value of improved seed, which he distributed in the refugee settlements. According to Schanche, he attempted one experiment to find a substitute for opium as a cash crop, persuading one village to grow sweet potatoes instead.[36] The attempt failed because the product could not be moved to market. More successful was a program to encourage the digging of fish ponds which were stocked with tilapia, a fish that grows rapidly on a diet of refuse and human excrement. Some effort was also made to improve the breeding stock of swine.

At the time of the signing of the Geneva Accords, the refugee population peaked at about 125,000. It then began to go down and despite the resumption of fighting in 1963 it declined to about thirty thousand in 1964.[37] In effect, although new refugees were created, older refugees continued to be taken off the rolls at a faster rate. It remained at that figure until 1967, when it began to rise again. By now it should be clear that the term "refugee program" is a misnomer, and that there is no available term to describe the effort except for "counterinsurgency program," as we have defined it. Once the refugees could feed themselves they were still of concern to Vang Pao and to Buell and his staff. Contact was maintained for the purposes of the public health, education, and agricultural programs. Annual "draft calls" were issued to participating communities, and, indeed, in those where many or all of the able-bodied men were away fighting, the village was maintained on the rice distribution lists. According to indirect evidence, the population supplied regularly for this reason remained at a steady one hundred thousand throughout the program, except for the earliest year or two.[38] That figure is not incorporated in the totals given earlier in this paragraph for it is not clear when the practice began and because the group cannot be accurately described as refugees.

Not all the "nation-building" was the work of USAID and the refugee program. The availability of aircraft and a myriad of landing strips (at one time numbering nearly three hundred) had some secondary impacts on the quality of life in the widely scattered villages and refugee centers. The tiny STOL aircraft, for one thing, began to carry mail and packages as well as people, and before long a rather sizeable postal service emerged without cost to the users. Letters were written by scribes for the illiterate and the service was widely used, helping to weld together the widely distributed population in a way that had not been possible before. A similar effect resulted from carrying private passengers, a service for which no fare was charged. It was limited to those vouched for by local village chiefs or other authorities.

The pilots of these aircraft were obliging young men who were fascinated by the ways of the people they were serving. They often used their own judgment in deciding who would or would not be carried, and without doubt they unknowingly moved opium about in the packages that their passengers carried. Although this violated their company regulations and the terms of the contracts between company and government, it probably happened frequently. Seldom, however, was it done knowingly or did the pilot benefit.

The existence of opium production and trade in the tribal areas later became, in the minds of some, a major charge against the U.S.'s involvement with the tribespeople in the "secret war" in Laos. The issue became especially inflamed after the arrival of American troops in South Vietnam and the diversion of Southeast Asian opium to this market, often in the form of heroin. A complicating factor was the role of some senior Lao officials—including, notably, senior generals of the Royal Lao Army—in the movement of opium out of the area to their considerable financial benefit. The Meo made no more money out of this trade than they had before it existed and had no involvement in it other than as primary producers who turned their product over to the traditional middlemen, often Chinese traders. Indeed, the turmoil of the war and the movement of populations sharply reduced opium production in the Meo areas.

The policy of the American agencies working with the Meo was to turn a blind eye to the Meo involvement with opium and, to the extent that they could control the contacts of their personnel, to have nothing to do with the growth and movement of the product. Nevertheless, as the public attention and interest in the tribal program grew, grave charges of complicity and neglect were brought against such agencies as the CIA and the State Department. As for complicity, no substantial evidence has ever been adduced, and the author during his years of involvement learned of no facts to support the charge. Although it is impossible to be certain that no individual American or other foreign national employed in the large, remote areas of the project did not take advantage for his personal account of the opportunities afforded by the availability of both opium and transportation (and the author is aware that some did), every effort was made to discourage it. As for the charge of neglect, it is certainly true that the policy of the U.S. government in Laos was to focus on the war and not be diverted into attempting to suppress an immemorial practice which no Lao saw as improper. Those critics who were opposed to the war naturally did not agree with these priorities, but they were nevertheless inevitable in the circumstances.

In 1965 an economic program sprang up based on the availability of cargo space. The regular payroll of the irregular units generated cash purchasing power—a ready-made market with no goods to soak it up. To meet the need (and no doubt to turn a profit) the Meo elders organized a trading company and obtained permission (presumably from the CIA) to bring consumer goods to the mountains on available aircraft. As a result, a bustling market sprang up at Long Tieng, where the wares included anything from frying pans to opium, gun powder to paste jewelry. Peddlers and traders could buy stocks from the trading company at Long Tieng and, as was traditional in the mountains, carry their wares from village to village on pack horses.

In time, Long Tieng, with its markets and schools and military facilities, grew to be one of the largest towns in Laos, with a population estimated at forty thousand. It was a strange city indeed, with no paved streets, no street lights, and hardly any vehicles, but with a sophisticated telecommunications center and a three-thousand-foot landing strip on which an aircraft landed or took off every few seconds. A road was built by USAID in 1966, zig-zagging across the ridge to Sam Thong. Work then started on a road leading out of the mountains to Route 13 and

Vientiane. Small buses appeared, and before long several hundred motor vehicles began to ply the roads. A variety of forces thus began to work on the population clustered around the two towns and other nearby settlements, pushing them into the modern world while at the same time improving their status and quality of life in ways that answered to long-felt desires. Perhaps the acme of this kind of satisfaction came at Meo New Year in January of 1966, when the king paid a formal visit to Sam Thong and the ceremonies were attended by the diplomatic colony flown up to Sam Thong for the occasion. The new *groupe scolaire* was dedicated on the occasion, all the Meo wore their brightest costumes, and the air was full of tiny aircraft delivering or picking up their distinguished passengers. To the tribespeople it no doubt seemed a vindication of their decision to join the resistance, in spite of the high price many of them had paid.

MEO LEADERSHIP

It is quite impossible to separate out of this program the share of responsibility attributable to Americans, Thai, Meo, and Lao. Each needed all the others, but little could have been accomplished had it not been for the particular strengths of the Meo and their leaders, Vang Pao, Touby, and other elders. Vang Pao's leadership was certainly the critical ingredient in maintaining the aggressiveness and spirit of the movement in spite of the many setbacks that eventually befell it. Part of his hold came from his relationship with the Americans and his ability, with their support, to respond with almost magical promptness to sudden crises. A horde of refugees in desperate flight might be located in the morning; a helicopter would appear with a Meo- or Lao-speaking American and a Meo or Lao representative on board. Frequently by the same afternoon rice and other supplies would begin dropping from the sky, wounded and ill were evacuated, and plans were being made for permanent resettlement. The promptness and sensitivity of the response had an extraordinary effect on the tribesmen, who until then in most cases had never in their lives received benefits from outside sources.

All of this activity was done in Vang Pao's name (although he also made it clear that he was an agent of the government and of the king), and he made full use of this ability to command American support as a means of strengthening his own appeal and his hold on his people. Much of that hold, however, grew out of his own character, which was open, direct, and volatile, but also firm. He shared the dangers of battle and appeared entirely fearless. He was generous and incorrupt; his personal fortune was considerable for a Meo but was not gained by taking "squeeze" in the immemorial fashion. The money promised to his men was paid to them, his rolls were not padded, and he saw that death benefits were distributed and dependants cared for when a family suffered loss. His honesty and faithfulness to commitments made him an entirely unusual military figure in Southeast Asia and accounted in good part for the willingness of his U.S. partners to support his movement generously.

At the same time, Vang Pao was not a Westerner but a Meo from Xieng Khouang who had come up through the ranks in the French and Lao armies. He understood his people and knew what impressed them. He punished cowardice, desertion, or betrayal severely, often by execution. His units sometimes took prisoners but often did not—a trait not uncommon in guerrilla movements. In extenuation, it should be noted that prisoners were particularly burdensome in the Lao mountains, where the normal structure could be penetrated by a fist or a stone. They were commonly kept in holes in the ground. Vang Pao also acted on occasion to cut off a village's rice supply if it had failed to meet its commitments, particularly in providing men for his military units. Nevertheless, he usually acted in accordance with Meo tradition, arriving at major decisions in council, after full discussions.

In spite of these qualities and his canny use of American support, Vang Pao was unable to unite the Meo, and some, even in areas to which he had good access, such as Sayaboury province and the strip of ridges just north of the Vientiane Plain, rejected his approaches. The fact is, the Meo of Laos had never been united, and deep clan divisions still separate them. Members of his own or Touby's clan joined readily enough, and those who had no clan reasons for standing aside were attracted for all the reasons described above. But some, for clan reasons, remained hostile and tried to keep their distance from both Vang Pao and the Pathet Lao. Still others could not be induced to give up their loyalties to Fay Dang and the PL. Even within his own movement, Vang Pao was challenged from time to time by groups who disapproved of his aggressiveness, his insistence on taking the offensive whenever he could, and baiting the enemy in his lairs. They viewed this as too costly in lives, and as time passed and the battles became ever more bloody, those of this persuasion grew more restive under his leadership. To the end, however, he maintained his position, and his appetite for battle; but on this issue he had some disagreements with Touby and lost some popular support. The numbers of soldiers he was able to field declined, not only because of heavy casualties but because some villages refused to send their quotas of men. In fact, reports were heard in Vientiane that some Meo had voted again with their feet and returned to their original homes, accepting PL rule rather than continue the fight. No figures are available on this trend but it undoubtedly took place. Toward the last years of the fighting, Vang Pao's forces dipped well below their maximum figure of about thirty thousand and were supplemented, as we shall see, from other sources.

Despite the presumed limitations of his background, Vang Pao had good understanding of the broader issues and thus perceived the futility of dreaming of Meo independence. Although often resentful of the Lao and scornful of Vientiane, he was loyal to his Lao friends—superiors and subordinates—and fitted readily enough into the loose military structure of the FAR. When his former patron General Phoumi Nosavan attempted a *coup d'état* in August 1964, Vang Pao refused his appeals and supported the government of Souvanna Phouma of which, as commander of the Second Military Region, comprising Xieng Khouang and Sam Neua, he became a pillar. He also had a particular sense of attachment to the king. When, in 1965, he came into possession of a shortwave transmitter and was able to organize regular broadcasts, he called it the "Radio of the Union of Lao Races." It broadcast news and propaganda in Lao and Lao Theung as well as Meo.[39]

Although we have spoken throughout this discussion of the "Meo resistance," the movement from its early days attracted Lao Theung and even some Lao who lived in the areas affected. While the native leadership and the driving force came largely from the Meo, many thousands of non-Meo hill people threw in their lot with the resistance, participated in the refugee program, and sent their men to fight in Vang Pao's units. Specific statistics are not available, but overall the refugee population of Laos in 1970, for example, was comprised of 40 percent Meo, 30 percent Lao Theung, and the remainder of other tribes and of Lao. The appeal of Vang Pao to these people, at least until 1967, would appear to reflect the desire to avoid Pathet Lao control and to share in the benefits the Meo movement was able to confer. In subsequent years, the intense bombing by U.S. aircraft added another motive, which was asserted by some to be the principal reason for the entire movement of refugees. One fact is certain: there were many refugees before bombing began and many more during the years when it was relatively light. Those who see the movement of the hill people as caused by U.S. bombing have greatly exaggerated some facts and have ignored the entire history here recounted.

The Lao Theung joined, as did the Meo, by decision of the entire village. Their men were incorporated into fighting units with the Meo and they provided some of the combat leadership. Numbers of Lao Theung were employed in the refugee and public health programs. Vang Pao's notion of a "union of Lao races" came close to realization in Xieng Khouang during the few years when the Meo resistance seemed on its way to success.

Was it Counterinsurgency?

If there is justification for considering the entire movement a counterinsurgency as well as a popular resistance effort, the positive programs provide it. Reverting to the earlier discussion of counterinsurgency doctrine, we can identify the factor of modernization, of combined American programs to engage the population in a multifaceted effort at the improvement of living standards and security to the point where the people are able and motivated to defend what, with American help, they have been able to achieve. On the other hand, although the program was in some ways a good illustration of the doctrine, too much should not be claimed for established American policies, planning, and concepts. The Meo resistance was entirely unplanned and grew out of a series of fortuitous accidents. Among them were the cultural traits and aspirations of the Meo people and the presence of native leaders who understood and were able to express those aspirations. Another was the presence of certain Americans, some of whose names are known and some not, who not only understood the needs of the situation but commanded the resources to permit the resistance to continue and did it with remarkable sensitivity to the special needs of the tribespeople. All of this was achieved with no conceptual baggage or conscious patterning on a theory or doctrine. It was a form of creative opportunism which nevertheless exemplified some of the underlying principles of the doctrine.

Still another factor responsible for the ability of the U.S. side to innovate effectively was the type of organizational arrangement which sprang up in the mission in Vientiane. The degree of unforced cooperation in the field was matched by the exceptionally close interaction of agencies in Vientiane to an extent not always found in U.S. missions abroad. Partly this was the accidental result of particular personalities preferring cooperation to competition, a quality which, however, varied as the personalities changed. What remained constant was the assertion of authority and close attention to management by strong ambassadors with a mandate from Washington to keep matters under their control. Ambassador William H. Sullivan explained to a Senate subcommittee in 1969 that to avoid the disunity that had characterized the Laos mission in earlier years, he, his predecessor, and his successor were all under instructions to maintain close control of U.S. personnel and operations. He also pointed out that owing to the absence of a U.S. military command in Laos, matters which were normally the responsibility of military commanders also came under the ambassador's authority. To make certain that all involved elements of the mission were fully aware of each other's activities and of his instructions, he held a daily meeting of agency heads, a most unusual practice which was continued by his successor.[41] The meeting was symbolic as well as functional, and when the rare officer appeared who did not understand the kind of cooperation expected of him, he was removed. Another series of accidents, therefore, brought about in Laos the centralized style of management that the doctrine held to be necessary to weld the heterogeneous efforts into a single program.

THE WAR RESUMES

The lull in the fighting that followed the signing of the Geneva Accords was briefly broken several times in early 1963 in skirmishes between the Meo and the PL/DRV. Then, in March 1963, fighting broke out between the PL and the neutralists on the Plain of Jars. Kong Le's units were driven from the eastern two-thirds of the Plain and persistent attacks were made against Meo positions. Although a patched-up cease-fire lasted unevenly on the Plain for another year, in the mountains overlooking the Plain and on the road leading to North Vietnam (Route 7), where the Meo had established themselves, the Communists attacked persistently with no pretense of cease-fire. The Meo soon abandoned their defensive posture and resumed the program of harassment which had been suspended the year before. (Quite certainly this was done with U.S. approval, for otherwise they could obtain no ammunition.) In August 1963, Meo units managed their largest exploit to date. At a point on Route 7 near Vang Pao's home village of Nong Het, and only a few miles from the North Vietnamese border, they destroyed a kilometer-long section of the road, blowing portions of it down the steep hillsides and causing rock slides to cover it at other points.[42] Although spectacular, the episode took place during the rainy season, when the road was not much used. Before the end of the year the damage had been repaired. The temporary loss of the road may have slowed the start of the 1964 dry-season offensive but it was not a serious blow.

The resumption of fighting also brought a resumption of recruitment by Vang Pao with U.S. approval. The general and his advisers had used the lull to reorganize the irregular forces, culling out older men and the physically unfit, and creating out of the remainder two categories of units, regional platoons and companies assigned to local tasks, and a species of strike force called a Special Guerrilla Unit, or SGU. This was a battalion composed of three line companies and a headquarters unit. Its arms were upgraded to include bazookas, medium-sized and even a few heavy mortars. Later it received pack artillery of the famous 75mm caliber and ultimately 105mm howitzers—truly an unusual weapon for guerrillas. These guns were moved by helicopters after being knocked down and were usually placed on hilltops to fire directly at their targets—a practice to make a professional artillery man cringe. The SGUs were directly under Vang Pao's headquarters and were used for major offensive or defensive purposes. In time they numbered over ten thousand out of a total irregular force of about thirty thousand.

Although setbacks occurred, the military trend in the ensuing period was narrowly favorable. After the mining exploit on Route 7, the PL/DRV concentrated on securing the vital section of that road connecting the Plain with North Vietnam. Methodically they moved against each of the Meo strong points, clearing them out one by one. Particularly south of the road, the area was too close to North Vietnam and to enemy bases in Laos, and could not be defended. In 1964 most of it was permanently lost, but a large part of the population left at the same time and resettled in areas around Long Tieng.

Somewhat farther north, however, Vang Pao discovered a soft area extending from the ridges overlooking the Plain deep into Sam Neua province. The PL/DRV presence was thinly spread in this zone and the population was ready to shift allegiance. While losing most of the area south of Route 7, the resistance movement balanced this off with a significant expansion into Sam Neua which continued in subsequent years until Vang Pao came into possession of the high ground overlooking Sam Neua town, the PL capital. His success was partly the work of a most unusual Lao soldier, a colonel named Thong who had been left behind and virtually forgotten by the FAR in the area of northern Xieng Khouang and southern Sam Neua provinces. Vang Pao reestablished contact with him and discovered that he and his men, together with another volunteer battalion under a Major Khamsao, had survived by living off the country and fighting a guerrilla-style war against the PL. With Vang Pao's support, Thong and Khamsao formed the spearhead of the return of government authority to Sam Neua province.

THE ANNUAL EXCHANGES

In the meantime, events in the area north of Vientiane in the spring of 1964 had left that capital city somewhat exposed. The final rupture of cease-fire took place in May when another PL/DRV offensive on the Plain of Jars virtually pushed the neutralist forces of Kong Le off the Plain, leaving them precariously perched with enemy both in front and behind them, for the PL still occupied an isolated enclave including the junction of Routes 7 and 13 and extending to within about thirty miles of Vientiane itself.

This situation brought on an unusual event in the rainy season (June to November) of that year. Government forces, both regular and irregular, abandoned the custom of remaining in their camps until the ground dried up and instead took to the offensive with surprising effectiveness. In normal circumstances offensive activity during the rains had been virtually precluded throughout Laos for lack of all-weather roads. The rains turned roads into quagmires and washed out bridges, thus preventing aggressive military activity. The factor that changed the pattern in 1964 was the availability of air transport by helicopter, STOL aircraft, and airdrop in support of the RLG's forces. Although clouds were heavy in the rainy season, the air was clear and visibility adequate for the low- and slow-flying aircraft in use. Indeed, it was better than during most of the dry season, when ground haze and smoke from the fires set by the tribesmen to clear their fields filled the air. Supported by the Americans, the RLG launched an operation to retake the junction of Routes 7 and 13, and reestablish ground links to Kong Le's forces perched on the western edge of the Plain at Muong Soui. Vang Pao's units participated in this offensive, which unrolled against virtually no opposition, for the zone had poor communications with Communist base areas and the North Vietnamese had withdrawn for the rainy season, expecting no serious military action in the wet months. As a result, the FAR initiative took all the objectives, gaining considerable material and territory.[43] Similarly, Vang Pao returned to the attack south of Xieng Khouang town and retook several locally important villages and positions.

Thus began a pattern that continued for five more years. The Communists sought to reduce Meo positions (and RLG-held areas elsewhere in the country) when the roads were passable, for they had become an entirely road-bound army, dependent upon wheeled vehicles to move their heavy weapons and to bring up their rice and ammunition. Because of these requirements, however, they were unable to move very far into the roadless hills in pursuit of the Meo before outrunning their supply lines. Their gains during the dry months, therefore, were limited to retaking certain accessible centers and were far from striking a mortal blow. Then, when the roads again became impassable, they withdrew the bulk of their strike forces and assumed a defensive posture. At this point the irregulars took up the attack and, facing a defensive-minded enemy, were often able to regain much of the ground lost during the earlier part of the cycle, thanks to their ability to move men and supplies by air. In effect, the war was largely confined to marginal areas between the heartland of the opposing sides, which, in some cases, changed hands twice annually.

Some commentators have described this recurring cycle as an accommodation, an unwritten agreement between the two sides to avoid causing each other serious damage. There is no evidence to support such a description which, besides, greatly underestimates the bitterness and determination of both antagonists. The pattern resulted from a condition of alternating marginal superiority briefly enjoyed by each side during the season that favored its particular strengths. Nor was the stalemate at the same level of intensity each year. Increases in firepower and troops by the PL/DRV in each dry season were balanced by increases in U.S. support to Vang Pao's forces to stiffen their defense and increase their offensive punch during the wet season. The pattern began to change only when the DRV undertook the expensive and burdensome task of building all-weather roads and also increased their forces to a point where they were able to leave their roadheads and move into the hills, depending on their own troops to porter the supplies necessary to maintain the offensive.

THE MANY ROLES OF THE U.S. AIR FORCE

Another major actor on the U.S. side entered the scene in 1964. With the resumption of hositlities in that year, the U.S. moved to strengthen the tiny Royal Lao Air Force by adding to its offensive arm a powerful World War II training aircraft, the T-28. At the same time, additional T-28s with RLAF markings but flown by Thai pilots were deployed secretly, mostly in support of Vang Pao's operation.[44] Both these activities were financed and guided by the U.S. through the agency of the USAF. Then, in 1965, regular bombing operations by the USAF itself against PL/DRV supply lines commenced in Laos, carried on by the 7/13th Air Force from bases in Thailand and, to a limited extent, by naval aircraft from the 7th Fleet in the Gulf of Tonkin. The USAF aircraft were stationed in Thailand for the purpose of bombing North Vietnam but some capability was available for use in Laos as a secondary mission.[45]

Thus began the curious marriage of high-performance jet aircraft with tribal guerrilla ground forces. The USAF greatly augmented the air support provided by the Lao and Thai T-28s; it also provided spotter aircraft to guide the high-flying jets. USAF personnel were assigned to Long Tieng to work with the intelligence staffs there, developing target information. Maintenance crews were also needed, as well as pilots, and gradually the numbers of air force men at Long Tieng increased to a sizeable figure, although precise numbers are not available.

Finally, some limited facilities were provided by the Meo resistance to assist the air force in its missions against North Vietnam. Thus, at several of the Meo forward bases, U.S. helicopters were stationed on standby to rescue downed American pilots in North Vietnam as well as in Laos.[46] Of greater significance was the decision to locate a navigational beacon and later a radar unit atop the 5,600-foot mesa of Phou Pha Thi, a notable geographical feature of Sam Neua which was a sacred mountain to the Meo. USAF personnel were permanently stationed at this outpost, guarded by a detachment of irregulars.

The involvement of Lao, Thai, and American air power served as an equalizer in the years 1965 to 1968, making it possible for the relatively lightly armed irregulars to slow down PL/DRV offensives in the dry months and regain much of the lost territory during the rains. The battles sometimes became intense slugging matches, with the irregulars performing rather like conventional infantry, attacking well-fortified and heavily defended hill positions and, with the help of the bombers, literally blowing the North Vietnamese out of their entrenchments. The air support was of a high standard, due in part to the terrain wisdom of the tribesmen and the excellent communications between ground and air. Some Meo became air guides, flying along in the spotter planes, and, after this experience, a few went on to become combat pilots in the RLAF.

This type of fighting, however, had a negative side for the Meo. The toll in lives was heavy and began to raise questions among some of the population. Furthermore, the use of irregular forces for such tasks was a misuse, strictly speaking, and when it succeeded beyond expectations it created an exaggerated notion of their capability. In truth, these battles were all very small affairs of at most one or two battalions on each side, and, as time was to prove, the irregulars could not be effectively used against competent regular forces of regimental or division size. Even though they might be able to concentrate sufficient numbers, they lacked the firepower and the experience in maneuvering sizeable forces.

THE POLITICS OF THE STALEMATE

Clearly this strange military sideshow cannot be explained except by reference to the larger purposes of the two principal powers involved in it. For the United States, in addition to such useful but secondary by-products as the radar and helicopter rescue facilities, the Meo resistance contributed importantly to its purpose of sealing off the Mekong Valley to afford a buffer for Thailand. It also served to insulate the Vientiane government from a direct Communist threat. Finally, it was a drain on North Vietnamese manpower and resources during the years when the strategy of the U.S. in Indochina was to grind up enemy fighting men until Hanoi's resources were exhausted.[47] On the other hand, the U.S. had no intention of seeking a military decision in Laos to determine the future of that country. The fate of Laos, it was assumed, would be decided by the outcome of the war in Vietnam—a position clearly stated, for example, by Ambassador Sullivan to the Senate Foreign Relations Sub-Committee.[48] Moreover, for the U.S. the most critical portion of the country was the region of the Ho Chi Minh Trail in the eastern panhandle, and here far more resources were lavished in the attempt to interdict the traffic than were invested in the Meo resistance. Unfortunately for U.S. purposes, the Meo did not live in the area of the Trail, and so the interdiction effort relied largely on air power, which, while it took a toll, did not succeed in cutting that vital artery.

As for the PL and the DRV, their interests did not entirely coincide, for the area was far more important to the former than the latter. Hence the long years of seesaw stalemate during which at any time the DRV could have, but did not, insert overwhelmingly superior force to eliminate the Meo resistance. As for the reasons for this restraint, we are able only to speculate, but logic suggests at least two factors at work. First, the DRV underestimated the difficulties. While it did steadily increase its inputs of men and resources into Northern Laos, it failed to anticipate the effect of U.S. escalations or judge accurately the increasing capabilities of the Meo. Secondly, even after the need became apparent, it did not accept the necessity for diverting the larger resources called for until the situation appeared to pose some degree of threat to the homeland. During the years 1962–1968 the DRV's minimum objectives in Laos, i.e., the use of the Ho Chi Minh Trail and control of all territory along its borders, were assured, and it too saw the war in Vietnam as the priority arena which would determine the fate of Laos. Very possibly the stepped-up air campaign and particularly the stationing of a U.S. military unit—the radar station at Phou Pha Thi—only a few miles from the DRV, finally raised the seriousness of the threat to a point which appeared to demand a strong response.

THE NORTH VIETNAMESE STRIKE FOR A DECISION

It is outside the purpose of this narrative to relate in detail the military course of the Meo resistance. We will therefore sketch only briefly the final tragic act of the drama. In the early dry season of 1967–1968 it became clear that a major Communist push could be expected in Sam Neua. Among the signs were major road-building activities which in these years became a prelude to large-scale PL/DRV moves. Later it was learned that substantial additional Vietnamese reinforcements, amounting eventually to eleven battalions, were being moved in.[49] In anticipation of a heavy attack, a decision was made to start evacuating the population, a tactic already tried on a small scale in previous years, and which now became a common practice.[50] The tactic had several advantages in that it avoided the mass panic that accompanied many earlier retreats and it reduced the hardship on the refugees. There was some military advantage as well in reducing the population base available to the enemy, particularly for service as porters, for this increased his dependence on roads and reduced the range of his attacks.

The 1968 offensive dealt a heavy blow to the Meo and to the United States as well for it resulted in the loss of Phou Pha Thi, including the U.S. Air Force installations there. Thirteen Americans were killed. The losses included most of Sam Neua province held by the irregulars, and although many positions were retaken in the following rainy season, they were held only briefly.

In 1969 a final break occurred with most previous restraints on both sides. The North Vietnamese brought into Laos the entire 316th Division, which had borne the heavy fighting in Laos but had usually been moved in and out in small detachments.[51] The timing of this movement made it clear that the North Vietnamese were prepared to stay in Laos and fight through the rainy season. They cleared the Meo from their flanks and pressed right across the Plain of Jars to attack the neutralist position of Muong Soui, symbolic of the neutralist claim to their former position of primacy on the Plain. They pressed the attack through the start of the rainy season and won the prize, whereupon Vang Pao fell upon their rear in the last major offensive he was able to mount. He put pressure on Route 7 near the Vietnamese border, and, after an intense air bombardment of the Plain of Jars in the first general air attack carried out against that target, he moved onto the Plain, completely surprising the enemy. The entire Plain and the town of Muong Soui were taken, along with much war booty.

It was the last great military success of the irregulars. As soon as they could rebuild their forces, the PL/DRV resumed the assault, this time augmenting their 316th Division with a large part of the 312th.[52] Their attack began in February 1970 and, despite heavy air support and adequate warning, General Vang Pao was unable to delay them even briefly. The irregulars had for some time and with some success been employed as shock-infantry in small battles and more was expected of them than they demonstrated on the Plain of Jars in February 1970. No doubt war-weariness had considerable influence on their performance, but in fact their units were not trained or equipped to meet a competent, professional enemy of division size on equal terms, and it was unrealistic to expect them to do so. If the retaking of the Plain of Jars is viewed as a major harassment, it was a partial success. Seen as an effort to take and hold key ground—as some saw it—it quickly failed.

Having retaken the Plain and Muong Soui, the North Vietnamese were for the first time within striking distance of the centers of the Meo resistance at a time of year when the weather favored them. This is the measure of the failure to delay the invaders on the Plain of Jars. If the irregulars had been able to fight a strong delaying action, the good weather would have ended once again before the enemy could strike at the heart of the resistance. As it was, the North Vietnamese had ample opportunity to move down on Sam Thong from the north and came so close that a hasty evacuation was ordered. Yet, as an indication of the difficulties the invaders had been struggling with for years in the inhospitable mountains, military observers estimated that of their twelve thousand men deployed against the Meo fastnesses, only two thousand were actually in the front lines pressing the attack. The rest were committed to portering supplies from depots at the roadheads.[53]

Nevertheless, the force was sufficient to cause grave upset to both the population and the headquarters of the Meo. The entire refugee population which had resettled around Sam Thong and neighboring Long Tieng—an estimated 110,000 people—was forced into a tragic exodus.[54] For many of them it was the third or fourth such experience. A new refugee relief center and government headquarters was quickly improvised in the mountains to the south, at a place called Ban Xon, but military headquarters, although reduced in size, was not moved. The defenses at Long Tieng were stiffened by the arrival of Thai volunteer battalions who were incorporated into the irregular forces under the command of Vang Pao and began to play an ever more prominent role in defensive operations.

For, as was frequently reported by the press at the time, the years of war had taken such a toll that the Meo resistance had exceeded the limits of its strength and was flagging. The steady drain of casualties had forced Vang Pao to call up thirteen- or fourteen-year olds. The veterans who still survived were weary and had little stomach to continue a fight which increasingly began to seem both endless and hopeless. The remedy adopted by the U.S. was to increase the intensity of the bombing, employing B-52s for the first time in the north and to bring in more Thai. The latter are estimated to have numbered as many as seventeen thousand at their peak in 1972. By these means, another stalemate was achieved. Sam Thong was retaken and lost again. Long Tieng, although seriously threatened, subjected to small-scale raids and mortar fire, never fell. When the cease-fire of early 1973 went into effect, the fierce seesaw fighting of the previous two years had produced little change in the battle lines. The principal effect had been to force most of the population that supported the resistance back into refugee status at a painful price in suffering and death.

THE COSTS AND ACHIEVEMENTS

Looking first at the impact of the experience on American objectives, the Meo resistance made significant contributions but also brought with it some clearly negative effects, making the net difficult to draw. The effect on internal Lao events was positive from the American point of view in that the resistance protected the Souvanna regime by holding off the Pathet Lao from the environs of Vientiane, permitting it to function free of an immediate military threat to its existence and of the undermining political effect of such a threat. Throughout all the long years of seesaw fighting and political maneuvering this had been the preeminent American objective in Laos: to keep in being the precarious neutralist solution which depended entirely on Souvanna Phouma, the symbol and embodiment of a middle way for this unhappy buffer state caught between two large spheres of influence. Unfortunately, as matters turned out, Souvanna at some point became unacceptable to the Communists, whose commitment to a truly neutral solution is subject to serious question. Nevertheless, on the international scene—the court of "international public opinion"—he and his regime still enjoyed the benefits of neutral coloration. The survival of the arrangement was also important because it avoided for the U.S. the difficult choices a right-wing regime, determined to confront and do battle with the PL, would have forced upon it.

The Thai also benefited, enjoying respite from the danger they saw were a Communist regime to be seated all along the further bank of the Mekong—and this was, of course, a matter of some importance to the U.S. as well. Finally, the U.S. gained from the drain upon the resources of its principal enemy, the North Vietnamese, particularly from the losses Hanoi suffered in manpower, which over the years certainly rose to a figure of many thousands. The short-term value of these positive factors was considerable, although they were far from being decisive gains and could not have been. On the other hand, the direct costs to the U.S. were not high and were largely in terms of money and material. Using criteria which were common at the time but have since fallen into disfavor, this secondary theater of the Indochina war was the most cost-effective. There were, however, indirect costs, to which we will return.

Shifting the appraisal to the point of view of the principal players, it is apparent that the Meo lost a great deal and that what they gained was certainly not worth the high price they paid. In terms of physical facilities, much that the tribesmen of the resistance had achieved—hospitals, many schools, dispensaries, markets, and the rest—has disappeared. Indeed, in the last few years of the fighting the battle had been so desperate that most of the positive and nonmilitary aspects of the resistance faded out. Vang Pao and his lieutenants were increasingly preoccupied with targeting air strikes, managing the details of the Thai influx, and directing large military operations. They had little opportunity to give thought to restoring the losses in education and the like.

At the same time, many of the gains could not be eradicated quickly. In effect, the resistance had flung the population of the north into involvement with the best and the worst of the modern world, death and suffering on a mass scale, along with mass education, public health services, organizational skills, and agricultural services which, although primitive, were a large step forward in contrast to what the people had known before. Although the tribespeople suffered extremely heavy losses, certainly well over twenty thousand dead from all causes connected with the war over a twelve-year period, and although many had elected not to stay the course and had filtered back to their original homes, accepting PL rule as the lesser evil, the experience made it certain that they would not again lapse into their traditional ways, content to remain in the mountains apart from the mainstream. They had lived through too much and had proved to themselves and to the other peoples of the region that they were able to master the demands of a more modern way of life.

Still, of equal importance to many of them was the fact that they had failed to achieve the goals for which they fought: equality and self-determination in local affairs. At this writing, the PL has achieved complete control of the Lao government and confronts the former participants in the resistance with only two choices: reeducation in camps established for that purpose followed by return to their home areas to live under PL domination, or flight and exile in an inhospitable Thailand. Increasingly, many are choosing the latter as the lesser evil, but the outlook for them in Thailand is poor indeed, for the government does not wish them to come or stay, and funds for their relief are steadily declining. The fortunate ones were some ten thousand—including all the principal leaders—whom the United States assisted at the time of the peace agreements and resettled in the United States or other countries of their choice.

Thus this tiny ally of the United States has been brought to a rather desperate pass while its powerful senior partner has little leverage left to protect and assist it. Among the indirect costs to the U.S. therefore, are the aftereffects of the ambiguous result of the Meo resistance. There is very little the U.S. can do to meet the undoubted moral obligation it has incurred, not so much because of monetary costs but because of its sharply reduced ability to intervene in the area. Unhappiness with this outcome has led some to criticize the U.S. sharply for involving the Meo in an unequal battle against a superior enemy, on the grounds that Washington should have been aware that the fight was hopeless, whereas the Meo, with their limited understanding of the total scene, could not have made their decision to join in full knowledge of the consequences. But, of course, at the time Washington did not know that the cause was hopeless. It saw the resistance as part of the larger battle against North Vietnam, and that was one in which it expected to gain the upper hand. In other words, this miscalculation was part of a larger one and only hindsight would argue that the opportunities offered by the Meo resistance should have been refused.

A criticism with more weight concerns the unplanned and improvised nature of the involvement and of its purposes which changed character several times, moving from a limited and provisional action related to internal Lao affairs to an open-ended campaign tied to the U.S.'s general objectives in Indochina. It has also been pointed out that the Meo resistance was a war fought as no other war in American experience, directed not by the military but by an ambassador and his staff, by a secret intelligence agency with the assistance of a relief and development organization. The characterizations are true but they are only criticisms to those unalterably wedded to the conventional ways of conducting government affairs. Others would say that it was only the unconventional and improvised nature of the resistance that made it possible. For such is the nature of large government bureaucracies and their tendency to follow established and familiar paths, that the Meo resistance would quickly have evolved into a simulacrum of the Vietnam war had it been planned and managed in conventional fashion, with the same inexorable tendency to draw the U.S. military into full involvement. Most certainly, the qualities which made it a counterinsurgency effort owed everything to the improvisations of talented American civilians in the field reacting sensitively to the exotic requirements of the program, without much thought to standard norms and expectations. This aspect would quickly have been smothered if the unique political context of the Geneva Accords, combined with Washington's intense focus on other theaters, had not left the field operators free to improvise and had not kept the military hierarchy out of the picture.

Among the indirect costs to the U.S. was eventually to have these achievements misunderstood while the Meo resistance was caught up in the public attack on all aspects of the Indochina war, its unique factors ignored, its nature distorted and misrepresented. The secrecy of activities in Laos was partly responsible, a secrecy which could not last and which ended at a time when the irregulars were in retreat, depleted, and weary, while the population was fleeing once again, with no end in sight to its sufferings. It was during this phase that the veils began one by one to be lifted. When the press and Congress and the public began to perceive the picture in some detail the critics of the war were not prepared to make any fine distinctions. Much attention was focused on the alleged role of opium in the conflict and on the impact of the bombing in creating refugees. The Meo irregulars were described as mercenaries, one item of proof being that they were paid slightly more than Lao regulars, and Vang Pao was depicted as a traditional warlord, concerned with power and pelf. The idea that the Meo had a right to fight and sacrifice for their own vision of their future was dismissed as unreal and the U.S. decision to support them as contemptible. In addition to ignorance of the origin and course of the resistance, these criticisms reflected the venom of the opposition to Vietnam and the ambiguous outcome of the resistance. Failure was an orphan in Laos as everywhere else.

Against the background of the facts, the Meo resistance is seen to have been a popular counterinsurgency movement which, in the context of a war of large dimensions, could not prevail against its enemies without greater help than the United States was prepared to offer. To say it should never have been permitted to exist and grow is to apply a lavish hindsight without regard to the realities of the time it was undertaken. And to dismiss it in the terms applied by the critics is particularly unjust to the sacrifices of the Meo people themselves in a cause which was also, at one time, ours.

6

Thailand: The Effort to Learn by Experience

★ ★ ★

The first signs of incipient insurgency in Thailand were noted by Washington in the early sixties, coinciding with the beginnings of the high-level interest of the Kennedy Administration in the problem. At the time, no overt violence was evident and Thailand to many observers appeared an unlikely scene for a repetition of the traumas of Vietnam, Malaya, and Laos. The Thai Communists were considered to be a tiny handful of whom virtually nothing was known except that they had no capability to effect the somnolent political life of Bangkok and even less to establish themselves in •the remote and primitive areas on the country's borders. Under ordinary circumstances, the initial reports of illegal propaganda and agitation centered in the northeast, near the Thai-Lao border, would have excited little interest, but, given the counterinsurgency sensitivities of the administration and the deepening crises in nearby Vietnam and Laos, Washington reacted promptly. Thailand was placed on the first list of countries whose situations were to be followed by the Special Group (C.I.)[1] and from this initial decision there stemmed a regular flow of reporting and program activity designed to prevent the situation from burgeoning into a full-scale threat.

In other words, the insurgency in Thailand was signaled and the signals were noted in the embryonic stage. Actions considered suitable to the threat were rapidly launched, well ahead of any serious crisis. In the years since, the situation there has at no time partaken of the crisis-ridden and often desperate tension typical of counterinsurgency elsewhere. Thailand was a place where a test was possible of the view that early prophylactic action is the secret of successful counterinsur-

169

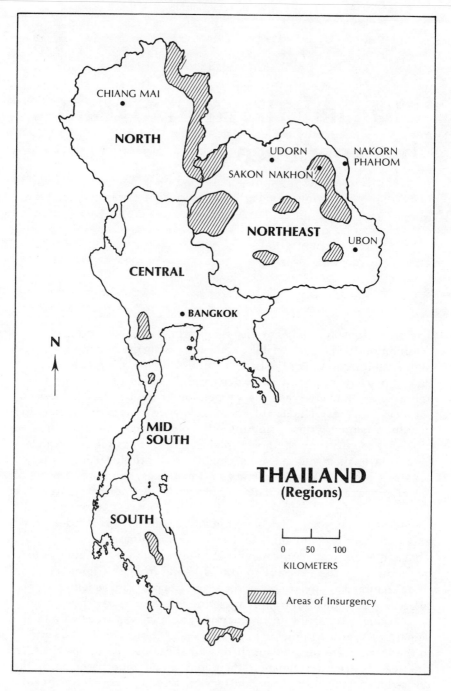

N

CHIANG MAI

NORTH

UDORN

NAKORN
PHAHOM

SAKON NAKHON

NORTHEAST

UBON

CENTRAL

BANGKOK

MID
SOUTH

SOUTH

THAILAND
(Regions)

0   50   100
KILOMETERS

Areas of Insurgency

gency. Now, after sixteen years of effort—declining in intensity since about 1970—the verdict can only be that counterinsurgency is a Chinese puzzle of dilemmas, where problem solving cannot follow a straight line between cause and cure, and that both the Thai and U.S. governments are far from mastering the methods by which their own prescriptions can be brought to bear. In both cases the realities of long-lived institutional inertia, of covert, unacknowledged priorities and persistent habits of mind, thwarted precisely the qualities of sensitive, innovative response, unified and controlled action on a broad front, which the varying doctrines call for.

Still, the insurgency, too, has moved slowly. It has suffered setbacks and, although growing, is today still a remote and minor problem for the government and much of the population. Apparently, the Thai jungle warriors bearing on their banners Mao Tse-tung's strange device have found their own country to be a puzzle, inhabited by people difficult to arouse and mobilize, who refuse, in fact, to respond in sizeable numbers as the doctrine calls for them to respond. Still, their theory prescribes "protracted war," which is an open-ended concept, infinitely extensible, and the loyal cadres do not flag in their efforts. Probably they will not until they win or die, or until, more remotely, their theory changes and they desist from insurgency to try some other approach.

The U.S. counterinsurgency effort in Thailand was not a major undertaking and should not delay us long before we turn to the largest and most difficult of all U.S. involvements, namely the second and enormously enlarged effort that was carried out in Vietnam. But precisely because it was deliberate and small-scale, the experience in Thailand is instructive. As in all our cases, however, some background is essential.

THAILAND IS DIFFERENT

The numerous surface similarities have misled many into seeing Thailand as posing a similar problem to the countries of French Indochina, with a similar fate threatening it. Thailand is in fact rather fundamentally different from Vietnam or Laos in ways bearing closely on the chances of Communist insurgency in the pattern of people's war.

All students of Thailand rightly dwell on the fact that in contrast to its ill-fated neighbors it has a relatively homogeneous population with a well-developed sense of nationhood and a common ethos centered around Buddhism and the king, who is a revered symbol of the values and traditions which most Thais accept. A concept exists of a "Thai way of life," which respects decorum and deference within an established hierarchy but also demands reciprocal support between levels and ranks of the system. National identity and ethos are thus firmly established.

The Thais also differ from their neighbors in having avoided absorption into the overseas empire of a European power during the age of imperialism. By adroit maneuvering between England and France, the two empires encroaching toward Thailand from opposite directions, Bangkok gave up some territory but gained acceptance by all parties as an independent buffer state. Limits were imposed on Thai sovereignty, but these were all lifted well before the Second World War. The experience has had psychological as well as other benefits. Thai relationships with modern Western powers are not shadowed by recollections of past inferiorities and slights; the Thai sense of identity was not crippled by the dominating presence of a powerful alien culture. Today, Thai governments deal easily with foreign guests and take for granted that they are masters in their own house. Moreover, dissidents and revolutionaries have not had the enormous advantage of a nationalist grievance against a foreign ruler to fuel their protests.

Whether for this reason or for others, Thailand seems, up to now, to have managed its modernization without suffering the dislocations and deep traumas that have occurred elsewhere. This may be because modernization moved slowly and, for the most part, involved a small elite centered in Bangkok, leaving the hinterland hardly affected in its fundamental attitudes and concerns. Nevertheless, under the leadership of their absolute monarchy, the Thais evolved Thai versions of all the modern institutions—military services, communications, government services, education, police, and courts. All this was done with the help of hired foreign advisers but under Thai direction, modified to suit Thai tastes. It worked reasonably well but cannot, for example, be compared with the revolutionary transformation of Japan from a traditional to a modern society. The Thai elite did not have the competitive drive of the Japanese and were satisfied with a system that left most of the country still living in traditional style.

THAI MINORITIES

Despite this considerable achievement, there are, of course, still many unsolved problems in modern Thailand. Most of them need not concern us, but others are highly germane to the origins of the insurgency, notably the existence of minorities which see themselves as disadvantaged compared with the majority. The Thai population divides into a mainstream and a group of minorities which geographically and politically are remote from the centers of influence and wealth. The mainstream Thais—the population of the great central plain extending north from Bangkok—enjoy a relative prosperity with rather little abject poverty and a reasonable social equilibrium. They also look upon themselves, and are regarded in Bangkok, as the "real" Thailand, inheritors of the country's proud religious and cultural traditions. In contrast, Thais in the great hinterlands of the northeast, the north, and the south, deep in the Malay Peninsula, are country cousins and have historically complained of the neglect and disdain that characterizes Bangkok's attitude toward them. Particularly in the northeast, where strong differences of dialect set apart the Thai-Lao inhabitants from Thais of the central plain, there is a tradition of bitterness and dissidence directed at Bangkok. This is nourished by the fact that the population and territory of the area are about a third of the whole, while the share of attention and funds from the central government is far from proportionate. The poverty in the northeast, where rainfall is lacking, is noticeably more general than in the central plain.

Added to the problem of "first-class" and "second-class" Thais is a further problem of non-Thai minorities, many of them hill tribes who inhabit the borderlands running along the frontiers with Burma, Malaya, Laos, and Cambodia. In the south we find Malay-speaking Moslems. Along the border with Laos and Burma the same hill tribes inhabit both sides of the frontier, including Meo and Yao, and the same is true of the Cardamon range of hills between Thailand and Cambodia. Toward all of these people Bangkok has commonly displayed an attitude of neglect and indifference. Certain laws fall particularly heavily on the northern hill tribes. Thus the regulations designed to maintain the productivity of the teak forests prohibit unauthorized felling of trees, which cuts across the practice of slash-and-burn agriculture by the tribesmen. The same is true of the prohibition against the cultivation of opium, which is the only feasible cash crop for numerous tribal villages. Such laws are not always enforced; often they are used as a threat by local officials to extract a bribe. Either way, they represent a highly resented burden.

The minority cultures in Thailand have no status protecting their language or affording special representation. The status of minorities as Thai citizens is not always clear and until recently some were simply considered illegal immigrants, who arrived unasked, pay no taxes, and are not entitled to government services. In general, few services are provided to any of the tribespeople although a recent decision was taken to grant citizenship to some. All dealings are in Thai, which few can read or write, and avenues into government or even public education are virtually closed. The resentments bred by such treatment have made certain of the tribespeople a potential source of support for an insurgent movement which could clothe its appeal suitably to their situation.

Other minorities of interest include approximately fifty thousand Vietnamese living in the Mekong River towns to which they fled thirty years ago when the French returned to Laos. They are not particularly welcome guests in Thailand since their loyalties are to Hanoi, and they have therefore been extremely careful not to play any overt role in the insurgency. The Chinese minority in Thailand is much larger, numbering several millions, and plays an important economic role in the business life of the country. It is considered one of the most assimilated Chinese communities in Southeast Asia, but it has also provided much of the leadership of the Thai Communist Party. Finally, we should note that the rural population of several provinces in the far south, bordering Malaysia, is largely Malay and Moslem. Here the government has made a somewhat greater effort to accommodate the special needs of this foreign culture. Nevertheless, a separatist movement flourishes and Communist influence has grown.

PATTERNS OF GOVERNMENT

During the postwar years government in Thailand rapidly evolved and expanded. Certain traditional patterns persisted, however, contributing to the resentments of the minorities and interfering with the impact of measures to deal with the insurgency after it broke out. These are the qualities we shall note, acknowledging that there is a great deal more to be said in a full treatment of the subject, which this does not purport to be.

The Thai government during most of the postwar period has been a nominally constitutional monarchy with actual power concentrated in the hands of a few senior military officers. During brief periods, a National Assembly has also existed, but each time it achieved some real power the military intervened and dissolved it. The latest such episode occurred in November 1976, ending three years of parliamentary rule. Atypically, both the overthrow of the military in 1973 and its recent return were accompanied by considerable bloodshed.

The government that emerged was in fact a dictatorship of bureaucrats—most of them military but some civilian—who maintained themselves in power by promoting the interests of the separate bureaucratic empires on whose support they relied. As one of the students of Thai government has pointed out, the principal private goals of a career bureaucrat are the undisturbed enjoyment of office, regular promotions, and, in status-minded Thailand, the unchallenged enjoyment of rank and its privileges.[2] The Thai government was thus not inclined to "clean house," or "crack down" on the large ministries or departments, nor undertake any reorganizations which were likely to change the distribution of resources or the weight of one group as against another. Stability was a prime objective of those who sat at the controls.

Another was the prevention of coups by political rivals. The entire bureaucracy, but particularly the police and the military, were under constant surveillance by various intelligence services to detect and neutralize plotting. In addition, the leadership took care to avoid giving serious offense to major supporters with control of significant resources (notably the police) or creating centers below themselves where major power elements could be linked together in a potentially threatening combination. By the process of occupying all key positions themselves, in fact, they insured that the power threads remained firmly in their grasp. For example, General Praphat Charusatharien during the final period of his years in power was deputy prime minister, commander-in-chief of the Royal Thai Army (RTA), minister of interior, and director-general of the Police Department. This device also served to avoid upsetting the intricate balance of power within the regime by bringing new potential competitors into the arena. As we shall see, these characteristics of the Thai system bore directly on the ability of the regime to react effectively to a challenge such as that posed by the insurgency.

Another quality of similar effect was the prevalence of corruption at every level of government administration.[3] Corruption has been the cement holding together the various cliques that form the building blocks of power. At higher levels of government it is associated with powerful industrial and commercial groups, many of them Chinese, who need favors to make large profits and are willing to share the proceeds. At the level where government services and public interact, it becomes a matter of small bribes for routine services. For those at the bottom of the heap, and particularly the villagers, this practice is often painful, especially in the villages where the police are frequently the culprits and where they sometimes engage in petty gangsterism. Such behavior does not build loyalty toward the representatives of government when insurgents appear and begin making their appeals.

The relationship between the center of government and the remote rural areas is another element in the complex of factors opening the way to insurgency. The regime, the bureaucracy, and the entire establishment are Bangkok-centered. Assignment to the provinces, especially in the police, has been traditionally considered an exile for which the only compensation is the chance to exact some tribute from the local populace. Although recently these attitudes have begun to change, it has been difficult for the leaders of the regime to accept the fact that events in the remote countryside and the attitudes of illiterate peasants can pose a serious threat requiring major governmental exertions. The neglect of such areas as the northeast and the remote south are very apparent and result in part from this attitude and also from the economic tendency to focus investment in the only area of the country—the capital region—where a large market and a strong infrastructure already exist. While the Bangkok area has grown strikingly since World War II, most other regions saw little improvement until after the insurgency began.

INSURGENCY BEGINS

As we have noted, dissident organizing activity began to be reported from the northeast as early as 1961, and in early 1962 Washington took its first steps to attempt to deal with it. Information was scanty at the time. Shadowy groups calling themselves by various names were denouncing the government as corrupt and indifferent to the needs of the people of the region. The Bangkok regime was attacked as a puppet of the Americans and the people were asked to support a movement to get rid of it. Propaganda, including "armed propaganda," recruiting, and training were the main dissident activities. Information developed later indicates that a meeting of the tiny Thai Communist Party, believed to have been held in 1961, adopted a decision to prepare the ground for armed insurgency in the Chinese pattern and that recruits were guided out of the country, across Laos and into North Vietnam for a course in guerrilla operations that lasted six to eight months.[4] This phase continued in the northeast for at least four years. Then, in 1965, the first armed outbreaks involving attacks on police posts, ambushes, and assassinations, signaled the start of active guerrilla warfare. The area initially affected was a remote jungle zone in the Phu Phan mountains comprising parts of several northeastern provinces. The scale was small; no more than a few hundred armed dissidents seemed to be involved. The pattern, however, seemed precisely based on the Maoist formula for people's war. In addition, a clandestine radio calling itself the "Voice of the People of Thailand" began broadcasting in 1962 from outside the country, reiterating the themes of the dissident propaganda activity.[5] It was at first thought to be transmitting from Hanoi but later evidence suggested China.

Indeed, it appears that the outbreak of armed dissidence was no surprise to the Chinese government, for Chen Yi, then foreign minister, had actually advised a French diplomat in Peking that precisely that would happen in Thailand in 1965.[6] This and other evidence has removed any doubt that the insurgency in Thailand is the work of the country's small Communist Party. It, in turn, has a close relationship with the Chinese Communist Party, which nurtured it into life and growth from its earliest days.[7] In early 1965 the "Voice of the People of Thailand" announced the formation of a new organization, the Thai Patriotic Front. Some time later, propaganda began referring to the insurgents as the Thai People's Liberation Army. In the villages where the movement was active the outline of a typical array of front organizations, grouping youth, women, farmers, and the like, became apparent.

In one important respect, the Thai insurgency differs from the expected pattern. It consists of several widely separated centers of activity, so scattered that little possibility exists of mutually supportive operations. Although part of the same movement, each of the separate components seems to have a separate line of communications and supply. Although we must assume a central direction existing at an unknown location, possibly as far away as Peking, the geography of the country and the location of preexisting dissident attitudes among the minorities on the periphery placed a major obstacle in the path of a tightly knit organization of the type preferred by the Communists. If they wished to proceed, however, they had no choice but to accept the handicap. Each of these dissident actions is a different war, and so we will discuss them separately.

The Northeast

The initial insurgent area, the northeast, has remained one of the two most serious local situations. From an estimated two hundred in 1965, armed guerrillas are currently estimated to have reached between fifteen hundred and two thousand.[8] The insurgents are favored by the existence of groups of villages where the population has long been alienated from Bangkok, and by the proximity of the area to Laos and to Pathet Lao–controlled territories which for years have reached close to the Mekong and today are firmly established along its banks. Their supply lines are thus reasonably assured. The Communist organization here has reached its highest point of development, especially in the range of hills called the Phu Phan, which are remote if not rugged. An estimate by Bangkok observers in 1972 placed the number of villages under insurgent control at 150, which would bring the northeast population governed by the insurgents above one hundred thousand.[9] The figure has probably increased in the intervening years. Also reported from the northeast is the existence of a part-time militia, groups called Village Military Units which, although as yet unarmed, supplement the full-time guerrilla force and maintain Communist authority. Terrorism clearly plays an important role in keeping many of these communities in line, for this technique of people's war is also a common tool of the Thai insurgent organization.

The first government reaction in the areas of the northeast where armed violence first appeared took the form of military sweeps which, however, were soon abandoned on principle for a more considered approach under a new organization described below. By 1967—that is, after two years—there was a noticeable falling off of insurgent activity, an unexpected development since the suppression campaign had not, in more obvious ways, appeared to be as effective as the results suggested. Insurgent activity continued at the same low level for more than three years, leading to some puzzlement and even premature self-congratulation. In fact, however, what seems to have happened was rather different from the appearance. When Bangkok reacted quickly to the outbreak of armed violence, many of the villagers involved in the support structure panicked, abandoning their homes and joining the guerrillas in the jungle, thus suddenly enlarging the forces which required support from the villages while simultaneously reducing the numbers providing support. Faced with a need for reorganization, the leadership in the northeast reacted coolly, withdrawing into their base areas where they proceeded to purge their ranks by sending those they found unfit back to their homes, in the meantime intensifying the training of the remainder until they felt ready to resume the initiative. In 1970 they quickly reestablished their continued capability by returning to the attack and have maintained an attacking posture ever since.

The episode suggests an answer to a debate which had been going on among analysts since the late 1960s, namely, whether there was a direct connection between the outbreak of the insurgency in 1965 and another event which began earlier in that year, the bombing of North Vietnam from bases in Thailand. On the one hand, it is clear that preparations had been under way for several years and that violence would have broken out at some point without reference to U.S. bombing. On the other hand, it appears that the decision to begin in the year 1965 was influenced by some event or consideration which caused the recourse to arms to be undertaken before the preparations were complete. Although we cannot be sure, it is possible that, as some claim, the extrinsic factor was the commencement of bombing, for there is no other event that provides an adequate justification for the considerable risks involved. But could there have been any serious hope that the bombing program would be affected by the insurgency of a few hundred poorly armed guerrillas? Probably not in so categorical a form. But as a harassment, aimed at distracting and giving pause to the government of Thailand in its commitment to the U.S., it may have seemed a profitable risk. We may speculate that this grasping at a straw was a gesture by their Chinese and Thai Communist brethren offered to—or insisted upon by—the North Vietnamese in return for help given in the past and promised in the future. A few small and ineffective attacks on American air bases were attempted in ensuing years, so halfhearted as to cast doubt on how seriously they were intended. By and large, we are safe in assuming that the Thai guerrillas had no intention of seriously provoking the United States in a direct way, given the embryonic state of their movement.

Be all this as it may, after some eleven years of violence, the insurgents, or Communist terrorists (CTs), as the government prefers to call them, have a small but firm organizational base, a military arm, and a political infrastructure in the northeast which continues to increase slowly in size. They control base areas in the Phu Phan area and provide a competing government authority for a certain number of rural villages. Although harassed by the government they have not yet received a mortal or even a crippling blow and give every sign of intending to persist in their efforts as long as necessary.

THE NORTH

At about the same time that violence began to drop off in the northeast, insurgency made its appearance in a new area, the far northern provinces, particularly Nan and Chiengrai, both lightly popu- lated, remote, and rugged regions bordering the Mekong. The insur- gents here were not Thai but tribesmen, mostly Meo. The areas across the Mekong in Laos from these centers of insurgent activity were controlled by Pathet Lao, and logistics and safe training areas were thus assured. From a small beginning, this guerrilla nucleus grew steadily until it became the largest and militarily the most effective insurgent group. By 1974 the total number of armed men in the guerrilla forces was estimated at about twenty-five hundred with another eight hundred unarmed village militia.[10] Their weapons were up to date, including the Soviet-designed AK-47 assault rifle, rocket-launchers, and mortars. By 1972 the guerrillas had moved their base areas and training sites into Thailand from Laos, and some seven districts of Nan and Chiengrai had been virtually abandoned to insurgent control, government forces only venturing there in heavily armed contingents. The government has tried a variety of approaches (described below) from bombs and napalm to resettlement. It finds the tribal guerrillas an extremely tough military nut to crack. Moreover, it has made no notable progress in finding a place for the tribesmen in the Thai scheme of things, so they have remained susceptible to the appeals of the insurgents.

For the Thai government, however, an important consolation is the apparent inability of the insurgents to expand their movement from its limited tribal support base to include the Thai population living in the upland valleys of the north. Very likely because the movement appears to the local Thai as an affair of the tribesmen, an obstacle has been created to broadening the appeal to include the main ethnic group whose support is essential if the insurgency is to spread. The dilemma was not unlike that that brought failure to the insurgency in Malaya, where ethnic cleavages barred the spread to the Malayan majority of an essentially Chinese movement.

One area of tribal insurgency was of especial concern to the Thais. It comprised parts of three provinces (Loei, Petchabun, and Phitsanulok) between the north and northeast centers of guerrilla activity. Here, violence in the now routine pattern broke out in 1968. Although smaller than the outbreak in the neighboring areas, it was of special concern because the area bordered on the central plain and represented the closest approach of the insurgency to the Thai heartland. The terrain is exceptionally difficult, and a large military operation undertaken in 1972 failed to reduce the CT redoubt area. (The operation had some significant implications and will be described later.) The total number of insurgents operating here is not known, but the best guesses place it in the region of four hundred.

THE MID-SOUTH

This area, in the elbow of the Malay Peninsula, is also remote from Bangkok, and its Thai population considers its treatment by the government to be that of second-class citizens. Estimates place the number of insurgents at about four hundred, a figure that has been virtually static for some time.[11] These insurgents are not well armed compared to their comrades farther north, for they are remote from any ready source of supply. Nevertheless, they are a tough and determined group, having survived against the efforts of the most effective of Thai regional commanders, General San, who alone of RTA field leaders maintained a consistent and coordinated attack. San kept the guerrillas on the run, arresting the growth of the movement; but in spite of these problems the insurgency retained its hold on its followers and maintained an aggressive posture.

FAR SOUTH

This area of Thailand is not only distant from Bangkok but economically and ethnically resembles neighboring Malaysia more than it does the rest of Thailand. Rubber plantations and tin mines provide the basis of the economy, and the population includes large numbers of Chinese and Malays. It was here, in jungle areas along the Malaysian frontier, that the Malaysian Communist Party took refuge in the late 1950s after its insurgency was suppressed. Since that time it has not only maintained its existence but increased in size, exploiting its foothold as a base for operations back into Malaysia. The group numbers close to three thousand armed men, and, despite joint operations of the police of both countries, they have never been in serious danger of suppression. Bangkok pays lip service to the goal of suppression, but avoids serious pursuit of this determined force, accepting the excuse that it is not directed against the Thai government and therefore represents no threat. For some time the MCP has been organizing among the Malay-speaking Moslem communities of the area to broaden its base. The combination of Chinese guerrillas with Malay community support could pose a serious threat if it were turned against the Thai authorities. Since this has not happened, the far south can be considered a special situation without direct relation to the insurgencies proceeding elsewhere in Thailand.

In sum, then, the four centers of dissidence just described, together with a few other small and scattered nuclei, comprise the Communist insurgency that has been active in Thailand since 1965. The total number of regular armed guerrillas can be estimated at between fifty-five hundred and six thousand (disregarding the MCP contingent), and, in addition, there are some thousands of part-time village militia. The population base which supports this guerrilla force may be in the neighborhood of two hundred thousand. Such a movement would not seem to amount to a serious problem for an authoritarian regime controlling a population of forty million, with a modern army of nearly one hundred and fifty thousand men as well as a considerable air force and a police arm of over seventy thousand. In addition, since the insurgency began the Thai government has enjoyed hundreds of millions of dollars of American military and economic aid, not to mention advice and technical assistance in the training and application of its men and resources. Nevertheless, the insurgency has maintained itself, refined and improved its organization and skills, and grown slowly in size. The difficulties it has faced seem related more to the equilibrium and stability of the Thai society than to the countermeasures of the government.

THE COMMUNIST SUPPRESSION OPERATIONS CENTER

The reasons for the failure of the Thai government to master the insurgency are complex. To understand them, we need to look at both the Thai effort and that of the United States, which made important contributions and had substantial influence over the Thai. The Thai response developed in several phases; as the problem became more serious, changes were made in the government's approach, and in time a doctrine was elaborated which showed some American influence but also reflected uniquely Thai attitudes and concerns.

The first Thai counterinsurgency measures came very early in the first phase of insurgency—so early that one is entitled to ask whether it reflected a genuine acceptance of the threat or an effort to please and impress the new Kennedy Administration. In 1961, Field Marshal Sarit Thanarat proceeded to form a new component of the Supreme Command of the Armed Forces (something like the American Joint Chiefs of Staff) called the National Security Command (NSC) and assign to it responsibility for dealing with the first manifestations of insurgency then beginning to be reported from the northeast. The program activities of this command reflected the new emphasis on military civic action in the United States armed forces, not surprising in view of the close relationship between the U.S. and the Thai military systems and the steady flow of Thai trainees through U.S. military educational and training centers. The chief activity of the NSC was the Military Development Unit program (MDU). Teams were formed, largely of military personnel, to provide assistance to remote villages in the form of small-scale public works, medical services, education, information and propaganda, and the like. An MDU would move into a group of villages and stay for some months; and, in fact, in later years they began to be virtually permanent. About three teams a year have been formed since 1962, and the total is now nearly forty. The program was well intended and has grown steadily, but even now, after more than fifteen years, no one can say much about its impact on the insurgency. It would appear, however, that the scope is still too small compared with the need for it to be considered more than a partial success.

An even more ambitious program that was launched before the outbreak of active insurgency also attempted broad improvements in the rural environment in affected areas. Started in 1964 and called Accelerated Rural Development (ARD), it was designed to equip provincial government with the resources and skills to carry on permanent, medium-scale public works such as road building and well digging. The U.S. mission had considerable influence in bringing the Thais to perceive the need for exceptional efforts in rural development as a prophylacic measure against the threat of insurgency. No doubt the offer of substantial assistance to get the program under way was an important factor in persuading the Thais to move ahead at a time when the threat was far from serious.

We will have more to say about ARD shortly. At this point we wish to note several characteristics of the program which revealed themselves at the beginning. First, of course, is the early start, a factor which should have conferred advantages. Second is the emphasis on rural development and on propaganda and information even before a fully worked out doctrine existed. Third is the failure to establish a single organization under a leader with full powers over all aspects of the program. Thus the MDUs were under the Supreme Command. ARD was first located under the logical office, the Department of Local Administration (DOLA) within the Ministry of Interior, of which the minister was General Praphat Charusatharien, who at the time was also deputy prime minister and one of the two men at the head of the regime. When it became clear that long-standing interagency rivalries were interfering with ARD's effectiveness, Praphat solved the problem by moving the new activity into the prime minister's office and appointing himself head of the policy committee.[12] This device was a typical solution, for it avoided upsetting delicate power balances among existing institutions and kept the threads in the hands of those at the top. But since the leaders of the regime were unable to devote their full attention to the problem, the result was the scattering of the new resources among different departments which were not effectively coordinated. Some of the advantages of an early start were thus lost, sacrificed to the higher-priority political objectives of stability and power balance.

After the commencement of the violent stage of the insurgency, the Thais quickly realized that rural development and propaganda were now insufficient. After a brief period of resort to the reflex action of military sweeps in the affected area of the northeast, a decision was taken to establish yet another new agency while leaving the existing organizations to continue their work largely as before. The new entity was named the Communist Suppression Operations Command (CSOC)* and its main responsibility was to plan and conduct suppression activity nationwide, although it, too, had funds for small-scale rural improvement and propaganda. Most important, in its early phase CSOC was given an unusual delegation of authority, namely, command and control of the police and military units placed under its authority.

CSOC was largely the work of Saiyud Kerdhpol, a young army general who had spent several years in U.S. military schools. He had also been influenced by studies of the British experience in Malaya, and the organizational scheme he worked out reflected that background. The central concept was the establishment of a framework for a coordinated effort by civilian, police, and military services linking Bangkok to regional headquarters and then to the combat areas. The system, called CPM, established suppression centers, usually under a military officer but including representation from local government and the police, in all the affected provinces and regions. Several regional intelligence offices (Joint Security Centers, or JSCs) were also established to combine the inputs of the various intelligence services working in the affected areas. In Bangkok, the heart of the system was an operations center with intelligence and psychological warfare centers attached. General Saiyud was director of operations, reporting to a chief of staff who (in a fashion typical of the Thai system) was also chief of staff of the Royal Thai Army.

Formed in late 1965, CSOC organized itself in 1966 and drew up an ambitious operational plan for 1967. It was based on the concept of target

*After the overthrow of the military regime, it was renamed Internal Security Operations Center (ISOC). For simplicity's sake, we will refer to it throughout by its original initials.

areas—groups of villages that were geographically linked and similar in other ways. Local defenses were organized based on an existing militia strengthened by police personnel. Propaganda campaigns were begun along with efforts to improve the local invironment with small-scale projects. As intelligence developed, platoon- and company-sized units were supposed to begin seeking out the guerrilla bands.

There were many flaws in the execution of CSOC's plan (called 09/10 from the years of the Buddhist calendar during which it was to unfold). Intelligence was faulty, and, despite the efforts of the command, pressure on the insurgents was intermittent and cooperation between services was lacking. Nevertheless, it represented in concept a sound realization of the essence of most counterinsurgency doctrines. The suppression effort was multifaceted and theoretically unified under a single command. The tactics prescribed were those of the guerrilla; air power and artillery were deemphasized. Small units of foot soldiers were the main reliance in carrying the battle to the enemy, avoiding the civilian population. CSOC, however, stumbled over an obstacle that had little to do with doctrine or execution. As the campaign wore on through 1967, Saiyud called on the regular army for the assignment to his command of more infantry, having considerably underestimated the requirement. This gave his opponents, some of whom felt the approach to be far too gingerly and others of whom were personal enemies and members of opposing military cliques, to point out that Saiyud and CSOC were acquiring an undue degree of power and that the RTA was losing control of too many of its own troops.

To avoid a serious split within his major constituency, Praphat again reorganized. Once more, he left the new entity to continue aspects of its work, but CSOC lost its command authority and became a planning and advisory staff. Although it disposed of a sizeable budget, operational control was transferred to the Thai Army and exercised through regional military headquarters. Within their regions (called Communist Suppression Operations Regions, or CSORs) the Army commanders were given authority over all resources related to insurgency suppression, including the CPM centers and the JSCs. In theory they were proconsuls, in control of the police, the civilian participants, and all CSOC assets.

Praphat's reorganization was a polished stroke of bureaucratic politics. He had left the body of CSOC untouched, merely removing the heart. Authority and control were now in the hands of traditionalists who were also prime beneficiaries of the "bureaucratic polity." Although if sufficiently stung by the guerrillas CSOR commanders might react violently, for the most part they would be reluctant to use their nominal authority aggressively or to insist upon full cooperation and support from other services. Such behavior was contrary to custom, disturbing to the smooth functioning of the system, and might bring the instigator to the unfavorable notice of Bangkok. Moreover, the incurring of casualties was also frowned upon. Being primarily a political instrument, the RTA did not see its routine duty to lie in fighting and other forms of martial behavior. For the most part, therefore, the managers of the counterinsurgency apparatus were content to go through the motions, reacting defensively when attacked, but avoiding the discomfort and tedium involved in keeping up a steady pressure on the enemy.

A FORMAL DOCTRINE

During this period a more formalized counterinsurgency doctrine was evolved and promulgated. As a formal statement of intent it was quite enlightened although in actuality it was often ignored or casually brushed aside. Broadly, the doctrine separated the effort into two types of activity—passive and active. The former covered programs directed at improving living conditions in the affected areas, and the latter included suppression activities and related programs such as intelligence. The "active" aspects were to be based upon the guideline "the people are the target," the enlightened view that operations were to be conducted so as to spare the people and if at all possible in a manner to engage them in the cause of the government. Underlying the doctrine was a strong feeling that it was wrong for Thais to undertake systematic violence against other Thais, often rationalized with the claim that the insurgents were, after all, not really Thais at all. In practice, the Thai counterinsurgency effort carried out the "passive" aspect of the doctrine with consistency and a considerable cumulative input of resources. On the suppression side, however, the doctrine was used to excuse the persistent failure to maintain steady military pressure. The preferred approach of most CSOR commanders consisted of propaganda combined with attempts to seal the loyalty of the villages by good works. The problem, needless to say, lay in the serious commitment to violence of a small group of men on the other side who could not be persuaded of their errors by means short of effectively used military power (not, of course, to be confused with indiscriminate exploitation of superior firepower).

At the same time, the Thai military did occasionally lapse into the unleashing of its firepower in a set-piece conventional operation. Usually it was aroused to such measures by frustration or impatience and usually the area selected was the north, where the opponent was not Thai but a variety of hill tribes. When the violent phase of the insurgency spread to the north in 1968, the military's first resort was to unobserved artillery fire, air attacks on villages with napalm, and the forced movement of populations into refugee camps. After a few months Bangkok called a halt to such aberrations from the doctrine, a commendable decision which, however, was not followed up by any systematic tactical effort.

The suppression effort then became a matter for each regional commander to work out according to his own concepts of what his situation called for and his capabilities permitted, within the general confines of the doctrine. In the northeast, the pattern established by CSOC's original 09/10 plan was maintained, new target areas being added as necessary, but in other respects little was changed except that the driving spirit once imparted by General Saiyud was absent and the program became routine and defensive. In 1970 the Cambodia crisis led the regime to withdraw some of the RTA units assigned to suppression operations in the northeast and to concentrate them along the border with Cambodia, thus further limiting the capabilities of the regional commander to operate aggressively. In the north, where the military situation was even more difficult, little was done in terms of active suppression operations, although a plan existed calling for an "oil-spot" technique, building strength outward from the Thai-inhabited upland valleys.[13] In the mid-south, as we have noted, General San was able to generate more consistent pressure, working closely with the police and civilian authorities. But his example had little effect on his fellow commanders in the more critical areas. Indeed, he was subject to some criticism in Bangkok for being overly aggressive and suffering casualties as a result.

Beyond these regular suppression activities, the RTA did begin a pattern of annual large-scale but short-term operations which were in part considered training exercises. The largest of these took place in early 1972, when the entire RTA First Division, an elite unit normally quartered in Bangkok, was moved to the north central region with the objective of attacking a guerrilla concentration estimated at four hundred and seizing its base area, a rugged redoubt called Hin Long Khla. The First Division moved out with all its equipment and copious air support and promptly bogged down. The operation was extended repeatedly, losses mounted, most of them from land mines and snipers, and finally it was terminated around midyear with public claims of victory. In fact, the redoubt area was not taken, no known casualties were inflicted on the insurgents, and the First Division lost between three hundred and six hundred men killed and wounded.[14] Later annual exercises were not quite so ambitious, and one conducted in 1973 was more successful, but the technique had little permanent effect. It was conventional in concept; reliance was on firepower and battalion-sized operations. When the military left the scene the guerrillas were quickly able to reestablish themselves. The principles supposedly underlying the counterinsurgency effort—combined and unified programs, focus on the population, persistent pressure—were all ignored. They were too complex and too unconventional for the system to carry out in the absence of leadership that understood them, endorsed them, and gave them priority over other goals.

This tactical aspect of suppression was without doubt the weakest side of Thai counterinsurgency, which taken as a whole was broadly conceived and not unimaginative. Although the weakness was critical, it is unfair and inaccurate to dismiss the whole effort as ineffective because of this failure. In both the "active" and "passive" sides, the Thai government made serious and in many cases effective efforts to improve the capabilities of the relevant government services—notably the police, local administration, propaganda, and information. It was in this area, and in the military, that the United States made its largest counterinsurgency inputs in material assistance, training, and advice. The various aspects of the U.S. program had differing degrees of success, but without doubt the overall contribution was a significant one. We turn therefore to the American effort, dealing first with the organization which was designed to combine and unify the contributions of the separate agencies.

The U.S. Organization

As we have pointed out, the counterinsurgency program in Thailand developed after considerable experience in Vietnam and embodied some of the lessons its designers believed had been learned in the larger arena. A principal figure in these events was the ambassador, Graham Martin (who served from 1963 to 1967), a strong believer in ambassadorial control over all parts of his mission. In 1966 he established an office called the Special Assistant for Counterinsurgency (SA/CI) and made in writing an unusual grant of authority to its head, delegating "complete responsibility to insure that there would be a single American voice speaking with those elements of the Thai government also concerned in counterinsurgency operations."[15] A memorandum by Martin's successor, Leonard Unger, stated that the SA/CI "will have the responsibility, under my supervision, for formulating and defining counterinsurgency doctrine, developing new programs, coordinating field programs, assessing and reporting on the prospective course of insurgency and assuring the consonance of all Mission programs and activities with that doctrine."[16]

Officers and other staff assigned to SA/CI eventually numbered about seventeen. The first incumbent, Peer de Silva, detailed from CIA, and his successor, George K. Tanham of the Rand Corporation, were senior men with previous experience in Vietnam. Both believed strongly in the principle of a unified program and labored in different ways to establish a firm centralized direction over the highly varied U.S. program mix. This task of unifying the American voice was accomplished, as were most of the other goals. The mechanism faltered, however, in the gray area discussed in an earlier chapter, that of creating a centralized command. Here the perennial problem remained that of the authority of an ambassador to control or manage the resources of an independent agency accountable to a separate command in Washington.

Nevertheless the SA/CI was able to police such matters as adherence to a cardinal principle of successive ambassadors which was also based on experience derived from Vietnam: the avoidance of direct U.S. participation in operations. "I do not think," said Ambassador Martin to a Senate subcommittee in 1969 "that when the Americans, who are an impatient people, become involved that we must necessarily take over."[17] As officially pronounced, "Advisers are specifically forbidden to go below battalion level, to go on any CI operation whatsoever, or enter by any means areas where fighting is going on or danger is imminent. Advisers do not plan or engage in military operations. They may give general advice but do not devise plans."[18] Military leadership enforced these restrictions (without necessarily agreeing with them) and they were generally honored.

The policy had the additional purpose of asserting civilian control of the program. The designers of the SA/CI system were convinced that the dominance of the military in Vietnam was responsible both for the overmilitarization of the program there and for the assumption by Americans of responsibility and initiative which belonged in the hands of the threatened government. To this purpose of preventing military dominance, the SA/CI organizational device made a major contribution. During the years when the huge military presence loomed over every other institution in Vietnam, the counterinsurgency support effort in Thailand was managed by civilians, with the military filling a carefully limited role.

A further theme of the SA/CI, especially under the second incumbent, George K. Tanham, was emphasis on the development of "human resources," in contrast to the tendency of most U.S. aid programs to focus on the transfer of hardware and equipment. In practice, the policy came down to according priority to training programs as a principal activity. The theme was formalized in the slogan "train the trainers," with a view to eliminating the need for U.S. involvement as early as possible. One instruction on the matter read: "All personnel engaged in formulating and implementing U.S. training programs should work toward the primary objective of training Thai instructors to train Thai. Direct training is an exception to policy; any exception must be approved by the Embassy."[19]

To provide a tool to establish a common understanding of the various policies and for enforcing them, the SA/CI developed and promulgated a set of written guidelines. The device seems an obvious one, but in fact it was never adopted in similar circumstances elsewhere because of the difficulty of bringing about agreement on the details by all concerned. That fact alone suggests the nature of the problem the guidelines set about to solve. They emerged from a lengthy drafting and coordinating process which tended to confirm the doubts of the skeptics, but, nevertheless, once completed they proved useful in assuring compliance with the rules and principles of the program.

Other devices were adopted to the same purpose, such as regional meetings of American field personnel, and met with success, although there were some instances where insufficient resources or interest brought failure. All in all, within the limits resulting from the concept itself and the nature of the ambassador's authority, the SA/CI imposed necessary discipline and unity upon the U.S. effort.

Its achievements were particularly noteworthy in view of the absence of any counterpart organization in Washington to support its views and policies within the Washington bureaucracy. Despite this handicap and due largely to the persistence of the two successive incumbents, the SA/CI imposed a notable restraint on American counterinsurgency activities in Thailand together with, or perhaps as a result of, continued civilian dominance. The adoption of the "Guidelines" was a genuine achievement, and its tough restrictions were made to stick by virtue of persistent policing by the SA/CI. Among examples that could be cited were its insistence that the Thais be assisted only to the point where they became capable of relying upon themselves, whereupon the assistance was withdrawn. U.S. help for the CI Training Center which retrained the entire Provincial Police was withdrawn after the commitment to "train the trainers" had been met. U.S. military attempts to develop and prolong U.S. civic action in the vicinity of air bases was resisted and discontinued.

Less tangible but equally important was the influence achieved over the Thais by the device of centralizing U.S. advice on counterinsurgency through a single channel. Thus the CSOC northeast operational plan of 1967 (which continues in effect at this writing), with its emphasis on combined efforts and small-unit operations, was shaped by the advice of the SA/CI.[20] The same was true with respect to continued emphasis on the CPM concept and the avoidance of reliance on firepower alone and to other salutary aspects of the Thai program.

After some four years of experience, the SA/CI was dissolved. The duty of coordinating the effort on behalf of the ambassador was assigned to the deputy chief of mission while a small staff continued to monitor programs and keep track of Thai activities. This represented a downgrading of the function and an end of the experiment of an ambassadorial alter ego focusing full-time, with the aid of an adequate staff, on the unifying, policy-formulating, and monitoring functions. The concept had never aroused enthusiasm among the foreign service professionals. Its elimination was a reversion to a pattern more agreeable to them and to their understanding of their traditional function as coordinators, i.e., the negotiation of treaties among independent entities.

We should be clear, however, that the SA/CI was itself only a partial realization of the concept of centralized authority for counterinsurgency. It went as far as the ambassador could take that purpose without presidential support and congressional consent. The next step toward more complete unification was to give to a new central entity control of the resources, personnel, funds, and equipment of the participating agencies, involving it in the day-to-day management of operations. Such a radical departure from government norms needed a true and a major crisis before sufficient support could be generated to break through the barriers of established practice and interests, something which happened only once—in Vietnam in 1967.

THE PROGRAMS OF THE THAIS AND THE AMERICANS

A few Thai counterinsurgency programs were initiated and carried on with little or no American involvement. One program—information and propaganda in the provinces—was initiated by the Americans and carried on for some seven years largely by the Americans on behalf of the Thais. These were atypical, however, for most counterinsurgency programs have been joint, with the U.S. providing advice, equipment, and training, and the Thais providing and paying personnel and assuming other local costs. In some cases the U.S. took the initiative in proposing ideas which the Thais endorsed more or less enthusiastically. There have been cases, however, when the Thais have gone along without enthusiasm merely because the Americans were anxious to launch the proposed effort and were willing to pay the costs. An example is the Military Research and Development Center. The concept of research as a tool in dealing with insurgents was not an obvious one to the Thais and seemed, in fact, a very American notion with little point in Thailand. Eventually it won their support and became a permanent institution, but initially they went along because it cost them little, brought them some equipment, and pleased the Americans.

IMPROVING RURAL LIFE

The counterinsurgency programs fall into two categories which in Thai parlance were designated "passive" and "active" and which Americans usually called development and suppression. The first category had the purpose of drawing the rural population closer to the government by improving the standard of life in a wide variety of ways. In some development programs the emphasis was on a quick, one-shot injection of assistance with little local input, such as the civic action work of the Military Development Units. Others carried out major, long-term projects such as highway and dam construction. Still others focused on creating or improving institutions serving the rural areas.

There is no need to describe all of these programs in detail. We will simply list and briefly note the purpose of the most important. Heading the list is Accelerated Rural Development, which we have already mentioned, and to which we will return shortly. Another early program was called Community Development, an effort to develop a capability in the villages to organize and carry out small projects desired by the villagers. Propaganda and psychological activities comprised a group of programs, including an American-run activity in the provinces which was eventually taken over by a new Thai entity, the National Information Psychological Organization. At one time USIS operated eleven outposts in the countryside and supported a sizeable program of Mobile Information Teams traveling throughout the affected areas. Also under this heading we should note CSOC propaganda activities closely related to the suppression effort and several radio broadcasting stations operated by the National Security Command.

A key institution in the rural areas, the Department of Local Administration, was brought to recognize the need to improve its capabilities and performance. On its own it founded a *Nai Amphur* (District Chief) Academy, to modernize and institutionalize the training of district chiefs. Later a course was set up at the academy for deputy *nai amphur* and a program evolved for a course for provincial governors. These were examples of Thai initiative with little U.S. input. Similarly, DOLA began a program of regular meetings of the representatives of the many ministries (Health, Education, Agriculture, and the like) stationed in the provinces.[21]

Finally, we should note the existence of the Public Welfare Department, relevant because it was responsible for some of the limited government efforts to cope with the problems of the tribal populations. Its tribal programs, consisting of development centers and resettlement centers for refugees, were unfortunately poorly funded and unevenly administered, but they did constitute recognition that a problem existed and were a basis on which better programs could be built.

In addition to this array, all of which sprang up in response to the insurgency, the conventional activities of the old-line ministries and departments—highways and other aspects of the Ministry of National Development, Health, Education, and Agriculture—were all gradually increased and refocused to reflect in some degree the new urgencies.

Much of the response to insurgency, therefore, was in these less apparent but no less important routine functions.

Of this entire span of activity, the most important to both Thais and Americans has been the Accelerated Rural Development program. It was designed to be a multipurpose response to the virtual government vacuum which existed prior to 1964 over large areas of the countryside. The system of local government which had sufficed for many decades assigned to the province governor neither staff nor adequate funds; he merely presided over the DOLA apparatus of district chiefs appointed by Bangkok and the village and cantonal heads selected by himself. Representatives of other ministries working in his province were independent of him and he had no capability to develop projects or respond directly to the needs he perceived in the province. Today, as a result of ARD's activity, "the governors . . . have up to 250 people on their staffs, a million dollars or so worth of equipment and a vastly increased budget. . . . [ARD] has also expanded its activities to include Mobile Medical Teams, a District Farmer Group Program (co-operatives), a youth program, a Potable Water Program and an information effort."[22] With these resources, the governors have been able to build two thousand kilometers of feeder roads as well as numerous other small-scale public works, e.g., wells, dams, and ponds.

Spelled out in these terms, the program is impressive, particularly in comparison with the vacuum that preceded it. Nevertheless, this twelve-year effort fell short of developing to the size and effectiveness necessary to make itself felt positively in the thousands of remote villages where the harsh conditions of life were still hardly altered. Indeed, the same was true of all the many development efforts combined. Very large areas were involved, with populations in the millions. The resources that were invested, which appear quite sizeable in abstract, were still too small to have the intended effects on the daily lives of the whole population of the affected areas. But to raise and deploy the necessary resources would have required a wrenching change in fiscal policy, particularly taxation, which could only have been carried out as part of a national mobilization far beyond the power of any modern Thai government to conceive, justify, and implement. This does not mean, however, that the cause was hopeless, for the Thais have had the great advantage of facing no immediate crisis. A gradual increase over, say, a decade would have done much to meet the need. Although there were great risks to such an approach, it was of necessity the one followed.

The developmental effort also suffered from the same enfeebling pattern of organizational manipulation to maintain the stability of the regime that we noted earlier. There was no single point below the highest levels where the development effort was coordinated and managed by a senior official with this as his full-time responsibility. To do so would have endangered the balance of the system as it existed up to 1973, and it does not seem that the short-lived Thai parliamentary regime was able to change this pattern. The result was a scattered and diffuse effort, with less impact than the same resources would achieve under centralized management.

Finally, and most important, in spite of some new departures and tentative efforts, the entire set of development programs reflected the traditional Thai government approach that "Bangkok knows best." Most of these programs represented what the central government apparatus and its experts (and foreign advisers) believed to be required in the countryside rather than what the villagers believed they needed. (An exception was the small Community Development program which was but a minor aspect.) As has often happened elsewhere, the Thai program tended to lose sight of the purpose of the development effort, which was to change village attitudes and build loyalty and commitment to the government cause. This long-range goal, however, is intangible and difficult to measure. Inevitably in such cases, focus shifts to what the institutions know best, namely, how to do their particular specialities. In the process, the system forgets the principal target—the villager—and fails to consult or involve him adequately. Yet experience also shows that doing things—even important and useful things—for people without bringing them into the process often leaves them as alienated as ever. It also can result in their gaining some facility they believe they need far less than another one the government overlooked. Less important, in fact, than the actual development project is the process by which it is brought to realization, the interaction between government and governed. Here is where the great gap between the educated, city-bred official and the barely literate peasant requires bridging if counterinsurgency is to achieve its goals. As yet, the Thai regime has not managed a consistent attack on the problem, and, until it does, the spread of worthy and useful development programs which, with considerable American help, it has deployed will fall short of their goal.

SUPPRESSION: THE OTHER SIDE OF THE COIN

We have noted that Thai counterinsurgency doctrine gives more emphasis to development and propaganda than to the tedious business of chasing and physically eliminating guerrillas. Indeed, from the point of view of any of the various versions of American doctrine, the Thais do not give sufficient attention to this task. Their answer to American criticism is a shrewd one. As Tanham states, he was told on more than one occasion that the Thais prefer not to follow the American practice they saw in operation in Vietnam which amounted to smashing a village with overwhelming firepower to get at a few Viet Cong, a process which, to say the least, did not help improve the villagers' attitudes toward the government.[23] There is, of course, an intermediate position, which is vigorous pursuit of the guerrillas with light, mobile forces, eschewing air and artillery bombardment, keeping the enemy on the run, and closing in on him when (as will happen only occasionally) he is cornered. It is in this phase of the task that the Thais have lagged most seriously.

Nevertheless, their doctrine does call for suppression, and programs were developed with considerable American urging and support to improve the services whose responsibility it was. The task involved the police, the intelligence services (largely police and military), the army, and various paramilitary formations under the control variously of the police, the army, or even of DOLA.

THE POLICE ROLE

Most theorists of counterinsurgency view the police as a critical suppression arm, and some, such as Sir Robert Thompson, believe that it rather than the military should be the principal reliance of suppression activities.[24] The Thai police service was not prepared to assume a major new role in the early sixties. It was under a political cloud and had been severely cut back in importance and resources. It was (and continued to be) associated with petty corruption, and its relations with the public were poor. This was particularly true in the countryside where, of course, an insurgency is fought. The Thai police is a unified national system called the Thai National Police Department (TNPD), with various branches performing specialized functions. One of its weaker branches, the Provincial Police, had the responsibility of maintaining law and order in the countryside together with the Border Patrol Police, which functioned in the frontier areas. The Provincial Police was, and remains despite considerable growth, far too small for its task of patrolling and maintaining security throughout the vast Thai hinterland. Moreover, it has long been looked upon as a poor relation compared to the city-based branches such as the Metropolitan Police and the Special Branch (which handles internal security). Morale has been poor, corruption common, and efficiency at a very low level. U.S. and Thai efforts, which go back to 1957, have improved the situation, but the problem remains a major one in Thai counterinsurgency.

Much of the increase in the size of the TNPD, which grew from fifty-one thousand in 1965 to a current total of over seventy thousand, has taken place within the Provincial Police. The main effort has been to establish *tambon* (cantonal) police stations in affected areas, each manned by a dozen or more constables. A goal was established of about one thousand of these stations by 1971 but that figure has not yet been reached.

Another counterinsurgency project brought into being in the Provincial Police a Special Action Force comprised of tactical platoons armed with light infantry weapons. Fifty have been created, theoretically to give the police the capability to react quickly to the presence of hostile armed bands. The Provincial Police in 1969 also began to receive draftees who were given the option of volunteering for two years of police service near their homes in lieu of entering the army for the same period. With these men a program of *tambon* police patrols was organized, providing a regular link between selected *tambon* police stations and the villages for which they were responsible.

The Provincial Police has also benefited from a rather intensive retraining program with emphasis on counterinsurgency. Five new training centers were established. Instructors for the program were trained by U.S. Special Forces, who then phased out, leaving a new facility capable of carrying on without assistance.[25]

The Border Patrol Police (BPP) is a specialized force organized on a platoon basis which can be deployed tactically when required. It is far smaller than the Provincial Police and was organized originally to deal with banditry and border incursions along the frontiers of the country. At one time it had elite status, with its own air arm, heavier weapons, and higher recruitment standards than the Provincial Police. Beginning in the early sixties, the BPP developed special programs among the hill tribes in the north and quickly became the only RTG service to enjoy any kind of rapport with the tribal communities. It established and manned two hundred schools as well as dispensaries and development centers with garden plots and the like. This Remote Area Security Program, as it was called, had the purpose of developing intelligence on subversive activity among the tribal peoples. In time it was supplemented by the recruitment of tribal volunteers into a police auxiliary service called Border Security Volunteer Teams.

There is evidence in the *Pentagon Papers,* specifically in the memorandum by General Lansdale quoted several times in the preceding chapter, that U.S. support for the BPP was conducted by CIA.[26] This, however, apparently came to an end in the mid-sixties.[27] Since then the advisory role for both the Provincial Police and BPP has been performed by USOM which has representatives working in the remote areas. For the specialized functions of the Remote Area Security Program, the AID mission contracted with a private American firm to provide the personnel and skills required to work effectively in the tribal villages. Still later, a Thai firm took over the contract.

The overall performance of the Thai police on the suppression side of counterinsurgency was undoubtedly improved as a result of these programs, but it remains one of the weaker links in the chain. The Thai Army remained suspicious of it as a potential rival for resources and political power and did not agree with plans to enlarge it to the size necessary to achieve its tasks. It was still viewed as corrupt by most of the public, and performance levels of the Provincial Police remained inadequate. It offers a prime example of the difficulties of institutional reform in the "bureaucratic polity."

THE COORDINATION OF INTELLIGENCE

Competent intelligence work is a major factor in successful counterinsurgency. Without it, the suppression effort spends itself in futile thrashing through vast remote areas, meeting the enemy only by accident. It is also essential to get at the organized political structure of the Communist apparatus, the so-called infrastructure, which is the directing mechanism without which the insurgency would fall apart. The intelligence task is a complex one, for many agencies are usually involved, producing a mass of paper which must be combined and analyzed professionally before it can be exploited. In Thailand, information on the identities, size, movements, armaments, and operational patterns of the insurgents was collected by these police services: BPP, Provincial Police, and Special Branch. (The latter is the senior police intelligence service but concentrates largely on the Bangkok area. It does have a small section working in the affected areas.) Army field units also had intelligence staffs supplemented by several staff elements in Bangkok, and, finally, the provincial administration collected information informally in the course of its normal duties. A civilian Directorate for Central Intelligence also existed in Bangkok but had no representation in the provinces and was little concerned with insurgency.

The professional level of these organizations was low, except for the Special Branch, which on occasion performed well. Their security was poor, resulting in a high rate of compromise of sources lost through assassination. But they nevertheless produced a large amount of low-level information which was useful when professionally handled and promptly exploited. This was the task of the Joint Security Centers (which also produced information themselves, especially from prisoner interrogations), and the CPM centers set up under the CSOC mechanism. Here, unfortunately, the system too often broke down. The sharing of information is not something intelligence services do cheerfully; they are disinclined to trust each other's security and discretion, and the question of credit for an intelligence coup also enters into the picture. A really important intelligence report will be sent first to the collector's own headquarters to be sure that he gets the recognition he feels entitled to. These tendencies exist everywhere, not only in Thailand; but there, success in overcoming them remained limited for lack of sufficient concern and priority. Similarly, operational commanders (which under the CSOC system meant the military) tended to look with mistrust upon information provided by nonmilitary sources. When operations were conducted it was ignored. When the system provided targets for operations, the operations were often not launched. The effort to combine all relevant intelligence and make it promptly available for well-conceived operations made some progress but remained a long way from the level required for successful counterinsurgency.

Existing sources say nothing about the U.S. agency working to develop and improve these intelligence efforts, but that very fact suggests that the task was performed by the CIA. Indeed, it appears that for a decade, the CIA's involvement in counterinsurgency in Thailand was limited to the intelligence side and did not include the paramilitary type of program it initiated in both Laos and Vietnam.

MILITARY ASSISTANCE

The Thai government had few new military programs specifically related to counterinsurgency, the MDU's being the outstanding example. This, of course, is not the same as saying that the military's role was not important. The decision, strongly supported by the JUSMAAG, was to treat counterinsurgency as "a lesser included capability" of the armed forces which, if they were up to standard, they should be able to accomplish without specialized units. The military aid program therefore concentrated on bringing the Thai armed services up to the performance standards held to be necessary for all its roles, without differentiation for its counterinsurgency tasks. This approach, of course, is entirely consistent with the U.S. Army view that counterinsurgency combat is very little different from other forms of combat and calls for the same skills and emphasis on the concentration of firepower at the right times and places.

Much of the military aid went into the supply of weapons and, not always to its liking, the JUSMAAG felt obliged to meet the insistent demands of its Thai counterparts for modern and sophisticated weapons, particularly tanks, artillery, and jet aircraft, which are not particularly well suited to counterinsurgency. These demands stemmed from the Thai military's view of the prestige to which it felt entitled. Since, during the period of heaviest U.S. involvement, the regime was dominated by the military, satisfaction of these demands seemed necessary. Some cynics in the American mission described the jets and tanks provided under military aid as a "rent" paid for the use of the Thai military bases on which the U.S. relied so heavily during the Vietnam war.

Besides weapons, the JUSMAAG focused largely upon training, which is a never-ending task in a conscript army. Training was performed largely by a company of U.S. Special Forces stationed in Thailand since 1967. It was counterinsurgency-oriented in the U.S. Army's understanding of the term. The MAAG also provided advice to Thai units at battalion level and above, but, as we have seen, this was done under carefully drawn guidelines to avoid any direct U.S. involvement in operations.

In these two latter tasks, the JUSMAAG was constantly thwarted by the political nature of the Thai armed forces in the regimes that flourished until 1973. A few examples will illustrate the problem. The combat units of the RTA in the provinces were usually led by older men because the young and ambitious officers preferred service in Bangkok where life was more interesting and chances for promotion were better.[28] Units were formed for the purpose of training together and then broken up again and redistributed to their original assignments; it was considered unfair to their commanders to lose their men permanently. No central basic training facility was ever established despite much urging by MAAG. Recruits were assigned to units near their homes and trained there by part-time trainers. The incurring of casualties in combat was looked upon as a failure of the commander who thereby caused much discomfort to the service. Such attitudes permeating the armed forces reflected other priorities than military competence and success in the mission of defending the security of the realm. They are another example of the workings of the "bureaucratic polity" when faced with new and demanding tasks.

The impact of any single example of this type is difficult to estimate and is certainly not decisive. The cumulative effect, however, is probably the largest single factor in explaining the puzzle of why a government with all the assets possessed by the RTG found it impossible to deal a crushing blow to so small an insurgency. Nor did the presence and aid of the U.S. significantly improve the capability of the Thai armed forces to meet the insurgency challenge. No doubt the Thai military became more professional in general. The staff work and logistics skills—and, of course, the weapons—were of a higher standard as a result of American aid. But leadership, aggressiveness, and general combat-worthiness showed little improvement. Moreover, the American military was in a weak position in regard to advice, for the Thais did not accept U.S. military counterinsurgency doctrine. As we know, they rejected, in theory at least (although not always in practice), the use of concentrated firepower as the proper means for dealing with guerrillas. In other words, the Americans gave the wrong advice which the Thais, with occasional exceptions, sensibly ignored. They had their own views on what to do but they were not able to do it effectively, and here the Americans were of little help. The result, particularly in the north where a very difficult military problem exists, was a policy of drift. On the military side of the task, the Thais were thoroughly baffled and (with rare exceptions) reduced to defensive maneuvers, routine patrolling, and hitting out at targets of opportunity. The guerrillas, as a result, retained the initiative and control of the scope and tempo of the fighting.

PARAMILITARY PROBLEMS

The threat posed by insurgents operating stealthily and in small groups cannot be defended against everywhere by the regular military and police without an impractical expansion in size and costs. The answer is to recruit local auxiliary forces, train and arm them, and assign to them the responsibility of the initial defense of their villages. In some versions, these local forces serve part-time and continue to farm or do other work. In others they are full-time, uniformed auxiliaries of the suppression forces. The Thai practice tends toward the latter and relies heavily on a preexisting militia called the Volunteer Defense Corps (VDC). Under the CSOC campaign plan, small groups of VDC have been placed under police leadership to form Village Protection Units, and this has been the common form in the northeast. In the north, the Border Patrol Police employed tribal volunteers as auxiliaries and the military organized similar units under its own command.[29] The Department of Local Administration also developed a version of its own which in time it deployed on a small scale. In other words, no single pattern evolved, and this for several reasons. First, the notion of distributing arms to villagers, although controls were provided, created uneasiness among the authorities. Secondly, the creation of a new institution in the countryside, and an armed one at that, threatened the balance of power between the institutions which shared authority in the provinces: the TNPD and DOLA. At one point a project pushed hard by the Americans for a nationwide program of Village Security Forces under the Department of Local Administration seemed on the verge of realization. Funds were set aside in the USAID budget in fiscal year 1967 to assist its formation, but in the end the regime felt obliged to abandon it because of the resistance of the police to this buildup of its rival. As a consequence, the counterinsurgency structure created by the Thais remains incomplete in the area of village security, although the various expedients adopted provide coverage of sorts. Of some importance in mitigating the problem has been a gradual improvement in the quality of the Volunteer Defense Corps, the existing militia, thanks in part to U.S. military assistance.

AN ASSESSMENT

The Thai insurgency fortunately remains a relatively minor threat to the stability of the regime, but one which continues to grow and could eventually become far more serious and costly to eradicate. On both the American and Thai sides this has been understood, and efforts encompassing the entire gamut of counterinsurgency were launched and persistently nourished over a period of thirteen years and in some cases even longer, actually antedating the outbreak of armed violence. The programs are linked with a comprehensive doctrine which is both sophisticated and humane. Thai efforts throughout the period have been encouraged by the U.S. and supported materially and with technical advice. The effect of all this has been some noticeable improvement in aspects of rural life and services, in the equipment and training of military and civilian services, and in the ability of the government to respond to attack. But in the specific areas where essential payoffs were to be looked for—the strength and size of the insurgency—the entire effort has had little measurable effect. It has probably increased the already considerable difficulties of the insurgency, but these remain attributable far more to the indifference of the Thai people than to the obstacles created by the government, and despite all the obstacles the insurgency continues to grow.

Given the low point from which it started—its poverty and lack of cohesion in contrast to the resources and organizational strength of the government—the insurgency's survival and growth raises evident questions. No doubt many at this point would say that the Thai government needs merely to carry out clearly indicated reforms to satisfy the people who respond to insurgent appeals, and those appeals would then fall on deaf ears. In actual fact, with the clear exception of the tribal grievances in the north, this is precisely what the government has tried to do, but the changes required are vast, and the costs, unless spread out over decades, are prohibitive short of a radical reversal of priorities and, indeed, of a social overturn unlikely to be either orderly or uninterrupted. Nor is it probable that committed revolutionaries and their guerrilla supporters would lay down their arms and suspend their operations merely because the government undertook major reforms. Without effective suppression the guerrillas would continue to be a worrisome threat for an indefinite time.

The problem does not lie in concept and doctrine but in execution and direction. Given the nature of the Thai regime and its methods of retaining power as these existed until the overthrow of 1973, counterinsurgency needs were fitted in as could be among higher priorities on the regime's list. Included in these were balance and distribution of power and stability among the various component elements of its political base. Such factors made it unwise for the leadership to concentrate power over all the elements of counterinsurgency in the hands of a single full-time manager. The factor of stability was particularly damaging. It meant "business as usual" within the military and civilian bureaucracies, and that in turn meant unaggressive suppressive operations, poor intelligence collection and exploitation, continued corruption in the rural police, indecision on such questions as the formation of a village militia and a national information service, and many more grave defects of performance and management. To remedy any of these defects, disturbing changes would have been necessary, altering established expectations within the groups supporting the regime, probably causing them to reexamine the basis of their support. We have returned in fact to the problem anticipated by such experienced participants as U. Alexis Johnson during the early enthusiasm of the Kennedy Administration. As he cautioned then, it could very well prove impossible for the threatened regimes to reform themselves in the midst of crisis, for their power base was built on an established distribution of rewards.[30] It is possibly no accident that Johnson had been ambassador to Thailand throughout the late fifties.

These factors in the background also explain to some extent the reasons for the persistent downgrading of the threat by the regime. The insurgents were sometimes dismissed as another variety of the bandit gangs that historically have preyed upon the remote rural areas—and indeed, the toll of lives and property was not seriously higher than occurred in the past during severe outbreaks of banditry. The claim was also made that no "true Thais" had succumbed to Communist appeals, that only minority groups and foreigners (i.e., Chinese and tribespeople) were involved, sustained by foreign support. That claim, too, had a certain plausibility, although it was quite untrue in the northeast and the mid-south. Although incorrect, both arguments served to reduce the urgency of the government's attack on the problem and excused an attitude of "business as usual."

A further factor reducing the priority accorded to the insurgency is noted by Tanham. This was the distracting effect on the regime of the Vietnam war and the associated crises in Laos and Cambodia.[31] Issues related to the Thai contingent in Vietnam, the use of Thai territory to base the bombers flying over Laos and North Vietnam, and the various Thai involvements in Laos monopolized the attention of Thanom, Praphat, and their associates and left them little time to devote to the complexities of counterinsurgency.

In this regard, the U.S. itself contributed heavily to the distraction by the pressures it brought to bear to involve the Thais more deeply. Beyond this, the U.S. effort, while carefully conceived and carried on with admirable discretion and restraint, suffered from some major defects, none of which can be laid at the door of individuals but rather reflect systemic weaknesses. The concept of a centrally organized field office was indeed sound but ran counter to established lines of authority which could not be easily altered. In fact, the special assistant for counterinsurgency, when confronted with differences with or among participating agencies touching on the sensitive areas of resources or prerogatives, had to fall back on the traditional "coordinating" devices of bargaining and persuasion. Moreover, he had no counterpart in Washington to speak for him in the councils of the foreign affairs community. By this time the Special Group (C.I.) had ceased to exist, and the forums which replaced it had far less influence.

In spite of its early efforts and good intentions, that organization left behind no binding or authoritative doctrine which dealt with an increasingly glaring deficiency on the American doctrine (or doctrines). This, of course, was the continuing U.S. Army emphasis on concentration of force and firepower in the suppression role. Regardless of how civilians might view this, and regardless of considerable civilian power to restrain military involvements, which, as we have seen, was effectively wielded in Thailand, the system gave no sanction to civilians to interfere in matters of military doctrine or the content of instruction and advice given to the Thais. President Kennedy himself had stumbled in attempting to persuade the military that counterguerrilla warfare was different from conventional infantry combat.[32] It should not be surprising, therefore, that in Thailand the JUSMAAG cheered on the Thais in such large-scale operations as the 1972 attack on Hin Long Khla, which produced no results, and systematically discouraged thoughts of developing special Thai units to assume the counterguerrilla burden. It was absorbed in the Sisyphean task of turning the entire RTA into a recognizable facsimile of a U.S.-style military machine—committed, aggressive, and technically skilled—and remained unwilling and probably unable because of internal pressures to admit that this goal was chimerical. U.S. doctrinal failures therefore weakened the impact of its advice which had little practical effect in resolving Thai bafflement on how to handle the task of guerrilla suppression.

All U.S. advice and influence were adversely affected by the further need to maintain Thai cooperation on matters affecting the basing of U.S. forces. Faced with the need to present a constant stream of requests for additional concessions or commitments in these areas, the mission was obliged to keep always in mind the importance of maintaining Thai receptivity, of avoiding offense or pressing too hard on sensitive matters involving the peculiarities of the Thai system. The tendency of the Thai military to ignore military effectiveness in conducting their affairs was therefore not seriously challenged. If persuasion failed, stronger methods, such as withholding aid that was likely to be wasted, could not be considered. Some exceptions, which keyed U.S. inputs to the accomplishment of specific performance levels, remained exceptions. In effect, the U.S., too, had its conflicting priorities which reduced its ability to concentrate its influence on the counterinsurgency task.

The net conclusion that one may draw from the less than successful results so far achieved against people's war in Thailand is that in that country mastery of the required skills and procedures eluded both governments and, further, that the absence of crisis pressures may actually hinder rather than help in dealing with the manifold difficulties of administrative reform and modernization as well as social and economic reform. Most significant has been the clash between the regime's view of the political urgencies of stability and power balance versus the need for administrative improvement and concentration of authority.

Does this suggest that the Thai system as it existed until 1973 was fundamentally unequipped to deal with the problem and that the U.S. was unable to fill the gaps in the Thai effort because of its inadequacies? If the Communist threat were more impressive that might have been the only possible conclusion. Given the limited size of the insurgency and its inability to make headway, however, it is also possible that some relatively superficial improvements could have delivered a serious setback to the insurgents. One such device was the relatively simple one of recruiting a lightly armed special force of counterguerrilla units outside and separate from the political system that dominated the military and muffled its capabilities.

As matters stand at this writing, however, the issue of insurgency and the proper means of dealing with it have been submerged by other, far more serious problems in Bangkok. The process of modernization has finally begun to take its toll in Thailand. The end of the Vietnam war and the withdrawal of American forces abruptly ended the years of prosperity and of sustained growth which accompanied them. Economic distress created new pressures on the regime coming not only from students and the nascent labor movement but also from the rural areas which have been aroused from their traditional political apathy by the sudden development of unprecedented land problems.[33] The pressure on the land of high population growth and of spreading tenancy have aroused the farmers as never before. These factors, among others, have entirely changed the political climate and apparently have put an end to the underlying stability of the Thai political system. The possibility looms of an insurgency which may be able to exploit the new cleavages in the structure, which may even be able to develop an urban arm and bring significant pressure at the seat of power in Bangkok. Whatever happens, it seems that a new set of problems exists today, and that the old approaches will no longer suffice.

In the meantime, in the United States the outlook has also changed, and public attitudes will no longer support an involvement similar to that attempted in the 1960s and early 1970s. Those changes, in fact, began to have their impact some years ago. After the departure of the second incumbent in mid-1970, the U.S. embassy abolished the office of the special assistant for counterinsurgency and abandoned the notion of concentrating authority in a special officer of high rank. Dominating in the embassy was the not implausible view that the threat was not of a size to cause immediate concern and that no need existed to press the Thais to exertions they were not prepared to take of their own initiative. We may note that this is an implicit abandonment of the theories that dominated U.S. thinking in the early sixties regarding the proper approach for dealing with insurgency. It does conform to the mood of the country and to the general skepticism regarding the prescriptions with which the counterinsurgency policies of the Kennedy Administration was launched.

That mood, of course, was not shaped by events in Thailand so much as by the far more traumatic and tragic developments in Vietnam. To this tangled subject we now turn, seeking to follow the thread of counterinsurgency doctrine and policy through the maze of competing and conflicting preoccupations in that arena.

7

The Revival of Counterinsurgency: Vietnam, 1963-1967

★ ★ ★

The American counterinsurgency efforts in Laos and Thailand attracted but a small share of U.S. resources and attention, which increasingly, as the sixties progressed, became bound up in Vietnam. Counterinsurgency, however, benefited only rhetorically from this focus. The collapse of the Diem regime was also a collapse of the counterinsurgency program identified with that regime, the strategic hamlet program. The ensuing period confirmed the fears that had kept the U.S. committed to Diem and Nhu long after they had lost the ability to master their country's problems. The successor regimes were so feeble politically and administratively that U.S. attention was monopolized by the need to find and legitimate a stable political structure without which progress in other fields was out of the question.

But the weakness and instability that paralyzed American efforts was precisely the mixture most helpful to the enemy. The Viet Cong, although slow to move during the confusion of the period immediately before and after Diem's overthrow, began to attack energetically in the countryside within a short time. Its offensive progressed to the point where the ARVN was pressed back toward the major cities and a few principal arteries. Increasingly the population in the countryside came under full-time VC control. This happened despite a continued high level of U.S. military assistance and advice, including helicopter and covert combat air support. To stop the military disintegration the U.S. resorted in early 1965 to regular bombing of North Vietnam and, later in the year, to the introduction and deployment of U.S. ground combat forces in the South.

These events preoccupied the policy levels of the government to the virtual exclusion of counterinsurgency despite repeated rhetorical commitments in general policy statements. At the operating levels in Vietnam, the agencies concerned, with little central guidance or planning, attempted to pick up the pieces of the disintegrated strategic hamlet effort while some of them quietly experimented with new departures attempting to apply the lessons of the debacle of strategic hamlets. Then, toward the end of 1965 and early 1966, interest at the White House and the cabinet level began to revive in what came at the time to be called "the other war."[1] A gradual and lengthy buildup took place of the programs now more formally called pacification, and they steadily absorbed greater attention and resources. In time it became the most serious, prolonged, and costly U.S. effort to realize the concepts and goals of counterinsurgency.

PACIFICATION TO THE FORE

The task the U.S. had set for itself in Vietnam was formidable. It was to step into the center and try to alter the outcome of a conflict in which the enemy was well organized, well attuned to local needs and attitudes, self-confident, and certain of its purposes and the road to their achievement; whereas the friendly side was a deeply flawed society, politically disorganized, weak, and uncertain of how to proceed, militarily unprepared for the kind of war it was involved in, and administratively unequipped to cope with the tasks of routine government, much less the fearful complexities of massive civil insurgency. Moreover, the U.S. faced a host of difficulties in shaping its role to suit the peculiarities of the area, the people, and the conflict. Among the most important was the need to avoid obvious offense to the sovereignty of this new and highly sensitive nation, the unfamiliarity of the terrain and the culture into which it was deploying its efforts, and, of particular interest to us, its uncertain grasp of the concepts and doctrine developed to deal with the problem of Communist insurgency. The failure of the strategic hamlet program had not resulted in any significant revision of approach or scrutiny of assumptions. Most important, the differing military and civilian approaches remained as far apart as ever, while there was little appreciation at the highest levels of government that such a difference existed, that the Kennedy White House had, in effect, failed in its highly publicized effort to produce a doctrinal revolution in the United States armed forces. In a comment written several years later, Roger Hilsman set forth the two distinct approaches followed by separate groups within the Kennedy and Johnson Administrations, dubbing one "political" and the other "military."

> Although the initial policy decision favored the political approach, it is a comment on the pluralism of the American government that the implementation was never clear-cut. In general, the military representatives in Saigon continued to recommend the essentially "military" approach to the Vietnamese; the representatives of the State Department and the Agency for International Development (AID) continued to press for the political approach; and the American mission lacked any clear line of authority and command that could control and coordinate the representatives of the often rival American departments and agencies. Partly for this reason . . . the result was frustration for the advocates of both the "military" and the "political" approaches. [2]

Events were to show that the new president, while accepting the rhetoric of his predecessor, did not appreciate the extent to which it had remained rhetoric as far as the military establishment was concerned, or that any real change would probably involve a public clash with the army leadership and some forced resignations. If he had, it is doubtful that he would have entertained the prospect. In the event, the new president dealt with the problem of counterinsurgency by relying heavily on his predecessor's appointees and particularly General Maxwell Taylor, who had become chairman of the Joint Chiefs and later was sent by Johnson to Vietnam as ambassador. Taylor, although considered a loyal Kennedy follower in counterinsurgency matters, was an advocate of the military approach, before and after American troops were committed. He could no more accept than most other generals the proposal that the army, which he had fought to modernize and improve in terms of mobility and firepower, must become not more sophisticated but more primitive in order to deal effectively with the Viet Cong. Under Johnson, McNamara, and Taylor, therefore, there was little prospect of significant change in the confused state of U.S. counterinsurgency doctrine.

Thus, when the commitment to the Vietnam conflict was assumed and broadened by the Johnson Administration for domestic and international reasons with little real grasp of its perils and pitfalls, along with it the administration took over an unexamined and poorly understood commitment to counterinsurgency. In the two years of acute political confusion that followed the fall of Diem in Vietnam, the U.S. regularly urged upon the GVN the need to battle directly with the Viet Cong in the villages, and it continued the programs of rural assistance which had been launched to support the strategic hamlet program. Indeed, the resources and the numbers of Americans involved steadily increased under the continuing momentum of the earlier commitment. All of this accomplished very little—indeed, less than nothing—for the Viet Cong made rapid progress in the prevailing confusion. Nighswonger's estimates, derived from various sources, show the number of claimed hamlets completed dropping from eighty-five hundred in November 1963 to three thousand in December 1965.[3] Some of the reduction resulted from more realistic reporting and some of it reflected the collapse of the program under pressure from the VC as well as the government's new policy of deliberate withdrawal where it felt overextended. Although the GVN (under the Khanh regime, which replaced the original coup group in January 1964) developed a new version of rural defense called the New Rural Life program, simplifying the criteria and eschewing forced resettlement, and claimed to have a National Pacification Plan, the actuality was chaotic and ineffective. Province chiefs were sometimes changed three times in a few months, cadres and regular civil servants went unpaid for long periods, and materials provided by the aid program gathered dust in warehouses when they did not simply disappear. Perhaps the only form of progress one could discern during much of 1964 was a somewhat increased realism on the part of both Vietnamese and Americans concerning the unpleasant facts of the situation.

The heart of the problem, fully recognized by the Americans concerned, was the absence of any political foundation for a program purporting to engage the population on the side of the government. As Ambassador Maxwell Taylor reported in November 1964, "Perhaps more serious than the downward trend in the pacification situation, because it is the prime cause, is the continued weakness of the central government."[4] General Khanh, in his early months of power, was quite skillful at sensing what the Americans wished him to say concerning, for example, national mobilization, pacification, improved administration, and other general matters. But his performance was woefully short of his stated goals and, indeed, regardless of his intentions, could hardly have been otherwise. He was without political experience, organization, or following and had no particular political talents except the kind of cunning that brought him to the top of the circle of generals who dabbled in *coups d'état*. Yet the U.S. leadership felt it had no alternative but to support him and reassure him publicly and privately in order to bolster his confidence. It also urged him to improve his political image and attempted to help him with information and propaganda activity, including personal appearances by his side of the secretary of defense, Robert McNamara.[5] This fumbling for levers and devices to produce instant political legitimacy in a country that was a blank mystery to most Americans contrasts sadly with the purposefulness and grasp of the party of Ho Chi Minh.

Nevertheless, despite the depths of South Vietnam's political confusion, the U.S. felt obliged to persist in a program of which the essence was successful political activity penetrating the depths of the remote countryside. The anomaly was well understood, and the documentation spread out in the *Pentagon Papers* made it clear that the program of pressure against the North and the later involvement of American troops grew out of this frustration with the intractability of the realities in the South and the hopelessness of affecting the necessary improvements before the VC swept all before it. Attention therefore shifted to the purely military measures which were intended to buy the time considered necessary for a stable political structure to grow in the South. But even though public and press attention thus shifted, the U.S. civilian apparatus in Vietnam was in place and committed to programs designed to improve the situation in the countryside. With considerable resources and experience behind them, working in the knowledge that in the higher levels of government many still saw the war in the countryside as the long-term heart of the matter, the civilians quietly launched a wide variety of tentative, experimental projects, improved on older programs, and laboriously evolved a far more elaborate, complex, and sophisticated pacification program which, in fact, did not reach its full scope and intensity until 1969. The effort was characterized by organizational upheavals and innovations and was on a greater scale than any other similar program attempted by any government anywhere in the world. It was the climax of the counterinsurgency policy of the United States, representing its best achievements and, in some respects, its gravest inadequacies.

Experiments and Small Beginnings

Thwarted by the confusion and weakness in Saigon, some U.S. agencies searched for alternative ways of making at least a start toward the goal of strengthening the government in the countryside. They looked for nuclei of political solidity upon which some form of local armed village defense movement could be based. In some ways the process resembled the early beginnings of the strategic hamlet program which had taken advantage of the cohesiveness of two minorities, the Catholics and the hill people, although in this case other minorities were involved. CIA was particularly active in the search. In the course of 1964 and 1965 it evolved several programs which were the seed of much larger efforts in the future. One of the more important was called People's Action Teams (PATs), launched mostly in Central Vietnam with the cooperation of local political authorities and of the Office of the President in Saigon. These were groups of about forty cadres, recruited for local service, carefully trained and indoctrinated and armed. Their training focused on ideology and on communication with the village populations from which they were drawn. They were to perform as village protectors and were also to assist the villagers in their work and in taking advantage of the numerous assistance programs which were intended to reach down into the villages but often did not.[6]

Where they were most successful, the PATs were allied with long-established political groups, notably the two old nationalist parties, the VNQDD (a Vietnamese version of the Kuomintang) and the *Dai Viet.* Both dated from prewar years and in their decades of activity had succeeded in building some strength in the central provinces. In effect, the PATs gave the local political bosses of these groups a means of directly countering the VC's use of violence and propaganda. Where the leadership was capable and the villagers amenable, they had considerable success in securing villages and hamlets. According to one authority, the PATs numbered 14,500 men by 1965.[7] Few other particulars are available on the numbers of such teams or their costs. They probably never numbered as many as four hundred and never developed more than a local importance. But they were one of the few progovernment efforts at the time to accomplish appreciable results in the critical village arena of war. Thus, when the GVN began casting about for a vehicle to launch a major new pacification effort, the concepts and techniques developed by the PATs were seized upon and made the basis of a greatly expanded program.

A second source of the same program was an experiment undertaken locally by officials in Binh Dinh province on the coast of Central Vietnam. Its leader was the deputy province chief, a Major Nguyen Be. Be had been a Viet Minh battalion commander during the first Indochina war, and what he taught, in fact, was the substance of the Communist village program shorn of such aspects as terrorism. He, too, based his program on a cadre-team organization selected from local youths who were trained and indoctrinated in a relatively lengthy course (eventually standardized at thirteen weeks) to do no less than completely reform the hamlets and villages to which they were assigned. They were dressed in black pajamas, lived with the villagers, and helped them in their work and, where possible, were assigned in the localities of their origin. Thus, in many ways, the program was similar to that of the PATs, and the two were readily enough combined at a later date.

By mid-1965, a new Saigon government, whose premier was Air Vice Marshal Nguyen Cao Ky, had accepted the concept underlying both programs as the centerpiece of a new national approach to pacification. All cadre programs, which now had become numerous and thoroughly confused, were merged into one, and a National Training Center was built at the resort city of Vung Tau. To it, all the old cadres were sent for retraining, and a steady flow of new trainees was recruited to establish the program throughout the country. Once again small local experiments supported by CIA had, as in the case of the strategic hamlets, become the basis of a large national effort. The recurring pattern was unpremeditated and was a reflection of the fact that counterinsurgency was not the province of any established agency, that cut-and-dried advance formulas could not be devised for each situation but had to be worked out on the scene, and that CIA had both the motivation and the flexibility to experiment and improvise until some solution had been found, whereas the more conventional agencies were held more closely to fixed programs. On the other hand, CIA's improvisations were based on special local conditions, the cohesiveness of selected minority groups, and the like. They could not always easily be transformed into national programs.

A rather different initiative attempted by the CIA during this period brought some success but considerable trouble in its wake. The concept was that of answering VC terrorism in kind to produce a climate of insecurity in enemy-controlled areas and to capture or kill identified members of the VC organization. The program was called Counter-Terror Teams (CTTs), not a happy name, as the CIA was to find. The teams were organized at province level under the direct authority of the province chief. Recruitment criteria emphasized the qualities thought necessary for personal combat, training was rigorous with emphasis on leadership, initiative, and discipline, but the results were highly uneven. In some cases, disciplined and formidable units of six or a dozen men carried out carefully planned forays into enemy territory, capturing or killing identified local Communist figures. Sometimes they struck silently and at other times they made brief public appearances in a VC-controlled community. Here and there such raids had a startling if short-lived effect, and the programs spread until almost all provinces had a unit of this type.

In some provinces, however, control was inadequate and the quality of the recruits was poor. They might simply be used as bodyguards by the province chief or, what was worse, might indulge in petty gangsterism in friendly villages or serve as "enforcers" for the dominant local political group. The program, in fact, grew too fast for the existing control mechanism and was already headed for trouble when it struck a reef. Publicity on the CTTs began to appear in the U.S. press, emphasizing and exaggerating the lurid aspects of its work—silent assassination and terror in enemy-held territory. The publicity suggested and stated, in some cases, that the teams were instruments of generalized mayhem visited upon villagers in the enemy's territory. Before long the CIA began a reorganization and trimming of the effort which eventually transformed it into a different and more manageable instrument. The refurbished Counter-Terror Teams became the Provincial Reconnaissance Units (PRUs), which will be described more fully in due course.

The next experiment in this series was anointed with the curious title of the Census/Grievance and Aspiration Program, usually shortened to the mysterious-sounding "Census/Grievance." Despite its title, it was not a program to identify popular grievances against the census. Rather it was intended to provide each participating province chief with a tool to establish a reliable village head-count that also identified the loyalties of the villagers while simultaneously checking on both corruption and on village aspirations—be it for a school, a market, a well, or similar small-scale public works. The census function was genuine, but it also provided a cover for interviews with each villager. Thus protected by the fact of universality, he could be asked delicate questions with some hope that he might tell the truth. The information was then collected and forwarded directly to a center at the province capital, skipping the intervening district office. There it was screened and distributed, with any information about corruption or village abuse going directly to the province chief. The work in the hamlet was performed by a resident selected and trained for that purpose. He remained in place permanently and sent periodic reports to his superiors.

This curious device was an expedient substituted for what should have been the normal functioning of local authorities—police and village councils. As was the case with all the cadre programs, it responded to the American sense of urgency about the need to take action immediately to avoid catastrophe, rather than patiently attempting what seemed the near-hopeless task of assisting the conventional arms of government to meet the demands of the crisis. When local conditions were right—a competent and interested province chief, adequate American advisory assistance, and so on—Census/Grievance was a useful adjunct of pacification, and particularly so in the intelligence it produced. It was, however, not a critical contributor to success or failure.

THE CONVENTIONAL PROGRAMS PUSH AHEAD

The cadre programs just described did not exhaust CIA's involvement in the layered growth of pacification, for it also worked in more conventional modes with focus on intelligence. The National Police had been reorganized after the collapse of the Diem regime. U.S. assistance no longer came from Michigan State University but from AID, with the exception of two areas where CIA was heavily involved. First was the expansion of the Police Special Branch (formerly the *Sureté*) from an urban security police centered in Siagon to a nationwide service represented in each province capital from which it attempted intelligence collection on the Viet Cong in the countryside. (The Special Branch was responsible for internal security and the collection of intelligence against subversive organizations.) The program took several years to reach the goal of nationwide expansion and even longer to begin making a useful contribution. The kind of professional intelligence activity aimed at calls for well-trained officers and much patience and thoroughness, qualities which do not flower overnight.

At about the same time, CIA assisted the Special Branch to build and staff a Prisoner Interrogation Center (PIC) in each province capital in the country. The intent of the project was to facilitate the professional interrogation of higher-level VC prisoners who frequently, for lack of facilities and properly trained interrogators, were sent directly to detention centers with no effort to obtain from them the wealth of knowledge about their organizations which they had stored in their heads. CIA's concept was the accepted routine function of any professional counterintelligence service worthy of the name: painstaking, patient questioning, checking and requestioning in circumstances calculated to emphasize the prisoner's helplessness and dependence on his captors. Psychological pressure is part of the concept but not physical duress. The interrogation doctrine of professional intelligence services in democratic countries stresses that torture is unreliable as well as repugnant and illegal as a means of obtaining accurate information. Notwithstanding this intent, the American adviser assigned to the PIC as one duty among many was not in control of the facility, and much went on of which he did not know or approve. As elsewhere in Vietnam, events and conditions in the PICs were beyond foreign control, and there is no doubt that torture was employed.

Given the kind of war this was, that fact is not surprising, although even the desperate circumstances of insurgent war do not justify it. CIA had the practical choice of giving up the quest for better intelligence to prosecute the war, or persisting despite the brutality of some of the PIC personnel while striving by persuasion and such leverage as was available to ameliorate or change it—sometimes successfully, sometimes not. It chose the latter, being committed, as was the rest of the government, to getting on with the war with the means at hand. That purpose overrode the dubious complexities of the situation and, in this instance among others, ran athwart the broad intent of the U.S.—to assist the GVN to establish a popular rural base—making that task more rather than less difficult.

Be all this as it may, one effect of the several CIA programs just described was a considerable increase of intelligence on the Viet Cong, some of it of local tactical and law-enforcement interest, some of it leading higher. At the same time, other intelligence programs—such as the military collection effort conducted largely with the Vietnamese armed forces, and the creation of a civilian Central Intelligence Organization in Saigon—also added to the mountain of data regularly pouring forth on the enemy. Moreover, one of the by-products of military operations against the insurgents was a vast hoard of enemy documents, for the VC organization proliferated paper due to its insistence on disciplined, structured, and fully analyzed organizational performance. (It was, in addition to its many other faces, a complex bureaucracy.) A Joint Translation Center in Saigon, operated by MACV and ARVN, translated the documents and attempted to distribute rapidly any information of tactical interest to the affected operating unit. Thus, the attempt to develop better intelligence, which for years had been a recurring theme of the American side, began to bear a prolific harvest—without, however, bringing the dramatic improvement in operations that had been anticipated. Attention then shifted from the collection to the exploitation process—the rapidity and effectiveness with which the intelligence was utilized. In this preoccupation lay the genesis of what later became the Phoenix program, the most controversial element of the later pacification effort.

That problem lay in the future. At this time (1964 and 1965,) energies were focused on the search for an improved programmatic basis for pacification. USAID bore the burden of supporting and improving many of the established programs and also innovated in the search for new solutions to unfamiliar problems. After becoming a USAID responsibility, the conventional police program grew steadily, and the National Police reached a total of about seventy-two thousand (up from twenty-one thousand in 1963) in the years we are discussing.[8] As the police began to function deeper in the countryside, attention centered on building a police-run Resources Control Program to choke the flow of supplies from government-controlled centers to the Communist military and civilian apparatus. In the thinking of some specialists this was a major goal which, if achieved, would strike a mortal blow at the insurgency. They saw it as an answer to a painful dilemma that was beginning to be apparent, the fact that any increase in economic aid, and thus in the availability of goods of all kinds, would also benefit the enemy, who existed symbiotically within the body politic, nourishing himself from the same sources that nourished the people at large.[9]

The concept of resource control also owed a good deal to experience in Malaya, where it had effectively choked off the insurgents and weakened them seriously. Checkpoints began to spring up on roads leading to and from market centers, and the population submitted more or less patiently to the searches of the police, although years were required to build up the effort to a level at which it became more than a nuisance to the VC. Indeed, it is not possible to say with any certainty that the program ever did become more than that, but it was seen as a necessary effort if only for symbolic reasons and was pursued systematically. The great difficulty with it lay in the fact that any business transaction anywhere could possibly have been conducted for the Viet

Cong, and the surveillance task was thus beyond the resources available; nor were there many "choke-points" where supply movement was concentrated and easily intercepted. The circulation of supplies to the Viet Cong was very like the capillary system of the body, broken down into myriad channels where goods moved in small increments intermingled with the regular flow of commerce. The government and the U.S. could and did claim that the blockade effort worked and cited statistics of goods seized in support of the claim.[10] But no one could say what proportion of the total was seized and thus determine the effect of the effort. Since the VC never seemed to suffer from critical shortages except in limited special situations, the program could not be described as a success.

The National Police also endeavored to carry out an identification card program intended eventually to supply to each Vietnamese a tamper-proof ID card enabling the police to identify any citizen anywhere. The program was not a new one. It had begun during the Diem regime but encountered a variety of problems, including the mechanical one of devising a card which could not be easily altered or duplicated by the Viet Cong. There were also false starts and delays occasioned by police reorganizations—itself a function of the instability of the various regimes that succeeded Diem—and so several years were to elapse before noticeable progress was achieved.

Another police program aimed at the insurgency was the establishment of a paramilitary police, called the Police Field Force (PFF), organized in one-hundred-man mobile companies of which eventually at least one was to be assigned to each province in the country. The purpose was to give the police the ability to respond quickly to attacks too large for the ordinary police or local defenders to deal with. It reflected the view that insurgency suppression is properly a police rather than a military function. This was a principle of what we have called the British school of counterinsurgency theory and it was not coincidental that the AID advisory group assigned to work with the PFF included a few Australians. In fact, however, the actual pacification program had long focused on the military as the chief actor on the government side. The police had nothing like the resources necessary to play a major tactical role. Moreover, its field force could not easily carve a niche for itself in assuming responsibility for small-unit operations in competition with the cadre, the Counter-Terror Teams, and the "regular" paramilitary, now called the Regional Forces and Popular Forces. The mission that finally evolved for the PFF was a compromise. They were given the VC control apparatus—the so-called infrastructure—as a target, and they were also assigned to protect National Police units as the service expanded its role in the countryside.

Besides these programs specifically oriented toward pacification, the

Public Safety activity of AID invested heavily in an effort to raise the general level of the police and its capability. This took the form of training and the formation of a National Police Academy, development of telecommunications, and improved central files—all of which were intended to impact on the insurgency as a particularly aggravated problem of law enforcement. Directly related to enforcement of the government's writ in the villages was the decision to place at least one two-way radio in every village and hamlet in the country to assure that help could be summoned in case of need. Although not part of police-managed communications, the task had been assigned to the Public Safety Division of AID which persisted in it until many years later it had emplaced no fewer than forty thousand sets, or more than three per hamlet.[11] While no doubt important as a means of tying hamlets and villages to higher government centers, the radios were only a channel of communications. Their effect depended on the reaction of the authorities to the information communicated, and often this was slow or nonexistent.

The combined U.S. and GVN effort with the police was thus a broad one and had many unconventional facets. Despite criticism that all this activity was fastening a police state upon the communities of rural Vietnam, it is difficult to challenge the need for an energetic effort to expand the law-enforcement capability of the police if the crisis were to be surmounted. It was also futile to have expected in the circumstances a punctilious regard in all cases for the niceties of the civil rights of suspected insurgents. What one was entitled to expect was that the police would not generally behave toward the public in a manner that contradicted and negated the basic goal of pacification which, to repeat, was to create a base of popular support in the countryside. Unhappily, the police as an institution was a troubled one, deeply involved in the politics of the regime. It participated in corruption, was accused (and was often guilty) of petty gangsterism, and was often arbitrary and hard-faced in its dealings with the general public. The U.S. did attempt to improve the quality of the service through training and advice and by preaching against corruption. There were also many honorable exceptions among the police to the unsavory norm. The problem remained: too many police were involved in activities that undermined the broad purposes of pacification. In its origins, the problem was similar to the one we have several times noted in other insurgency situations. Far-reaching reform was required and was pledged but, if carried out, threatened to undermine the arrangements, the deals, and the political understandings that precariously held the regime together—and so never went far enough. The police, inevitably in politically underdeveloped Vietnam, were very much part of the political system. And so, with American help, they expanded and improved in technical capability, but, because of their weaknesses, each expansion and technical improvement brought them into contact with more of the public and presented more opportunities for misbehavior. The dilemma was not easily solvable under the circumstances.

Beyond the Public Safety Program, AID had many other responsibilities relating to pacification, some more or less directly connected to its principal mission of development, and some assigned to it because they did not easily fit anywhere else. One of the latter was the effort to induce defection from the VC on a large scale, a program launched in principle in the last year of Diem's regime but which had many problems getting started, the most important being the difficulty encountered in persuading GVN officials that it made sense to offer your enemy anmesty and rehabilitation merely for the asking. Nevertheless, under American urging, the point was gradually made and eventually accepted and the *Chieu Hoi* or Open Arms program became an established and generally useful arm of the pacification effort. Genuine progress, however, did not come quickly but had to await, on the Vietnamese side, the stabilizing of the regime and, on the American side, the results of various studies which convinced the policy level that its promise justified a higher priority. These factors came together in 1966 when, in the words of its historian, the program "took off."[12]

Among the factors influential in persuading the GVN were the requirement that each *hoi chanh* (one who had rallied to the government side) cooperate voluntarily in supplying all useful information available to him about the enemy and undergo a period of indoctrination during which his attitudes and political understanding were to be revised in the appropriate direction. During the renovation of pacification that gradually evolved in 1964–1965, the Chieu Hoi program advanced from an appalling state of disarray (four thousand would-be defectors who volunteered en masse in the delta region in 1964 slipped through the government's fingers for lack of preparation and understanding of the program) to a nationwide structure which provided at least a basis for the later takeoff. This involved the training and deployment of Vietnamese and Americans in most provinces of the country, the refinement of propaganda appeals and techniques, and the construction of rehabilitation centers in every province.

AID had other sizable programs related in some way to pacification of which the most burdensome was the refugee program, a never-ending tragedy resulting from the impact of the war, and particularly the bombing, on the rural population. In truth, it was a peripheral effort in its relationship to pacification, and we need primarily to note it as a continuing preoccupation of many of the same Americans and Vietnamese who were also involved in pacification itself. In the early Diem years, refugee resettlement had been a major U.S. effort largely completed by the time the regime collapsed but which had to be regenerated on a larger scale when the U.S. intervened with armed force in the mid-sixties. The creation of a mass of new refugees was to some extent inevitable but was seriously aggravated by the style in which the U.S. felt obliged to fight the war, notably in the heavy use of air power and artillery—neither of which, despite the efforts made to control them, could under battlefield conditions be wielded with the degree of accuracy required. The resulting population movements had a major impact upon the VC, and accusations have been made that "refugee-generation" became a deliberate goal of the U.S./GVN war effort. If that were true, and the accusation remains unproved, it cannot be described as part of pacification as conceived and implemented by those who had responsibility for the effort but an overlay applied by the military which amounted to a gross distortion of the program.

With all these related responsibilities, AID also continued to support the disorganized nationwide pacification efforts that succeeded the aborted strategic hamlet program. A Province Coordinating Committee[13] continued in existence in each province. It had three members, the province chief, the AID representative, and the MACV sector adviser assigned to each province. After an annual budget had been approved in Saigon and an agreement drawn up covering the commitments of each side, funds could be released on the signatures of the three principals. During a brief reversal of policy, American involvement in the release procedure was suspended in 1965 on the grounds that it usurped GVN authority but was restored permanently in 1966. The funds went into small public works of which roads, bridges, and public buildings were the most common. Among other typical projects were training centers for farmers, agricultural extension work, fertilizer distribution, rural electrification, dispensaries, medical technician training, and much more. A share of this activity was based on "self-help," meaning that a given project would be supported by the Saigon government and AID on the understanding that the villagers would contribute their labor to realize it. Self-help projects usually came closer to realizing the true aspirations of the villagers than those selected by the government bureaucracy, which too often followed its own ideas of what was suitable, i.e., what would enhance its standing or produce graft on the side.

As far as concerned AID and the American mission, much pride was taken in doing good works, even though, admittedly, a sizable amount was lost to the Communists or wasted owing to corruption and inefficiency. The problem which was not often addressed was how all this related to the objective of affecting loyalties and changing attitudes in the countryside. To many it appears self-evident that a government that brings good things to the people, be it fingerlings for fishponds or schoolteachers for a school, must be improving its hold on the people's loyalties. This view, which is frequently considered axiomatic (sometimes modified to require that security be established first before good deeds can work their spell), leaves out several dimensions of the act of giving assistance, namely, the process by which decisions are arrived at and the style in which each project is carried out.

The essence of the rural political problem of the GVN was the cultural gap between its apparatus and the population, the lack of communication across that gap, and the resultant sense of insecurity of the peasant who saw the ruling power as arbitrary, capricious, and inscrutable when it was not nakedly exploitive. The ingredient essential to change that picture was a means by which the peasant could to some appreciable extent control his destiny and conclude that there were levers in his hands which produced responses to his needs. It is perhaps here that we find the true importance of land reform as a way of changing peasant attitudes. By transferring title to the land to the man who tilled it—providing the terms were seen as fair and the government protected the title effectively—the authorities in the most direct and elemental way gave assurance of fundamental security to and control of his future by the peasant himself. When the matter involved was in the category of incremental village improvements—a paved road, a small canal, a dispensary—it had little real impact unless the peasant saw the need himself and could influence the choice of improvement and details of location, material, and the like. Sometimes the process involved negotiation, lengthy explanations, and some education. If this were done in the right way, it could eventually have the desired effect. All too often, however, the peasants were manipulated or merely pushed aside. They were presented with a gift and expected to be suitably grateful even though they may have preferred something else or the location interfered with convenience or custom or they really did not see the need for the improvement at all. The help provided did nothing to strengthen loyalty because the process merely reinforced the villager's feelings of helplessness.

In this light, efforts to improve standards of living in the countryside were irrelevant unless they also reduced the villager's sense of insecurity that came from feeling defenseless in a hostile world, whereas the desired feelings could be produced by means which did little to improve the standard of living. Thus, if a villager whose daughter had been abused or whose chickens had been stolen by ARVN soldiers could report the matter to company headquarters and receive restitution or see the culprit punished, his personal sense of worth and his respect for the system that defended it were strengthened. This effect was obtained at no or little cost yet it had more real consequence for village attitudes than an expensive public-works project carried out arbitrarily.

The "self-help" portion of the rural program was thus a useful technique as far as it went. Nevertheless, the program at this time achieved little in the way of changing attitudes, although this fact—obvious in view of the continued decline of government control in the countryside—cannot be blamed on the rural aid program. Conditions in those chaotic years could not have been worse for the supporters of what began to be called the "hearts and minds" school of counterinsurgency. Security was fragile everywhere and nonexistent in most places. The GVN was in disarray both in Saigon and the countryside; whole ARVN battalions were being put out of action at a frightening rate. The pacification effort had no leadership or élan, plan or doctrine. In short, there was little basis for judging the success of any single aspect of an effort which had to be multifaceted to succeed. Nevertheless, the point is an important one: process was the key to success in rural assistance rather than the volume of projects, the flow of commodities, or similar material matters.

Meanwhile, despite the discouraging atmosphere, the piecemeal evolution of an array of programs proceeded. Thus, the American view of counterinsurgency attached importance to the use of information and entertainment media to spread the word of the government's good works and intentions. The United States Information Service had long been occupied in building up the GVN's ability to do that job, having had a major role in the development of a Vietnamese Information Service (VIS), the spread of a government-controlled radio network, and the beginnings of television. It also put out its own magazines in Vietnamese and supported (along with AID) province newspapers and mobile information units to show films and present drama teams which were a kind of native cabaret. All of these spread a message along with the news and entertainment. Besides USIA, the U.S. military and AID both worked in the psychological (military) and media (AID) fields. To concentrate and improve the impact of this three-agency activity, a new combined organization dubbed the Joint United States Public Affairs Office (JUSPAO) was put together in 1965, headed by the USIA director in Vietnam. It partly unified the field activity in the provinces and some information activities in Saigon. It was, in fact, a precursor of later, more sweeping reorganizations affecting the whole of pacification.

Propaganda and information services can be of great value in any conflict, but practitioners are well aware that actions and words explaining them must dovetail if their efforts are to make a difference. The peasant will not accept verbal assurances and promises if his eyes and ears are delivering a different message. Describing the information booths that were built in each hamlet in Quang Nam province, Nighswonger writes: "[They] were often poorly located in the hamlet and the posted materials were rarely up-to-date. The condition of the structures suggested to this observer that they were rarely used and little appreciated by the hamlet people. They were empty symbols of community deference to external authority."[14] Not all of the effort was quite so irrelevant. The entertainment teams and mobile film programs were welcome and appreciated in most cases, for the villagers were starved for entertainment. But propaganda cannot accomplish much on its own in a political vacuum, and that, too often, was the state of affairs in rural Vietnam in those years.

THE SLOW PROCESS OF INTEGRATION

This survey of activity during the 1963–1965 period of political drift demonstrates that there was no lack of energy and resources invested in pacification. Although extremely small in comparison with military input, the investment was as much if not more than the demoralized Vietnamese government apparatus could absorb and use, and it kept growing. It was, however, a scattered deployment of separate programs, lacking any integrating strategy and low in priority. When General Khanh was importuned by the Americans to meet the need, he renamed strategic hamlets the New Life Hamlet Program and issued a "Victory" plan *(Chien Thang)* but this merely put a new name to the lagging effort and left it virtually unchanged. Clearly, the Vietnamese side of pacification was woefully disorganized and limp. But the U.S. side was hardly better. Although not lacking for lip service to the principle that popular support was essential for victory, the U.S. effort, by the measure of resources and attention committed, placed pacification in the lowest rank of priority and the military effort first. There were some, however, who were not satisfied with this state of affairs, and they gradually acquired influence as time passed and the military effort brought no real solutions. An uneven and fumbling progress occurred toward a higher priority, a better integration, and a more unified organization of the U.S. approach, culminating at last in a sweeping reorganization and reformation that finally emerged, after prolonged labor pains, in May 1967.

Why did it take the U.S. so long to bring about changes whose need was recognized by some as far back as 1962? There were many reasons, but chief among them were bureaucratic pride and inertia. As stated by one analyst of the matter who was also a key figure in the reorientation of the U.S. approach:

Counterinsurgency was never tried on a sufficient scale because it was not part of the institutional repertoire of most GVN and U.S. agencies involved. . . . It fell between stools and so was overshadowed from the outset by the more conventional approaches of the major GVN and U.S. institutions which were playing out their own institutional repertoires. The military institutions in particular knew how to mobilize resources, provide logistic support, deploy assets, manage large efforts. So they employed all these skills to develop irresistible momentum toward fighting their kind of war.[15]

And despite the unsuitability of the military approach, the weight and prestige of our military leaders in dealing with lethal conflict—a shooting war—gave their conventional perceptions enormous authority. Reinforced by the vastness of their resources, the military overshadowed the civilian contribution and resisted the criticisms of the "counterinsurgents." Still, the feeling persisted that something had to be done to focus and energize pacification, and so the search began, with no sure grasp of the nature of the problem and, at this stage, no comprehension of how far-reaching were the changes required.

Casting about for some means to focus pacification, the Americans hit upon the notion of identifying a single important area and concentrating sufficient resources and personnel there to achieve a clear and impressive victory. The program was dubbed *Hop Tac* (Cooperation) and the objective was to drive the enemy from the seven provinces immediately surrounding Saigon and keep him out permanently. A special *Hop Tac* command center was created in MACV and a counterpart center in the Vietnamese military staff. Plans were drawn up for a military sweep followed by a large dose of the entire range of existing pacification programs. The hastily concocted plans were launched in September 1964 and for several years afterward *Hop Tac* was considered a major feature of the U.S. effort in Vietnam. In fact, however, it achieved none of its goals and was eventually quietly submerged in a new nationwide plan developed in 1966.[16] According to a mission postmortem, its failure derived from the fact that it had never had more than token endorsement from the Vietnamese, to whom it seemed pointless and purely an American exercise to which they needed pay only lip service. The ARVN *Hop Tac* staff was a powerless office created merely to satisfy the Americans. The Vietnamese military in Saigon had the priority mission of guarding against a coup attempt and nothing was permitted to interfere with that overriding task. Without the cooperation of ARVN, pacification was, of course, an impossibility, and so the environs of Saigon remained for many years one of the least pacified rural areas in the country.

Hop Tac was proposed by no less a figure than Ambassador Henry Cabot Lodge, although he had completed his first ambassadorial stint and left before it was initiated. Lodge was one senior figure who maintained a serious commitment to counterinsurgency and took every available opportunity to advocate a greater emphasis and more effort in the cause. Unfortunately, his talents and concept of his job did not lie in management or in careful study of the realities confronting the concept. For example, he described the first step of an effective pacification program in these terms: "Saturate the minds of the people with some socially conscious and attractive ideology which is susceptible of being carried out."[17] Clearly implied is the feeling that ideologies are something like consumer goods, that sophisticated merchandising techniques could persuade Vietnamese peasants of the truth of any set of high-sounding ideas. In fact, as we have seen, words alone could have little impact on the masses of people adrift in the fast-changing currents of rural life; nor were programs themselves as important as style, process, and coordination of numerous activities to produce a unified effect, all very difficult for Americans even to grasp, let alone carry out. But in the search for a handle on the elusive problem, it was not surprising that some Americans would seize on hasty improvisations, of which *Hop Tac* can stand as an example. The building of a serious pacification program in Vietnam was in one aspect a progressive disillusionment with one such scheme after another.

Nevertheless, Lodge did succeed in maintaining rural pacification as high as possible on the list of goals in Vietnam, given the preoccupation with preventing complete collapse. On his return to the mission as ambassador in the summer of 1965 he indicated that his view of the priorities had not changed for he brought with him a staff officer who had become identified with the subject, Major General Edward Lansdale, returning to a Vietnam much changed from the early years of Diem when he had last served there. Accompanied by a small group of colleagues, some of whom had served with him ten years earlier, Lansdale did not request and was not given any operations to handle but was directed to focus on two tasks: political action in Saigon (presumably to help strengthen and improve the government of Prime Minister Ky) and, in Lodge's words, "to get pacification going."[18] In the latter role, the general was named the U.S. mission's contact with the new Ministry of Rural Construction. Lansdale was thus on the scene at the birth of a new Vietnamese approach to the subject which gave some signs of improved focus and seriousness. The process, however, was already under way before he and Lodge returned, and what, if anything, he contributed is difficult to say in the absence of specific evidence. In pursuit of his mission "to get pacification going" his ability to move government leaders in Saigon was limited for he had no programs or apparatus in the countryside. His influence was therefore based of necessity on intangibles. Still, he was able to unify somewhat the American voice—at least the civilian element—in its dealings with the Vietnamese on pacification, and that had utility. Perhaps his appointment, which was attended by much publicity, had the additional benefit of serving as a signal to both the U.S. mission and the GVN of the increased importance attached to pacification by influential Americans, with the ambassador at their head. Nevertheless, the appointment and the accompanying fanfare was another example of the unreality of Lodge's approach. He added a fifth wheel to a machine which was working poorly already and assumed that the benefits would automatically flow without further overhaul. If anything, Lansdale became a vague irritant to the other, more substantial parts of the faltering machine but in other regards had little influence on them.

By the time Lodge and Lansdale arrived, however, the GVN had already made some headway in the desired direction. It appeared that the new government of Prime Minister Nguyen Cao Ky had begun to move on long-delayed changes in policies and performance, of which pacification was one major example. The changes still consisted largely of preparatory actions, but in contrast to the leaderless confusion of the preceding twenty months, they held out the possibility of significant improvements. One reason was the critical factor of relative stability. The fall of Diem had left a political vacuum which only the generals who had brought him down could fill. The ensuing period of kaleidoscopic political turmoil resulted from deep divisions within the military, pitting various generations and cliques against one another. One difference that distinguished the Ky government from its predecessors was the relative unity (and it was only relative, for more than once coups were attempted and the regime seemed threatened) of the generals in support of the regime. There also appeared to be a greater seriousness of declared policies which emphasized "revolution," "anti-corruption," and more vigor in prosecuting the war. Time was to prove both the unity and the commitment to noble ideals to be considerably less than appeared but nevertheless there was improvement over the lassitude and confusion of the preceding regimes.

Within a month of his accession to office he and the new chief of state, General Nguyen Van Thieu, were briefing a visiting party led by Secretary of Defense McNamara on a new approach to pacification which in American parlance became "Revolutionary Development."[18] The novelty of the plan lay in two factors: It was to proceed by annual national plans, carefully developed well in advance and, it was said, realistically based on an appreciation of the situation and of the government's capabilities. Secondly, the cutting edge and impetus of the program were entrusted to a reorganized, retrained, and redeployed national cadre which was to absorb all existing cadre formations—a concept which, as we have noted earlier, emerged from experiments with the People's Action Teams and their analogues. Within this framework, the established rural improvement programs were to continue. The concept called for the Revolutionary Development Program to reestablish the government's authority throughout the countryside, hamlet by hamlet, village by village, spearheaded by the new cadre who, in turn, would be supported by all the existing services, civilian and military, with responsibilities in the villages.

The Americans concerned naturally welcomed these signs of a more considered and thoroughgoing approach, although there was never any unanimity on these matters and many skeptics viewed Revolutionary Development as an impractical and unsound diversion of resources. The advocates won the argument, however, because their proposals were concrete and in motion and they could point to some successes already gained by the new-style cadres. The opponents, on the other hand, were not united and had no concrete program to offer in place of RD. The decision was made to support the scheme because nothing else was tested and available, because the GVN was committed and because the specialists in the subject, in the embassy, in CIA, and in USOM, were enthusiastically in favor. Indeed, there is little doubt that the GVN's conversion to the proposal was also due in part to the coaching and persuasion of Ky and his entourage by contacts in the mission which included members of the CIA. Once committed, however, the GVN proceeded with some persistence to develop the details, the operational plan for 1966, the training school, and the new Ministry for Rural Construction[20] to which the program was assigned. This new ministry assumed the responsibilities and assets of various predecessor organizations and was placed under a civilian, Nguyen Tat Ung, who shortly thereafter died in an air crash. His replacement, General Nguyen Duc Thang, was a member of the ruling military group and chief of operations of the Joint General Staff, a job which he retained.

Revolutionary Development

The new program was the culmination and distillation of all previous experience with cadre schemes in Vietnam. It therefore amounted to a major commitment to the controversial philosophy underlying all versions of that approach: that the road to success in counterinsurgency in the circumstances existing in Vietnam, where a successful insurgency threatened to sweep all before it, was the forced draft development of a national corps of specialists who were to bring effective government directly into the hamlets and do it on a scale which would eventually reach everywhere in the country. All of the functions of the cadres were actually normal for existing arms of the administration or could have been assigned to them as extensions of normal responsibilities along with the additional personnel and other necessary means. Indeed, some maintained throughout these years that special cadres were not the best solution to the problem, that the same efforts invested in the regular government agencies would achieve the same results, achieve them more quickly, and leave as a valuable dividend permanent improvements in the regular civil service. The "British school" in particular saw a competent, professional public service as a key to counterinsurgency and special cadres as a costly diversion from that goal.[21] As we have seen, however, the dominant American theory favored a cadre approach and had done so for many years. Although the reasons for this approach were never explained authoritatively they seemed to reflect the sense that shortcuts were necessary to head off defeat, that a desperate situation called for urgent measures with immediate impact, that the regular ministries and government services were mired down hopelessly in red tape, timidity, and corruption—and, in fact, hardly functioned in the countryside—and so some substitute had to be devised. The cadres were intended to bring to the people a fresh, helpful, and supportive impact, to do it quickly, and, by combining many functions under one umbrella organization, to do it more efficiently than could have been done by a half-dozen separate agencies.

On the Vietnamese side, we know little about the motivations of Ky and his associates other than that they were influenced by the American enthusiasts and that they spoke often of a "revolutionary" approach to the country's problems. The program very likely appealed to them for the same reasons it appealed to the Americans, since none of them had confidence in the capabilities of the regular government services. There was also a small corps of true believers on the Vietnamese side of whom the most noted was a former province chief, Colonel Tran Ngoc Chau. Later Chau was to become the center of a *cause célebre* when, as a Vietnamese deputy, he attempted to thwart President Thieu's control system over the legislature, finally ending up in jail. In 1966, however, he was in favor with the regime and became the first director of the cadre program. Under him was the large new training center at Vung Tau, designed to be the means by which the new-style cadre program was to be set and kept upon its new course. Assisting him as director of training was first a certain Major Mai who had helped to devise the People's Action Teams. In 1966, however, he was replaced because of suspicions that he was attempting to exploit the cadres as a power base in support of Dai Viet party ambitions. He was replaced by Major (later Colonel) Nguyen Be, an intense and eloquent former Viet Minh officer who became the ideologist of the program. Be, as noted earlier, had designed one version of the new approach and had tested it in action in Binh Dinh province. His thinking owed much to his Viet Minh experience and to his conviction that the peasants could be brought to support the regime only by a thorough cleansing of local government and by substituting self-governing peasant communities for the existing system. He was, in fact, highly critical of virtually all aspects of the regime he served and did not always enjoy its favor.[22] His responsibilities under the program were limited to training the cadres, and he was never permitted to develop an independent power base built upon the cadre organization.

To the training task Be brought a personal charisma combined with some depth of experience, beginning with his service in the Viet Minh. The training was not only rigorous but featured some of the successful techniques of the Communists, including self-criticism sessions, a communal style of living, and an intense focus on a simple, repetitive set of principles stressing "the concept of fidelity . . . in personal relations and to the national cause."[23] By these means the course sought to "internalize" in the candidate cadres the basic elements of the approach. Like most earlier cadre programs, the new one also issued the standard peasant clothing of black cotton tunic and trousers, and in its early days, at least, stressed the recruitment of peasant youth who were then assigned back to their home provinces after completing the course.

Graduation came after thirteen weeks, and in a short while the facility at Vung Tau was turning out nearly five thousand men (and a few hundred women) every five weeks. The graduation ceremonies included speeches by senior officals, a solemn torchlight parade, and an impressive massive oath-taking. Every device the designers could invent was utilized to assure that the men and women who left Vung Tau to return to their home provinces were imbued with the creed of service to the people, reform, and improvement in peasant life. The extent to which they carried out the creed is another and far more complex question, but the training program at least was well conceived to form a dedicated and responsive body of men and women in the service of the new program.

At this time, the team structure was fixed at fifty-nine men, of whom thirty-four were specifically charged with assuring security. The entire team was armed with light weapons, but three eleven-man squads had the assignment of setting up and manning hamlet defenses, training villagers to form a self-defense force, and making the arrangements to tie in hamlet defenses with the nearby militia posts (Regional and Popular Forces) and the regulars of ARVN. In theory, the hamlet defenders were expected only to be able to hold off small squads of VC. If attacked by larger forces they were to be reinforced by RF/PF or ARVN units designated ahead of time and prepared to provide that service as required.

Meantime, the remainder of the team—twenty-five men and women—was to be performing the other tasks called for in the program. A civil affairs unit and a Census/Grievance unit were compiling a census, issuing identity cards, interviewing all hamlet residents to identify both VC supporters and government officials against whom the people had serious complaints, and determining the aspirations of the people for community improvements. When the team had completed its work and moved on, normally in six months, a permanent Census/Grievance representative stayed in place to continue the monitoring function, sending his reports to the Census/Grievance center in the province capital.

The civil affairs squad also proceeded to organize a new hamlet government. The appointed hamlet chief and his deputy were replaced by elected officials who were then trained in their new responsibilities, usually at the district capital. (Later they were sent to Vung Tau for a special course.) The teams were also required to set up functional groups—farmers, youths, and women being the most important—in frank imitation of the VC village organization. Such groups were intended as vehicles for further indoctrination and mobilization of the population. Another squad worked at social and economic development. It carried on with literacy programs, schools, small public works, and agricultural training and assistance, usually on the basis of self-help. The scheme also called upon the team to "carry out the land reform," a rather ambitious injunction which in reality meant something like this: establish the extent to which the land reform of 1956 had actually been carried out, identify the local obstacles, and remedy them to the extent that remedies lay within the power of the team.

Finally, the teams were trained and organized to collect information of intelligence interest and to conduct psychological warfare, propaganda, and information activities. They included several trained medics, usually women, who could treat minor illnesses, set up dispensaries, and train permanent medical technicians to remain in place when they moved on. The formal procedures laid out no fewer than ninety-eight tasks the teams were to undertake in a "Real New Life Hamlet" *(Ap Doi Moi)* to achieve eleven specific goals or criteria, beginning with the identification and destruction of the VC underground, ending with the "meritorious treatment of combatants," and including such vague injunctions as "rejuvenation of hamlet morals," as well as the very specific "eradication of illiteracy" and "development of a communication network." Other types of hamlets existed in which the approach was streamlined, but most required the full course of actions.[24]

This bare description of the team and its duties does not do justice to the fervor as well as the practical organizing effort that went into it. Training emphasized the "three withs"—"eat together [i.e., with the people], live together, and work together"—a formula lifted bodily from the Viet Cong. The manual of the RD Ministry, issued in 1966, stated in its first sentence, "We are determined to realize a social revolution in rural area [sic], aiming at destroying the present gloomy, old life and replacing it with a brighter and nicer new life." It went on to state that "each cadre should have at least three families that love him and treat him as one of their relatives. Cadres should stay long to help the people and never disturb them. Cadres should do first, enjoy later, and win the hearts and minds of the people."[25]

Nor, in concept, was the program simply a means for carrying out good works on a one-time basis. The goal was to put the hamlet upon the road to self-determination, to establish a process whereby it could take control of its own governance and, within limits, its own defense and its own standard of living. All these activities took place approximately at the same time, with, however, some priority going to defense at the earliest stage, consistent with the view commonly accepted by most theories of counterinsurgency, namely, that without security none of the other aspects of the program could be expected to have their intended impact. A team was normally given six months to complete its program in a single hamlet and would then move on to another one, usually nearby. The annual plans assigned priorities to certain areas of the country with some attention to the "oil-spot" principle of building out from secure areas and gradually expanding the secure zones until the whole country was covered. Follow-up after a hamlet had been completed included return visits by the team, further administrative training for the new officials, and incorporation of the Census/Grievance cadre into the permanent province administration in addition to routine administration of continuing aid and other civil and military programs.[26]

To manage the activity within each province a structure was set up which tied the teams into the civil government and security system, monitored their performance, and cleared the way for them with the governing authorities. At the province capital, a cadre control group sat in proximity to the province chief and participated in a province pacification committee headed by the province chief or his deputy. All relevant arms of the government in the province were represented in the committee.

The machinery was reasonably complete and workable. As an administrative design, RD benefited from years of trial and error, of partial, local experiments, and of the numerous failures that had preceded it. It also relied heavily on American aid and advice. CIA was designated the responsible U.S. agency, and in Saigon, Vung Tau, and each province capital, CIA advisers worked with the RD leadership (except for the liaison with the minister which, as already noted, was in General Lansdale's hands). Equipment, supplies, and, in fact, all material needs except salaries came from this source. The commitment of the regime leaders to administrative support was demonstrated when two-year draft exemptions were granted to cadres who had completed the training successfully and stayed with the program. Cadre pay also increased substantially in 1966.[27] The regime appeared to look upon the program as a good deal more than a token effort or a propaganda device. The initial annual target, established for 1966, was nineteen hundred hamlets concentrated largely in four priority areas.[28] By November 1966 the GVN acknowledged that these goals would not be met.[29] The regime wished to make clear the contrast between the sobriety of its approach and the irresponsibility of its predecessors.

Such factors suggested better auguries for this latest in a long line of strategies to wrest the initiative in the countryside away from the enemy.

The moment we are describing was the start of a long road, and many changes lay ahead. Without seeking to assess the program at this early stage, we can look for certain features which would eventually be essential for success. The program sought to alter attitudes in the villages by going directly into the target areas and changing the terms of existence there for the better. It was a scheme to affect government relations at the grass roots by stirring around among those roots. But if the problem grew out of the sum of government relations with the villagers, a plan to alter these relations would need to extend beyond the village, for many of the obstacles to political support originated else-where. Corrupt officials or ARVN soldiers preying upon a community could only be dealt with further up the chain of command. A predatory village official often was protected by a patron at district level and above. One question then was whether the RD program was accompanied by parallel improvement throughout the government structure. Put differ-ently, was the military regime serious about reforming itself?

A second question related to the economy of the village, and here, while there were many facets to the problem, the principal issue was land reform. Because of the preoccupation of the Vietnamese peasant with the ownership of the land, land redistribution had more political impact and permanent effect than any other measure contemplated. Although American enthusiasm for land reform waxed and waned over the years, and there was some tendency during these years to dismiss its impor-tance, the issue was permanently on the agenda because the Viet Cong kept it there. Nothing made the government cause more unpalatable in the village than the knowledge that restoration of government control meant the return of the landlords and the collection of back rents. The violation of rent restrictions which went unpunished was another facet of the same problem. At its inception, Revolutionary Development had little to offer on the subject, other than requiring the teams to monitor the enforcement of the law to the extent of their limited power. The government's approach to land reform was thus a matter not included in the RD program but which was nevertheless important for its success.

Again, the effort would rest in part on the active support of the military and paramilitary forces controlled by ARVN. The RD teams and the hamlet defense units they formed were not expected to provide security against large-scale or persistent attacks. If such attacks came, the teams—and later, after the teams had left, the hamlet defenders—were to be linked by radio to heavier units which were supposed to move quickly to their support. Underlying this plan was the assumption that the regular forces had a commitment to react to the call for help regardless of the time of day or night or other circumstances. In their relationship to the hamlet defenders they were a fire brigade. Moreover, the knowledge that reliable help was not far away would certainly affect the morale and determination of the part-time village defenders, as would the other services for which the hamlet soldiers depended on the regulars and the province administration: weapons and weapons replacement, ammunition resupply, inspection, and training. The defense system therefore depended as much on the regulars as it did on the irregulars, and the question raised was how seriously did the regular forces take the commitment.

Finally, we come to the complex matter of the hamlets' and villages' sense of their place in the dispensations of the new government. As we have seen, much of the VC's success came from its systematic effort to create among the villagers a sense of participation in decisions that affected their lives—some of that stemming from the fact that local men could rise to important rank in the system, thereby ameliorating the old state of alienation between the urban elite that controlled the administration of laws and the general population. It would indeed have been a revolutionary change for the Ky regime to have sought to alter the scheme of things in the countryside to the extent of recruiting district-level or province-level officials from the villages. They never contemplated such a drastic reordering of affairs, nor did the Americans seriously propose it. Both tended to see education as the most important criterion for civil service recruitment, thus automatically ruling out most peasants. American ideas run on different lines in such matters, and the preferred solution to the problem was to build democratic political processes and self-government in Saigon. This, no doubt, was an approach which in theory might also have worked to produce the desired results if the delicate growth of democratic process could have been brought about in the midst of war in a countryside with no previous democratic experience. It was clearly a course filled with difficulty, but, as we shall see, it was the route chosen. How well it achieved its aims would also impinge on the success of Revolutionary Development.

Thus, while the concept, as well as public discussion, of Revolutionary Development focused heavily upon the teams, their recruitment, training, and performance—in fact, the program's success—depended as much upon the rest of the government, on its ability to reform itself, to generate a greater dedication from the military and civilian services, as it did on the fifty-nine-man teams. It was a test, in fact, of the ability of the South Vietnamese to rise to the needs of the crisis and of the Americans to manage their support to maximize its effect in the critical areas which would determine success or failure.

THE TAKEOFF AT HONOLULU

The apparently stagnant years of 1964 and 1965 were, as we can now see, actually a time of gradual development of a new attack, more complex and more thoroughgoing, on the problems of the countryside.

However, the process had been quiet and, partly because CIA was involved, deliberately obscure. In fact, nothing more than a beginning had been achieved. In the meantime, in Washington, attention had finally ceased to be riveted on the course of the war and on the threat of political collapse. With the insertion of American troops, the military emergency had eased while in a short time it became clear that the war would not end quickly. The new government of Ky and Thieu offered somewhat encouraging signs of an improved grasp of affairs and, as we have seen, took action on some of the stubborn and neglected problems of the country.

The attempt to disarm the political dynamism of the Viet Cong by offering a better life for ordinary Vietnamese had always remained one of the rhetorical commitments of the U.S. In the latter part of 1965, as fears of disaster eased off, impatience began to be evident in the press and the Congress that too little was being done to fulfill that commitment. It was, for example, one of the themes of Senator Fulbright in his growing skepticism about the war and promised to be fully aired in a new series of Senate Foreign Relations Committee hearings scheduled for February 1966.

President Johnson, of course, was sensitive to the growing pressure. A message from the State Department to the Saigon mission in late 1965 said, "There is continuing concern at the highest levels here regarding need to emphasize our non-military programs in Vietnam and give them maximum possible public exposure."[30] This steady buildup of public concern was apparently the motive behind the president's sudden decision in February 1966 to call a meeting on very short notice between himself and his principal aides and Prime Minister Ky and his lieutenants. The location was Honolulu and the participants had no more than two days to prepare themselves to "discuss the political and economic future of the country." Obediently, Ky and his aides flew off for two hectic days of meetings with Lyndon Johnson and several dozen of his principal advisers which produced a long communiqué and many words stating the renewed commitment of both sides to improving the ordinary Vietnamese's lot in life.

The Honolulu conference was thus hastily organized and conducted in considerable confusion. It did succeed, however, in making clear to senior members of both governments that the president of the United States was serious in his commitment to improving the lot of the Vietnamese people. Promises were made and activity launched across the gamut of social, economic, and political needs of the battle-scarred country, and, among the programs which received much emphasis, emerging from the Honolulu sessions with a new and far higher priority, was pacification. From that time onward, all Americans involved with Vietnam understood this fact. The details agreed upon there to implement the decisions taken were quickly superseded, but the impetus given to pacification by the unprecedented gathering of high officials lasted for the duration of the war.

The Road to CORDS

Governments demonstrate the seriousness of their good resolutions by reorganizing. There are sound reasons for this, not the least of which is to signal to the bureaucracy itself that more than mere words is involved. In the case of the U.S. organization for pacification, moreover, reorganization was overdue. From the days of strategic hamlets, critics had pointed out that the Saigon mission was not sufficiently unified to perform at best efficiency.[31] In the years since, no far-reaching changes had been made. Thus, General Taylor, although empowered by a sweeping delegation of authority from the president to gather all the threads, military and civilian, into his hands,[32] did not fulfill the proffered role of proconsul. He left military matters to the new COMUSMACV, General Westmoreland, whom he had handpicked himself. He did rename the Country Team the Mission Council and systematize it with prepared agendas and detailed follow-up by a secretariat, but each agency retained separate responsibility for managing its own operations and for its own organization, which reflected the sense of urgency (or lack of it) of the separate chiefs. The unidentified author of the chapter "Re-emphasis on Pacification: 1965–67" in the *Pentagon Papers* describes the situation with a clarity that suggests he probably knew it from the inside:

> Each agency had its own ideas on what had to be done, its own communications channels with Washington, its own personnel and administrative structure—and starting in 1964–65, each agency began to have its own field personnel operating under separate and parallel chains of command. This latter event was ultimately to prove the one which gave reorganization efforts such force, since it began to become clear to people in Washington and Saigon alike that the Americans in the provinces were not always working on the same team, and that they were receiving conflicting and overlapping instructions from a variety of sources in Saigon and Washington.[33]

As the same writer points out, pressure for reorganization came principally from Washington and was steadily resisted by the agency heads in Saigon who, in effect, were being asked to curtail and merge their own authority. Finally, after Honolulu, the president himself took a hand. In three stages an entirely new and unprecedented arrangement was hammered out which finally unified the pacification effort, although, even after it was completed, it still left intact the basic division in other activities between the civilian and military arms of the government.

The first step was the relatively simple one of making Deputy Ambassador William Porter, the second-ranking civilian in the U.S. hierarchy, responsible for coordinating the civil side of pacification and devoting himself full-time to this task with the assistance of a small staff. Porter remained the ambassador's only deputy and, more important, he limited his own role to coordination, to negotiating agreements among the various participating agencies which remained unaffected in their internal arrangements; and that was the heart of the problem.

This step took place shortly after Honolulu as an organizational follow-up to the decisions taken there. In effect, it merely stiffened the apparatus for producing agreed decisions, and to the critics of the mission's organization it was merely a small step toward rational management. Before taking further steps, however, the president saw the necessity of putting his own house in order first. Some of the same defects that hindered the effort in Saigon existed in Washington: a cumbersome process of coordination under a low-ranking standing committee was the sole interagency unifying vehicle aside from the formal and informal meetings of principals that occurred regularly, for the Special Group (C.I.) had been disbanded by President Johnson, on the advice of General Taylor. In its place, a new series of regional committees had been established within the NSC structure to handle its (and all other routine) business, topped by a Senior Interdepartmental Group under the undersecretary of state.[34] Although, according to Taylor, his purpose in recommending this reorganization had been to strengthen the government's ability to deal with Communist insurgencies, the new system was given no role in Vietnam and showed "little interest in the counterinsurgency mission which the President assigned to it."[35] Something else was clearly needed to deal with the major preoccupation of the foreign affairs and national security communities in those years. It emerged quickly after Honolulu, taking the form of a special office in the White House created specifically for the coordination and energizing of civilian efforts in Vietnam. In NSAM 343, which set up this office, the president said:

> In my view, it is essential to designate a specific focal point for the direction, co-ordination and supervision in Washington of U.S. non-military programs relating to Vietnam. I have accordingly designated Mr. Robert W. Komer as Special Assistant to me for carrying out this responsibility.
>
> I have charged him . . . to assure that adequate plans are prepared and co-ordinated covering all aspects of such programs, and that they are promptly and effectively carried out. The responsibility will include the mobilization of U.S. military resources in support of such programs.[36]

The language, notably such words as "direction" and "supervision," which are highly charged terms in a bureaucracy, was sweeping enough. As in all such matters, however, the key decision was the choice of the individual to occupy the new chair. The president's selection, Robert W. Komer, had been a member of the NSC staff since 1961, specializing in matters other than Vietnam and known for the energy and self-assurance with which he tackled any task. He decided on only a small staff—a fact which immediately placed in question the seriousness of the terms "direction" and "supervision" in his mandate—but nevertheless moved rapidly to attempt to live up to his instructions.

Although he did not actually (and probably did not seriously aspire to) "supervise and direct" in the sense of detailed, day-by-day management of the Washington civilian apparatus, he nevertheless used his authority and his access to the president (also explicitly granted in the NSAM) to prod and urge the bureaucracy on with its tasks. His mandate was broader than counterinsurgency, and he devoted much effort to such matters as combating the inflationary impact of the American presence and breaking the bottleneck of the Port of Saigon. Two of the accomplishments of this new office were particularly important: Komer succeeded in maintaining and strengthening the newly acquired priority of civilian affairs, notably of pacification, and he played the key role in bringing about the successive reorganizations of the mission that culminated in the formation of a new structure that came to be called CORDS—Civilian Operations and Revolutionary Development Support. In addition, he concentrated attention and generated new activity on specific operational programs which were important components of pacification but had tended to be neglected. Among them were *Chieu Hoi*, land reform, and the RD cadre. By dint of a constant barrage of cables which often invoked the authority of the "highest levels of the government," of some seven field trips to Vietnam in the course of a year, and of a copious flow of memoranda and reports, he achieved an undoubted impact. Thus, land reform returned to the agenda as an immediate goal, and support for the cadre program became established as a first priority.

All of this activity naturally generated friction along with movement. Komer was not popular in the U.S. mission. This is not surprising since his approach was that of a gadfly which it is unsafe to ignore. Probably to the mission the least appealing aspect of his effort was his emphasis on improved organization. Americans in Saigon, as was understandable, believed that the newly intensified pressures from Washington were excessive and, having already reorganized once in response to the new mood, were inclined to feel that their structure should be given more time to prove itself. In the view of their Washington overseers, however, the designation of Porter as full-time coordinator did not sufficiently unify the effort.

Komer's focus on reorganization was reinforced by other voices. During the post-Honolulu period, U.S. operations in Vietnam were subjected to intense scrutiny by various study groups and by high-level visitors of whom the most important were Undersecretary of State Katzenbach and Secretary McNamara. In addition, a select group of officers which had been commissioned by the army chief of staff to study new actions to achieve U.S. aims in Vietnam submitted its report in March 1966. All of these various inquiries came to a similar conclusion on pacification—that it was lagging—and on the importance of reorganization.

McNamara's 1966 views on pacification are particularly worth considering in some detail, for they represent a grittily realistic survey of the scene as a whole with a new emphasis on that aspect at a time when criticism of the Vietnam effort was rising steadily even while the administration was insisting that progress was being made and that the problems were well within U.S. capability to manage. From the point of view of counterinsurgency, they are the sanest and most sober comment to be made during the period by a senior official.

> Pacification [he said] is a basic disappointment. . . . [It] has, if anything gone backward. . . .
>
> The large-unit war . . . is largely irrelevant to pacification as long as we do not lose it. By and large, the people in rural areas believe that the GVN when it comes will not stay but that the VC will; that cooperation with the GVN will be punished by the VC; that the GVN is really indifferent to the people's welfare; that the low-level GVN are tools of the local rich; and that the GVN is ridden with corruption.
>
> Success in pacification depends on the interrelated functions of providing physical security, destroying the VC apparatus, motivating the people to cooperate, and establishing responsive local government. An obviously necessary but not sufficient requirement for success of the RD cadre and police is vigorously conducted and adequately prolonged clearing operations by military troops who will "stay" in the area, who behave themselves decently and who show respect for the people.
>
> This elemental requirement for pacification has been missing. In almost no contested area designated for pacification in recent years have ARVN forces actually "cleared and stayed" to a point where cadre teams, if available, could have stayed overnight in hamlets and survived, let alone accomplish their mission.

After this grim sketch of the problems, McNamara turned to the remedies:

> The first essential reform is in the attitude of GVN officials. They are generally apathetic, and there is corruption high and low. Often appointments, promotions, and draft deferments must be bought; and kickbacks on salaries are common. Cadres at the bottom can be no better than the system above them.
>
> The second needed reform is in the attitude and conduct of the ARVN. The image of the government cannot improve unless and until the ARVN improves markedly. They do not understand the importance (or respectability) of pacification nor the importance to pacification of proper, disciplined

conduct. Promotions, assignments and awards are often not made on merit, but rather on the basis of having a diploma, friends, or relatives, or because of bribery. The ARVN is weak in dedication, direction and discipline. . . .

Furthermore, it is my conviction that a part of the problem undoubtedly lies in bad management on the American as well as the GVN side. Here split responsibility—or "no responsibility"—has resulted in too little pressure on the GVN to do its job and no really solid or realistic planning with respect to the whole effort. We must deal with this management problem now and deal with it effectively. [Emphasis added.]

The Secretary concluded his comments on pacification with a warning that echoes somberly even today. Of all of his recommendations, he said,

the most difficult to implement is perhaps the most important one— enlivening the pacification program. The odds are less than even for this task, if only because we have failed so consistently since 1961 to make a dent in the problem. But because the 1967 trend of pacification will, I believe, be the main talisman of ultimate U.S. success or failure in Vietnam, extraordinary imagination and effort should go into changing the stripes of the problem.[37]

This analysis was unusual in a number of ways. It clearly showed that pacification had, in fact, achieved the highest of priorities in the mind of the man who had become the principal director of the U.S. effort in Vietnam. This had not been the case in years past. Secondly, it spoke with a frankness about the defects of the GVN that was startling from an official of McNamara's rank. He was saying, in effect, that the U.S. was backing with American lives and wealth a corrupt and incompetent government which was failing in its basic duties. Had his views been made public at the time, they would no doubt have had an explosive effect on American opinion. Thirdly, his comments on the components of a successful pacification program amount to a doctrinal statement and show some breadth of understanding of the nature of the problem, although expressed in very general terms. What is absent from McNamara's comments is any suggestion that these problems have systemic roots which also need to be analyzed, that the deficiencies might not ultimately be susceptible to technical, administrative treatment, or to U.S. "imagination and effort" no matter how "extraordinary."

The lack was an understandable one, for to seek the roots of the problem was to come up against the fragmented nature of the Vietnamese society and the realization that the American investment was based on most unpromising social and political foundations whose weaknesses very possibly could not be cured by foreign efforts, no matter how benevolent or energetic. In other words it would have been defeatist, a viewpoint no one in McNamara's position could adopt and remain in the government. Another blind spot, needless to say, was the absence of reference to the tactical failures of the approach adopted by the American military—a point we will discuss in due course. Although he avoided defeatism, he came quite close in estimating the chances of "enlivening pacification" as less than even.

The national security community was free to accept or reject what it chose of McNamara's analysis, but his policy recommendations were another matter. His comments on reorganization, moreover, were echoed by most of the other high-level reviews noted earlier. Under the energetic orchestration of Komer, a consensus had developed among the president, McNamara, and the Joint Chiefs that unification of pacification was essential, and that, since the mission did not agree, the reorganization had to be brought about by presidential fiat.[38] On November 26, 1966, after several weeks of rearguard resistance, the mission bowed to the inevitable and accepted the changes which had been directed by the president. At the same time, this initial measure did not propose complete reorganization linking military and civilian efforts into one structure. That final step was left as a future possibility to be considered after a period of ninety to one hundred and twenty days, during which civilian control was to be given a chance to show its mettle.

The details of the reorganization as they were worked out by the mission bodily removed the field offices of all the civilian agencies—that is, all their provincial operations—from the control of the heads of the agencies and transferred them to a new entity, the Office of Civilian Operations (OCO) whose head reported to Deputy Ambassador William Porter. Pay for personnel and other support continued to be the responsibility of each agency, but the operations themselves were to be carried out under the direction and control of the new office. Similarly, the civilian personnel and activities of each agency in each province were unified under the direction of a single official who became the counterpart of the MACV province (sector, in military terminology) adviser and the Vietnamese province chief. A similar pattern was decreed for the four regional commands (also known as corps tactical zones). At the same time, General Westmoreland designated a brigadier general to be his special assistant for pacification and to provide liaison between his command and OCO.

Administratively, what resulted was a major upheaval producing much internal confusion at the start. The activity reached a furious pace, but it was largely internal to the U.S. mission, and necessarily so, as the new office sorted itself out, selected its staff, and developed its procedures. Visible progress in the war could hardly be achieved quickly in any case, but progress of any kind had to wait until the machinery was working properly. In the meantime, a deadline hung over the new arrangement and every day brought closer the threat of the transfer of all pacification programs to the control of the military command.

The deadline was unrealistic, and that fact gave rise to the view among those affected that the decision to leave the civilian apparatus under civilian control had not been a serious one, that the plan from the beginning had been to arrange a two-stage transfer. This, in fact, was correct. In order to reduce inevitable criticism by those who opposed further militarization of the effort in Vietnam, the civilians were given a last chance to achieve what would have been an administrative miracle, with a fallback position prepared in the event they failed, and such failure was assumed to be likely. As Komer stated later, "he [the president] stacked the deck."[39] Given the inability of the civilians to make any impact with existing pacification programs and the absence of any civilian figure who could have plausibly seized the reins over the military side of pacification, the decision would have had to be made sooner or later. Most important in the minds of Komer and others in Washington, only the military side of the U.S. effort controlled adequate manpower and organization to take it over and make progress quickly. In the event, as we shall see, the CORDS solution turned out not to be so much a military takeover as the creation of a novel hybrid, retaining civilian attributes and control within the military structure which the new entity used for its own purposes without being swallowed up.

The denouement of the organizational drama of U.S. pacification came in May 1967, shortly after Ambassador Ellsworth Bunker took over the mission from Henry Cabot Lodge. Claiming to have studied the situation carefully, he announced his conclusion that assignment of the pacification role to the U.S. military had become necessary. Presumably, Bunker had retained a veto if he had chosen to exercise it, but in any case he appears to have agreed strongly with the decision, which he saw as a necessary strengthening of management. At the same time, he announced his conclusion that the new arrangement did not necessarily have to amount to a complete military takeover. As he put it in a message to Washington:

> As senior U.S. official in Vietnam, I intend to keep a close eye on all U.S. activities, including pacification—I am not abdicating any of my responsibilities . . . during 34 years in the business world I have learned that unified management with clear lines of authority is the way to get the most out of large-scale and diversified programs. . . . I intend to see that the civilian element of the U.S. effort is not buried under the military—in many instances soldiers will end up working for civilians as well as the reverse.

CORDS Is Launched

For the second time in less than six months, the pacification machinery in the U.S. mission was plunged into the throes of reorganization. The results showed the shrewdness of the decision to make the change in two stages, for most of the more wrenching changes, those involving the severance of whole limbs and organs and combining them into a new entity, had already been made in the creation of OCO. The process, therefore, proved less painful and caused less upset to the programs than some expected. The major alterations occurred in the superstructure rather than the operating levels, which is not to say that they were unimportant, for they made it possible for the command to move and operate the U.S. pacification support mechanism as a single, fully combined unit.

CORDS combined all the civilian programs of OCO with the facilities existing in MACV to support pacification, including a major part of the military advisory apparatus. It placed a single individual in command of the combined facility, and supported him with a staff directorate in MACV, coequal with the conventional staffs of a joint command such as J-1, J-2, and the rest. This directorate reported to a deputy to MACV, a civilian with the rank of ambassador and the assimilated military rank of a four-star general. At the next level below Saigon—the four corps commands—the CORDS chief was a deputy to the corps commander, and at province and district level the entire military advisory staff was transferred to CORDS. The combined civilian and military apparatus in each province was placed under a single chief who might be soldier or civilian. One of the first tasks of the new leadership was to designate these CORDS province senior advisers, selecting on merit and experience, without regard to service status.

The man named to fill the position of deputy to COMUSMACV for CORDS was its chief architect, Robert Komer, who now shifted the scene of his activity from Washington to Saigon, bringing with him the same energy and direct form of attack that he had relied on as assistant to President Johnson. It was a natural choice, for Komer had early decided upon this solution to the organizational problem and had pressed for it against much opposition. Having played a major role in designing it, he was able to move rapidly to use the authority bestowed on him with no pause for "reading in." There is little doubt that this choice of leadership was a factor in launching CORDS with relative smoothness and speed.

Also a major factor in launching the new mechanism rapidly was the attitude of General Westmoreland. The U.S. commander not only accepted with good grace the unprecedented grafting of a civilian/military hybrid onto his command but supported Komer in his dealings with the MACV staff, extending to major policy matters where his military advisers opposed CORDS initiatives. He seemed determined that MACV not play the role of an obstacle to CORDS and thus be forced to accept the onus of possible failure. This attitude was clearly communicated to his command and was decisive.

A major question in discussions leading up to the CORDS decision concerned how the Vietnamese would react, there being some concern that the change might discourage the movement of the GVN—urged repeatedly by the U.S.—toward a civilian and constitutional regime, and thus bring on the further militarization of pacification. To head off such a movement, briefings and discussions were undertaken with the key Vietnamese. Initially it seemed reasonable to some of the GVN figures that they should undertake a parallel shake-up, placing all of pacification under the Ministry of Defense, but this was successfully opposed by the Americans.[41] One effect which became apparent only with the passage of time was a gradual increase in the importance attached by the Vietnamese to pacification. Although delayed beyond the American awakening as represented by CORDS, it was no doubt helped in that direction by the example.

The net result of the organizational upheavals of 1966 and 1967 was the knitting together of a dispersed and disparate group of programs into a unified management structure disposing of some sixty-five hundred people, military and civilian, and an initial budget of about $500 million in U.S. funds together with many billions in U.S.-owned piasters and in GVN appropriations.[42] The organization now extended down from Saigon through regional and province levels to the 250 districts in the country where subsector advisory teams operated in support of the district government and its security efforts. This apparatus supported and advised—in effect, guided—a variety of ongoing Vietnamese programs of which some were well under way and others merely limping along. The programs reached down even further into the rural heartland, conducting activities in many of the twelve thousand hamlets which were the frontline of the war. A single official presided over this entire advisory structure, supported by an adequate staff to give him control of his operations, to enable him to plan in detail and over a longer term than heretofore, and to support his field activities.

The solution appeared to respond adequately to the problem it was intended to resolve, although several flaws continued to hamper and embarrass the effort. For one thing, no counterpart organization to CORDS functioned in Washington. Komer's former office, the Special Assistant to the President for Vietnam Civil Affairs, remained in existence under a senior foreign service officer, but with Komer in Saigon it was overshadowed from afar and gradually atrophied. In effect, the deputy COMUSMACV for CORDS continued to orchestrate his Washington support by cable and occasional visits, a system which responded to his demands but did no more than was asked of it.

A second weakness stemmed from the ad hoc nature of the solution: CORDS existed by virtue of presidential fiat and had no basis in legislation. One could say, and some did, that it usurped the authorities and resources allocated by Congress to the separate agencies. This led to a degree of resentment and foot-dragging and also to some uncertainty about which portions of each organization remained under the authority of its statutory leadership and which had been loaned to CORDS.

But these weaknesses were minor and caused no serious obstruction to the effort. The U.S. pacification effort was now united as it had not been before, but still a major and significant gap remained at the top of the U.S. structure. The civilian side of affairs, still under the ambassador, remained separate from the military aside from the normal requirement that both sides coordinate their activities closely. Despite the incorporation of CORDS into the military organization and the considerable influence it was able to bring to bear from within MACV to modify military practices which impacted unfavorably upon pacification, no element existed inside or outside the military to prevail on fundamentals. The military continued to fight in the fashion it was familiar with and preferred. Given the reluctance in the U.S. and the lack of support in public or in Congress for the unprecedented move of placing strong civilian restraints on the military in combat, the concept of a proconsul in the style of General Templer in Malaya was not attempted. The creation of CORDS was the final organizational innovation attempted by the U.S. in Vietnam.

The events of May 1967 were thus the climax of a lengthy—far too lengthy—process by which the U.S. converted the nominal priority of pacification in Vietnam into an actual priority. Events confirmed the view that organization as well as resource allocation must reflect policy if the latter is to represent more than a pious hope. The actions which followed upon the reorganization and made a reality of the priorities will be the subject of the next chapter.

8

CORDS in Charge: Vietnam, 1967–1972

★ ★ ★

In the pages that follow, we will trace the course of the action program undertaken by the new CORDS organization with an inevitable emphasis upon American measures and policies, for this is the principal interest of our study, and, besides, the record is clear that pacification was, in the entire period from 1963 to the end, an American initiative. The Americans developed virtually all of the programs and concepts (sometimes, as in the case of Revolutionary Development, in collaboration with some exceptional Vietnamese), established priorities, and contributed most of the resources. On the other hand, it remained entirely an advisory program which would succeed or fail to the degree that the GVN willingly and energetically carried out its share which was, in number of people involved, overwhelmingly the larger part of the effort. The Americans could advise and prod and persuade but they could not do the job themselves. The story of the CORDS phase of pacification is thus the story of how the Americans organized, managed, and implemented an effort to induce the Vietnamese to do the right amounts of the right kinds of things so as to secure the countryside and gain the willing support of the rural population.

PROJECT TAKEOFF

Komer did not delay in putting to use the powers and resources of his new office. He moved rapidly to obtain certain policy decisions which were critical to his concept of the needs of pacification and to fill obvious gaps in the program array with new or revised programs. One such gap which had long concerned all participants was the absence of continuous security for the hamlets. In an attempt to provide the needed security capability he sought a major policy decision at the start, assigning to CORDS responsibility for support, advice, and training of ARVN's paramilitary auxiliaries, the Regional and Popular Forces. The decision was a critical addition to CORDS' ability to affect directly the security environment in the countryside and it led to a greatly enlarged program of support and development for these neglected rural units. Numbers were steadily increased, reaching a half million in 1970; weapons, which had consisted of World War II leftovers, were replaced by the M-16 and other modern light armament. The entire paramilitary force was re-trained by five-man mobile advisory teams, eventually numbering 355. They conducted the training in the field and often served in an advisory capacity to local commanders. ARVN was persuaded to upgrade its RF/PF staff and replace the colonel commanding with a lieutenant general.[1]

The decision was an early example of the value of the CORDS concept, for it is unlikely that MACV would have agreed otherwise to turn control of such a large military advisory program, intimately involved with ARVN, to a civilian pacification management. Even more remarkable was Westmoreland's agreement, early in the life of CORDS, to remove the MACV sector advisory teams from the chain of command which tied them to the division advisory teams and thus to the regular ARVN command channels. ARVN division commands, closely control-ling the pacification activities in each province, had become enmeshed in province politics and power rivalries to the detriment of both their primary functions and of pacification. Although the Americans could not directly change ARVN's internal arrangements, the argument was made that ARVN would eventually follow any pattern established by MACV. Komer therefore made the recommendation and Westmoreland, previ-ously opposed to the change, now accepted it.[2] Ultimately, ARVN did the same. Both chains of command were now in tandem and had eliminated a purely military link at a critical level.

These were significant improvements, although their impact should not be overstated. The RF and PF were substantially improved in the ensuing years and came to be a major factor in establishing better rural security; improved capability, however, by no means always guaranteed improved results. The better-trained and better-armed militia performed unevenly, depending on the quality of local leadership. Often they continued to button themselves up in their fortified outposts at night instead of patrolling and laying ambushes. They were sometimes slow to respond to calls for help from hamlets, especially at night, and they were frequently used for personal security and static duties at the pleasure of the province or district chiefs. Although division commands played a reduced role in local security arrangements, the local government was still in the hands of ARVN officers on active duty. CORDS could and did attempt to transfer individuals who had behaved corruptly or otherwise demonstrated incapacity, but changing individuals did not change the system. In addition to being a national defense force, ARVN was also a political cabal whose first priorities were to perpetuate the system and to protect the safety, livelihood, and future prospects of those who controlled it. CORDS was thus able to bring about changes which were out of the reach of any previous American organization, but that very fact tended to highlight the outer limits of the technical, administrative approach to the fundamental problem of Vietnam which was, first and last, a political problem.

The Origins of Phoenix

Such considerations anticipate somewhat. Returning to our account, CORDS, while busying itself with the establishment of a headquarters staff, managed also to move systematically on substantive programs, committed to the principle that American resources, skills, and dedication, effectively focused, would eventually prevail upon the Vietnamese to alter their behavior patterns.

One of the early priorities was the attempt to improve the exploitation of the growing volume of intelligence on the Viet Cong and to focus that process on the most important target, namely, the enemy's directing organization, the government organs and structure of the Viet Cong. Earlier we noted that an elaborate and sophisticated network based on the People's Revolutionary Party organization managed all VC activity. Within the American bureaucracy it was dubbed "the VC infrastructure." In 1967 the CIA proposed that all U.S. intelligence agencies pool their information on the VC infrastructure at the district, province, and Saigon levels and agree on assigning responsibility for exploitation. Permanent centers were proposed at province and district levels staffed by the participating agencies. At Saigon, a permanent staff was to be established, headed by a CIA officer, to whom other agencies would also assign staff. Its function would be to support, monitor, and guide the local centers in the field. Exploitation—that is, the taking of action on the intelligence screened, collated, and put into usable form at the district centers—was the responsibility initially of the subsector adviser, who was to avail himself of the most suitable resources in the area. In a large number of cases the Provincial Reconnaissance Units were most readily available, for the Americans had a more direct role in their control, but police and military units could also be called on. It should be made clear at this point that this entire U.S. structure was intended to support and advise Vietnamese operating units. From the beginning of Phoenix, the Americans proposed but the Vietnamese disposed of the operating units and used or, as often happened, mis-used them in accordance with their own notions. At the outset no effort was made to persuade the Vietnamese to establish a counterpart staff structure.

This program in its origins was entirely American and largely the initiative of the CIA. It was first called the Intelligence Coordination and Exploitation Program (ICEX) and began to take shape in the regions during the last months of OCO. The Vietnamese were advised of the plan but were not pressed immediately to adopt it as their own. That, in brief, was the origin of the most controversial of the U.S. pacification efforts, the Phoenix program. To its originators it seemed the essence of straightforward common sense, a managerial device to pull together a scattered and diverse effort by often competing and duplicating units, to focus it, eliminate inefficiencies, and direct it precisely against what many believed to be the enemy jugular. In this spirit, Komer enthusiastically adopted it, obtained COMUSMACV's endorsement, and assigned it a high priority. For a new, more impressive name, he chose Phoenix, an approximate translation of Phung Hoang—"all-seeing bird"—already being used by the Vietnamese. He began discussions with the Vietnamese leading to their adoption in 1968 of a counterpart staff structure also bearing the name Phung Hoang. CORDS also proposed for it one of its preferred management techniques, that of assigning quotas of Viet Cong Infrastructure (VCI) members who were to be "neutralized," i.e., eliminated by whatever means (they were not specified), in each month.

This decision can stand as a symbol for the mismarriage of enthusiastic American managerial technique with Vietnamese indifference that produced the Phoenix failure. Phoenix made certain unexamined assumptions which proved to be damaging to its purposes and to pacification. These assumptions were shared by all of those who saw effective counterinsurgency as the heart of the matter in Vietnam, including the British experts led by Sir Robert Thompson.[3] The concept, in fact, owed much to British experience in Malaya and to the belief, frequently voiced by Thompson, that a program which ignored the enemy infrastructure was doomed to failure in the long term, if not the short. For, the theory held, the infrastructure of dedicated Communist cadres gave the enemy his staying power, his ability to adapt to new conditions, to regenerate his strength, and to stay the course of a "protracted war." The threat, therefore, could not finally be disposed of while the VCI survived intact.

Among the unexamined assumptions made by the program were several that related to operational matters. Thus, it was assumed that the various competing and jealous Vietnamese intelligence services could be forced to cooperate, share information, and contribute qualified personnel to a combined effort. In the event, lacking the power of command, the U.S. was unable to force co-operation. The sharing of information was meager and the Vietnamese police and military tended to assign their least valued personnel to the district and provincial centers. They had more urgent priorities, including the goal of advancing their own positions in competition with rival services. Pooling of effort in a center where service identity was merged in a larger whole did not serve that purpose. The Police Special Branch, which should have been the key to an improved effort, was a serious offender.

Again, it was assumed that the arrest of infrastructure members would remove them from the picture. The reality was quite different. The judicial and correctional systems were inadequate to cope with a large new influx of prisoners. Bribery and official indifference together with the shortage of facilities led to many prisoners being released soon after their apprehension. One estimate made by Phoenix advisers stated that in 1969 only 30 percent of the suspects brought in through the Phoenix mechanism were eventually sentenced and served jail terms.[4]

But the most serious misconception underlying Phoenix lay in the belief that the purpose of the Vietnamese police and intelligence services was the same as that of the Americans. With some honorable exceptions, it was the same as that of ARVN described above, to preserve the system and its benefits for the individuals and groups that controlled it, the benefits being understood to include in many cases the opportunity to squeeze the population and to appropriate the resources made available by the Americans. By establishing a nationwide organization and system and bringing pressure to bear through it upon the police everywhere, Phoenix was forcing the police and the local authorities to assume a task which those concerned apparently considered unrealistic and far too difficult. They believed, it would appear, that the Viet Cong infrastructure was so well dug in and so effective as to be beyond the reach of any tools available to them. To satisfy the demands of Phoenix, they merely had to fulfill a quota which they proceeded to do by a variety of techniques, the most common of which was to list as VCI individuals killed or captured in routine military sweeps. Although the purpose of the system was to generate *targeted* operations against specific high-level VCI members, a large number of each monthly "bag" was made up, in fact, of untargeted suspects labeled as VCI after the fact. Another technique that helped fill the quota was to arrest as VCI the low-level peasants who merely paid taxes or joined VC mass organizations because they had no choice. In fact, they were not VCI at all. Moreover, it later turned out that some of the VCI "eliminations" were completely faked.

Although, therefore, Phoenix was not a viable concept in the Vietnam of the 1960s, many misconceptions have seriously distorted its intent and structure. Thus, it was not a new organization or activity but a staff whose purpose was to rationalize and focus a confused tangle of on-going police and intelligence operations against the Communist apparatus. It was not a large effort in terms of manpower and other resources: under five hundred advisers were assigned to it, most of them from the Army. Furthermore, while the concept was American, the execution was largely Vietnamese. The Americans had only the control they could generate through their corps of advisers at various levels. Often this amounted, in effect, to no control at all.

More remains to be said on the subject at a later point. In any event, the apparently reasonable and straightforward case for a major effort against the VCI was embraced by the CORDS leadership, and the program became a priority in "Project Takeoff," the initial set of goals set for the new organization to be accomplished in 1967. In his account Komer summarizes these goals as "aimed principally at improving 1968 pacification planning, accelerating the Chieu Hoi program . . . mounting the new attack on the VC infrastructure, expanding and improving RVNAF support of pacification—especially RF/PF— expanding the RD effort, stepping up aid to the mounting number of refugees, revamping and strengthening of the police and land reform."[5] The priorities comprised the most pressing immediate problems or represented essential foundations for future progress. "Project Takeoff" had the further purpose and effect of impressing upon both Americans and Vietnamese that a serious new effort was under way to realize the goals of pacification.

THE HES DILEMMA

Much prominence also came to be given at this time to a new addressing of the perennial problem of how to measure such progress— or lack of it—as the program may have achieved. The goal of pacification was to change attitudes and thus behavior. Good management practice requires that the managers of such a complex enterprise have readily available a measurement of how well their efforts are succeeding, if possible with sufficient accompanying detail to permit the pinpointing of problem areas. But attitudes, especially in so exotic a culture as Vietnam, are not easily pinned down and measured, much less as promptly, frequently, and comprehensively as the managers required. After unhappy experience with such devices as measuring incidents of violence, captured weapons, and the like, or of counting U.S. inputs (dollars, tin roofing, cement, and so on) a new approach was attempted. Down at district level, the U.S. staff (MACV advisers under CORDS) were given a list of factors, eighteen in all, which they were to rate on a six-point scale (A through F). The factors corresponded roughly to the criteria of the RD teams. Six concerned security, six social and economic factors, and six political factors. In effect, they evaluated some elements of village conditions relating to pacification, and they measured administrative success or failure in carrying out the requirements of the program or VC success in subversion and terrorism. The ratings were then averaged to produce a grade from A (secure) to F (VC-controlled) in some ten thousand hamlets throughout the country.

The effort was a bold and highly controversial attempt to become independent of the GVN. Its weakness lay in the fact that it depended on the inputs of hundreds of subsector advisers who were in effect judging their own work, whose tours were short, and who were often inexperienced. On the other hand, it strove, unlike earlier systems, to measure elements that were meaningful in relation to the goal. As a management tool it had its usefulness, especially over time, in indicating general trends; but as an absolute measurement of success, a way of determining how close or how far off lay final victory, it was inadequate. Unfortunately, this was the interpretation most often placed upon the figures in public discussion. Later, a more sophisticated version, called HES/70, developed over several years of experimentation, was put into operation. It was more reliable because it attempted to eliminate subjective judgment in assigning grades and simply posed questions of fact with the grading done in Saigon, using a "weighted formula not known to the field."[6]

HES attracted a great deal of attention and represented a considerable effort, but its main interest for us is as a symbol of the dilemma the U.S. found itself faced with in Vietnam, especially in regard to pacification, which was supported and advised but not managed or controlled by the Americans. Under such circumstances, a properly functioning allied government, reaching down to all levels of the rural community, should have routinely been able to provide the kind of rough-and-ready indicators that would adequately depict the trends in security and development and even in attitudes that CORDS needed to know. But the Vietnamese apparatus could not cope with the reality of its problems in the countryside, for the system, in effect, did not wish to know and confront the hard facts. Left to its own devices, it would simply produce the kind of information desired by the regime with little reference to actuality. The Americans were therefore obliged to institute a large new program which could only be a clumsy substitute for the natural feedback of functioning local government. The problem, in truth, traced to the rural/urban gap which split the governors from the governed and which underlay all the bitter dilemmas of Vietnam.

THE MILITARY SIDE OF THE COIN

The organization of CORDS in mid-1967 gave pacification activities a notable increase in relative importance, in visibility, and in vigor of address against the problems of the countryside. Although much of the activity was internal to the American mission, there was, in Saigon at least, a sense of progress which reflected organizational improvements as much as anything else. One indicator—the figure of persons rallying to the government side in 1967—showed a dramatic increase in the first half of the year and this contributed to the feeling of growing success, leading some to talk of "the smell of victory" in the air.

Pacification was only one element in the complex situation—although the critical one—and remained, despite its growing importance, a relatively minor facet of the war in terms of numbers of men, resources, and attention it absorbed. In 1967, U.S. armed strength in Vietnam increased by one hundred thousand reaching 486,000 by the end of the year.[7] Other Free World forces reached fifty-nine thousand.[8] The combat operations of these forces monopolized the attention of the press and the world in general. Several large operations in 1967, particularly those called "Cedar Falls" into the "Iron Triangle" and "Junction City" into "War Zone C," seemed to be major victories. They took the U.S. and accompanying ARVN units into zones which had long been enemy strongholds, caused heavy enemy casualties, and resulted in the capture of major supply caches, headquarters areas, tunnel complexes, and the like. Such operations contributed heavily to the feeling that success was near.

The strategy followed by the military was now firmly established. The bulk of the U.S. firepower and about half its combat force would be directed against Communist main force units to prevent them from concentrating for attack and to "drive . . . [them] away from the priority pacification area."[9] This "search and destroy" mission represented the offensive side of the military strategy and reflected the traditional U.S. Army concept of the proper use of its great superiority in technical capability, firepower, and mobility. It was used with the actual purpose of inflicting such heavy casualties on the enemy that he would be unable to sustain them and thus be forced to yield. In the absence of any other measure of how this phase of the war was succeeding (terrain, in this type of conflict, being irrelevant), the military focused on enemy casualties, or "body count." It was a notoriously inaccurate measurement, prone to exaggeration or even fabrication. In the pursuit of such goals, the troops were copiously supported by artillery and air power, including B-52 bombers which were used virtually as a tactical weapon in support of troops. These fearsome aircraft could each drop 100 five-hundred-pound bombs. Released in carefully timed sequence, the bombs from one flight could churn up the earth for a square mile and do it with great precision. They flew at such great heights as to be inaudible and invisible from the ground and the sudden eruption of frightful destruction from a silent sky struck terror in the hearts of the victims. The use of chemical defoliants to strip the jungle of its cover, of Rome plows to clear large jungle areas which had been enemy sanctuaries, of helicopters to move troops into and out of quick-striking attacks, these were some of the technical triumphs deployed in the effort to punish the enemy so heavily that he would be unable to sustain his losses over any considerable length of time. In order to employ such techniques effectively, the Army preferred to operate in remote, thinly populated areas. Said General Westmoreland, "This would enable the full U.S. fire-power potential to be employed without danger of civilian casualties."[10]

Some Vietnamese units, comprised largely of specialized elite units such as marines, airborne forces, and rangers also participated in the attempt to search out and destroy the enemy force. But in 1966, the Vietnamese command had, under American urging and with some reluctance, agreed to consecrate the bulk of its regular forces to the support of pacification, stationing them in populated areas where they would be available to protect the hamlets undergoing the process of reclamation from VC control. Other American and allied units, constituting more than half of their combat strength, were supposed to be assigned to work with them in this task.

This division of labor seemed a reasonable one to the Americans. It used superior American firepower and mobility against the toughest element in the enemy array—the main forces—while it deployed the ARVN's divisions in intimate contact with their own people, whose language and customs they understood. At the same time these ARVN units benefited from considerable American support in their assignment although the numbers never actually came up to the half share promised.[11] Throughout 1967, therefore, while American and allied strength grew to over a half-million men and the ARVN was substantially upgraded along with its paramilitary auxiliaries, the new strategy and division of responsibility was put into effect. Firepower and its use in offensive operations was never greater; a great buildup of logistic capability was carried forward and pacification enjoyed more substantial and better-managed support than ever before. Yet shortly after the end of the year, at the beginning of Tet, the Vietnamese 1968 New Year holiday, the enemy unleashed a general offensive throughout the country which, while immensely costly for him, nevertheless showed the opposite of the declining power and capability one would have been led to expect from the massive effort carried on for more than a year against him. This surprise attack turned out to be a political and psychological blow from which the Americans never recovered. It changed the war, causing abandonment of the assumption that U.S. power could win in a time span and at a cost acceptable to the American public. After Tet, the Americans no longer talked of victory as the objective but of other, lesser goals.

Although many continue to maintain—and no doubt always will—

that this outcome resulted from the restrictions placed upon the military for political reasons, the analysis and description we have offered lead to another conclusion: U.S. military concepts and the style in which they were carried out were simply off the mark, played into the enemy's hands, and gave him the opportunity to bring Goliath down. Put differently, the course of the war would have at least been substantially altered—although one still hesitates to assert that it could have been won outright relying on purely military means—by a more sophisticated and flexible use of U.S. strength, avoiding the known pitfalls of counterguerrilla warfare. This would have required making the undoubtedly painful changes in the American approach which had long been formally and verbally accepted as the appropriate tactic but never carried out—fight the enemy with his own weapons, "set guerrillas to catch guerrillas."

What actually happened in the two phases of the war, the offensive "search and destroy" campaign in remote areas, and the close-in phase of pacification? In the first phase, immense areas of jungle were pitted with bomb craters and swept with shrapnel, and substantial enemy casualties were inflicted, but they were spread out in time, never concentrated to the point that large units were overwhelmed and disappeared or a cost exacted that could not be sustained. The American style prevented such an outcome, in part, at least, because it required a softening-up process to precede each attack, thereby giving due warning, even if the enemy intelligence system had not already learned of an attack from its massive penetrations into the ARVN. By and large, then—and this is the essence of the VC/NVA's ability to survive in the teeth of American superiority—the enemy was able to control the pace and scope of combat and thus the level of combat losses by evading contact when it did not suit his purpose. By this means, he managed to keep losses within his capability to replace them, even despite the length of his supply and replacement lines and his lack of mobility and of heavy firepower. Generally alerted in advance to American intentions, he avoided battle until he was ready. To him, losses—at least up to a rather high level never actually reached—did not matter, terrain did not matter. What mattered was to keep the main force in being, its morale high, and its minimum supply requirements assured—and to exact a price from the Americans which in the long run would be felt painfully. To explain in detail how the VC/NVA was able to do this in 1967 and after would take us too far afield, but one thing is clear: during this phase of the war it could only assure the essential intelligence, supply, and manpower from the South Vietnamese population, and that required a substantial degree of local support secured by all the means described earlier.

The same factors were of importance in the close-in, pacification, phase of the war, but an equally critical element was the performance characteristics of the ARVN and the U.S. military. The regular ARVN units assigned to "support of pacification" maintained the predilection, derived from their training and doctrine, to operate in large units, to rely on air power and artillery to soften up the target prior to the attack, and to carry out set-piece attacks with concentrated force; and the Americans involved in the same mission for the most part did the same. Although nominally dedicated to pacification support—a type of duty that rarely called for as much as a battalion to fight in any action—the ARVN remained organized into divisions and the divisions into corps. Commanders were free to interpret "pacification support" as might suit them. Frequently they diverted companies and battalions on pacification duties to such tasks as securing roads and canals or reinforcing large-scale attacks which had only a tenuous relationship to pacification. In fact, the pacification support mission was not popular with ARVN commanders who, naturally, derived their values from their American mentors. It seemed demeaning compared with the main-force war. It also called for tedious, very basic, small-unit operations with little opportunity for dramatic battles using the full panoply of weapons at their command. Success in pacification did not bring glory and promotions. It brought hard, tedious work, nighttime operations, and casualties. Division and regimental commanders generally contrived to slight it without directly opposing it. At the same time—and in spite of continuing U.S. training and support efforts—ARVN performance standards continued low. Reluctance of commanders to close with the enemy, corruption in handling pay and other requisites, poor combat leadership, poor troop behavior toward the population—all remained common characteristics of most units.

The Americans involved in close-in operations followed a similar pattern, although performance standards were, of course, higher and there was usually no reluctance among the Americans to close with the enemy. Nevertheless, the pattern remained one of keeping large units together to seek out and hopefully to destroy large enemy units, and of copious use of artillery and air power to soften up the target before the attack. The desire to use firepower freely led to the declaration of "free-fire zones," areas where no friendly population was believed to exist and where any human observed was subject to attack without warning. Populations were sometimes moved from their homes and resettled to permit the declaration of such a zone.

Another tactic frequently employed was "harassment and interdiction fire," the unobserved firing of artillery at night at targets believed to be in the vicinity of enemy concentrations, installations, or lines of communications. An enormous weight of shells was expended in this fashion. By the nature of the technique, results were unverifiable and the risk of hitting innocent civilians was great. Nevertheless the practice continued.

All regular forces—American, Korean, and ARVN—also conducted sweeps of areas where the enemy were suspected of hiding among the civilian population. These were usually called "cordon and search" operations and were often preparatory to the introduction of pacification teams into new areas. They called for the sealing off of an area with troops, searching all structures, and screening the entire population to comb out enemy weapons, supplies, soldiers, or infrastructure members. Surprise was sought though not often achieved. Again the fault probably lay with the penetration of ARVN staffs by Communist intelligence; usually the enemy's adherents were alerted and slipped away. Even if some of the enemy were caught, his organization was soon mended. The troops left, pacification units moved in, and the submerged and scattered VC waited—as the population was aware they did—for their opportunity to return. Often, before they left, they summoned the people and told them that they were going—but would be back. The purported goal of such operations, to "clear and hold" territory infested with VC, was thwarted by the failure of troops to stay and patiently and persistently patrol the area as long as necessary to establish true security. This was not seen as their proper mission and tended to be left to paramilitary forces, which in pre-Tet years were inadequately trained and led, together with the pacification teams, while the regulars moved on to additional "clear and hold" activity or to larger, set-piece operations against VC/NVA main forces in their area of responsibility.

It was in this phase of the war, namely, pacification support, that the military demonstrated most clearly its inability to grasp the nature of the conflict it was attempting to fight. Studies of the Vietnamese war carried out long afterward and based on careful analysis of all statistics available in the Pentagon demonstrate conclusively that the military machine, in spite of all verbal assurances to the contrary, simply performed in Vietnam according to its normal and conventional combat repertoires. By far the largest part of the resources expended in South Vietnam were dedicated to the air war. The huge numerical superiority of the anti-VC/NVA forces was illusory because so many of the troops were involved in logistics, the air war, and other noninfantry combat activity. In 1971 the overall strength ratio of the two opposing forces was 6 to 1, but the "foxhole" strength ratio was a mere 1.6 to 1. Even more striking is the fact that combat results measured in terms of casualties improved *after* the U.S. had withdrawn the bulk of its combat forces because, at the same time, efforts to improve and enlarge Vietnamese territorial forces (the RF, PF, and People's Self-Defense Forces) reached their peak.[12] Pacification support was a bitter failure of both the U.S. Army and the ARVN. It never enjoyed the troop allocations claimed, and those troops which were employed in this duty, by the style in which they fought, made the pacification task more difficult rather than helping to advance it.

The futility of attempting to fight a guerrilla enemy with the wrong techniques, the poor psychological preparations of U.S. units, and the stark strangeness along with frequent hostility of the people whose rescue from Communist rule was supposed to be the purpose of all the sweaty, toilsome, and frequently bloody effort—these were the chief factors responsible for the poor morale, declining discipline, and grave operational lapses of U.S. forces, of which the My Lai episode is the best known. The troops—among the best-educated infantry ever put into the field—quickly learned that their dangerous work was not accomplishing its purpose, that the task was endless and the people unwilling, that, in fact, they were accomplices in a fraud being perpetrated upon the Vietnamese and American people by an army leadership which did not grasp the fundamentals of what it was supposed to be doing. Heroin addiction and a growing frequency of "fragging" episodes (a surreptitious attack upon an American officer by his own soldiers) against combat leaders were some of the eventual results.

The Impact Upon the People

The tragic irony of the regular military effort, particularly in the close-in operations which were intended to support pacification, was that the manner in which it was carried out assured that the goals of pacification, instead of being brought closer, would be made vastly more difficult. That goal was to gain the willing support of the government's cause by the people brought into the pacification process. Instead, large numbers of them were bombed or shelled, forcibly resettled, or caught in the cross fire as contending forces clashed in or around their homes. Wherever American troops were stationed they had an inevitably powerful effect on the economy and social fabric of the surrounding communities. Inflation rates soared, "strips" featuring bars and bar girls sprang up, and a flow of ready cash overturned accustomed expectations and fostered a class of entrepreneurs battening on the Americans. For those shrewd enough to exploit the situation there was opportunity for fast profits, but for most it was simply a rather obscene assault on moral standards and an uprooting of normal life that brought few rewards.

The style of war of the regular forces thus, in a variety of ways and without anyone deliberately willing it, reinforced the sense of helplessness, of alienation from the authorities, of the Vietnamese caught in the powerful wake of the war machine. The tendency among military leaders was to dismiss the civilian toll as an unfortunate but inevitable cost of war, something that always accompanied battle, and to point to directives and practices MACV instituted to minimize it to the extent possible. Their case was seriously weakened, however, by their inability to bring about a decisive military result following the strategy and tactics they had adopted. It is impossible to measure the precise impact of the phenomenon we are discussing upon attitudes in the countryside and thus to suggest the extent of the damage done to the effort by the way the military played its role. One must appeal finally to common sense: If the target was truly the people, was this the way to reach them?

COMBINED ACTION PLATOONS AND CIDG

Within the military itself there were many who questioned the conventional wisdom, and there were significant efforts to change the pattern. The one which came closest to answering the need involved the marines, who throughout their heavy combat commitment in the northern part of the country set aside a small group of men to work integrally with Vietnamese paramilitary units at hamlet level, performing the basic security tasks in communities undergoing pacification. These Combined Action Platoons came into existence in 1965, not long after marine combat units arrived in force. The marines operated in I Corps, the northernmost provinces of South Vietnam, in areas where the countryside had long been dominated by the enemy. They early discovered that the Viet Cong controlled villages on the margins of their bases and that local security forces were unable to dig them out. An experiment was launched to determine whether American soldiers assigned to selected hamlets to work with the local Popular Force militia could bring about a significant improvement. The results of the early experiments were encouraging, and a slow expansion of the program took place, reaching eventually a total of 114 Combined Action Platoons.[13] This small effort is nevertheless worth exploring in some detail for it represents the only sustained effort to fight guerrillas with guerrillas undertaken by any part of the United States armed forces in Vietnam. The experiment thus demonstrated the problems and the potential of such an attempt.

Each unit consisted of a squad of marines (fourteen men) under command of a sergeant, assigned to live and work with a Popular Force platoon of thirty-four Vietnamese. One navy corpsman was also included in the American component. The marines were volunteers and were required to have had previous combat experience in Vietnam. They were screened before acceptance with emphasis on eliminating those who disliked or were unable to work with Vietnamese. They received several weeks' training which tended to emphasize the basics of small-unit combat with a limited amount of attention to civic action. The trainees were then assigned to their locations which were usually selected because of proximity to an important military objective such as a base or a major road. The formal mission of the platoon was the same as that of the Popular Forces they worked with except that they had the additional task of improving the performance of the PF units themselves. That mission included—besides the obvious tasks of destroying the VC organization, protecting the government organization and installations, and enforcing law and order—the formation of "people's intelligence nets" and civic action and propaganda. [14]

Regardless of the formal goals, the marines focused on patrolling the hamlets at night, on setting up ambushes, and, in whatever other way they could, preventing the enemy from moving in and out, collecting taxes, recruiting, or gathering information. They brought a higher degree of professionalism to the PFs as well as better weapons and support, particularly medical evacuation by helicopter. One of the superior combat narratives of the war, *The Village,* by F. J. West, Jr., [15] gives a vivid account of the work of a single CAP assigned to the village of Binh Nghia in Quang Ngai province. It is very largely the story of a series of night patrols, many of them ending in no contact, during which marines and PF, in groups of six or eight, stalked an elusive enemy through the pathways and backyards of a handful of adjacent hamlets, finally forcing him to abandon the village which, thanks to persistent night patrolling by the CAP, had become exceedingly hazardous to him. This success took over a year to accomplish and was costly in American lives relative to the size of the unit. During the entire year, the village was not once bombed from the air, and only once did the CAP request artillery support. On that occasion, a single shell was fired, well off target, destroying a house and killing two villagers. Artillery was never again called in by the marines in Binh Nghia. Moreover, neighboring regular American units were instructed to leave Binh Nghia alone and only occasionally lapsed. On one occasion, an Army battalion attempted a sweep, using tanks, one of which slipped off the dike road into a rice field, where it stuck. That ended the sweep.

After seventeen months, the marines at Binh Nghia reported that the local PF platoon, with which they had worked so closely, was fully capable of maintaining security without their help. The village officials were staying in the area at night, VC contacts occurred very seldom, and there was little left for the marines to do. They were transferred to a neighboring village and the militia was left to do the job on its own. The PF unit had difficulties at first which, its leaders claimed, were due to their inability to get quick reaction support from the Americans now that no American soldiers were stationed in the village. They dealt with that problem by organizing and arming a People's Self-Defense Force to supplement their own firepower. Under the leadership of the battle-tested PF, this solution worked and Binh Nghia remained secure.

The Village is a superb case history of the kind of tactics which, if used on a wider scale, could have made a vast difference in the war for the countryside. There were problems and weaknesses, of course, even in the small program that was actually carried out. The CAPs were not uniformly successful. Their lack of language capability was a serious handicap, training was inadequate, and confusion often existed about the purpose and mission of each unit—a matter the marines usually solved by focusing on combat as their *raison d'etre* and letting the rest go. More serious was the failure of the command to link the various CAPs together into an interlocking and mutually supporting network. They were too scattered and isolated to have maximum impact.[16]

Small as they were, the CAPs drew considerable command attention. Generals often dropped in by helicopter to be briefed by the units, for the experiment intrigued and puzzled the command levels. The combat record, the "kill ratios," and the fact that American soldiers were living and fighting in intimate contact with Vietnamese, all suggested an interesting phenomenon, but, despite this interest and its achievements, the program was kept small. The commanders were unable or unwilling to accept the conclusion implicit in the success of the CAPs, which was that their vast resources, equipment, and technology were essentially irrelevant to the kind of war they faced. Some months after the CAP program was launched, the marines noted a growing enemy buildup in the Demilitarized Zone, the northern frontier of South Vietnam. They shifted the axis of their effort to dealing with that threat and from then on the CAPs were considered a limited sideshow to the main-force war. What would have happened if the army had also adopted the experiment and if it were given a priority call on manpower up to, but not beyond, the point where the combat divisions could no longer shield the CAP areas from heavy-unit attacks? All that remains a matter of speculation. It would certainly have been a different war.

THE CITIZENS IRREGULAR DEFENSE GROUPS

Throughout Vietnam, and indeed Southeast Asia, the majority of the people occupy lands suitable for the cultivation of "wet" rice. The vast mountainous areas are lightly populated by the more primitive tribal communities, and between the two lie age-old animosities encouraged by the colonial powers to ease their task of ruling huge territories with a handful of administrators. In South Vietnam this pattern prevailed throughout the mountainous provinces along the lone, remote frontier with Laos and Cambodia. Literally dozens of small tribes practiced shifting cultivation (slash-and-burn) remote from the densely populated Mekong Delta and coastal plains and were, until 1954, shielded by the French from penetration by the lowland Vietnamese. With independence these barriers were lifted, and Vietnamese began to filter into the upland valleys, a movement encouraged by the Diem government which sponsored resettlement projects in tribal lands. Inevitably, the tribal peoples felt victimized and exploited and became readily susceptible to Viet Cong appeals.

To the Communists the area was of critical military importance, controlling the entry points of their supply lines into the South and providing enormous remote areas for bases, supply dumps, and concentration points. They quickly became active among the tribes, preaching a form of autonomy and employing cadres who spoke the tribal languages and were familiar with tribal ways. The VC did suffer from several disadvantages: they spoke for a Vietnamese authority, and their intentions, which could not always be concealed, amounted to the establishment of a kind of control over the tribes which the latter had instinctively and traditionally sought to avoid. Into this rather explosive mix the CIA moved in the early sixties, establishing the first of the armed village programs which were described earlier.[17] In 1963 the CIA relinquished management of the tribal programs to the U.S. Special Forces which conducted them from then on in the role of advisers to the Vietnamese Special Forces. What had originally been a system of interlocked village defense groups supported by strike forces drawn from all the villages in the group became a rather different type of program. The CIDG volunteers became full-time soldiers numbering eventually some fifty thousand in all. They were stationed at special camps built in remote areas from which they patrolled, identifying targets for air strikes and conducting raids against VC installations. Their families usually lived in the camps with them, but in other respects the CIDG were full-time professionals fighting under the command of the Vietnamese. Fighting was an occupation to which the tribal populations took with more ease than the Vietnamese, especially in the mountains which were their homeland.

In the prevailing conditions of the highland areas, disrupted as they were by war and political turmoil, service in the CIDG became a means of livelihood for the troops. The commitment was by no means a political one, for the GVN was dilatory and inconsistent in evolving a program that went even part of the way to meet tribal demands for equality, representation, and some control of their own affairs. The CIDG soldiers were, in effect, mercenaries who performed useful service in the remote areas where otherwise the enemy would have had virtually a free hand. (In passing, we should note that in more stable and settled tribal communities closer to province towns and Vietnamese centers of population the Revolutionary Development program was active in a slightly modified form. Here the RD cadre were called *Truong Son*.) Similar forces had been used in insurgent and other types of war from time immemorial, and there was nothing particularly innovative about the device, although it was not one the U.S. had often employed in its previous martial experience. Nor did the CIDG in this latter form make any particular contribution to counterinsurgency as we have defined it.

The role of the Special Forces in this conventionalized war was therefore different in important ways from that envisioned in the early sixties, when they were seen as a key counterinsurgency force. Essentially, they trained and advised the Vietnamese Special Forces who, in turn, organized the CIDG. This, at least, was the formal relationship, although in the early days of USSF responsibility the Vietnamese role was often minimal. During this very confused period (1964 and 1965) the Special Forces, in fact, were caught in a major political confrontation between the Vietnamese government and CIDG units who were demanding autonomy or even independence. This tension was eventually resolved, but the episode had the effect of reducing the direct role of the USSF in the program.

Although the Vietnamese were thus mollified and accepted the program, it remained one conceived and planned largely by the U.S. The pattern it finally took thus inevitably became one that fit U.S. military criteria and met U.S. norms. The CIDG Strike Forces, as they were called, were simply light infantry companies constituting a military auxiliary organized to conduct scouting and raiding activity from fixed bases in difficult terrain. The Special Forces, in effect, devoted the larger part of their effort in Vietnam to a variant of standard military operations with a distinctly limited counterinsurgency function—a far cry from the role originally anticipated for them.

Some of the other missions they undertook were less conventional in nature. For example, they organized long-range patrols, small units operating for relatively long periods away from their bases. As the main component of the Special Operations Group (SOG) they were also deeply involved in the so-called 34A Operations, comprising secret raids and harassment into North Vietnam. None of this altered the fact that as a small specialized force the USSF in Vietnam had a restricted role compared to earlier expectations, the reason being the need to conform to prevailing military concepts in a command dominated by the regulars.

Indeed, something similar could be said of the entire U.S. military effort in Vietnam. Despite the public fanfare surrounding the "new form of warfare" with which the Vietnamese involvement began, the essence of the effort remained very much the old familiar form of warfare for which the military were long prepared. We can sum up by saying that counterinsurgency was not seriously attempted on a large scale by the U.S. combat forces in Vietnam. It was left to a few thousand civilian and military advisors with some military support, but they had only a limited influence on the way in which the military command, with its vast resources, conducted the phase of the war which it had defined as its responsibility. The war, in fact, was fought as two separate conflicts despite the fact that it was only one. What was done by the military in pursuit of victory over the main force impacted severely on the populace, so severely that we can conclude that the regular army's side of the war not only did not constitute counterinsurgency, it was a massive obstacle in the way of successful counterinsurgency. That is what the "new form of warfare" came to represent in the largest of U.S. involvements in people's war.

THE TET EARTHQUAKE

The massive nationwide Viet Cong offensive that began on January 30, 1968, ended the first phase of U.S. military involvement and began the long second phase of gradual withdrawal which finally played itself out in April and May 1975. The Tet offensive and its aftermath affected every phase of U.S. activity in Vietnam, pacification included. By the time the shock waves receded and the U.S. and GVN restored the losses of the attack, it was a much-changed war, most particularly in the countryside, where initially all the painfully won gains of the previous year seemed to vanish in a moment, until the reality of the changed situation dawned on all concerned: as a result of Tet, the government was stronger, not weaker, in the villages and hamlets. Many things which before had seemed impossible were now within reach and merely had to be energetically seized.

We need not rehearse in detail in this history the events of Tet 1968. Suffice it to say that, with a large degree of surprise, the VC/NVA forces unleashed coordinated attacks on thirty-four cities, Saigon very much included.[18] The focus of the "General Uprising and General Offensive," as the Communists called it, was the cities, hitherto largely exempt from the havoc of war. Most urban areas in the country and most towns were assaulted, as the major part of the armed strength of the enemy was moved up from remote bases and close-in hiding places and flung against the superior American and South Vietnamese firepower. Relying on surprise and on the massive nationwide fury of the assault, the Communists—for reasons still not well understood—took an incredible gamble. How one judges the results varies with the time scale and vantage point from which the judgment is made. No doubt, now that the war has ended victoriously for them, the Communists are entitled to view the gamble as a success. It was the turning point of U.S. involvement, and they had no chance of victory while the U.S. remained in strength. But there is also no doubt that as a result of the Tet gamble the relative strength of the two sides altered significantly in favor of the government and that by the end of 1968, psychologically as well as materially, the government side confronted new opportunities.

The initial impact of the Tet attacks in the countryside seemed to be a victory for the Viet Cong for the reason that the security forces were immediately preoccupied either with defending the embattled towns or preserving their own lives and left the villages with greatly reduced defenses. The relative vacuum that resulted partly reversed the gains of the reorganized pacification effort. But these initial results were, in a matter of months, rapidly overtaken by a new reality. With the reestablishment of security in the cities, units were released and returned to their original posts in the countryside. In the meantime, the recklessness of the offensive had taken an enormous toll of the enemy, a figure estimated at forty-five thousand men lost through the end of February 1968 out of a total deployment of eighty-four thousand.[19] This figure was put together from probably exaggerated body counts and needs to be discounted. Nevertheless, subsequent developments confirm that the losses were enormous. The larger part of the Communist forces committed (though by no means all) comprised Viet Cong local and main force units whose losses were staggering and left them seriously depleted. A second wave of attacks occurred in May and increased the toll. A third wave, scheduled for August, was a hardly noticeable ripple. Hamlet Evaluation Survey statistics, which are useful to illustrate this kind of trend, tell the story concisely. At the end of 1967, HES reports showed over two-thirds of the hamlets (67.2 percent) in the secure or relatively secure category, the rest being contested or under VC control. At the end of February 1968, that figure had dropped by 7 percentage points to about 60 percent and was at the same level as the beginning of 1967. By the end of November, however, the total number of hamlets in the secure and relatively secure category was 73 percent, higher than it had ever been before.[20] The Tet losses had set back the Viet Cong in the countryside far below their strength at the time they had launched the offensive. Moreover, the enemy was not only physically but also morally depleted. The sacrifices called for at Tet had been justified in advance as a final, all-out surge which was to bring victory quickly.[21] But after the slaughter was over and victory still had not arrived, the VC faced the necessity of a period of retrenchment and rebuilding to restore enthusiasm and commitment.

Some students of the war point out that the Tet offensive was a strategic victory although a tactical defeat for the VC/NVA. They suggest that it is entirely plausible that Vo Nguyen Giap and his associates were not surprised by the heavy losses, having discounted them in their planning in order to achieve a result which would shock American opinion and greatly undermine support for the war.[22] This interpretation is plausible, although we will probably never be certain. In any event, the results were a major and significant blow to the VC organization in the South which, as we shall see, precipitated important changes in the course of pacification.

In the meantime, after some months of shock and confusion, the GVN side began to pull itself together. Encouraged by the fact that the government and the armed forces remained intact and had held on despite the ferocity of the attack, Saigon recovered its poise and gained increased confidence from the Tet ordeal. Although their performance was uneven, many ARVN units had fought well during the crisis with their backs to the wall. The government continued to function under adverse circumstances, and Communist propaganda calling for a nation-wide popular uprising to greet and support their general offensive proved unavailing. These among other factors encouraged the GVN to take measures long urged by the U.S. but put off because of political sensitivity. In effect, the enemy's loss of morale was paralleled by an eventual increase in morale on the GVN side and a turning point of sorts occurred which had major consequences for pacification.

NATIONAL MOBILIZATION

The drafting of men of military age was a perennial U.S. recommendation that no South Vietnamese government had felt strong enough to endorse. The effects of Tet and the popular reaction to it emboldened President Thieu to proceed where he had earlier hesitated. One feature of the reaction to Tet had been a sudden increase in volunteers for the army and, most noteworthy, demands from many areas for arms for the people. The National Mobilization Law of 1968 emerged from this experience, requiring all able-bodied men of military age to serve in the armed forces. This long-delayed mobilization resulted in the eventual increase of the armed forces to a million men and had the unintended beneficial effect for pacification of absorbing much of the manpower pool on which the VC as well as the government had depended.

Another important post-Tet decision, again at U.S. urging, was the creation of a nationwide program to arm villagers and city dwellers alike in units now called People's Self Defense Forces (PSDF). Although lip service had long been paid to the concept of arming the population, the national government now seemed to be serious about it. The new law required that all men of military age who were not in the armed forces participate in the defense of the country by joining the PSDF. Provision was also made to accept voluntary participation by women, old people, and children as young as twelve in noncombat support roles. By 1970 some three million persons were claimed to be enrolled in the PSDF.[23] The figure was undoubtedly inflated, but some four hundred thousand arms were distributed, and this figure can be accepted with more certainty.

The PSDF was responsible to village chiefs and they in turn had the duty of assuring that the members received training and that their activities were effectively coordinated with the militia. American advisers, especially the Mobile Training Teams assigned to work with Popular and Regional Forces, were of assistance in many localities in putting the program on its feet. As did every other such activity in Vietnam, PSDF varied greatly in quality and performance but it had an undoubted impact. The spread of these rather informal and unmilitary village-based armed groups was one of the causes and, in turn, one of the most important indicators of improvement of the situation in the countryside. The act of issuing arms to the population was symbolic of a growing awareness of the importance of popular engagement in the government's cause and of the willingness of the government to take some chances to make progress along that road.

COUNTEROFFENSIVE IN THE COUNTRYSIDE

By the end of 1968 the government was sufficiently recovered to plan and launch a systematic pacification offensive to recover lost ground and exploit the Tet-generated enemy weakness in the countryside. The drive, called the Accelerated Pacification Campaign was Komer's final initiative. It was motivated in part by the realization that the opportunity to gain ground might be fleeting. It also stemmed in part from events in Paris, where peace talks appeared about to begin. The GVN wished, in the event of a cease-fire, to have established its presence in as many villages as possible. To release additional forces for this purpose, the RD team structure was altered and the teams reduced in size. In effect, a standard team no longer included a squad whose main duties were military. Instead, the reduced team—now consisting of thirty-five men and later reduced to thirty—was tied in more closely with the local militia platoon, which took over the defense functions. This step was made possible by the increase and improvement of the RF/PF militia. It permitted the rapid creation of additional teams needed to launch the Accelerated Pacification Campaign.

The campaign progressed rapidly, and soon the government, against little opposition, had moved back into all the communities it had abandoned at Tet and penetrated into areas over which its hold had never been reestablished. Originally scheduled to last only three months, the Accelerated Pacification Campaign became the basis for a far more vigorous and successful phase of pacification which had as its key a substantial upgrading of the process by President Thieu and his immediate advisers. For whatever reason—and some suggested that it was the galvanizing effect of the reality of gradual American withdrawal— President Thieu from 1968 to 1970 took decisive action on major issues which had caused pacification to lag in the past. As important was his personal involvement in the decision-making process, manifested by his presiding regularly over the Central Pacification and Development Council which coordinated the work of the various GVN agencies involved. He set the goals and helped to shape the details of the 1969 plan and those that followed. By personal appearances in the villages and at the training camps he sought to emphasize and reemphasize the priority he and the government attached to the program.

This commitment by the regime gave to the program a critical ingredient which had hitherto been absent—Vietnamese initiative and convinced leadership at the highest levels. In all of its many aspects, as we have noted, pacification was—and of necessity had to be—a Vietnamese program, with the Americans serving as advisers, expediters, and suppliers of material resources. Too often in the past, the ideas, initiatives, and sense of urgency had been contributed by the Americans, with much of the program considered by the Vietnamese to be an American hobbyhorse. Such a division of labor ill-suited an activity which sought to deal with the most intimate aspects of social life in thousands of Vietnamese communities. By making the program his own, President Thieu resolved some of the anomalies that had dampened the impact of the effort and gave it an injection of sorely needed élan. On the other hand, while his personal involvement had a noticeable impact, the resulting improvement—as always in Vietnam—remained relative to the earlier low levels of performance, efficiency, and honesty of administration.

Sweeping policy decisions continued into 1969 and 1970, focused on the village and aimed at the goal of giving the villagers greater control over their affairs and resources. First, the process of village elections to select a governing council, instituted in 1967, was pressed forward vigorously. By the end of 1969, 95 percent of the villages of Vietnam had elected their own councils which, in turn, elected the village chief.[24] By a decree of April 1, 1969, the elected village governments were given control of local armed forces which by now included the PF, PSDF, RD cadres, and police (where assigned to villages).[25] Village government was enlarged to handle the new responsibilities. A deputy chief for security managed the security forces, another deputy was created for administration, and a secretariat assisted village officials in processing their paperwork.[26]

The same decree delegated to the reorganized village governments control of a development fund which initially was set at one million piasters annually and later increased. This was to be spent at the discretion of the village council for local development with the proviso that the villagers themselves contribute their labor or other resources to each project. During the same period, reflecting the increased responsibilities of the village regimes, training of village officials became a large-scale program, mostly carried on at the RD Training Center at Vung Tau. In 1969 a total of seventeen thousand hamlet and village officials passed through the center, receiving instruction in the requirements of effective local government and indoctrination on nationalist themes and goals.[27] Persisting in his new pattern of personal involvement, President Thieu addressed each graduating class of village officials in succession.

Perhaps the most far-reaching policy initiative of this whole period of renovation of pacification, however, was Thieu's decision to throw his personal prestige and influence behind a new and sweeping land reform program. The passage of the new land reform law was delayed in the legislature and did not come until March 1970, but in its final form it was one of the most thoroughgoing undertaken anywhere. Its critical provision reduced landholdings to fifteen hectares per farmer and awarded title to that amount of property without cost to the new owner, the government assuming the burden of compensating the landlords.[28] Moreover, local land distribution under the reform became a responsibility of village government, which thus acquired a major new power over a critical aspect of village life. Long-delayed as it was, true land reform finally became a firm feature of GVN policy. Once passed, the law was implemented with a degree of vigor that surprised both Americans and Vietnamese. According to one authority "three years after the bill was signed, the GVN had redistributed nearly one million hectares of farmland. Well over two-thirds of the tenant farmer families in South Vietnam were to be significantly affected by the measures."[29]

Accompanying these basic structural changes in the government's rural policies was a steady improvement in levels of economic activity, reflecting better security as well as the payoff from many years of increasing development inputs and, not least important, the ingenuity and hard work of the peasant population. Among the most important material factors involved were the reopening of roads and canals, the spread of the so-called miracle rice of the IR5 and IR8 strains developed in the Philippines, and the spread of small tractors along with gas-powered irrigation pumps in the Delta. Official estimates placed the number of tractors in the Delta in mid-1970 at thirty-four hundred, representing a doubling of numbers in a little more than a year.[30] The decline of South Vietnamese agricultural production which had continued steadily since about 1960 was reversed, and signs of new prosperity and growth were visible almost everywhere. The prosperity was not evenly distributed, of course, and many, especially the refugees, continued to lead a life of hardship. Nevertheless, the trend was apparent and contributed significantly to the improved rural picture. These results were an outstanding success for CORDS which had invested a far larger proportion of its resources in such activities than in those such as Phoenix, which attracted more attention.

IMPACT ON THE VIET CONG

One significant political development that accompanied and underlay these changes was a sharp decline in the fortunes of and popular support for the Viet Cong. The Tet spasm backfired seriously in terms of popular faith and confidence in VC promises. The manpower losses resulting from Tet, together with the government's mobilization of the entire national manpower pool and the movement of population away from the scene of heavy fighting, had depleted VC ranks and made the recruitment of replacements exceedingly difficult. Loss of support meant loss of funds; consequently VC taxation in areas to which they still had access became so high that the peasants found the burden far greater than in government-controlled areas. Forcible recruitment into VC ranks became more common—in effect a form of a kidnapping which did not produce reliable adherents. In many provinces the VC concentrated merely on maintaining its organization, undertaking little aggressive activity. During 1970, for example, aggressive operations by the insurgents were concentrated in eleven provinces, while in the remaining thirty-three they were reduced to occasional harassment.[31] In 1969, forty-seven thousand VC personnel, mostly low level, voluntarily went over to the government side through the Chieu Hoi program. In 1970, the figure was thirty-two thousand.[32]

Nevertheless, despite the undoubted decline of the VC's hold, it would be an error to conclude that it had been defeated as an insurgency. As had happened more than once in their history, the Communists had sustained a serious setback but, as before, they adjusted rapidly to the new circumstances and developed a new set of tactics to deal with them. Their goal now appeared to be that of maintaining the existence of their organization at the least cost in manpower and to wait for the withdrawal of the Americans and the new situation that would then prevail. In the meantime, the burden of aggressive operations and of keeping up the pressure was assumed by the North Vietnamese, who also provided replacements for the depleted VC units.

In effect, the war entered a new phase of a markedly different character. Insurgency-style guerrilla warfare was no longer the prevailing mode of Communist operations, although it persisted in a few provinces where the capability still existed. In most areas, the VC conducted the minimum of operations necessary to maintain a reduced organization. Periodically, a regional or nationwide "highpoint," a flurry of mortarings and ambushes, would be carried out, often by North Vietnamese units. In effect, the war was conventionalized to a considerable degree in that the political link between the enemy and the population withered away, and forces which were largely foreign to the area conducted operations which more and more resembled incursions from outside. The North Vietnamese did not have the same capability as the VC to melt away when pursued and took greater risks in their operations for that reason. Believing it essential to keep up some pressure and to give evidence of continued strength and effectiveness, the Communists nevertheless took those risks.

CHANGE AND PERSISTENCE IN U.S. OPERATIONS

In the aftermath of Tet, U.S. forces also began to change their tactics, although there does not appear to have been a direct connection between one side's changes and the other's. The changes followed and reflected the rotation of commanders when General Creighton Abrams took over from General Westmoreland as COMUSMACV in June 1968. Under Abrams's leadership, U.S. forces modified their tactics to patterns more in keeping with the kind of war they faced. By mid-1969, most American units committed to locating and attacking large enemy units in remote areas were shifted from that duty. Instead, they were conducting saturation, small-unit operations in populated areas, working closely with ARVN and, particularly, with the regional and local paramilitary platoons and companies.[33] Constant patrolling by squads was ordained by the command and, according to one observer, many units were "entirely on night shift, as in one division where three battalions operate exclusively during the hours of darkness and schedule nothing but rest during daylight."[34] General Abrams also placed considerable command emphasis on military support for the Phoenix program although it remains unclear how army support of a police program was intended to function in practice. Certainly large numbers of troops were not an essential or even a useful ingredient for Phoenix purposes.

The implication of these changes is that General Abrams had formed certain convictions during his years as deputy to General Westmoreland relating to the appropriateness of U.S. military tactics in Vietnam. Some observers hold that the actual motivation was the instructions he received to hold down casualties during the U.S. withdrawal. In any event, the impact of the changes he made does not seem to have been great. The new emphasis on saturation patrolling and the accompanying deemphasis of "search and destroy" was in several respects ineffective. The commanders found that to change the tactics of an army already in the field was not merely a matter of issuing new orders. Frequently the new instructions, which violated ingrained habit, were given token compliance while the worst features of the old approach continued to be followed. "General Abrams," wrote one analyst of the problem, "has only partly succeeded in making his own ideas prevail over the traditional doctrine."[35] And again, "Our military institution seems to be prevented by its own doctrinal and organizational rigidity from understanding the nature of this war and from making the necessary modifications to apply its power more intelligently, more economically, and above all, more relevantly."[36] What this meant, among other things, was that the military forces often continued to operate against the enemy regulars as the primary target, concentrating firepower for this purpose and attempting to wear them down by exacting an intolerable rate of casualties. In the process, the population was victimized and the goals of pacification undermined. Within the military and CORDS many individuals, notably the veteran pacification expert John Vann, sought to alter this costly procedure, but the system, for many reasons, proved impossible to change fundamentally.

Within CORDS there were also changes in command personnel but no major alterations in the program or the organization. Robert Komer left Vietnam in late 1968 and was replaced by his deputy, William E. Colby, a senior CIA officer with many years of involvement in Vietnam affairs. Colby continued and refined the CORDS structure and program array that he had inherited. He sought to maintain a lower profile than his predecessor but doggedly pursued the main lines already established. Under his management, CORDS grew moderately in size, reaching an authorized personnel level of seventy-six hundred in 1970 with a budget of $891 million. This represented a near doubling of the U.S. contribution to pacification over the level of CORDS' first year. In the same period, the GVN total also doubled, from the piaster equivalent of $307 million to the equivalent of $628 million.[37] We have no information casting light on Colby's role in bringing about the GVN's policy departures of 1968–1970 other than that his public testimony suggests strong support for all of them. He also endorsed and strongly defended the Phoenix operation in congressional testimony and public statements during the years when it came under increasing public criticism.

Assessing the Achievement

Pacification in Vietnam reached a plateau of achievement in 1970. The Hamlet Evaluation Survey for June of that year rated 91 percent of the hamlets in the country as "secure" or "relatively secure," 7.2 percent as "contested," and only 1.4 percent as "VC-controlled."[38] The evidence is impressive that a completely changed situation prevailed in the rural areas and that the insurgency in the countryside—the people's war—was effectively contained. This was certainly the impression of observers on the scene based on indicators evident to all. As early as October 1969, the *Washington Post* reporter in Saigon, like most American journalists a highly critical observer, prepared a series of three articles on pacification which he called "The New Optimists." It is largely a rehearsal of the facts summarized in the previous section—the new vigor of the government, the success of its changed policies, the improving prosperity of the population contrasting with the surprising weakness of the Viet Cong and its failure to respond vigorously to the spread of government presence and activity.[39] Quantitative measurements confirmed such impressions. In addition to the evidence of the HES, the number of internal refugees declined from the enormous total of 1.5 million in February 1969 to 217,000 in mid-1970, much of the improvement resulting from a movement of population back to homes in the countryside. Komer also notes the decline of the enemy-initiated incident rate and the localization of insurgency-type activity in some eleven provinces among other suggestive indicators of the reversal of the situation.[41]

Moreover, similar evidence confirms that these gains were firmly established and that the situation did not significantly change until shortly before the sudden collapse of 1975—underlining again the changed nature of the conflict in which conventionalized enemy tactics carried out by North Vietnamese replaced the techniques of people's war. From one viewpoint, by 1975 the situation in the countryside had become irrelevant to the outcome. This happened only after the enemy had lost the ability to prosecute a people's war and only after the departure of U.S. forces, which would have relished the challenge of meeting the NVA in conventional combat. The irony was no accident, of course. The enemy would not have risked meeting American forces "one on one," but felt no inhibitions about such a confrontation with ARVN. Thus, although the war continued for over four more years, the story of U.S. counterinsurgency policy and practice in Vietnam can be concluded in 1970. In the years that followed, there were few innovations or departures from the pattern already described other than the orderly winding down of programs and the reversion of special organizations like the RD teams and the PRU to more normal formats.

To sum up, by 1970 a considerable measure of security had been restored and the ability of the insurgency to affect events, to mobilize the population, to fight, tax, and recruit had been eroded to the point where it was a manageable threat. On the other hand, neither in 1970 nor afterward was the VC apparatus—the infrastructure—dismantled or destroyed. It retained its structural integrity, albeit at far lower levels of strength and capability. And it still managed in a variety of ways to impress upon the population that it lurked in the wings, an alternative authority which could again become a threat. This residual presence was of importance to the enemy, for it maintained some credibility to the VC claim to represent the people and constituted a shadow government that, in the event of a sudden improvement of fortunes, could quickly provide a basis for a provisional Communist regime. Nevertheless, the population had substantially abandoned the VC cause which, it would appear, in the very same villages where once it had held on despite the overwhelming strength of its enemies, had now lost the "mandate of heaven."

At this point we face the question of the extent to which the pacification program could take credit for this outcome—and, in addition, whether the results represented a full achievement of the goals of the program. The first question has already been answered. VC errors and particularly the moral and material effects of the Tet gamble had a large but not precisely measurable share in the reversal of the situation. At the same time, however, the GVN moved effectively and broadly to exploit those errors and, in the process, jettisoned many of the political albatrosses that had hampered it in the past. It had also—urged on by the Americans—developed an organization and a series of programs which, under the improved circumstances of 1969 and 1970, realized broad gains. Not all of the programs were equally important or effective, as we will discuss at greater length below. But the combined impact of VC failures, an improved political approach, and improved programs vigorously prosecuted was responsible for the effects we have described.

A more difficult and complex matter is the extent to which the goals of the program were fully achieved. Specifically, the question is whether the GVN had succeeded in enlisting the voluntary support and commitment of a major part of the peasant population to its cause. This, of course, is a difficult question to answer convincingly, for it involves speculation about the attitudes and inner feelings of Vietnamese peasants. The conclusion of independent observers who studied the matter most thoroughly was that, while the VC lost much of its hold, the government was not able to replace it with a new loyalty to its cause. Thus, Samuel L. Popkin, a social scientist who conducted detailed interviews with some four hundred peasants in 1969, stated, "The increase in GVN control results in large measure from a drastic decline in the appeal to peasants of life in areas controlled by the Viet Cong, and from the grave danger of fighting for them."[42] In this writer's opinion, the effect of the programs and events described earlier was to develop a peasant opinion which was neutral with regard to national-level issues and thus considerably short of the goal of popular engagement on the government side. This view stems from the analysis given earlier and from the fact that the new autonomy of the villages had obvious limitations to go along with its advantages. In actual fact, the reformed

village governments were forced into an overall structure which remained largely unchanged and which came into frequent conflict with
the new aspirations of village self-government. At district level and in the
province capital, the ARVN officers holding the key positions and
responsible to an ARVN chain of command still dominated the power
structure. The gap between peasant and urbanized army officer still
existed. Favoritism, corruption, and manipulation of the laws for private
purposes were the rule in this system. Despite persistent efforts by
CORDS and by the Presidential Palace to remove the most notorious and
ineffective of local and provincial officials, the system remained largely
unchanged—the higher-caliber replacements still had to wink at corruption even if they did not participate, or risk earning the hostility of the
command structure.

As a result, the villagers still saw themselves as being in the grasp of
an alien power structure with little legal recourse. The ability of the
peasants to influence the terms that shaped their lives was still severely
circumscribed despite manifest improvements at the village level.

Some American observers thought that Vietnam's new
constitution—despite the domination of the provincial structure by
ARVN appointees—nevertheless offered a serious possibility of balancing the inequalities of rural power through the elected National Assembly. And indeed, a number of representatives systematically organized
constituency services and began to act as a channel whereby villagers
could obtain remedies for their grievances against the provincial government.[43] They remained a minority, however, and their efforts had
limited effect. Thus, although the American view that a democratized
government would eventually compete with the appeal of the VC system
to the peasants began to demonstrate some validity, it was a long-term
process requiring many years to bear fruit—too many, in fact.

The process, which was of vital importance to the goal of a committed
peasantry, could have been greatly advanced if the central government
had given positive encouragement to rural-based political organizations.
Although President Thieu made several beginnings in that direction, he
never followed through and eventually abandoned them all.[44] Without
official encouragement no political group could survive the hostility of the
provincial government. In the end, the peasant was left to his own
resources, with no organization to speak for him above the village level.
The government thus failed—despite the economic and development
benefits of its programs, despite the increased security in the
countryside—to create among the peasantry a strong, positive motivation to engage in the struggle on the official side. It was still, in peasant
eyes, a government of "them," remote, arbitrary, and often abusive.

How could the same government which made such strenuous efforts
to shore up its rural base have failed to get to the heart of the matter and

left the peasant in a political limbo where he remained indifferent to national appeals and commitment? The answer seems to be the same as the one given earlier to the question of why President Diem, despite heavy pressure, had been unwilling to reform his overcentralized and increasingly isolated regime. Thieu could not change the system without putting his own position in serious jeopardy. His first political constituency was the military: if he attempted to strip it of power and privilege and access to wealth, he risked the development of a serious opposition to his leadership within the armed forces which could eventually bring him down. He seems to have considered more than once replacing his military base with a more open and broadly supported structure, but in the end he shrank from the risk. No doubt it was a real risk which would have required some daring and skill and perhaps some luck for him to succeed. The main justification for taking such risks in the mind of a practical politician would be the greater risk of not acting—but Thieu did not see matters in that light. The problem of self-reform in a situation of crisis, of fundamental change in a fragile political structure under great hostile pressure, remained as difficult as ever in the Vietnam of the 1970s.

REVOLUTIONARY DEVELOPMENT: AN UNREALIZED IDEA

The matter of political commitment concerned pacification in its broadest sense. Most of the American side of the effort had been invested in specific programs designed to accomplish specific goals in the area of performance which then, it was hoped, would change attitudes. Of these, the two that attracted the most controversy, though they were not the most important, were Revolutionary Development and the Phoenix program. How had they fared?

At the heart of Revolutionary Development was a fundamental dilemma which was never resolved. The teams were trained, indoctrinated, and deployed in order to assist the villagers to take control of their own affairs, provide for their own defense, reorganize their government, cleanse the local power structure of corruption and abuse, and so on. But, according to the original concept, they were to do all this as an instrument of the province and district authorities who were themselves interested in retaining control of the village and, more often than not, in exploiting their power for personal advantage. Similarly, their role in local defense depended heavily on the support of the regular forces, which was often reluctant and delayed. These two factors, which we noted earlier as critical problems facing RD, were never satisfactorily resolved. After the revised strategies of 1968 and later, the RD teams were reduced in size, local defense was stiffened by the improvement and expansion of the militia, and control of the teams was assigned to the village chief. At this point the RD concept lost its central position in pacification, and the teams reverted to the role of an extra contribution of trained manpower at the disposition of the village government. As such they were helpful but not critical to pacification.

The RD program, in other words, had served as a device for mobilizing and organizing the pacification effort for a preliminary period, after which better means were found to do the job. The revised system developed in 1968 was better because it was simpler, more straightforward, and easier for all concerned to comprehend—and it conformed more closely to the realities of village life. The idea that an elite corps of some fifty thousand young men and women could be recruited, trained, and sent into the village to change the bases of life there in a period of six months to a year was attractive but quite unrealistic. Very soon the pool of suitable manpower was exhausted. The ranks of the RD teams were filled up with youth from the main towns of the province who lacked familiarity or even sympathy with village life. In many cases they obtained their assignments through favoritism; the position of RD cadre was, after all, a government job with steady pay and exemption from the draft. Once in place, the teams often lacked effective military support and, in many cases, were unable to do more than a token or cosmetic job in meeting their objectives. The system worked better after the teams were reduced in size and placed at the disposition of the village chiefs. With less responsibility they were still able to be useful, and although their contribution now became less critical it remained of substantial assistance.

PHOENIX: A CUCKOO IN THE NEST

The outcome of the Phoenix program was less constructive. There seems to be considerable agreement on one score, at least, and that is on the matter of Phoenix's lack of efficacy. Robert Komer, who had endorsed and successfully proposed it to the GVN, became an outspoken critic of it on grounds of ineffectiveness after he left the government. "To date," he said, writing in 1970, "*Phung Hoang* has been a small, poorly managed, and largely ineffective effort."[45] We have already discussed the reasons for this failure: they ranged from the inadequacy of the detention system to the lack of seriousness in the commitment of the Vietnamese services involved. The results were commensurate with the quality of the effort, namely, very poor.[46]

But there remains another and even more serious criticism of Phoenix to be dealt with. This is a charge maintained not by journalists, whose opportunity was slight for in-depth study of a specific subject, but by a number of social scientists who focused their researches on the rural areas. It is the allegation that Phoenix became a serious and additional obstacle in the pacification process. Here is the testimony of one such observer, based upon "several hundred discussions" with rural, political, and religious leaders with the object of identifying the principal problems of the peasant population:

> During 1969, the primary problem faced by the rural population involved the injustices suffered under the administration of the "Phoenix" program. . . . Often "Viet Cong" are arrested on the basis of anonymous denunciations received by the police from those who bear personal grudges against the "suspect." Of greater concern, however, are the large numbers of persons arrested in connection with the efforts of each provincial security agency to fulfill the quota assigned to it, regardless of a suspect's political affiliation, and it has not been unknown for province or police chiefs to seek each month to exceed their quotas in order to demonstrate their competence. With large numbers of helpless persons detained in province or district jails, opportunities for corruption have proliferated. In some provinces the Phoenix program has been turned into a money-making scheme through which a villager's release can be obtained for the payment of a bribe, usually about $25 to $50.[47]

This is a very serious criticism indeed. It charges the pacifiers with controverting the purposes of their own program by mistaken zeal in pressing the attack against the infrastructure. Whether the actuality was fully as serious as charged remains questionable, for CORDS had its own means of checking public attitudes and problems and detected no such phenomenon.[48] We may with some plausibility conclude, however, that Phoenix did become a major problem to the peasantry in some areas where individual officials behaved abusively, but we question whether it was as general a matter as Goodman and others alleged.

As for the even more extreme charge that Phoenix was merely a machine for torture and murder, that it was responsible for the outright slaughter of some twenty thousand Vietnamese for political reasons, it should be clear from what has already been said that these charges were highly distorted and largely imaginary. The figures came from GVN claims which in turn were based largely on military actions, the labeling of the casualties as VC infrastructure being done after the fact in order to boost the quotas of the local authorities. This fact, of course, does not justify Phoenix, for it was a system seemingly made to order for manipulation and misinterpretation.

Clearly, then, Phoenix failed to eliminate the infrastructure that remained after the heavy losses of Tet and contributed to some degree to the difficulties confronting pacification. There is little evidence to suggest that it resulted in more eliminations of important infrastructure members than would have been achieved by conventional police operations. The advocates of Phoenix at the time of its inception, and the author among them, were therefore mistaken in the belief that, in view of the critical role of the infrastructure in the enemy's system, the insurgency could not be brought under control without the elimination of the VC organization which directed it. From this belief, the concept of a hierarchy of local and regional centers where the work was to be done on a full-time and urgent basis emerged more or less naturally as simple administrative common sense. On the other hand, the author does not share the view that the members of an organization efficiently going about the destruction of an entire social system, and incidentally using terror and assassination routinely, are entitled to be dealt with gently, in accordance with the full protections of the Bill of Rights. The crime of Phoenix was not the use of harsh methods to apprehend or destroy the enemies of the GVN. Its crime was ineffectiveness, indiscriminateness, and, in some areas at least, the violation of local norms to the extent that it appeared to the villagers to be a threat to them in the peaceable performance of their daily business. The Americans involved erred in failing to appreciate the extent to which the pathology of Vietnamese society would distort an apparently sound concept. The GVN was guilty of both misfeasance and malfeasance in executing the program.

Believing what they did about the importance of the elimination of the infrastructure, those responsible thought they had no choice but to attack that objective with all the weapons they could devise. They did have an alternative, however, and that was to accept the unreality of the objective for the time being and concentrate on perfecting the tools before going at the target at full strength. This would have required a longer view and a more patient approach than prevailed at the time, delaying the final elimination of the infrastructure to a last "cleanup" phase after the main objectives of pacification had been completed.

Both Phoenix and Revolutionary Development suffered from a similar defect: a simplified view of the complexities of village life in Vietnam and of the ability of the central authority to intervene directly in the internal arrangements of thousands of villages simultaneously. Yet they were also overly complex programs for the American and Vietnamese personnel who were required to carry them out, demanding too much trained and dedicated manpower and a subtle approach which was only possible if attempted on a small scale. On the other hand, the programs which succeeded were more direct and straightforward in concept. Unfortunately, they evolved only after the Vietnamese leadership, particularly President Thieu, came to see pacification as an urgent and major priority, far too late for rapid achievement of the goals envisioned.

DID PACIFICATION SUCCEED OR FAIL?

A final judgment on the effort is not a simple matter, for it depends on how one sees the goals. The events of 1968 to 1970, of which pacification was a major element, broke the hold of the VC on the rural population. A striking contrast was established between the well-being enjoyed under government protection and the dangers and hardships of life with the Viet Cong, and certainly the pacification effort could take some if not all of the credit for that. According to a broader concept of pacification, however, the final goal of willing identification by the peasant of his interests with those of the government remained unachieved because of the regime's failure to devise a political framework that could express and bring the aspirations of the peasantry to bear on national decision-making. The government hold was extensive but thin, a little like Mark Twain's description of the Platte River: "an inch deep and a mile wide."

No doubt, on the other hand, the development of such a deep commitment was beyond the capability of a U.S. advisory and assistance program such as CORDS and depended upon the generation of indigenous, purely Vietnamese initiatives and leadership. These not only never emerged but were discouraged by the regime, which feared political movements it could not control and the threat they posed to its stability. The ultimate goals of pacification were thus beyond the reach of the program and depended on factors over which it had little influence.

It is problematical whether any foreign government could, under the circumstances of Vietnam, have brought into existence the indigenous policies and leadership required, but the American policymakers did not seriously try. They were convinced that stability was the first requirement for progress in any other field and therefore refrained from a persistent and determined attempt to force the Thieu regime in the desired direction, pinning their hopes on persuasion and on a gradual evolution toward democratic norms which never materialized. But as Thieu increased the repressiveness of his hold on political life, he fanned the flames of opposition in the United States to the Vietnam involvement. The upshot was the crisis of early 1975, which was precipitated by the refusal of the United States Congress to provide an assured supply of military aid in the amounts required. The tragic collapse of South Vietnam was ultimately a product of the crucial difficulty we have noted frequently on these pages, that of reforming and redistributing power in a political system under severe internal stress. If Thieu had gambled upon such a redistribution and won, his regime would both have answered the criticisms that undermined his support in the U.S. and deepened his hold upon the population in Vietnam. If he had gambled and lost, his honor would at least have shone a good deal brighter in exile, and he would have lost nothing he did not finally lose in any event.

The programmatic aspects of pacification in Vietnam were therefore a substantial success, but they were unable to come to grips with the most deep-seated problems of rural life in Vietnam. These could only have been solved by providing the villagers with political levers linked to the national political process, creating what one observer has called a "political community."[49] This failure lays bare in stark outline the basic dilemma implicit in counterinsurgency policy which was never seriously grappled with by U.S. policymakers, a matter which goes far beyond the programmatic and organizational questions that preoccupied the national security community during the "counterinsurgency era." Effective programs require governmental stability, but successful counterinsurgency requires granting the rural population a strong voice in its own affairs. Steps toward the latter appear to threaten the former and are usually pushed aside with ultimately disastrous effects on counterinsurgency.

These considerations will be examined in more detail in what follows. As far as concerns the counterinsurgency in Vietnam, we may conclude that after unconscionable delays which granted the enemy an almost insurmountable head start, his own mistakes combined with—at long last—a revived and greatly strengthened "new model" U.S. pacification effort and a greatly improved GVN appreciation of the requirements, brought pacification a considerable degree of success. But pacification was only part of the story, and the total effort was still short of what was needed to sweep the enemy off the board or convince the American public of the value of its burdensome involvement. The limited nature of the success reflected, among other things, the inability of the U.S. to establish within its own apparatus a clear, consistent, and firm understanding of the needs of the situation, most notably to knit together successfully the civilian and military efforts. In turn, that failure permitted the military to perform in a manner which aggravated the problem and brought public revulsion in the U.S. The mixed outcome also reflected the intractability of the political dilemma of Vietnam, the tension and opposition between political reform and stability. These failures brought the effort down in ruins and quite obscured the real accomplishments of the pacification effort, which were, in contrast to the rest, a notable achievement in a dark, confused, and tragic imbroglio from whose consequences it will take this country many years to recover.

9

Denouements

★ ★ ★

LATIN AMERICA AND CIVIC ACTION

The involvement of the U.S. in pacification in Vietnam was the largest such involvement anywhere. It was not only costly but complex, a natural outcome of the attempt to spread its effects everywhere and to transform the daily lives of a large population through the intervention of the government. The involvements in Laos and Thailand were small relative to Vietnam, but both called for complex programs which posed considerable challenges to the U.S.'s ability to coordinate and to respond flexibly in a wide range of activity, some of it (notably in Laos) entirely unprecedented in our history.

These episodes in Southeast Asia do not by any means exhaust the U.S. counterinsurgency experience, but they absorbed and deployed the greatest amounts of resources and attention. The threats that developed there were assessed to have a degree of seriousness not found elsewhere, and particularly not in Latin America, which is where almost all other such activity was concentrated.

It is true, however, that for a brief period in the early and mid-1960s insurgent activity in Latin America seemed to be a threat of major proportions. The urgings and appeals of Fidel Castro plus the indications that Cuba was providing training, weapons, and other assistance to insurgent groups were viewed in Washington as alarming. The countries where such signs were assessed as most threatening were Venezuela, Colombia, Peru, and Guatemala. Later, of course, Che Guevara's quixotic sally into Bolivia briefly revived concern. All these and other minor attempts to start Cuban-style insurgencies in Latin America quickly petered out in failure and disillusionment or else sputtered along

279

uncertainly at a low level of activity, posing no credible threat. After a while the arguments for continued U.S. concern no longer seemed compelling. During the time of greatest concern, the U.S. involvements never advanced beyond the transfer of relatively small amounts of military aid, training by Mobile Training Teams, and by the assignment of Latin American officers to military schools in the Canal Zone and the continental United States, and police training and advice by both USAID and CIA. For this purpose AID made use of an international police school which it had established in Washington.

WHY CASTROISM FAILED

Various explanations have been advanced for the failure of Castro-style insurgency in Latin America. One study puts it simply in terms of the absence of a revolutionary situation in any of the countries of the area.[1] As we have seen in Chapter I, however, the theory developed by Castro, Guevara, et al. was designed to overcome that problem and to create a revolutionary situation by the activity of one or more guerrilla *focos* which would awaken the peasants to the possibility of achieving an overturn of existing authority by violent revolutionary action.

That theory failed entirely to prove itself for a number of reasons. One explanation, acknowledged by the Cuban leaders, was the absence of the element of novelty which, in Cuba itself, had seen the revolt against Batista develop rapidly and succeed before either Cubans or foreigners were aware of the seriousness of the threat or even that a Communist revolution was contemplated. To this day, in fact, many analysts believe that Communism was not Castro's conscious goal until some time after he came to power.[2] The effort to apply the tactics of the Cuban victory to other countries met with a far more alert and vigorous response by both the United States and the regimes concerned and shut off the possibility of a repetition of the Cuban surprise.

Equally important was the absence in these attempts of either a Castro on the side of the insurgents or a Batista in the seat of power. Castro's talents as a dramatic symbol of popular aspirations and as a figure around whom the opposition of all hues could rally was an essential ingredient of success in Cuba. It was lacking in all the other countries. Similarly, Batista's political and military ineptitude was a priceless asset to the Cuban revolutionaries. In contrast, we find in Venezuela, for example, the politically adept Romulo Betancourt, first freely elected president in his country's history, conducting a skillful campaign to isolate the revolutionaries and largely succeeding. Similar, if not so impressive, reactions resulted in the containment and isolation of revolutionaries in Colombia, Peru, and Bolivia. The Guatemalan situation has been more complex since the government at various times has tried different prescriptions ranging from the enlightened to the brutal. After much bloodshed a persistent guerrilla infection continues but makes little progress.

One of the shrewdest observers of these phenomena notes another major flaw in the revolutionary approach, namely, the origins of the revolutionists among the urban educated classes which made them, in the eyes of the peasantry, an alien force with little appeal.

> By and large they [the peasants] preferred to keep the little they had in life rather than to risk it in battle against the *patron* and his army. They believed it wiser to hope that those in power would grow more benign, rather than struggle to alter the hierarchy of things. Even where the peasants had already been politicized . . . they tended to look on the revolutionary insurgents as aliens. In most cases, the peasants would probably have preferred not to take sides; but when they did they usually favored the army with the information and co-operation needed to hunt down the guerillas.[3]

A final point in explaining the failure of Castroism to catch on in Latin America is the large question which can be raised about the extent to which the revolutionary principles abstracted from their experience by the Castro group and broadcast far and wide as a surefire method of acquiring power in Latin America were actually responsible for the victory in Cuba. More important than the few *focos* fighting in the hills, according to some, was Castro's political skill which brought him the support of the anti-Batista forces throughout the island and resulted in the victory being handed to him after Batista fled, although at the time his guerrilla forces controlled only a small territory. The romantic predilection of the Castro brothers and Che Guevara for guerrilla heroics and—probably more important—their desire to take all the credit led them to attribute this success to the magic of guerrilla operations, but the story is far more complicated and probably not fully understood to this day.[4]

THE AMERICAN ROLE

The U.S.'s share in all of this was clearly secondary but nevertheless of some significance. The rash of Castro-style insurgencies coincided with the development, under President Kennedy's urgent insistence, of an interest and a capability on the part of the foreign affairs and national security agencies to guide and assist threatened governments in meeting the challenge. Missions were dispatched to survey the scene and to recommend U.S. assistance programs. In accordance with the procedure promulgated by the Special Group (C.I.),[5] the U.S. missions in designated countries developed Internal Defense Plans whose purpose was to design and put into effect an integrated program involving contributions from all concerned agencies. This then could provide a basis for monitoring and managing the ongoing American assistance effort.

Among the goals of the U.S. program was the education of the military leadership of the threatened countries in the concept of counter-insurgency as, among other things, a test of the army's ability to establish an improved relationship with the rural population. Civic action was one key concept of the prescription, along with rapid action to smother the insurgency at the earliest possible stage in its development and close pursuit to keep up the pressure. Of these, civic action received a large share of attention and resources—and also of the publicity. Presumably this was because it was considered an attractive concept with appeal to the public and thus a decorative embellishment of the armed forces' public image. It was, of course, also seriously intended as a counterinsurgency measure, and, in fact, as the decade progressed, the older justification of military aid to Latin American countries as a contribution to "hemispheric defense" was entirely superseded by the newer objective of improved internal defense against subversion of the Cuban type with emphasis on civic action. In a review of the military aid program, an assistant secretary of state for Latin American affairs said in 1969, "It is not . . . a program based on such an outdated rationale as 'hemispheric defense.' " And he added, somewhat more positively, "One primary purpose of our military aid program has been and is to help our Latin American neighbors to attain socioeconomic development by systematic evolution rather than in the volatile atmosphere of destructive revolution."[6] During much of the period roughly 15 percent of military aid was allocated to civic action. The total for all Latin America in 1964, a fairly representative year, was about $14 million.[7]

On the civilian side of the effort the most specifically counterinsurgency-oriented program was the police training activity of USAID. For this purpose, AID established an International Police Academy, first in the Canal Zone and later in Washington. The six-week basic course was given in Spanish. This was embraced within the larger Alliance for Progress programs which themselves were aimed at heading off insurgency by promoting development. In other words, one could look on the entire program of the U.S. in Latin America during these years as a broad counterinsurgency program at least in a preventive sense. We will not, however, include it as part of our story, for we are primarily concerned with actual insurgencies and the measures taken to deal with them.

As we have seen, all the Castro-inspired guerrilla insurgencies failed, and in most cases the U.S. contribution played a part, albeit a limited one. To review these episodes briefly, Venezuela was an early case and one in which the insurgents came closer to succeeding than anywhere else—although they did not actually come very close. It was not typical of this series of episodes in that, in the early phase, urban rebellion played a major role in the revolutionary scheme and rural guerrilla warfare was secondary. Clearly, Romulo Betancourt's contribution was essential, whereas that of the U.S. was merely useful. No civic action funds were committed in Venezuela during 1962 and 1963, although military aid was sizable. Probably the most important aspect of the American effort was the police program. The Venezuelan police were a principal target of the urban guerrilla operations. They were in woeful condition at the beginning of the insurgency for lack of training and because of the low quality of personnel, a condition due to the poor repute in which the police were held. Police programs were initiated by the U.S. (and also, curiously enough, by Chile) and carried out by both AID and CIA. Improvements, especially in equipment, were noticeable.[8]

All this was no doubt helpful to Betancourt, but not critical. The insurgency in Venezuela went through several phases, but an early turning point was the election of 1963 when a successor to Betancourt (Raul Leoni) was chosen in free national elections and then assumed the office as provided in the constitution—an unprecedented accomplishment in Venezuelan history. The Communists focused on the goal of preventing this election and failed. In the political and counterinsurgency campaign preceding the election, Betancourt mastered his enemies on all sides and did so without violating the constitution or democratic norms. On election day, 91 percent of the electorate turned out, dramatically demonstrating the failure of the insurgent campaign. The Communists showed an appreciation for the reasons of their failure. They gave up urban insurgency and opted for "protracted war" in the countryside, which sputters on to this day. Meanwhile, democratic government has persisted in Venezuela, social and economic development have continued, and these have provided a political context in which the insurgency has been unable to flourish.

In neighboring Colombia the story is less dramatic and the role of the army more important. As recently as 1976 an American reporter in Colombia sought to develop an analysis to explain the failure of Castroite guerrilla warfare to progress in that country despite more than ten years of trying. She advanced such reasons as the traditional political loyalties of the population to either the Liberal or Conservative parties, the bloody years of civil war between 1948 and 1957 whose memory remains alive, and the shallowness of the commitment of the urban students to a cause which they quickly abandoned under pressure. Of considerable importance, she found, was the skill of the military handling of the peasantry.

The initial government response to guerilla action [she wrote] was careful, involving as much social and psychological action as military retaliation. The army . . . realized that "extremism feeds on broken promises," said one military source.

The army brought roads, clinics and construction jobs along with the state of siege when it fought guerillas in depressed areas. Soldiers were told to treat the population as allies against a few misguided but retrievable insurgents. Troops who manhandled villagers were court-martialled publicly in the towns where offenses occurred.[9]

This suggests that the training offered to Colombian officers at Fort Gulick, Panama, and Fort Bragg, North Carolina, was put into practice when they returned to their duty in Colombia. At the same time, another student of Colombia makes quite clear that the Colombian army had its own long and well-established tradition of civic action many years before it was exposed to North American concepts.[10] Colombia had been afflicted with bitter domestic violence and endemic banditry in the countryside for many years. Attempts to identify the underlying causes had led the military leadership to the concept that la Violencia reflected, among other things, social and economic disparities, and to the conclusion that the armed forces had a role to play in solving such problems. The theory was developed well before various leftist organizations moved in among the active guerrilla groups and became predominant in some of them. Nevertheless, there was close cooperation between U.S. counterinsurgency planners and the Colombian military in drawing up a comprehensive plan, called "Plan Lazo," which was adopted in 1962 and continued for three years. Although it succeeded in eliminating some of the bandit and guerrilla groups, it also appears to have had the effect of driving the remaining holdouts into the arms of the Castroites who, after 1965, became the dominant element in guerrilla activity.[11] The military continued, with some American help, the program of military pressure following a generally enlightened approach, and succeeded in reducing the threat to a lower but nevertheless persistent level which continues up to the present. As in Venezuela, the threat has been contained but not eliminated. American help, meanwhile, has been reduced to a trickle.

The experience in Peru was directly related to Communist exploitation of deep-seated peasant grievances in the department of Cuzco in the period 1963–1965. Spearheaded by the Trotskyist Hugo Blanco, there was an outbreak of strikes, demonstrations, and some violence against the authorities in the La Convencion valley which stimulated an army reaction characterized by both military repression and social action, including a local land reform, road-building, the opening of schools, and the like. Although the land reform was later criticized as being halfhearted and inadequate,[12] it succeeded for a while, along with the other measures taken, in dampening the revolt. Within a few years, however, another group of local Communists, this time modeling themselves on Cuba's fidelismo, launched an ill-timed and ill-led guerrilla-style revolt from the neighboring mountains. The leader was Luis de la Puente.

The tactic failed [writes the same reporter]. Peru's army, one of the best-disciplined in Latin America, had been getting ready for the guerillas since 1963. Many Peruvian officers and noncoms were among the eighteen thousand Latin American soldiers trained at the U.S. Army Counterinsurgency School in Panama. Thousands more have undergone Special Forces training in the United States. . . . In addition, many agents of the Peruvian Investigative Police have attended a counterinsurgency school run by the Central Intelligence Agency.[13]

The military first attempted to bomb the guerrillas out of their fastness but succeeded in wrapping up the revolt only after sealing off the trails that led in and out. The victory in this one-sided affair stemmed from the overwhelming force brought to bear plus the failure of the guerrillas to attract support during a period when peasant hopes had been raised by partial land reform and promises of more.

This entire experience convinced the military that Peru was in a state of "latent insurgency" and played a role in establishing the viewpoints among some Peruvian officers which led them eventually to seize control of the government and to institute a socialist regime under military domination which remains in power to this day.[14] Although the training and indoctrination received by Peruvian officers at American schools can hardly be held responsible for this outcome, it was one element among several that led them in that direction.

Guatemala, too, conducted counterinsurgency operations during these years which were to some extent influenced by American concepts. Guatemala participated in the various training programs and experimented with civic action, offers of amnesty, and has even tried the unique tactic of ignoring the guerrillas entirely. The latter have been divided among themselves and have gone through various phases in which one or another of the existing varieties of Communism was adopted as the current ideology. Neither the government nor the guerrillas has been strong enough to prevail, however, no matter what approach was taken. The bloodshed has been heavy for a small country, with the urban supporters of the guerrillas resorting to assassinations (including several foreign ambassadors) and the regime retaliating by sponsoring vigilante-style terrorism. In the midst of this reign of terror and counter-terror the principles of enlightened counterinsurgency were overwhelmed and forgotten.[15]

A final case we must note is that of Bolivia and of Che Guevara's fatal intervention there. This famous episode has been repeatedly described and analyzed and does not require detailed review for our purposes. (The account we found most useful is that of Daniel James in his introduction to an edition of Guevara's captured diaries.[16]) In virtually every detail, Guevara's final adventure was based either on faulty concepts or mistaken estimates of the situation or poor technique. The fact is almost incidental that the U.S. contributed to his defeat by hastily training a ranger unit of the Bolivian army which was deployed in August 1967 (the *foco* was discovered by the authorities in March), and finally destroyed both of Guevara's armed groups in October. Similarly incidental is the reported involvement of the CIA in close monitoring and advice on the intelligence aspects of the operation. The attempt was foredoomed to failure and would certainly have collapsed of its own errors, particularly in the choice of a location and a situation in which no likelihood of peasant support existed.[17]

These five cases represent the most extensive of the various insurgencies attempted in Latin America following the Cuban model and the theories of Castro and Guevara. Several of them continue at a low and unpromising level to this day, kept alive by the desperate commitment of their leaders to a revolutionary concept of dubious origin and highly exaggerated potency. The Latin American peasantry, largely Indian in origin and culture and isolated from the Hispanic mainstream of the ruling cultures, has so far rejected this effort to overturn the immemorial patterns of society in the remote countryside. In the meantime, after Guevara's debacle, the interest of the urban and educated adherents of revolution turned from Castroism to urban terrorism, a variety of insurgency which is remote from people's war and has so far also failed in its goals. At the same time, attitudes toward the insurgent threat began to change in the United States. The programs launched by the Kennedy Administration, which had a distinct if secondary role in thwarting the insurgencies, have declined in importance and have largely been terminated. For most purposes the counterinsurgency era in Latin America is at an end.

★　★　★

THE WINDING DOWN OF THE APPARATUS

If we confine ourselves to doctrine and theory, the interest in counterinsurgency of the U.S. military services, and most particularly of the army, remained high throughout the 1960s. A process of earnest study by military intellectuals of the available field experience, and reformulation of manuals and training courses in accordance with the lessons derived, went on throughout the decade and after. "Counterinsurgency" disappeared as a descriptive label to be replaced by "internal defense and development" as a general term for a whole range of activities related to assisting less-developed countries, and by "stability operations" to describe the specific operational activity of the armed forces. A field manual specifically called "Stability Operations—U.S. Army Doctrine" was prepared which gave liberal emphasis to noncombat roles for the military.[18] Among them were "civil affairs" activities which could encompass, among other things, the establishment of schools and public health systems, assistance to the police, or civic action by the army to improve the environment in a given locality.[19] All of this was to be fitted into an overall "internal defense and development plan" developed by the U.S. and the host government. In its elephantine way, the military system was attempting to adapt itself to the novel complexities of the new dispensation, but the adjustments quickly came up against unchangeable "laws" when the question of combat tactics arose. Unit integrity and the full use of available firepower, including armor, artillery, combat air support, and "aerial fire support" (armed helicopters) were all mandated.[20]

Even more novel notions began to emerge in some corners of the system. Serious staff attention was given to designing regional military organizations to be placed at the headquarters of some of the joint commands (e.g., CINCPAC in Pearl Harbor and CINCSOUTH in Panama) which would have a preplanned capability to intervene in insurgency situations. In association with these regional assistance commands, the planners talked of developing special combat units "as flexible and lightly equipped as possible. Light, fast, specially outfitted units are needed, rather than conventional fighting forces."[21] This concept, which has long been a secret dream of military men with an orientation toward counterinsurgency, never left the drawing boards. In fact, the notion of a regional assistance command, which was encouraged by General Howard K. Johnson when he was army chief of staff, died when General Westmoreland assumed that position in late 1968. The latter favored, instead, the development of a "nation-building" school.[22] There was, in fact, a brief period in the late 1960s when military intellectuals were advancing the notion that the U.S. Army was the arm of the government best equipped to carry out in the field the entire range of activities associated with "nation-building." According to two analysts who studied these trends:

> The new doctrine does, however, imply a greatly enlarged advisory role for the U.S. military, extending far beyond security and encompasssing, in some variants, virtually every facet of life in the rebellion-beset country, even such purely civilian efforts as assistance in the conduct of the country's fiscal and economic affairs. By the beginning of the 1970's many thoughtful Army officers believed that, in view of the difficulty that U.S. non-military agencies had in deploying well-trained civilian advisers for these functions, the Army itself should be prepared to provide such assistance.[23]

In actual fact, Fort Bragg, the home of Special Forces and the Special Warfare School, absorbed the Civil Affairs School of Fort Gordon and became the Military Assistance School. The change had limited impact for, at the same time, public support for all such activities dwindled steadily in reaction to the growing frustration and sense of futility generated by the stalemate in Vietnam. In truth, the army had reacted far too slowly to the pressures that had been brought to bear upon it during the counterinsurgency era. It had taken three or four years of costly exposure to the reality of the battlefield in Vietnam for the import of "revolutionary war," i.e., people's war, to have an impact. By that time an impatient public and a disillusioned press were unwilling to hear of innovations to make future interventions more effective. They wanted no more such interventions. By the early 1970s, the army, after a brief, unconsummated flirtation with the notion of fighting in new or, perhaps more accurately, in more primitive ways, slipped back with some relief to a more familiar posture. Its principal concern again became the preparation for conventional, high-technology war against a conventional enemy on the familiar battlefields of Europe. Less and less was heard about giving the U.S. Army a predominant role in nation building. But even the novel departures of the late 1960s missed the main point. They accepted new roles for the army other than the application of force, but, at the same time, with the exception of a few voices which had begun to speak of a special light infantry, they clung to the assumption that the principal role of *military force* in a counterinsurgency situation is to find and destroy the armed enemy rather than accepting the prior importance of protecting the population in order to separate the insurgents from their base. The latter was viewed as a defensive strategy and anathema was pronounced upon it. Finally, even the achievement embodied in the new field manuals was illusory, for as Heymann and Whitson state:

> Even as late as 1966, most American unit commanders and division staff officers arriving in South Vietnam were not familiar with the standard doctrinal literature contained in Army field manuals. . . . In the view of these officers, the focal division staff problem was not that of understanding the nature of the conflict, but one of managing a division's resources according to prevailing practice.[24]

The genuine accomplishments of the military in Vietnam described in the last chapter were not the work of the line commanders and their staffs but of military men detached from their units and assigned to CORDS to work as advisers and members of Mobile Training Teams developing the capabilities of Regional and Popular Forces and assisting village chiefs with their security problems. The line units, despite adjustments made by General Abrams, remained fixated upon the large enemy divisions as their preeminent responsibility to be discharged in traditional fashion by the concentration of overwhelming force.

UNWINDING THE CIVILIAN AGENCIES

In those civilian agencies which had participated heavily in the counterinsurgency effort, a similar process of deemphasis began in the late sixties, aided by the fact that they all had other major commitments and concerns which reasserted their priority. For example, in AID, where the police training and advisory activity continued well into the mid-seventies, it nevertheless succeeded in gradually shifting emphasis away from counterinsurgency concerns—rural police, combat police, and the like—to more conventional goals summed up in the term "institution-building." These comprised training, administration, and the improvement of police support activities such as communications. Concurrently, the overall emphasis shifted from counterinsurgency to law and order. AID as a whole reverted to economic development as its primary task and gradually subordinated or dropped entirely its interest in the problems of rural environmental improvement for the sake of cementing popular loyalties.

This concept had always been a dubious proposition based on the unsupported belief that economic and social improvement, if seen as having been brought about by the government's efforts, would induce people to throw in their lot with the government rather than its enemies. But others were soon pointing out that development, or economic and social modernization, was a highly disruptive process usually accompanied by social upheaval.[25] Another view held that small-scale investment in local improvement, if properly institutionalized so as to become a permanent ongoing function of the threatened government, was a more appropriate response to a Communist rural insurgency. But many problems developed out of this concept as well, among them the undoubted fact that the insurgents were often able to exploit the aid, diverting some of it for their own use, terrorizing recipients to make increased contributions, and benefiting in many other ways.[26]

Still another point of view held, as does this writer, that the critical aspect of rural development aid for counterinsurgency purposes was the process by which decisions were made and the aid distributed, that an important part of the answer to Communist challenges in the countryside was to devise a means whereby the government side brought those affected into the decision-making process, thereby giving them some control over the terms of their existence. Land reform could be a major contributing factor in such an approach, depending on the degree to which tenancy and land ownership were a serious problem. A voice in the selection of the local officials who administered the program would be another, as would the availability of channels whereby a community could make its views known to a higher authority. Such an approach, however, is exceedingly difficult for a foreign power to launch within a host country. Inevitably it merges into issues of political reform, of changing the local power structure, and becomes anything but a neutral, administrative, and technical matter. In other words, it is a program beyond the capability of a foreign technical advisory and training agency such as AID to administer. AID had been called upon to accomplish a highly political task with a repertoire of techniques—the delivery of materials, advice, and technical training—which were not appropriate to the task, and the agency was not loath to see the emphasis on counterinsurgency gradually eased, permitting it to concentrate its efforts in areas in which it felt more competent.

A somewhat similar process occurred in CIA, where gradually the focus shifted in the late 1960s to the intelligence and counterintelligence aspects of counterinsurgency and away from efforts to support local popular paramilitary forces to fill the gaps caused by the central government's failure to provide local security. Symbolic evidence of this shift came to public light when a lengthy CIA analysis of the Vietnamese situation leaked out to the press in 1970.[27] The study made an extensively documented case for the view that Communist strategy in Vietnam had shifted from active military confrontation to the quiet penetration of government services by an estimated thirty thousand agents under Lao Dong control. The goal of the strategy was to establish a strong position from which the Communist organization could work to bring down the South Vietnamese regime after the American military withdrawal had been completed.

This study was the apparent fruit of a laborious and thorough intelligence collection and analysis effort made possible by a shift of CIA resources from training and advisory roles to *independent* intelligence collection, that is, collection carried on separate from and without the knowledge of the South Vietnamese. That type of effort, while it had always been part of the CIA program in Vietnam, acquired a high priority only in late 1968 when the CIA station informed CORDS that it intended to withdraw the personnel who had been performing advisory and monitoring functions in the Phoenix program. CORDS replaced these officers with hastily trained army lieutenants and captains, and CIA put the personnel thus made available to work on the independent collection of information on the Viet Cong and Lao Dong. Similar transfers of effort took place as CIA and CORDS began the long process of withdrawal from the various cadre programs, particularly the Revolutionary Development teams. That shift represented the reassertion by elements within CIA of the preeminence of independent intelligence collection as the classic CIA function in any situation involving the U.S. national interest overseas. In effect, the lengthy report, completed in 1970, made the point by implication that the enemy had swept the boards in this subterranean contest of spying and counterspying and had thereby thwarted the immense and costly military and pacification efforts of the U.S. and South Vietnam. It stated that the enemy's penetration program had established Lao Dong–controlled agents at all key points in the South Vietnamese government structure, including the intelligence and counterintelligence services, and had done so in such strength that the very weapons by which they would ordinarily have been combated and neutralized were unable to achieve any lasting success against them. Whether or not that conclusion was true—and fragmentary reports from Vietnam since the Lao Dong victory tend to confirm it—it implies a pointed criticism of CIA, and indeed of U.S. priorities in Vietnam up to 1968, and demonstrates both the trend away from counterinsurgency involvement by CIA as well as some of the arguments underlying that trend.

The evolution of national security and foreign policy concerns away from preoccupation with Communist insurgency was also evident in the Department of State. Indeed, although its public commitment had been as firm as that of the other agencies, foreign service officers as a body had included from the beginning a large number of skeptics, especially among the more experienced members of the career cadre. This attitude had been generated by the precise question which U. Alexis Johnson— the senior active foreign service officer at the time—had sought to combat as early as 1961.[28] This was the doubt, born of experience, that ambassadors and their staffs could, with the means available to them, i.e., persuasion plus offers of aid, generate the enlightenment and breadth of view among host governments which were required to carry out a serious and effective counterinsurgency program. As Johnson himself had acknowledged in the early days of the policy, it was possible that foreign leaders might not be able or willing to take the risks of reforming their governments along the lines demanded by the urgencies of their situation.[29] Many foreign service professionals doubted that they would and remained quietly reserved toward the counterinsurgency enthusiasms of the moment, never taking their doubts to the public. An insight into this critical view was offered, somewhat after the fact, by Charles Maechling, Jr., who had served as "Director of Internal Defense" in the State Department during the Kennedy years, later left the government and in 1969 published "Our Internal Defense Policy—A Reappraisal," also in the *Foreign Service Journal*.[30]

Maechling's argument is a root-and-branch assault on the policy which he had played a senior role in implementing, and it strikes some shrewd blows. It suffers, however, from a failure to make adequate distinctions between differing situations and assumes an inability on the part of the U.S. to exercise choice between favorable and unfavorable circumstances. In fact, during the mid-sixties some advocates of the doctrine *did* more or less assume that counterinsurgency policies could be applied successfully anywhere, regardless of circumstances, but Maechling did not content himself with addressing the contradictions that resulted from this overly ambitious reach. He assumed that coun-tries like Vietnam were the predominant type among nations endangered by insurgency and dwelled on the frustrations of intervention in a situation where the government services are corrupt, the army indifferent to the fate of the population, and "the ruling oligarchy is numerically so small that it has to keep the political opposition . . . divided and neutralized in order to prevent being blown sky high." This is the government the United States has to rely on to achieve reforms that will make effective counterinsurgency operations possible. The result, in the author's view, "is the old horror of responsibility without authority, elevated to the plane of high strategy." The final and tragic contradiction emerges when the situation deteriorates to the point that the U.S. believes itself obliged to intervene with troops, for that introduces all the horrors attendant on modern warfare, and visits them upon the hapless population.

In sum, Maechling sees counterinsurgency as envisaged by the then avowed policies of the U.S. as inevitably producing at best a prolonged and costly stalemate. He attributes this result to the reliance upon mere advice and persuasion to resolve the complex internal problems of sore-beset underdeveloped countries and to the destructive impact of foreign military intervention. Clearly, he had Vietnam in mind in making this indictment, and it had much validity as applied to that country. The view was representative of the opinion of many foreign service professionals who feelingly echoed the conclusion that an ambassador armed with nothing but his own eloquence and some economic and military aid could hardly rearrange the intimate internal power relationships of a foreign country at a time of crisis.

The Department of State did not resist the gradual drawing back from the open-ended and global commitments implied in the earlier formulations of counterinsurgency policy. On the contrary, many welcomed the trend as a delayed acknowledgment of reality. One of the clearer expositions of the new policy came from the under secretary of state in the early years of the Nixon Administration, Eliot Richardson. It was a version of the "Nixon Doctrine" first expounded by the president at Guam in 1969. Without disavowing anything that had been done in the past, Richardson said that while the U.S. would continue to aid its friends and allies threatened by internal subversion, such aid would

> hereafter depend on the realities of each separate situation. In some cases aid in economic and political development would be enough. In other cases aid in the form of training and equipment may be necessary. But the job of countering insurgency in the field is one which must be conducted by the government concerned, making use of its popular support, its resources and its men.[31]

The implications were further expounded in a later sentence: "We cannot, it seems clear, do the job of fighting insurgency for someone else." That, in fact, was the only new element of the policy. Despite the implications of Richardson's remarks, the character of American aid had usually depended upon the nature of the given situation.

The State Department continued for a while to offer the "counterinsurgency" course which had been launched by President Kennedy. Successive reorganizations brought about the establishment of the position of "Under Secretary for Security Assistance," whose function was to coordinate both military and economic assistance programs at a higher level than hitherto. Such bureaucratic rearrangements had little impact upon the reality of a steady decline in interest and concern which was reflected both in a reduction in appropriations and in high-level attention. An example of the latter is evidenced in President Nixon's report to Congress on U.S. foreign policy delivered on February 18, 1970. This document was unprecedented in the completeness of its survey of both foreign policy and defense policy. When published and distributed it comprised 160 pages. In the entire document a mere two paragraphs cover the matter which had stimulated such a copious flow of verbiage in the preceding years. They appear in the section devoted to defense policy and specifically concerned with "general purpose forces." Here they are *in toto:*

> We cannot expect U.S. military forces to cope with the entire spectrum of threats facing allies or potential allies throughout the world. This is particularly true of subversion and guerilla warfare, or "wars of national liberation." Experience has shown that the best means of dealing with insurgencies is to preempt them through economic development and social reform and control them with police, paramilitary and military action by the threatened government.
>
> We may be able to supplement local efforts with economic and military assistance. However, a direct combat role for U.S. general purpose forces arises primarily when insurgency has shaded into external aggression or when there is an overt conventional attack. In such cases we shall weigh our interests and our commitments, and we shall consider the efforts of our allies, in determining our response.[32]

As we have already noted,[33] the reorganization of the National Security Council Staff by the Johnson administration had seen the dissolution of the Special Group (C.I.) set up by President Kennedy to oversee and energize the multiagency counterinsurgency effort. It had been replaced by a series of interdepartmental committees organized on a geographical basis, each one chaired by an assistant secretary of state. This structure ultimately disappointed its designer, General Maxwell Taylor, who had intended it as a means of concentrating effort and attention on the problems of Communist insurgency.[34] The result, he admitted, had been the opposite, not, one suspects, because of inherent defects, but because of the waning interest at the highest levels of the government after the departure from the scene of such true believers as

John F. and Robert F. Kennedy. This trend was somewhat abetted, however, by the diffuseness of the new multicommittee structure.

In a desultory fashion an effort was made to bring up to date the policy document that governed U.S. activities formerly called counterinsurgency and now known as the Foreign Internal Defense Program. A formal paper was srawn up, processed through all the agencies, approved by the NSC, and allowed to remain unimplemented.[35] It would appear that there was a reluctance at the higher levels of the system either to apply the global policies which remained formal commitments or to admit that they no longer carried the weight they once did. The rather indifferent and *pro forma* attitude of the policy levels is well illustrated by the language of the summation of counterinsurgency policy in the Nixon state paper cited above. The formula invokes the preemption of "wars of national liberation" through "economic development and social reform" and control "with police, paramilitary and military action by the threatened government." This approach was merely an iteration of conventional wisdom which ignored much of the hard-won experience of the preceding ten years, particularly the failure to establish any link between economic development and change in popular attitudes in favor of the government. It completely overlooks the political essence of the problem and once again implies that we are merely dealing with a technical and administrative matter rather than one that goes to the heart of the way power is distributed in the threatened country.

A final illustration of the eclipse of counterinsurgency as a foreign policy concern—without any public revision of the formal commitment—is an episode in which the author was personally involved. In May 1972, Henry Kissinger, then assistant to the president for national security affairs, signed an NSC Study Memorandum directing an interagency study of the insurgency situation in Thailand to include an array of U.S. government options for presidential decision. A study group was organized (the author was a member), traveled to Thailand, and began drafting its paper. By December 1972 a draft was circulating among the agencies concerned, but it did not complete the round of approvals. It simply disappeared into the bureaucratic maze and never emerged. For reasons still not clear, Dr. Kissinger lost interest and allowed it to expire for lack of high-level support. That experience convinced the author that no systematic program approach in this field could succeed without very high-level backing against the indifference of the bureaucracy to the subject as well as the resentment generated by the effort of the NSC staff to take the initiative in foreign policy formulation. Perhaps Dr. Kissinger concluded that any effort by him to bulldoze through the obstructions would probably not produce a worthwhile paper, or would take too much time and effort better spent on other matters, or, even if a workable policy emerged, it would be implemented half-heartedly—or perhaps his reasons partook of all three arguments. Not to be ignored is the possibility that concern over domestic political reaction was also involved, or even the impact on the new policy of rapprochement with China. At any rate, this abortive effort is the last initiative known to the author to generate new policy in the field of counterinsurgency. It represents the unmarked grave of a policy born amid much fanfare and high expectations twelve years earlier and now gone the way of "manifest destiny" and Theodore Roosevelt's Monroe Doctrine "corollary" and other forgotten policy urgencies in a changing world.

COULD COUNTERINSURGENCY BE REVIVED?

Behind the executive branch's retreat from counterinsurgency was the public identification of that policy with the involvement of the U.S. in the countries of former French Indochina and particularly Vietnam, an involvement which had generated such a powerful revulsion that any policy associated with it automatically shared the negative recoil. There were, however, less emotional reasons underlying the unavowed abandonment of the policy. Major changes had occurred in the world in the 1960s and in American perceptions of that world, changes which undermined most of the analysis by which the advocates had convinced two presidents of the seriousness of the threat and a third that enough of a residue remained to justify continued, if reduced, concern. No doubt the most momentous of these changes was the surfacing of the Sino-Soviet schism and the subsequent fragmentation of the international Communist movement. From a state in which the world was divided into two hostile camps and a third that strove to avoid commitment to either, one of the two major groupings, the Communist, split several ways and became polycentric. The hostility between the various centers made it appear certain that they could not combine their policies and resources against the United States and its allies, even though their verbiage continued to identify "imperialism" as a common enemy. Before this development, the power balance appeared to depend upon containing the threat of monolithic Communism and preventing it from spreading further. After the schism it no longer seemed momentous whether a given distant and obscure country became Communist unless some strategic or major economic factor also was apparent. The perception of the so-called domino theory—the belief that Communist victory in one country automatically placed its neighbors in immediate jeopardy—as an exaggerated extrapolation from questionable premises also played a part in allaying concern.

Sober second thought in the late sixties had also undermined the beliefs that the Communist world was unrelentingly expansive, that Maoist people's war was the preferred instrument of the Communists for the further expansion of their movement in the nuclear age which had rendered all-out war inconceivable, and finally that the less-developed world would be the scene of the critical struggle between Communist and non-Communist forces in which the side that mastered the secrets of people's war would win. Regarding Communist expansionism, the removal from the world scene of Khrushchev, together with his threatening bombast, made it easier to perceive and reflect on the fact that the Soviets were cautious rather than otherwise in taking risks for the sake of expansion, that they would become involved in extending their sway only if they could do so in a fashion so indirect that no provocation to justify war would be apparent. Nor were they at all wedded to people's war as a universal route to power. On the contrary, as we noted in the first chapter of this work, the Russians had never accepted the claims that Mao made for his formula for taking power in the less-developed world. Indeed, even China itself abandoned its immoderate pretensions to having devised an infallible method which all true Communists were obliged to put into prompt practice. Lin Piao, its great advocate, was disgraced and dead, and China had swung around almost 180 degrees in its approach to the United States. While guerrilla warfare and terrorism continued to be prominent features of the troubled world scene, more often than not they had become the instruments of extremist fanatics not only not under Communist discipline but looked upon by orthodox parties as both misguided and dangerous. Moreover, such failures of people's war as those of Castro in Latin America and the long-drawn-out but hardly significant efforts in Burma and Thailand, suggested that where the threat existed its success was far from guaranteed even without U.S. intervention, as was the case, for example, in Burma. A great deal depended on circumstances and on the capabilities of the two sides involved in the struggle. It began to be clear that the Communist movement, despite its sophisticated training and indoctrination methods and its tested organizational principles, performed unevenly throughout the world, and that in some countries its local representatives were downright incompetent.

Of these changes by far the most important was the split between the two major Communist countries. When the U.S. moved to take advantage of the schism by establishing contact with China and committing itself to "normalizing" relations, the fears of Chinese expansionism that had been a major justification for the Vietnam intervention were seen by all to have been more than somewhat exaggerated. As far as concerns his public commitment to the waging of unrelenting people's war until the West was surrounded and brought down, Mao Tse-tung himself, rather than the United States, was seen to have been the paper tiger.

Thus, in the mid-1970s, very little if anything remained of the analytical structure which constituted the justification for the gravity with which, in the 1960s, the United States had viewed the threat of people's war and the urgency with which it sought to counter it. Rarely has there been so complete a reversal of strategic views and assumptions by a great power within so short a span of time. Many serious observers and analysts now look upon the brief preoccupation with counterinsurgency as an aberration stemming from cold-war fixations combined with the Kennedy style of policy development, a style emphasizing enthusiasm and faddishness at the expense of sober reflection.

Although perhaps containing some truth insofar as applies to the headlong attack and the breathless pursuit of the goal by hastily concocted techniques, the view nevertheless is an exaggeration based on the clarity of hindsight. In the early sixties the threat of a monolithic and expansionist Communism was not so easily dismissed. The expansionist thrust of Khrushchev's rhetoric, his pressure on Berlin, and his later effort to implant ballistic missiles in Cuba could not be waved aside. His verbal commitment to "wars of national liberation" was easily misread as a new global initiative in view of events in Vietnam, Laos, and Cuba—not to mention earlier Communist victories in China and Yugoslavia and the rash of insurgencies that had swept through Asia in Stalin's last years. In all these countries, attempts had been made—some successful, some still under way, and a few thwarted—to bring Communist parties to power by effective exploitation of the techniques of guerrilla warfare combined with skilled political organization and terrorism, all dominated by a shrewdly calculated political strategy. New episodes continued to manifest themselves throughout the 1960s, and even today we see the Soviets in particular providing encouragement and support to outbreaks of a similar type in Angola, Namibia, Mozambique, and Rhodesia, although actual Soviet control does not exist. It may have been largely coincidental that the combination of events on the eve and immediately following Kennedy's inauguration loomed so threateningly. No doubt the threat was partly in the eye of the beholder, the president, whose life had been lived in a time when World War II and its lessons were assumed to apply to all messianic totalitarians. Nevertheless, it cannot be dismissed as a mere figment in a later decade made wiser by further experience.

Although such movements, for the reasons just noted, no longer appear to pose a serious threat to the United States and its interests, there is no guarantee that this will always be so. The world continues to change, and the prominent and seemingly permanent features dominating one epoch can and do suddenly disappear, leaving a completely altered landscape. It is fruitless to speculate what such changes might be, but even in today's world, a Communist-sponsored and effective guerrilla insurgency, encouraged by the Russians in, for example, Panama or

Mexico, could quickly reawaken U.S. concern. That being the case, it is not difficult to conceive of major changes in the world scene—a rapprochement between China and Russia leading to a close alliance between those two powers is one far-from-impossible development—under which a guerrilla insurgency even farther from our borders would have the effect of once again posing an apparent threat to vital interests.

In other words, it is imaginable, although far from likely in the near term, that some future White House may become interested in scrutinizing the counterinsurgency experience which we have been at some pains to recount and analyze in these pages, for lessons on both the pitfalls and the positive courses of action suggested by the successes and failures of the period. For several reasons it is much to be hoped that such does not turn out to be the case, and most especially for the reason that the lessons of our experience are clearly negative. Effective counterinsurgency, avoiding the brutalities of unadorned suppression, and seeking to deal with the genuine issues in a sophisticated manner which does no damage to our moral and democratic principles, is a complex and difficult maneuver for which the United States has shown no talent. Nevertheless, the world being the unpredictable place that it is, let us review the terrain we have traversed to identify the lessons that seem common to most of the involvements discussed.

COPING WITH THE MILITARY AND THE BUREAUCRACY

To begin at home, involvement in counterinsurgency in any depth immediately confronts us with very difficult obstacles internal to our government and growing out of the nature of permanent bureaucracies. It cuts across the norms and hierarchies of the concerned agencies in several ways. First, it forces them to do things which are only indirectly related to their basic missions. Second, if organized in a properly integrated fashion it short-circuits normal command channels in favor of a new, temporary command structure that grievously flouts institutional loyalties and prerogatives. Unless dealt with early and firmly, these difficulties will quickly result in an apparatus that is merely going through certain motions without a considered strategy or appropriate priorities or operations effectively coordinated in the field. The foreign aid apparatus will focus on development for its own sake, placing emphasis on the transfer of things and of skills rather than on changing popular attitudes, for this latter is a goal which is extremely difficult to get hold of and to measure. The military will inevitably attempt to build the host government's armed forces in its own image, to shape a conventional army able quickly to concentrate its forces and spew forth heavy fire upon the terrain regardless of what is there. These agencies, together with the

CIA and USIA, will be content to coordinate their operations at a regular committee meeting by a process of negotiation which leaves the internal and routine processes of their organizations undisturbed.

A central control point at a high level empowered to force new concepts through the system and monitor compliance is essential—even more so after the experiences of the counterinsurgency era than in 1962 when the Kennedy Administration innovated with the Special Group (C.I.). For the experience and lessons of the subsequent decade will largely be lost if no central authority exists to exhume them, reexamine them for lessons, and apply the lessons where appropriate. Not only is institutional memory in our government of two-year or four-year stints in office extremely weak, but each agency will have its parochial view of the past as well as the present. Each will also have its own doctrine so designed as to disturb the institution the least. A common doctrine must be developed and enforced or the effort will be neutralized. Awareness of these problems must exist at the highest levels, that of the president himself, and he must be willing to take the heat that will result from imposing the necessary changes. If he shrinks from the political costs then he should not launch the effort at all, for he is courting failure, which will produce higher political costs in the long run.

APPLYING THE LESSONS TO THE MILITARY

The decision-makers' knottiest problem in the hypothetical situation we are discussing will be fitting the military into a revised organizational and doctrinal approach. At this writing, the U.S. military, in particular the army, has not acknowledged any degree of error in Vietnam or anywhere else and has dismantled the centers and training programs that might keep alive in some corners of the system a commitment to the notion that counterinsurgency calls for some modification the prevailing wisdom of "find 'em, fix 'em, and fight 'em," or "git thar fustest with the mostest."

Indeed, the way through this thicket is not easy to see. The military notoriously offer great resistance to change, especially if imposed from the outside. Moreover, as discussed in Chapter III, counterinsurgency war poses a conundrum for the higher commands with no solution that readily satisfies conflicting urgencies. The "solution" adopted in the 1960s was simply to deny the problem, to insist that standard military doctrines could readily be adapted to counterinsurgency warfare with only minor changes. Three and a half million tons of bombs dropped in South Vietnam alone were a monument to the belief voiced, for example, by General Wheeler when he was chairman of the Joint Chiefs, that "the essence of the problem is military."[36] Clearly, the solution chosen was no solution at all, and the problem will confront any future leadership attempting to avoid the mistakes of the past.

How can the U.S. Army best accommodate a mission which runs athwart its permanent and essential commitment to conventional war fought at the highest feasible technological level, and calls for it to strip down to a primitive and basic mode of combat, relying on small units, light weapons, and precise, measured fire? The matter is even further complicated over the uncertainty about whether any given situation will yield to a combination of material assistance and advice and training or whether it will escalate in seriousness until it becomes necessary once more—and in spite of repeated commitment to the contrary—to contemplate direct intervention with American forces.

Taking the second question first, it is impossible to be absolutely certain ahead of time that changed circumstances will not eventually force the U.S. to think again about the "unthinkable" alternative of deploying combat forces. Clearly, however, it is decidedly preferable for the United States to abstain from direct intervention if it is possible to do so without suffering a major setback. The best, if far from perfect, resolution of these conflicting requirements is to focus in the first instance upon developing suitable training and advisory capability, while at the same time perfecting a doctrine and a suitable plan for implementation in the event that intervention becomes inevitable. Both the advisory and training program and the plans for intervention must be consistent with each other and share a common doctrine and approach.

As for the nature of the approach, there is no single best solution. The principal alternatives all have drawbacks. One can create specialized units specifically pointed at this kind of warfare, a solution disfavored by the military hierarchy but one which was pressed upon it by President Kennedy. Such a solution tends to restrict the requisite skills and techniques to the specialized units which in the Kennedy years were the Special Forces. If such forces were given the full responsibility for dealing with U.S. commitments in counterinsurgency situations the approach might indeed meet the requirement. The record, however, shows a great unwillingness by the military hierarchy to permit the Special Forces a free hand in advising friendly governments on counterinsurgency. Its role has been limited to training and advising a counterpart organization, or simply to training any units that are assigned to receive such training. The broader task of helping an ally to develop a suitable armed forces structure pursuing a suitable strategy and encouraging systematic use of tactics appropriate to counterinsurgency operations has been preempted by the regular military. They, regrettably, conceive of the task as that of creating a mirror-image armed force functioning to the extent possible as the U.S. functioned in Vietnam.

Other alternatives have been discussed but never tried. Thus, it is imaginable but unlikely that the United States Army could fight or advise its clients to fight as the British fought in Malaya—breaking divisions up into smaller units, eschewing almost all artillery and combat air support, and totally merging the military side of the effort into a combined police and civilian organizational structure under civilian control. This alternative, which in theory is the one best fitted to the task, would involve the president in attempting to force down reluctant throats a drastic alteration in the military's procedures, their concept of their mission, and their traditional doctrine. The reaction of the officer corps to such an effort is suggested by the explosive comment of one general on the problem of adapting U.S. military operations to the task in Vietnam. "I'll be damned," he said, "if I permit the United States Army, its institutions, its doctrine, and its traditions, to be destroyed just to win this lousy war."[37]

Even if cooperation from the military institution were forthcoming, the policy would call for preparing the army, or parts of it, to fight at least two different kinds of war, which is obviously an extremely difficult if not an impossible burden. The mind shrinks from the complexities and the inevitable confusion and error that would result.

Another alternative would be to assign counterinsurgency functions neither to the army as a whole nor to any part of it but to another service entirely, which, in effect, means to the marines. Being a smaller force with a limited mission in contrast to the army's global security responsibility, the marines actually seem best suited to a limited and specialized task such as counterinsurgency. In their favor is their demonstrated flexibility, as shown in Vietnam, and their history of involvement in "nation building" in the Caribbean and Central America. The solution would face some practical difficulties but is one that, we could hope, would be seriously studied should the government again be faced with the necessity of assisting a foreign government to deal with Communist rural insurgency.

Who to Help

The American side of the coin thus still presents many dilemmas and difficulties, all of which would tend to reinforce our initial hope that the necessity to deal with them never does come up again. If we turn now to some of the lessons that should be absorbed and applied in approaching the foreign government and people to be helped, the situation is no better. Moreover, generalizations are far more uncertin because no two foreign countries will present identical sets of problems, and what may quickly prevail in one country may equally quickly fail in another.

No lesson is easier to state and harder to apply than that a decision to become involved once again in a counterinsurgency situation should be preceded by intense and prayerful study. Moreover, such a study should be in the form of an honest appraisal of whether or not U.S. assistance, knowing what we should have learned of its limitations in affecting the internal political arrangements of any foreign land, can truthfully be expected to perform what will be demanded of it if the intervention is to be successful. Merely suggesting such an approach immediately brings to the mind's eye the pitfalls it will be forced to confront. Call it "the arrogance of power" or the unwillingness to accept limitations in America's ability to deal with the backward and small and weak "as a great power should," it is simply impolitic to tell a president or a secretary of state of the "most powerful country in the world" that all our skill and wealth and know-how are to no avail, that country X is beyond saving because its own leadership is not up to the task, and no foreign government can substitute its own will for that of the native leadership. Nevertheless, unless the decision-makers are willing to ask such questions and probe beyond the easy responses to come to grips with the core problem, then we again invite failure.

Let us pursue the question further by asking what were the particular problems of Vietnam (as distinguished from the internal U.S. governmental problems just discussed) that made a mockery of our vast power, advanced technology, and willingness to spend resources lavishly. Some of them are obvious and are generally accepted. One is the advanced stage of the insurgency at the time we intervened militarily, with the South Vietnamese on the verge of defeat and the Lao Dong organization fully developed, experienced, and skillfully led, and operating from a firm base in North Vietnam. Another was the issue of nationalist feeling which, by the massiveness of our presence, as well as by our lack of familiarity with the people and the culture, we managed to exacerbate and reinforce so tragically. But by far the most critical problem, and one we never mastered, was the failure of the government we were bolstering and guiding at such great cost to rise to the opportunity, take hold, and move ahead with the task in vigorous and capable fashion. From beginning to end it remained unable to confront its problems effectively and to elicit an acceptable performance from its services, and was therefore hesitant, dependent on the U.S., and afraid, despite its great superiority in weaponry and the availability of massive technical and economic aid, to contemplate going it alone. Its services—military and civilian—were eaten out with corruption, favoritism, and petty politics. Its leadership also led in those categories, but not in the qualities necessary to grasp the opportunities offered and move forward confidently.

Why was this the case? Many reasons have been adduced—cultural or historical or keyed to the personalities involved. No doubt they all played some role. Without delving any more deeply into causes, however, we would point to the underlying political structure of the government and its paralyzing effect with regard to the compelling need for self-reform of its services and their relationship with the public.

The word reform is often employed by the school which sees successful revolution as preventable only by "social reform" or "thoroughgoing reform" or some such formula. We have something more specific in mind. The problem stems from the precariousness of the regime's political base and the devices it employs to maintain itself in power. Three of the six governments in the case histories presented earlier were military dictatorships, and the fourth—the Philippines—was a corrupt civilian regime ruling, behind a constitutional facade, by means of graft and cronyism. The Diem regime had similar structural weaknesses. The problem arises when a regime relies for its continued survival upon powerful subordinates whose support has to be purchased and who have to be carefully balanced in order to prevent combinations that might be tempted to reach for power themselves. The phenomenon is clearly a feature of political underdevelopment where sources of legitimacy via traditional means or constitutional processes are not available. Military dictatorships which have come to power by *coup d'état* are particularly prone to this defect, for they have little moral claim to power and must devise a system to minimize the threat that others will attempt to duplicate their feat in seizing control by force and guile.

The effect upon the government's services of the system of purchased support is highly destructive of performance standards and of the relationship with the public, particularly in the armed forces and police, the two services which are closest to the leadership of a military regime and whose support is essential to any regime. At the top of any given service and filling the key posts are men who know that they enjoy their positions as a result of political loyalty and have been given within broad limits a free hand to make of it what they will. The quality of their performance has little to do with their continuance in office, and exploitation of their position for financial gain, if appearances are preserved, is expected rather than otherwise.

Once the top leadership of a service is of this character, it follows necessarily that the entire service will be permeated with the same attitudes. Subordinates down to the lower ranks are chosen to build a structure which will serve the private needs of their superiors. Their loyalties are purchased, too, thus permitting them to extract the most out of the bargain within the limits generally understood but never spelled out.

Even worse than corruption in its impact on the public is the effect of the system on performance. Part of the political bargain between superior and subordinate is the promise of prestige and ease of life, which reverses the normal order of the military in which the prestige is supposed to reward such qualities as courage, leadership, and competence in an arduous profession. When personal loyalty is offered in exchange for office, the martial qualities are the first to suffer. It is no part of the political bargain by which an officer obtains and keeps his job that he should take risks with his life, that he should work long and late, that he should put the comfort of his troops before his own, that the demands of duty, in other words, shall have first call on his time and energies. As a result, a political army—an army whose leaders play a critical role in keeping an existing regime afloat—is often a very poor army indeed. The low quality of its standards also impacts heavily upon the population it is supposed to be defending. Troops with poor leadership will normally not behave well in their contacts with the public, for their leaders are unconcerned and often take such poor care of the soldiers under them that the latter must steal in order to eat.

There are, of course, exceptions to this rule, most of which are found in countries with a proud military history and strong preexisting martial traditions. Pakistan is one such example, among several one could cite. Another exceptional case is Korea, whose present-day army is officered by men who survived and advanced during the testing time of the Korean War. Such countries as Laos, Thailand, and Vietnam, however, have no such proud past. Their armies had no traditions of valor and skill against which officers were judged and which they had to meet in order to be accepted into the charmed circle. Acceptability was determined by such criteria as class, family, relationships formed in military school, and the like.

In the case of Vietnam, these qualities persisted in the army and police throughout the long American involvement and proved impervious to the extraordinary efforts that were made to correct them. The ARVN combat patrols that were carefully signaled in advance to the enemy, the battalion and divisional commanders who were notorious incompetents but could not be removed, the frequent refusal to close with a trapped enemy, the great reluctance to risk casualties, and the apparent inability to raise the low standards of troop behavior toward the population, all were a result of the inherent flaws of a politicized army. They could not be eradicated unless and until the army had been removed from politics and entirely reformed by a firm leadership in the style of Magsaysay. When the ARVN fought well—and it sometimes did—it was usually because it had no alternative, as at Tet or during the Easter offensive of 1972, when it had to fight to survive. There were also exceptions which resulted from intense American pressure favoring particular officers who performed above normal ARVN standards. But when the American soldiers were gone and the Congress sharply reduced its logistic support, panic quickly set in—panic caused, one can only surmise, by the realization of the Vietnamese officer corps that it was really not up to its job. In the final analysis, those who had played out the charade had never been fooled by it. Only the foreigners had been deceived, and deceived largely as a result of their own blindness to the political realities of a land where they had lived and worked for so many years without learning the most elementary truths of the scene about them.

Very similar problems—although for obvious reasons on a lesser scale—also characterized the military and the police in Thailand. The Royal Thai Army was notoriously a garrison army and was not really intended by its superiors to fight in serious combat. The volunteer units sent to Vietnam, for instance, were quite inferior fighting forces. On the other hand, the volunteer units sent secretly to Laos were supposed to have given a good account of themselves. But these latter were not regular Thai units; the officers were RTA regulars assigned to the duty, while the men were volunteers. The accidental effect of this makeup was to produce a better-motivated and better-led force than the normal RTA regular battalions. The reason seems to have been that the officers were those with the least political influence in their original units. They could only hope that professional competence and a good combat record would help their careers in lieu of the political standing which they did not command.

Despite an enlightened doctrine relating to the role of the military in counterinsurgency, the Thai army has lapsed into firing into unarmed villages, and also into employing unobserved artillery fire and aerial bombardment against such targets. Such episodes violate Thai doctrine, but they nevertheless still happen on occasion. Notoriously, the RTA is reluctant to risk casualties. In one famous foray in 1971, the entire elite First Division sallied forth from its barracks outside Bangkok to eliminate an insurgent force in the northwest and returned months later without having accomplished its objective or having suffered a single casualty in direct combat; although losses were considerable, they all resulted from enemy booby traps and the like. Casualties, particularly among the officer corps, cannot be distributed in accordance with political influence, and so are to be avoided even at the cost of failure of the mission.

Examples could be multiplied, but the point is clear enough. When the services of a regime have been politicized, a strong risk exists that they will be inadequate to the demands of dealing with a Communist insurgency—or any other serious military challenge. They must be reformed if the regime is to succeed against a well-established and well-led Communist insurgent movement. Such reforms are easy to prescribe but difficult to carry out. In effect, they require that the regime change the base of its power, a most problematical course to follow, especially at a time of internal crisis. This is the problem of "self-reform in crisis," to which we have frequently referred in the course of this history.

Reverting again to the example of Vietnam, it is well established that more than once between 1969 and 1975 General Nguyen Van Thieu launched apparently serious efforts to build a popular political base as an alternative to relying on the purchased loyalty of the armed forces. (See the preceding chapter.) Each time, however, he quailed before the risks and abandoned the effort. No doubt he saw that his chances for success were quite small, while the risks of provoking another military coup were very real. Thieu has more excuse for his failure than has the United States for its persistence in the hope that lavish weaponry and supply and massive training and retraining programs would transform the Vietnamese armed forces into a tough, well-led, competent fighting machine and the police into an efficient, honest, and respected public service. Adding to the bitterness of the lesson is the fact that it is not understood or incorporated in any of the analyses of the Vietnam experience that have general acceptance.

The implications of this insight for any future involvement are not necessarily the imposition of a stark choice between intervention and abstention based on the political character of the armed forces of the threatened country. The matter is not that simple. What our findings mean is that an important additional consideration must be added to the preintervention analysis over and above such obvious considerations as the strength and quality of the Communist movement, the state of the threatened society, its cohesiveness, and its social and economic—as well as political—structure and state of health. For example, although it is quite clear that Thailand will never defeat its twelve-year-old insurgency unless it depoliticizes its armed forces and police, it is also clear that the insurgency is not quickly solving its problems and is making slow headway in a Thai society that retains its basic cohesiveness. Given the relatively weak condition of the insurgency, there may very well be a solution to the Thai problem which would quickly reduce the threat without the trauma involved in another major political upheaval—even in the unlikely event that the U.S. were able to induce the Thai leadership (since late 1976 once again a straight military dictatorship) to depoliticize the army. This would be to recruit a special paramilitary force under army sponsorship but—in the pattern of the units recruited especially for service in Laos—separate and apart from the internal political system of the armed forces.

This depoliticizing effect was accomplished inadvertently in the Laos intervention by *assigning* officers to what was understood to be a thoroughly dangerous and unpleasant duty rather than asking for *volunteers* as was done in forming the divisions sent to fight beside the U.S. Army in Vietnam. The Vietnam duty was not expected to be a particularly dangerous or arduous assignment, and there were known to be opportunities for profit from the easy access to PX goods. The complements were easily filled, and officers were accepted on the basis of political influence, which accounts for the inferior fighting quality of these units as compared with those formed for duty in Laos.

A unit recruited to fight against the insurgents inside Thailand on a basis similar to those sent earlier to Laos and totaling no more than a half dozen battalions would quickly reverse the slow growth of the insurgency and eventually reduce it to a hard-core remnant. Such a solution was opposed by the U.S. JUSMAAG in 1972[38] and probably would be opposed by the U.S. military today as being an unnecessary diversion from the priority task of building the Royal Thai Army into a proud and competent fighting force, at which point the insurgency would easily be mopped up. This view persisted despite the fact that some fifteen years of military aid had not had the desired effect.

The lesson suggested by these examples is the obvious one that the political structure of the country to be aided is of first importance in determining whether it can be successfully aided, and that the political role of the armed forces must be fully understood and taken into account in any aid decision. This view does not go so far as to insist that impeccable democratic credentials are essential for success in dealing with a people's war or that any degree of corruption will undermine the effort. If no political base exists other than the military, however, very grave questions are raised about the possibility of intervening successfully. At a minimum, the problem must be taken into account in reaching a decision and designing a program. A plausible solution must be proposed which goes to the central point and does not merely wish it aside by reference to training and advice to bring about better performance. Most discussions of counterinsurgency focus upon the programmatic details, and such matters do, indeed, have importance—the same importance that good tactics have in military conflict. But good tactics cannot prevail when embedded in bad strategy. The strategic factors in counterinsurgency relate to politics and not to military concerns. In most cases it will be found that the basis of a successful strategy is the development of a political base that willingly supports the regime against its Communist enemies and that extends beyond the purchased loyalty of the senior military and police officers.

Nor is it satisfactory to decide to intervene hastily in order to rescue a seriously threatened regime in the expectation that the political problems can be straightened out later. Once assumed, the commitment, as we know, is not easily abandoned. American lives may be involved, not to mention pride and political stakes at home. We risk very quickly becoming the reluctant prisoners of an unsavory and incompetent regime which we continue to aid despite its obvious failures because it is too difficult to back out. At that point our ability to argue and persuade the regime into reforming itself and its military services becomes virtually nil. The client sees our advice as forcing him to face unacceptable risks of instability and loss of power, and so he evades and maneuvers to avoid our pressures, satisfying our demands with token adjustments which leave essentials unchanged.

Once these strategic political considerations have been dealt with in a fashion consistent with the lessons of our experience, the tactical matters can be addressed. We have seen that competent, professional police and military services are essential, and that they must proceed in accordance with the principle of "making the people the target." Conventional military operations are unsuited to this goal. Heavy weapons, tanks, artillery, and jet aircraft are worse than useless in most cases, for they impact at great cost upon the population while the enemy can usually evade their power. Small, lightly armed units, pinpointed operations assisted by "hunter-killer" squads, imaginative psychological warfare operations—and all of this based upon coordinated collection and exploitation of intelligence—should be the main reliance of the military side of the effort. The police, if they have or can be brought to develop the capability, should play a major role in the intelligence effort and in other programs requiring frequent contact with the public. Both soldiers and police must be brought to recognize the overriding importance of good relations with the population and make consistent programmatic efforts in pursuit of that goal, which will probably include small-scale civic action. Part-time popular militia to maintain security in areas where the military have already done their job will also be essential. It is the best means of preventing the regular forces from being scattered about in static guard duties and it also serves to cement the population to the government's cause.

All of this still is not to suggest that counterinsurgency is, after all, essentially a military problem. As we have been at some pains to point out, competent and effective military operations are a product of a healthy political structure in which the army and police avoid behaving like an army of occupation and, instead, place themselves at the side of the people against a common enemy. Mere training and exhortation will not accomplish such a posture. It is a structural effect reflecting the fact that the power base of the regime is linked in some fashion to popular needs. Many brilliant students of counterinsurgency have somehow or other completely missed this point in their earnest and detailed advice to the U.S. and its clients on how to cope with insurgency. The last such effort was called *Rebellion and Authority: An Analytic Essay on Insurgent Conflicts* by Nathan Leites and Charles Wolf, Jr., of the Rand Corporation.[39] This erudite work dismisses the effort to gain public support for the purposes of defeating an insurgency—the so-called hearts and minds approach—as beside the point. It aruges that stimulating certain kinds of popular behavior is the objective of the program and that such behavior can be brought about by various means, most effectively by making contrary behavior unprofitable to the individual. It argues for approaching the insurgency analytically as a system and focusing on four types of action to damage and bring it down without wasting effort and concern for whether or not the population supports the government's cause as a cause. The four actions are: reducing the supply of insurgent inputs, interfering with the conversion process whereby these inputs are turned into outputs, destroying the actual outputs (troops, but more importantly, leadership), and reducing the effectiveness of the insurgency's actions. The reader will see from this that the level of abstraction of the Leites and Wolf study is impressive. What they do not explain, however, is how all of these complex tasks can be accomplished by a regime with a level of competence that is extremely low and which is kept that way by the system's political dependence upon the purchased loyalty of military and police officers whose first priority is their private well-being. That, of course, was the essence of the problem in Vietnam—a political problem from beginning to end which was never solved or even, in many cases, grasped by the most impressive official or academic minds.

This somewhat prolonged discussion of military aspects may give the impression that we see them as the major factor. In fact, they should be fully complemented by a program confronting the economic, social, and political problems of the affected regions, which, in the long run, is of equal importance. Military aspects have a priority in time, since other factors cannot progress far unless some measure of security exists. In the longer run, however, military and police operations, while they can greatly reduce and limit the insurgent movement, cannot be relied upon to eliminate it permanently. To do this, the regime must be shown to be deeply concerned about major popular needs and aspirations and also as able to do something effective to begin to meet them. Only in this way will the thrust of the Communist appeal be durably blunted and turned. For that reason, a successful counterinsurgency effort must combine the military and police actions already described with programs to tackle some of the serious problems pressing upon the rural population. In our opinion, major economic development programs are neither necessary nor, if they initially tend to disrupt the traditional patterns of rural life, desirable. The scale of rural assistance programs can be small if basic grievances are dealt with and if, in particular, the peasantry acquires, by means of the government's program, a role in determining its fate and its terms of living. How this is accomplished depends, of course, on the circumstances of particular cases. As we have already noted several times, land reform can be an important element, along with such reforms as rural self-government relating to local matters and an assured means of interaction between the local level and the higher levels of power and decision. Grievance procedures are also important, more so than the more common emphases on education, health services, roads, and the like, although these latter should not be ignored. In all these matters the process, to repeat what we have earlier stated more than once, is more important than the material details. It must be a process in which the beneficiaries are confirmed in their essential goal of achieving greater control over what is done for them and to them by the power structure.

Finally, all of this combined military, police, and civil effort must be managed and coordinated by a single civilian authority which has as its sole responsibility the task of assuring that the many parts of the complex effort mesh with each other, that a comprehensive plan is developed and faithfully followed. Simple efficiency requires such a management structure, but here, too, political obstacles exist. The authority which achieves control over such a major aspect of governmental activity automatically achieves great power within the system. Nevertheless, the highest levels of the threatened government must take the risk for the sake of an effective program which, after all, also has the objective of assuring its survival. Not to be overlooked is the fact that effectiveness also has political effect. A critical ingredient in gaining popular support—if you will, in winning hearts and minds—is competence on the part of the government and its services. The respect that is earned by a government which does the right amount of the right thing at the right time and place is more important to its cause than a vague liking or affection. Coercive measures such as forced population movements may also be necessary on occasion, and these need not harm the government's cause if they are seen to be controlled, fair and appropriate to the purposes sought. All of these factors go to underline the significance of a unified, well-managed effort, responsible to a single authority.

It should be starkly clear by now that counterinsurgency places unique demands upon a threatened regime, and that the governments which have most need of the courage, understanding, and cohesion required are the least likely to be able to muster these essential qualities. That, more likely than not, is why they have become targets of insurgency and why their defensive efforts will fail to the point where they require outside help. All the more reason why the United States, if it ever again sees its own vital interests intimately involved with the success of such a contest against a Communist people's war, should scrutinize the terrain with care, with an eye to the underlying fundamentals, and with a disabused realism in regard to its own abilities to provide suitable assistance.

THE AMBIGUOUS HERITAGE

The fundamental lesson to draw from our misadventures of the counterinsurgency era is the one already emphasized by many—the lesson of the limits of American power. It is also of importance that we should understand in what way our power, great as it is, can be challenged by a few thousand ragged jungle fighters armed with a dedicated leadership, a tested theory, and great patience. Too many have fallen back on the easy excuse that we failed in Indochina because our power was constrained and leashed, that more bombs, more destruction, more firepower was the answer. At the end of this account of what we tried to do, and how and why it fell short, it is to be hoped that some will be convinced that the failure was one of understanding: an inability to perceive the underlying realities of both our own system and that of the countries into which we thrust our raw strength. The scars of these failures will be a long time healing, but possibly, in time, understanding will take the place of revulsion in our thinking about the meaning of our unhappy experience. If, in addition, some turn of the wheel should once again bring us to the brink of such an involvement, the lessons which are our only return for all the blood and fortune that was spent will stand us in good stead, provided only that we finally have understood and digested them.

Notes

★ ★ ★

Chapter 1

1. Mao Tse-tung, *Basic Tactics* (Stuart R. Schram, ed.), Praeger, New York, 1966, pp. 21–22.

2. Mao Tse-tung, *Selected Works of Mao Tse-tung,* vol. 2, Foreign Languages Press, Peking, 1965, pp. 113–194.

3. Vo Nguyen Giap, *The Banner of People's War: The Party's Military Line,* Praeger, New York, 1970, pp. 82–84.

4. Mao Tse-Tung, *Selected Works,* op. cit., vol. 2, p. 224.

5. Chalmers Johnson, *Peasant Nationalism and Communist Power,* Stanford University Press, Stanford, California, 1962, especially Chapter I.

6. Ibid., p. 5.

7. Edward Rice, *Mao's Way,* University of California Press, Berkeley, 1972, p. 114.

8. Anne Fremantle (ed.), *Mao Tse-tung, An Anthology of His Writings,* New American Library, New York, 1971, p. xxxiii.

9. Ibid.

10. Cf., for example, Lucian Pye, *Guerilla Communism in Malaya,* Praeger, 1956, esp. Chapter 9.

11. Truong Chinh, "The Resistance Will Win," in *Primer for Revolt,* Praeger, New York, 1963, p. 116.

12. Chalmers Johnson, *Autopsy on People's War,* University of California Press, Berkeley, 1973, pp. 49–50.

13. Regis Debray, *The Revolution Within the Revolution,* Monthly Review Press, New York, 1967, p. 20.

14. Jay Mallin (ed.), *"Che" Guevara on Revolution,* University of Miami Press, Coral Gables, Fla., 1969, p. 98.

15. Ibid., p. 65.

16. Ibid., p. 62.

17. Chalmers Johnson, *Autopsy on People's War,* pp. 56–57.

18. J. H. Brimmell, *Communism in Southeast Asia,* Oxford University Press, New York, 1959, pp. 252–263.

19. The Philippines, where fighting was already going on, was an exception due to internal Communist dissension. Cf. Jay Taylor, *China and Southeast Asia,* Praeger, New York, 1974, p. 258.

20. Ibid., p. 193.

21. Rice, op. cit., p. 238.

22. Arthur M. Schlesinger, Jr., *A Thousand Days,* Andre Deutsch, London, 1965, p. 282.

23. Ibid., p. 274.

24. Chalmers Johnson, *Autopsy on People's War,* p. 21.

25. Lin Piao, "Long Live the Victory of People's War," *Peking Review,* September 3, 1965, p. 27.

26. Ibid., pp. 38–45.

Chapter 2

1. Lt. Col. Edward R. Wainhouse, "Guerilla War in Greece, 1946–49: A Case Study," in Franklin Mark Osanka, *Modern Guerilla Warfare,* Free Press, New York, 1962, p. 225.

2. Col. Napoleon D. Valeriano and Lt. Col. Charles T. R. Bohannon, *Counter-Guerilla Operations: The Philippine Experience,* Praeger, New York, 1962, pp. 48–49.

3. Alvin H. Scaff, *The Philippine Answer to Communism,* Stanford University Press, Stanford, California, 1955, p. 22.

4. Ibid., p. 27.

5. Ibid., p. 28.

6. Major Boyd T. Bashore, "Dual Strategy for Limited War," in Osanka, op. cit., p. 193.

7. Scaff, op. cit., p. 35.

8. Major General Edward G. Lansdale, *In the Midst of Wars,* Harper & Row, New York, 1972, p. 20.

9. Valeriano and Bohannon, op. cit., pp. 126–128.

10. Ibid., p. 133.

11. Lansdale, op. cit., p. 43. Magsaysay was supported by the U.S. JUSMAG in this demand.

12. Valeriano and Bohannon, op. cit., p. 207.

13. Ibid., p. 207.

14. Ibid., p. 107.

15. Scaff, op. cit., p. 45.

16. Lansdale, op. cit., p. 51.

17. Scaff, op. cit., p. 37.

18. Valeriano and Bohannan, op. cit., pp. 225–226.

19. Lansdale, op. cit., pp. 89–90.

20. Ibid., p. 100.

21. Scaff, op. cit., p. 36.

22. Lansdale, op. cit., p. 121.

23. Hans Heymann, Jr. and William W. Whitson, *Can and Should the United States Preserve a Military Capability for Revolutionary Conflict?* (R-940-ARPA), The Rand Corporation, Santa Monica, Calif., January 1972, p. 46.

24. Lansdale, op. cit., p. 2.

25. For an instance when he did not, see the *Pentagon Papers,* Gravel Edition, Beacon Press, Boston, 1971, vol. 2, p. 531.

26. This account relies particularly upon the following works: Brig. Richard L. Clutterbuck, *The Long Long War,* Praeger, New York, 1966; Lucian W. Pye, *Guerilla Communism in Malaya,* Princeton University Press, Princeton, N.J., 1956; Edgar O'Ballance, *Malaya: The Communist Insurgent War, 1948–60,* Faber & Faber, London, 1966; Robert W. Komer, *The Malayan Emergency in Retrospect: Organization of the Successful Counterinsurgency Effort,* R-957-ARPA, The Rand Corporation, Santa Monica, Calif., February 1972.

27. O'Ballance, op. cit., p. 119.

28. Cf. Dennis Duncanson, *Government and Revolution in Vietnam,* Oxford University Press, N.Y. and London, 1968, Chapters V and VI, passim.

29. Sir Robert Thompson, *Defeating Communist Insurgency,* Praeger, New York, 1966, p. 61.

30. Komer, op. cit., pp. 40, 41, and 48.

31. *John Fitzgerald Kennedy, A Compilation of Statements and Speeches Made During His Service in the United States Senate and House of Representatives,* United States Government Printing Office, Washington, D.C., 1964, p. 288.

32. Cf. Peter Paret, *French Revolutionary Warfare from Indochina to Algeria,* Praeger, New York, 1964.

33. Cf., for example, Max F. Millikan and W. W. Rostow, *A Proposal: Key to an Effective Foreign Policy,* Harper and Brothers, New York, 1957.

34. Quoted in W. W. Rostow, *The Diffusion of Power, 1957–1972,* Macmillan, New York, 1972, p. 283.

35. *Department of State Bulletin,* September 8, 1958, p. 376.

36. President's Committee to Study the U.S. Military Assistance Program, W. H. Draper, Chairman, *Composite Report,* U.S. Government Printing Office, Washington, D.C., 1962, vol. 1, p. 8.

37. Rostow, *The Diffusion of Power,* p. 112.

Chapter 3

1. Roger Hilsman, *To Move a Nation,* Doubleday, Garden City, N.Y., 1967, p. 413.

2. See Chapter I, p. 18.

3. Arthur M. Schlesinger, *A Thousand Days,* p. 274; and Hilsman, op. cit., p. 414.

4. Department of Defense, *U.S.-Vietnam Relations,* U.S. Government Printing Office, Washington, D.C., 1971, vol. 11, p. 17.

6. *John Fitzgerald Kennedy, A Compilation of Statements and Speeches Made During His Service in the U.S. Senate and House of Representatives,* U.S. Government Printing Office, Washington, D.C., 1964, p. 288.

7. Ibid., pp. 284–293.

8. John F. Kennedy, *The Strategy of Peace,* New York: Harper, 1960, p. 184.

9. "Two Communist Manifestoes," Washington Center for Foreign Policy Research, 1961, p. 52.

10. Cf. "Khrushchev's Speech of January 6, 1961, A Summary and Interpretive Analysis," Legislative Reference Service, Library of Congress, 87th Congress, 1st Session, Document No. 14, U.S. Government Printing Office, Washington D.C., 1961.

11. *Public Papers of the President, John F. Kennedy, 1961,* U.S. Government Printing Office, 1962, p. 336.

12. Ibid., p. 236.

13. Ibid., p. 397.

14. Theodore C. Sorenson, *Kennedy,* pp. 631–633; and Roger Hilsman, op. cit., p. 415.

15. David Halberstam, *The Best and the Brightest,* Random House, New York, 1972, p. 124.

16. Rostow, *The Diffusion of Power,* p. 284.

17. Ibid., p. 168.

18. In Lt. Col. T. N. Greene (ed.), *The Guerrilla and How To Fight Him,* Praeger, New York, 1962, pp. 22–36.

19. Ibid., p. 29.

20. Ibid., pp. 25–26.

21. Ibid., p. 31.

22. Ibid., p. 35.

23. Ibid., p. 35.

24. Maxwell Taylor, *Swords and Plowshares,* Norton, New York, 1972, p. 201.

25. *Foreign Service Journal,* July 1962, pp. 20–23. Johnson and many others preferred the term "internal defense" to "counterinsurgency." In his Oral History interview on file at the John F. Kennedy Library, he states that he was never fond of the latter term and commented on it unfavorably to General Taylor, "who indicated very much that this was the President's title."

26. *The Pentagon Papers,* The Senator Gravel Edition, Beacon Press, Boston, 1972, vol. 2, p. 689. (Henceforth referred to as *Pentagon Papers.)*

27. There is evidence in the Special Group (C.I.) files at the John F. Kennedy Library that the doctrine paper was actually drafted in the State Department, and thus that U. Alexis Johnson probably had a good deal of influence on its

contents. An unclassified note to McGeorge Bundy from his assistant Robert W. Komer, on July 10, comments on the attached Special Group (C.I.). Agenda as follows: "The hassle over State's doctrine paper has been resolved, I believe, with DOD now recognizing State's primacy in policy field."

28. For Schlesinger's view, see *No More Vietnams? The War and the Future of American Foreign Policy,* Harper & Row, New York, 1968, pp. 84–86; for Hilsman's, see his *To Move a Nation,* for example, p. 426.

29. *Foreign Service Journal,* July 1962, p. 23.

30. This has become the generally accepted view of the Kennedy (and Johnson) Administration's approach to Vietnam, particularly since the publication of the *Pentagon Papers.* See, for example, Leslie Gelb, "The System Worked," *Foreign Policy,* Summer 1971; Robert W. Komer, *Bureaucracy Does Its Thing,* The Rand Corporation, R-967-ARPA, August 1972, p. 2; and Richard M. Pfeffer (ed.), *No More Vietnams? The War and the Future of American Foreign Policy,* New York, Harper & Row, 1968.

31. Based on interviews with several participants.

32. *Pentagon Papers,* vol. 2, p. 660.

33. Maxwell Taylor, op. cit., p. 201.

34. Cf. for example, the Oral History interviews at the John F. Kennedy Library of U. Alexis Johnson and William Gaud.

35. *Pentagon Papers,* vol. 2, pp. 667–668.

36. This is apparent from the inventory of Special Group (C.I.) files maintained at the JFK Library. This unclassified list notes the subject of each memorandum in the files.

37. "Memorandum for the Special Assistant to the President for National Security Affairs, Subject: Summary Report, Military Counterinsurgency Accomplishments Since January, 1961," from the chairman of the Joint Chiefs of Staff, dated July 21, 1962, p. 2. Originally classified "Secret," it was declassified in May 1973.

38. Robert Amory, recorded interview by Joseph E. O'Connor, February 9, 1966, p. 99, John F. Kennedy Library Oral History Program.

39. JCS Memorandum of July 21, p. 1.

40. The writer was enrolled in this first running of the course. He recalls that the attorney general attended a lecture by Professor Lucien Pye, of MIT, on the role of the military in underdeveloped countries. After the lecture, he congratulated the speaker and pronounced the lecture "terrific."

41. *Washington Post,* July 4, 1962, p. 1.

42. The last running of the "Interdepartmental Seminar" took place in 1971.

43. Hilsman, *To Move A Nation,* p. 415.

44. *Pentagon Papers,* vol. 2, p. 689.

45. This description is based largely on the author's experience of how the foreign affairs community approaches such problems.

46. From NSAM 162, *Pentagon Papers,* vol. 2, p. 682.

47. This is a logical deduction from the John F. Kennedy Library's inventory of the Special Group (C.I.)'s files.

48. Originally classified "Secret" but now declassified.

49. Sorenson, op. cit., p. 632.

50. Special warfare, in army usage, comprised unconventional warfare, psychological warfare, and counterinsurgency operations. Unconventional warfare comprised guerrilla warfare, escape and evasion, and subversion vs. hostile states in time of war.

51. Lloyd Norman and John B. Spore, "Big Push in Guerrilla Warfare," *Army*, March 1962, p. 39.

52. Edward B. Glick, *Peaceful Conflict*, Stackpole, Harrisburg, Pa., 1967, p. 71.

53. Ibid., p. 72.

54. JCS Memorandum, op. cit., p. 8.

55. JCS Memorandum, op. cit., p. 10.

56. Ibid., p. 13.

57. Norman and Spore, op. cit., p. 31.

58. See, for example, Hilsman, *To Move a Nation*, p. 423.

59. *The Public Papers of the President, John F. Kennedy, 1962*, p. 454.

60. Cf. Walter D. Jacobs, "This Matter of Counterinsurgency," *Military Review*, October 1964, pp. 79–85.

61. Norman and Spore, op. cit., p. 34.

62. *FM 31-16*, Department of the Army, Washington, D.C., 24 March 1967, p. 18.

63. Ibid., p. 3.

64. Ibid., p. 43.

65. See, for example, Hilsman, *To Move a Nation*, p. 426.

66. Schlesinger, op. cit., p. 381.

67. See, for example, Schlesinger, op. cit., pp. 514–518.

68. Robert Amory, Oral History Interview, pp. 101–103.

69. *Pentagon Papers*, vol. 2, p. 681.

70. U. Alexis Johnson, op. cit., p. 23.

71. Cf. Lt. Col. Jonathan F. Ladd, "Some Reflections on Counterinsurgency," *Military Review*, October 1964, pp. 72–78.

72. Pfeffer, op. cit., p. 11.

Chapter 4

1. *Pentagon Papers*, vol. 2, p. 27.

2. See John C. Donnell, "The War, the Gap and the Cadre," *Asia Magazine*, Winter 1966, especially pp. 53–54.

3. Based on Robert L. Sansom, *The Economics of Insurgency*, MIT Press, Cambridge, Mass., 1970, especially Chapter 3, pp. 66–67.

4. See, e.g., Jeffrey Race, *War Comes to Long An*, University of California Press, Berkeley, Calif., 1972, David W. P. Elliott and W. A. Stewart, "Pacification and the Viet Cong System in Dinh Tuong: 1966–67," RM-

5788-ISA/ARPA, The Rand Corporation, Santa Monica, Calif., January 1969.

5. *The Vietnamese and Their Revolution,* Harper & Row, New York, 1970.

6. *Fire in the Lake,* Little, Brown, Boston, 1972.

7. McAllister and Mus, op. cit., pp. 59–69.

8. See Race, op. cit., pp. 167–171, for a discussion of these aspects of Lao Dong organization.

9. Quoted by Samuel L. Popkin, "Pacification: Politics and the Village," *Asian Survey,* August 1970, pp. 62–63.

10. Race, op. cit., p. 161.

11. Stephen T. Hosmer, *Viet Cong Repression and Its Implications for the Future,* R-475/1-ARPA, The Rand Corporation, Santa Monica, Calif., 1970, p. 9.

12. Ibid., p. 65.

13. Michael Charles Conly, *The Communist Insurgent Infrastructure in South Vietnam: A Study of Organization and Strategy,* Center for Research in Social Systems, American University, U.S. Government Printing Office, Washington, D.C., 1966, p. 45.

14. *Pentagon Papers,* vol. 2, p. 642.

15. Ibid., p. 25.

16. Ibid., p. 27.

17. Ibid., p. 24.

18. Ibid., p. 138.

19. Ibid., p. 437.

20. In Vietnam, "hamlet" and "village" are specific government units, the first being in our terminology a village and the second a township comprising several hamlets. "Hamlet" is always used here in the Vietnamese sense, but "village" is used in both senses, although the meaning should be clear from the context.

21. Dennis Duncanson, author of *Government and Revolution in Vietnam,* Oxford University Press, New York and London, 1968, of which see p. 314.

22. For an account of the agroville experiment see, for example, J. J. Zasloff, *Rural Resettlement in Vietnam, An Agroville in Development,* Department of State, AID, Washington, D.C., n.d.

23. Duncanson, op. cit., pp. 313–315.

24. See, for example, Duncanson, op. cit., p. 309, and the *Pentagon Papers,* vol. 2, pp. 50–51.

25. Details in this account are from "The Highlanders of South Vietnam," an internal CIA study declassified in August 1974 under Executive Order No. 11652.

26. Figures from an internal CIA memorandum dated 3 March 1965 and entitled "The Civilian Irregular Defense Groups (CIDG) Political Action Program." The memorandum was declassified in August 1974 under Executive Order No. 11652.

27. Hilsman, op. cit., p. 455.

28. The text of Thompson's delta plan is available in *U.S.-Vietnamese Relations,* U.S. Government Printing Office, Washington, D.C., 1971, vol. 11, p. 345, *et seq.*

29. *Pentagon Papers,* vol. 2, p. 141.

30. Hilsman, op. cit., p. 435.

31. See for example, Robert Scigliano, *South Vietnam, Nation Under Stress,* Houghton Mifflin, Boston, 1964, p. 32.

32. For a discussion of Vietnamese personalism see John C. Donnell, *Politics in South Vietnam: Doctrines of Authority in Conflict,* Ph.D. Thesis submitted at the University of Calif., Berkeley, 1964, especially pp. 77–123.

33. Ibid., p. 226.

34. William A. Nighswonger, *Rural Pacification in Vietnam,* Praeger, New York, 1966, p. 56. The policy was not enforced but is an example of the fascination Communist methods had for Nhu.

35. Milton E. Osborne, *Strapagic Hamhets in South Vietnam, a Survey and a Comparison,* Data Paper No. 55, Southeast Asia Program, Department of Asian Studies, Cornell University, Ithaca, N.Y., 1965, p. 29.

36. Nighswonger, op. cit., p. 56.

37. Douglas Pike, *Viet Cong,* The MIT Press, Cambridge, Mass., 1966, p. 67.

38. John C. Donnell, "Expanding Political Participation—The Long Haul from Villagism to Nationalism," *Asian Survey,* August 1970, p. 693.

39. Duncanson, op. cit., p. 313.

40. Nighswonger, op. cit., p. 55.

41. Duncanson, op. cit., p. 314.

42. John Mecklin, *Mission in Torment,* Doubleday, Garden City, N.Y., 1965, p. 45.

43. Nighswonger, op. cit., pp. 67–69.

44. *Pentagon Papers,* vol. 2, pp. 143–144.

45. Duncanson, op. cit., p. 316.

46. Osborne, op. cit., p. 27.

47. *Pentagon Papers,* vol. 2, p. 150.

48. *Pentagon Papers,* vol. 2, p. 150.

49. Pike, op. cit., p. 67.

50. George K. Tanham, *War Without Guns,* Praeger, New York, 1966, p. 7.

51. *Pentagon Papers,* vol. 2, p. 443.

52. Ibid., p. 443.

53. Hilsman, op. cit., p. 442.

54. Cf. Tanham, op. cit., Chapter 3.

55. *Pentagon Papers,* vol. 2, p. 177.

56. Hilsman, op. cit., pp. 442–444.

57. Ibid., pp. 465–466.

58. Statistics from Osborne, op. cit., p. 33.

59. Ibid., p. 32.

60. Duncanson. op. cit., p. 326; Osborne, op. cit., p. 36.

61. *Pentagon Papers,* vol. 2, p. 717.

62. Ibid., p. 175. The instructions were issued as early as July 1962.

63. Nighswonger, op. cit., p. 64.

64. Sir Robert Thompson, *Defeating Communist Insurgency,* Praeger, New York, 1966, pp. 141–142.

65. Osborne, op. cit., p. 39.

66. Thompson, op. cit., pp. 141–142.

67. Scigliano, op. cit., pp. 49–50.

68. *Pentagon Papers,* vol. 2, p. 123.

Chapter 5

1. The best and, in fact, the only scholarly discussion of the role of the North Vietnamese in the Pathet Lao movement is *North Vietnam and the Pathet Lao,* by Paul F. Langer and Joseph J. Zasloff, Harvard University Press, Cambridge, Mass., 1970. They document thoroughly what all observers of Lao affairs long have accepted, that the Pathet Lao has been guided and aided materially, militarily, and technically by the North Vietnamese since its inception.

2. The correct pronunciation of the "e" is as in "egg," rather than as the "a" in "bay." Another name, actually preferred by the Meo, is "Hmuong."

3. "The Meo of Xieng Khouang Province," by G. Linwood Barney, in *Southeast Asian Tribes, Minorities, and Nations,* Peter Kunstadter, editor, Princeton University Press, Princeton, N.J., 1967, vol. 1, p. 292.

4. Ibid., p. 275–277.

5. Alfred W. McCoy, "French Colonialism in Laos, 1893–1945," in *Laos: War and Revolution,* Nina S. Adams and Alfred W. McCoy, editors, Harper & Row, New York, 1970, pp. 80–81.

6. Ibid., p. 92.

7. Barney, op. cit., p. 274.

8. Ibid., pp. 289, 291.

9. Ibid., p. 292.

10. Langer and Zasloff, op. cit., Chapter 9.

11. Joseph J. Zasloff, *Pathet Lao, Leadership and Organization,* Heath, Lexington, Mass., 1973, pp. 67–68.

12. Barney, op. cit., p. 274.

13. Arthur L. Dommen, *Conflict in Laos,* Praeger, 1971, pp. 133–134.

14. Two such versions are: *Mister Pop,* by Don A. Schanche, McKay, New York, 1970, which seems to be based almost entirely on the recollections of Edgar M. Buell, associated with the Meo effort from its earliest days; and a series of articles by *Baltimore Sun* reporter John E. Woodruff, published in February 1971. Woodruff's source seems to have been Touby Lyfong.

15. Dommen, op. cit., pp. 157–158.

16. Barney, op. cit., p. 275. Say Kham later told another source that he had never made such a statement.

17. Ibid., p. 271.

18. See p. 140 below for further details on this civilian air activity.

19. Cf. Schanche, op. cit., pp. 64–65, and John E. Woodruff, "The Meo of Laos–II," *Baltimore Sun*, February 22, 1971.

20. *Pentagon Papers*, vol. 2, p. 646.

21. Ibid., p. 645. A denied area, in intelligence parlance, is a country where relations prohibit the establishment of an intelligence unit with the host country's permission.

22. Schanche, op. cit., p. 73.

23. Cf. Dommen, op. cit., pp. 183–184.

24. Charles A. Stephenson, *The End of Nowhere*, Beacon Press, Boston, 1972, p. 137. Stephenson's more recent research fills in some of the gaps in Dommen's pioneer account.

25. *Pentagon Papers*, vol. 2, p. 646.

26. Op. cit., p. 83.

27. Ibid., p. 84.

28. Hilsman, op. cit., pp. 140–141.

29. Hilsman, op. cit., p. 115.

30. Schanche, op. cit., p. 91.

31. Ibid., p. 93.

32. James Thomas Ward, "U.S. Aid to Hill-tribe Refugees in Laos," in Kundstadter, op. cit., p. 301.

33. Testimony of Dr. P. McCreedy in U.S. Congress, Hearings Before the Subcommittee to Investigate Problems Connected With Refugees and Escapees of the Committee on the Judiciary, U.S. Senate, 91st Congress, Second Session, May 7, 1970, *Refugee and Civilian War Casualty Problems in Laos and Cambodia*, U.S. Government Printing Office, Washington, D.C., 1970, pp. 46–47.

34. Ibid., p. 47.

35. Ward, op. cit., p. 300.

36. Schanche, op. cit., p. 131.

37. Senate Subcommittee on Refugees, 1970 *Hearings*, op. cit., p. 67.

38. Ibid., p. 63.

39. The technical skills required to produce these programs were provided by Thai hired in Bangkok.

40. Senate Subcommittee on Refugees, 1970 *Hearings*, op. cit., p. 69.

41. U.S. Congress, Hearings Before the Subcommittee on U.S. Security Agreements Abroad of the Committee on Foreign Relations, U.S. Senate, 91st Congress, First Session, October 20–22 and 28, 1969, *United States Security Agreements and Commitments Abroad, Kingdom of Laos*, U.S. Government Printing Office, Washington, D.C., pp. 517–518.

42. Schanche has a thoroughly garbled version of this event, which he places a year too early, op. cit., p. 162.

43. Stephenson, op. cit., p. 204.

44. *New York Times,* May 8, 1972.

45. Senate Subcommittee on U.S. Commitments Abroad, *Hearings,* op. cit., pp. 454–470, sets forth the pattern and organization of USAF operations in Laos.

46. Colonel Thong, Vang Pao's commander in Sam Neua, often served as a guide on such missions and was killed by ground-fire in the doorway of a helicopter over North Vietnam in 1965.

47. Cf. U.S. Congress, Hearings Before the Committee on Armed Services, U.S. Senate, 92nd Congress, First Session, July 14, 22, 1971, on *Fiscal Year 1972 Authorization for Military Procurement, etc.,* U.S. Government Printing Office, Washington, D.C., 1971, pp. 4268 and 4271.

48. Senate Subcommittee on U.S. Commitments Abroad, *Hearings,* op. cit., p. 391.

49. Ibid., p. 491.

50. Schanche, op. cit., p. 294.

51. Dommen, op. cit., p. 299.

52. Ibid., p. 302.

53. Ibid., p. 302.

54. Dr. Patricia McCreedy, from a personal interview.

Chapter 6

1. *Pentagon Papers,* vol. 2, p. 661.

2. Fred W. Riggs, *Thailand: A Bureaucratic Polity,* East-West Center, Honolulu, 1966, p. 326–329.

3. All students of Thai politics agree on this fact. See, for example, David A. Wilson, *Politics in Thailand,* Cornell University Press, Ithaca, N.Y., 1962, pp. 135 and 259.

4. U.S. Congress, Hearings Before the Subcommittee on United States Security Agreements and Commitments Abroad of the Committee on Foreign Relations, U.S. Senate, 91st Congress, First Session, Nov. 10–14 and 17, 1969, *U.S. Security Agreements and Commitments Abroad, Kingdom of Thailand,* U.S. Government Printing Office, Washington, D.C., 1970, p. 852.

5. George K. Tanham, *Trial in Thailand,* Crane, Russak, New York, 1974, p. 34.

6. Alessandro Casella, "Communism and Insurrection in Thailand," *The World Today,* May 1970, p. 197.

7. Tanham, op. cit., pp. 28ff.

8. Ibid., p. 57. These and other figures of insurgent strength cited herein date from 1974, but available information suggests there has been only minor growth since then.

9. David Morell, "Thailand, Military Checkmate," *Asian Survey,* February 1972, p. 159.

10. Tanham, op. cit., p. 62.

11. Ibid., p. 65.

12. *A Brief History of USOM Support to the Office of Accelerated Rural Development,* USOM/Thailand, September 1969, p. 2.

13. Tanham, op. cit., p. 99.

14. David Morell, "Thailand," *Asian Survey,* February 1973, pp. 161–163.

15. U.S. Senate Subcommittee of the Foreign Relations Committee, *Hearings on Thailand,* p. 893.

16. Ibid., p. 637.

17. Ibid., p. 700.

18. Ibid., p. 638.

19. Ibid., p. 910.

20. Tanham, op. cit., p. 135.

21. Ibid., p. 76.

22. Ibid., p. 75.

23. Ibid., p. 92.

24. Thompson, *Defeating Communist Insurgency,* Chapter 9.

25. Ibid., p. 148.

26. *Pentagon Papers,* vol. 2, p. 646.

27. Tanham, op. cit., p. 121.

28. Ibid., p. 81.

29. Some observers maintain, and the author is inclined to agree, that the only practical solution to the suppression problem in the north is large-scale paramilitary recruitment and deployment among the tribal population. Such a program would succeed only if accompanied by a significant redressing of tribal grievances and development activities in favor of the tribal villages, all of which are remote from prevailing attitudes and concepts.

30. See Chapter III, p. 65.

31. Tanham, op. cit., pp. 110–112.

32. See Chapter III, p. 80.

33. Clark D. Neher, "Stability and Instability in Contemporary Thailand," *Asian Survey,* December 1975, pp. 1100–1101.

Chapter 7

1. This serious misnomer was frequently denounced but never completely suppressed, for it corresponded to the general but faulty perception that the principal war front was where U.S. combat forces were active and that different criteria applied to these two "different" conflicts.

2. Roger Hilsman, "Two American Counterstrategies to Guerilla Warfare," in Ping-ti Ho and Tang Tsou (eds.), *China in Crisis,* University of Chicago Press, Chicago, 1968, pp. 289–290.

3. Nighswonger, op. cit., p. 63.

4. *Pentagon Papers,* vol. 3, p. 667.

5. Halberstam, *The Best and the Brightest,* p. 353.

6. Two USIS officers, Frank Scotton and Robert Kelly, are credited with initiating the first PAT. See John C. Donnell, "Pacification Reassessed," *Asian Survey,* August 1967, p. 572.

7. Lawrence E. Grinter, "South Vietnam: Pacification Denied," *South-East Asian SPECTRUM,* July 1975, p. 60.

8. Nighswonger, op. cit., pp. 45 and 138.

9. George K. Tanham and Dennis J. Duncanson, "Some Dilemmas of Counterinsurgency," *Foreign Affairs,* October 1969, p. 121.

10. See, e.g., the testimony of William E. Colby claiming that the program seized in 1969 over 1000 units of ordnance, 50,000 units of drugs, and 6000 tons of contraband foodstuffs. U.S. Congress, Hearings Before the U.S. Senate Committee on Foreign Relations, 91st Congress, Second Session, *Civil Operations and Revolutionary Development Support,* Washington, D.C., U.S. Government Printing Office, 1970, p. 721.

11. United States Congress, Hearings Before a Subcommittee of the Committee on Government Operations, House of Representatives, Ninety-second Congress, First Session, July 15, 16, 19, 21; and August 2, 1971, *U.S. Assistance Programs in Vietnam,* U.S. Government Printing Office, Washington, D.C., 1971, p. 5.

12. J. A. Koch, *The Chieu Hoi Program in South Vietnam, 1963–1971,* R-1192/1-ARPA, The Rand Corporation, Santa Monica, Calif., May 1975, p. 26.

13. See Chapter IV.

14. Nighswonger, op. cit., p. 155.

15. Robert W. Komer, *Bureaucracy Does Its Thing: Institutional Constraints on U.S.—GVN Performance in Vietnam,* R-967-ARPA, The Rand Corporation, Santa Monica, Calif., August 1967, p. 145.

16. For a more detailed analysis of *Hop Tac,* see the *Pentagon Papers,* vol. 2, pp. 521–527.

17. *Pentagon Papers,* vol. 2, p. 530.

18. Ibid., p. 530.

19. Chester L. Cooper, *The Lost Crusade,* Dodd, Mead, New York, 1970, p. 281.

20. Throughout the life of the program the U.S. and the GVN knew it by different names. "Revolutionary Development" was Ambassador Lodge's choice of a name in preference to the prosaic Vietnamese choice of "Rural Construction," which later became simply "Construction." Cf. the *Pentagon Papers,* vol. 2, p. 582.

21. Cf., as a good example, Thompson, *Defeating Communist Insurgency,* p. 80.

22. A good summary of Be's thinking can be found in Race, op. cit., pp. 242–249.

23. Donnell, *Pacification Reassessed,* p. 571.

24. VTC Study Aid, "Revolutionary Development/Pacification," Vietnam Training Center, Foreign Service Institute, Department of State, Washington, D.C., June 1969, p. 11.

25. "11 Criteria and 98 Steps," Handbook No. 12017, RD Ministry, Saigon, 1966.

26. Donnell, op. cit., p. 571.

27. Ibid., p. 570.

28. *Pentagon Papers*, vol. 2, p. 550.

29. Donnell, op. cit., p. 569.

30. *Pentagon Papers*, vol. 2, p. 543. "The highest levels" is a common euphemism in government correspondence for the president.

31. See Chapter IV.

32. *Pentagon Papers*, vol. 3, p. 79.

33. Ibid., vol. 2, p. 537. This writer has been advised informally that the author of the quoted words was Richard Holbrooke, a staff aid to Ambassador Lodge. At this writing, Holbrooke is Assistant Secretary of State for East Asia and Pacific Affairs.

34. Maxwell Taylor, *Swords and Plowshares*, p. 361.

35. Ibid.

36. *Pentagon Papers*, vol. 2, p. 568. The date was March 28, 1966.

37. *Pentagon Papers*, vol. 2, pp. 595–597.

38. Thomas W. Scoville, "United States Organization for Pacification Advice and Support in Vietnam, 1954–1968," Ph.D. thesis, MIT, 1976, pp. 183–186.

39. Ibid., p. 185.

40. Ibid., p. 618.

41. Ibid., p. 619.

42. Subcommittee of the Committee on Government Operations, Hearings on *U.S. Assistance Programs in Vietnam*, op. cit., pp. 181–182.

Chapter 8

1. Robert W. Komer, "Clear, Hold and Rebuild," *Army,* May 1970, pp. 20–21; and "Impact of Pacification on Insurgency in Vietnam," in David S. Sullivan and Martin J. Sattler (eds.), *Revolutionary War: Western Response,* Columbia University Press, New York, 1971, p. 52.

2. *Pentagon Papers*, vol. 2, pp. 620–621.

3. They were also shared at the time by the author.

4. *New York Times*, February 18, 1970.

5. Komer, "Clear, Hold and Rebuild," p. 20.

6. Komer, "Impact of Pacification on Insurgency in Vietnam," p. 57.

7. General William C. Westmoreland, *Report on the War in Vietnam* (As of June 30, 1968), U.S. Government Printing Office, Washington, D.C., p. 131.

8. Ibid., p. 156.

9. Ibid., p. 132.

10. Ibid., p. 132.

11. R. W. Komer in a personal interview. The commitment of over "half of the U.S. combat forces . . . in close proximity to the heavily populated areas of the country, targetted against the guerillas and local forces," is reported by General Westmoreland in his *Report on the War in Vietnam,* p. 132.

12. Data from Thomas C. Thayer, "How to Analyze a War Without Fronts," Washington, D.C., n.p., 1976.

13. Komer, *Bureaucracy Does Its Thing,* p. 109.

14. M. Doan Havron, William W. Chenault, James W. Dodson, and A. Terry Rambo, *Constabulary Capabilities for Low-level Conflict,* HSR-RR-69/1-Se, Human Sciences Research, McLean, Va., April 1969, p. 83.

15. Harper & Row, New York, 1972.

16. Havron, Chenault, et al., op. cit., pp. 102–105.

17. See Chapter IV.

18. The exact extent of surprise remains a matter of controversy. It varied from area to area, but even General Westmoreland admits that "we did not surmise the true nature or the scope of the countrywide attack." (*Report on the War in Vietnam,* p. 158.)

19. Westmoreland, *Report on the War,* p. 161.

20. Ibid., p. 199.

21. Don Oberdorfer, *Tet!,* Doubleday, Garden City, N.Y., 1971, p. 54.

22. Cf. for example, Bernard Brodie, "The Tet Offensive," in Noble Frankland and Christopher Dowling (eds.), *Decisive Battles of the Twentieth Century,* Sidgwick and Jackson, London, 1976.

23. Senate Committee on Foreign Relations, *Hearings on CORDS,* p. 719.

24. Ibid., p. 709.

25. Komer, "Impact of Pacification," p. 54.

26. Senate Committee on Foreign Relations, *Hearings on CORDS,* p. 719.

27. Ibid., p. 714.

28. MacDonald Salter, "Land Reform in South Vietnam," *Asian Survey,* August 1970, p. 732.

29. Grinter, "South Vietnam: Pacification Denied," p. 64.

30. Komer, "Impact of Pacification," p. 65.

31. Ibid., p. 63.

32. Koch, "The Chieu Hoi Program," pp. 48 and 53.

33. Richard L. Prillaman, "Vietnam Update," *Infantry,* May–June 1969, quoted in *U.S. Army War College Selected Reading, Course 4, Stability Operations,* Carlisle Barracks, Pa., December 1969, p. 238.

34. Ibid., p. 239.

35. Brian M. Jenkins, "The Unchangeable War," RM-6278-1-ARPA, The Rand Corporation, Santa Monica, Calif., September 1972, p. 5.

36. Ibid., p. 2.

37. Figures from Senate Committee on Foreign Relations, *Hearings on CORDS,* pp. 707 and 708.

38. Komer, "Impact of Pacification," p. 62.

39. *Washington Post,* October 29, 30, and 31, 1969.

40. Komer, op. cit., p. 63.

41. Ibid.

42. Samuel L. Popkin, "Pacification: Politics and the Village," *Asian Survey,* August 1970, p. 662.

43. See Allen E. Goodman, "Political Implications of Rural Problems in South Vietnam: Creating Public Interests," *Asian Survey,* August 1970, pp. 672–687.

44. John C. Donnell, "Expanding Political Participation—The Long Haul from Villagism to Nationalism," *Asian Survey,* August 1970, pp. 700–701.

45. Komer, "The Impact of Pacification," p. 53.

46. One persistent dissenter was Ambassador Colby who continued to see Phoenix as contributing usefully to the attack on the infrastructure. Cf. his testimony in Subcommittee of the Committee on Government Operations, Hearings on *U.S. Assistance Programs in Vietnam,* p. 184.

47. Goodman, "The Political Implications of Rural Problems," p. 677–678. In the same issue of *Asian Survey,* two other social scientists make the same point.

48. CORDS developed a Pacification Attitude Analysis System which used standard polling techniques modified suitably for Vietnam to measure public attitudes on major issues. Interviewers were Vietnamese who presented themselves as private persons.

49. Lawrence E. Grinter, "How They Lost: Doctrines, Strategies and Outcomes of the Vietnam War," *Asian Survey,* December 1975, p. 1115.

Chapter 9

1. David F. Ronfeldt and Luigi R. Einaudi, *International Security and Military Assistance to Latin America in the 1970's* (R-924-ISA), The Rand Corporation, Santa Monica, Calif., December 1971, p. 8.

2. Hugh Thomas, *Cuba or the Pursuit of Freedom,* Eyre and Spottiswoode, London, 1971, Chapter 85.

3. Jack Davis, *Political Violence in Latin America,* Adelphi Papers, No. 85, The International Institute for Strategic Studies London, 1972, p. 14.

4. Thomas, op. cit., pp. 1038–1047.

5. See Chapter III.

6. *U.S. Military Policies and Programs in Latin America,* Hearings Before the Subcommittee on Western Hemisphere Affairs of Committee on Foreign Relations, U.S. Senate, 91st Congress, June 24, 1969, U.S. Government Printing Office, Washington, D.C., 1969, p. 57.

7. Willard F. Barber and C. Neale Ronning, *Internal Security and Military Power,* Ohio State University Press, 1966, pp. 239–240.

8. *Castro-Communist Insurgency in Venezuela,* Georgetown Research Project, Atlantic Research Corp., Alexandria, Va., 1965 (ARPA Project No. 4860), p. 59.

9. *Washington Post,* October 7, 1976.

10. Richard L. Maullin, *Soldiers, Guerillas and Politics in Colombia* (R-630-ARPA), The Rand Corporation, Santa Monica, Calif., December 1971, pp. 41–42.

11. Ibid., p. 46.

12. Norman Gall, "Peru's Misfired Guerilla Campaign," *The Reporter,* January 26, 1967, p. 38.

13. Ibid.

14. Luigi R. Einaudi and Alfred C. Stepan III, *Latin American Institutional Development; Changing Military Perspectives in Peru and Brazil* (R-586-DOS), The Rand Corporation, Santa Monica, Calif., April 1971, pp. 27–28.

15. Jack Davis, op. cit., pp. 16–17.

16. *The Complete Bolivian Diaries of Che Guevara and Captured Documents,* Daniel James (ed.), Stein and Day, New York, 1968.

17. Jack Davis, op. cit., p. 17.

18. Department of the Army Field Manual FM 31-23, December 1967.

19. Ibid., p. 66.

20. Ibid., pp. 111–114.

21. George W. Ashworth, "U.S. Designs Forces to Nip Red Insurgents," *Christian Science Monitor,* July 5, 1968. (Reproduced in *U.S. Army War College Selected Readings, Course 4, Stability Operations,* U.S. Army War College, Carlisle Barracks, Pa., pp. 129–130.)

22. George W. Ashworth, "Have U.S. Officials Learned to Cope with Another Vietnam?" *Christian Science Monitor,* March 12, 1969. (Ibid., pp. 131–132.)

23. Hans Heymann, Jr., and William W. Whitson, *Can and Should the United States Preserve a Military Capability for Revolutionary Conflict?* (R-940-ARPA), The Rand Corporation, Santa Monica, Calif., January 1972, p. 31.

24. Ibid., p. 37.

25. Cf., for example, Edward Shils, "The Military in the Political Development of the New States," in *The Role of the Military in Underdeveloped Countries,* John J. Johnson (ed.), Princeton University Press, Princeton, N.J., 1962, p. 27.

26. Cf. George K. Tanham and Dennis J. Duncanson, "Some Dilemmas of Counterinsurgency," *Foreign Affairs,* October 1969, p. 120.

27. "CIA Says Enemy Spies Hold Vital Posts in Saigon," *New York Times,* October 19, 1970.

28. See Chapter III.

29. U. Alexis Johnson, "Internal Defense and the Foreign Service," *Foreign Service Journal,* July 1962, p. 23.

30. January 1969, pp. 19–21 and 27.

31. Eliot L. Richardson, "The Foreign Policy of the Nixon Administration: Its Aims and Strategy," *Department of State Bulletin,* September 22, 1969, p. 258.

32. Richard Nixon, *U.S. Foreign Policy for the 1970's, A New Strategy for Peace,* U.S. Government Printing Office, Washington, D.C., 1970, p. 127.

33. See Chapter VII.

34. Maxwell Taylor, *Swords and Plowshares,* p. 361.

35. Heymann and Whitson, op. cit., p. 93.

36. Quoted in Alastair Buchan, "Questions About Vietnam," *Encounter,* January 1968, p. 7.

37. Brian Jenkins, "The Unchangeable War," p. 3.

38. It was proposed informally by the author.

39. Publication No. R-462-ARPA, Santa Monica, Calif., 1970.

Selected Bibliography

★ ★ ★

BIBLIOGRAPHIC NOTE

The principal subject matter of this work, the development and course of U.S. counterinsurgency policy and operations, has not been discussed in its whole aspect in any other study. The primary sources, of course, are the government documents (including congressional hearings) in which the policy is expounded or stated or defended, many of them compiled in the *Pentagon Papers,* and in that way finally made public. Others remain classified and unavailable for study. The resultant gaps, however, are not critical to our understanding of the policy and how it developed.

The most useful secondary sources for this work have been the memoirs and articles written by participants. Of these, the writings of Roger Hilsman (especially *To Move a Nation*), of Robert W. Komer, George K. Tanham, and Sir Robert Thompson are the most valuable.

As far as concerns the case histories which make up such a large portion of this work, the episodes vary widely in the degree of thoroughness and authority with which they have been recorded and analyzed. The history of the Philippine counterinsurgency in the late 1940s and 1950s is poorly recorded, and, in fact, no complete and authoritative account exists. Valeriano and Bohannon's book is a discussion of counterinsurgency as practiced in the Philippines rather than a full historical account, but it is still the best available work on the subject.

The British experience in Malaya has attracted many more serious analysts and historians, of whose work this writer prefers Brigadier Clutterbuck's *The Long, Long War.* O'Ballance provides another useful short work.

With respect to Thailand, we are fortunate in having in George K. Tanham's *Trial in Thailand* an account by one of the principal actors which, although a memoir and analysis rather than a history, does give a fairly comprehensive survey of this limited episode.

Laos and the U.S. involvement there have attracted more study, but little of a serious nature has been written about the Meo activity. The most useful general survey of Laos since World War II, with emphasis on the U.S. entaglement, is that of Arthur J. Dommen. This is a careful account by a writer who successfully combined journalism with scholarly research. Nothing that is both thorough and reliable, however, has been written about the Meos, and, unhappily, the careless and sensationalized *Mr. Pop* by Don Schanche dominates the field for lack of competition.

Vietnam, of course, usually dominates discussions of counterinsurgency, but no complete accounts of pacification exist other than still classified studies not available to the public. Komer's Rand study, *Bureaucracy Does its Thing,* is an analysis of constraints rather than a history, but it does manage to touch at least briefly on most of the main themes. Another good analysis somewhat more negative than Komer's is Sir Robert Thompson's *No Exit From Vietnam.* Frances FitzGerald's *Fire in the Lake* has some good cultural insights which are spoiled by the excessive sentimentality of her views of the Communist side. *The Village,* by F. J. West, is a remarkably unsentimental account and the best case study of counterinsurgency in a specific area in Vietnam, being both true and readable at the same time. Jeffrey Race's *War Comes to Long An,* although marred by an unrealistic analytic approach, is an authoritative account of what happened in a single province with an unusually full treatment of the Communist side. Many other useful studies exist of particular time periods or programs within the pacification effort, but all are partial or fragmentary.

The Selected Bibliography which follows is not a listing of all the works examined but of those which provided some useful material in the preparation of this work—facts or background or analysis. It goes without saying that it is not a complete listing of all the material that bears on any of the many aspects of counterinsurgency. For example, an enormous library on guerilla warfare has been built up in the last twenty years, but the reader will find that only a few are listed, for most had little to offer on the specific subject of this work.

GENERAL
Books and Official Documents

ALMOND, GABRIEL A., AND COLEMAN, JAMES S., EDS. *The Politics of the Developing Areas.* Princeton, N.J.: Princeton University Press, 1960.

BARBER, WILLARD F., AND RONNING, C. NEALE. *Internal Security and Military Power.* Columbus: Ohio State University Press, 1966.

BELL, J. BOWYER. *The Myth of the Guerilla.* New York: Knopf, 1971.

BRIMELL, J. H. *Communism in Southeast Asia.* New York: Oxford University Press, 1959.

DEITCHMAN, SEYMOUR J. *Limited War and American Defense Policy.* Cambridge, Mass.: MIT Press, 1964.

DEPARTMENT OF THE ARMY. FIELD MANUAL *FM 31–16, Counterguerilla Operations.* Washington, D.C.: U.S. Government Printing Office, 1967.

DEPARTMENT OF THE ARMY. FIELD MANUAL *FM 31–23, Stability Operations: U.S. Army Doctrine.* Washington, D.C.: U.S. Government Printing Office, 1967.

EEKSTEIN, HARRY, ED. *Internal War.* New York: Free Press, 1964.

FITZSIMONS, LOUISE. *The Kennedy Doctrine.* New York: Random House, 1972.

GALULA, DAVID. *Counterinsurgency Warfare: Theory and Practise.* New York: Praeger, 1964.

GLICK, EDWARD B. *Peaceful Conflict.* Harrisburg, Pa.: Stackpole, 1967.

GREENE, LT. COL. T. N., ED. *The Guerilla: And How to Fight Him.* New York: Praeger, 1962.

HEYMANN, HANS, JR., AND WHITSON, WILLIAM W. *Can and Should the U.S. Preserve a Military Capability for Revolutionary Conflict?* Santa Monica, Calif.:The Rand Corporation Collection, R-940-ARPA, January 1972.

HILSMAN, ROGER. *To Move a Nation.* Garden City, N.Y.: Doubleday, 1967.

HUNTINGTON, SAMUEL P. *Changing Patterns of Military Politics.* New York: Free Press, 1972.

JOHNSON, CHALMERS. *Autopsy on People's War.* Berkeley: University of California Press, 1973.

JOHNSON, JOHN J., ED. *The Role of the Military in Underdeveloped Countries.* Princeton, N.J.: Princeton University Press, 1962.

KENNEDY, JOHN F. *John F. Kennedy: A Compilation of Statements and Speeches Made During His Service in the United States Senate and House of Represenatives.* Washington, D.C.: U.S. Government Printing Office, 1964.

KENNEDY, JOHN F. *The Strategy of Peace.* New York: Harper, 1960.

KLARE, MICHAEL T. *War Without End.* New York: Vintage Books, 1972.

KUNSTADTER, PETER, ED. *Southeast Asia Tribes, Minorities and Nations.* Princeton, N.J.: Princeton University Press, 1967.

LAQUEUR, WALTER. *Guerilla.* Boston: Little, Brown, 1976.

LEITES, NATHAN, AND WOLF, CHARLES, JR. *Rebellion and Authority: An Analytic Essay on Insurgent Conflicts.* Santa Monica, Calif.: The Rand Corporation Collection, R-462-ARPA, February 1970.

McCOY, ALRED W. *The Politics of Heroin in Southeast Asia.* New York: Harper & Row, 1972.

McCuen, John J. *The Art of Counter-Revolutionary War.* Harrisburg, Pa.: Stackpole, 1966.

Millikan, Max F., and Blackmur, Donald L. M. *The Emerging Nations.* Boston: Little, Brown, 1961.

Millikan, Max F., and Rostow, W. W. *A Proposal: Key to an Effective Foreign Policy,* New York: Harper, 1957.

Nixon, Richard M. *U.S. Foreign Policy for the 1970's: A New Strategy for Peace.* Washington, D.C.: U.S. Government Printing Office, 1970.

Osanka, Franklin Mark, ed. *Modern Guerilla Warfare: Fighting Communist Guerilla Movements, 1941–1961.* New York, Free Press, 1962.

Paret, Peter, and Shy, John W. *Guerillas in the 1960's.* New York: Praeger, 1962.

Pustay, Major John S. *Counterinsurgency Warfare.* New York: Free Press, 1965.

President's Committee to Study the U.S. Military Assistance Program, W. H. Draper, Chairman. *Composite Report.* Washington, D.C.: U.S. Government Printing Office, August 17, 1959.

The Public Papers of the President, John F. Kennedy, 1961. Washington, D.C.: U.S. Government Printing Office, 1962.

Richardson, Elliot L. "The Foreign Policy of the Nixon Administration." *Department of State Bulletin,* September 22, 1961.

Rostow, W. W. *The Diffusion of Power, 1957–1972.* New York: Macmillan, 1972.

———. *The Stages of Economic Growth.* New York: Cambridge University Press, 1960.

Schlesinger, Arthur M., Jr. *A Thousand Days: John F. Kennedy in the White House.* London: Andre Deutsch, 1965.

Sorenson, Theodore. *Kennedy.* New York: Harper & Row, 1965.

Sullivan, David S., and Sattler, Martin J., eds. *Revolutionary War: Western Response.* New York: Columbia University Press, 1971.

Taylor, Gen. Maxwell D. *Swords and Plowshares.* New York: Norton, 1972.

Thompson, Sir Robert. *Defeating Communist Insurgency.* New York: Praeger, 1966.

Trinquier, Roger. *Modern Warfare: A French View of Counterinsurgency.* New York: Praeger, 1964.

U.S. Army War College. *Stability Operations, Selected Readings, Course 4.* Carlisle Barracks, Carlisle, Pa., December 1969.

U.S. Joint Chiefs of Staff. "Memorandum for the Special Assistant to the President for National Security Affairs, From the Chairman, Joint Chiefs of Staff, July 21, 1962, Subject: Summary Report, Military Counterinsurgency Accomplishments Since January 1961." (Secret; declassified May 1973.)

———"Memorandum for the Special Group (CI), Subject: Counterinsurgency Organization, 17 July, 1962." (Secret: declassified May 1973.)

U.S. Senate. *The Speeches of Sen. John F. Kennedy, Presidential Champaign of 1960.* 87th Congress, 1st Session, Report No. 994. Washington, D.C.: U.S. Government Printing Office, 1961.

Wolf, Charles, Jr. *U.S. Policy in the Third World.* Boston: Little, Brown, 1967.

Articles

AHMAD, EQBAL. "Revolutionary War and Counterinsurgency." In David S. Sullivan and Martin J. Sattler (eds.), *Revolutionary War: Western Response* (p.v.).

BUCHANAN, WILLIAM J., AND HYATT, ROBERT A. "Capitalizing on Guerilla Vulnerabilities." *Military Review,* August 1968.

GARTHOFF, R. L. "Unconventional Warfare in Communist Strategy." *Foreign Affairs,* July 1962.

GELB, LESLIE. "The System Worked." *Foreign Policy,* Summer 1971.

HILSMAN, ROGER. "Internal War: The New Communist Tactics." In Lt. Col. T. N. Greene (ed.), *The Guerilla: And How to Fight Him* (q.v.).

———. Foreword to Vo Nguyen Giap, *People's War, People's Army* (q.v.).

———. "Two American Counter Strategies to Guerilla Warfare." In Ping-ti Ho and Tang Tsou (eds.), *China in Crisis,* vol. 2, (q.v.).

JACOBS, WALTER D. "This Matter of Counterinsurgency." *Military Review,* October 1964.

JOHNSON, CHALMERS A. "Civilian Loyalties and Guerilla Conflict." *World Politics,* July 1962.

JOHNSON, U. ALEXIS. "Internal Defense and the Foreign Service." *The Foreign Service Journal,* July 1962.

LADD, LT. COL. JONATHAN. "Some Reflections on Counterinsurgency." *Military Review,* October 1964.

LANSDALE, MAJ. GEN. EDWARD G. "Do We Understand Revolution?" *Foreign Affairs,* October 1964.

MAECHLING, CHARLES, JR. "Our Internal Defense Policy: A Reappraisal." *The Foreign Service Journal,* January 1969.

McCUEN, COL. JOHN C. "Can We Win Revolutionary Wars?" *Army,* December 1969.

NORMAN, LLOYD, AND SPORE, JOHN. "Big Push in Guerilla Warfare." *Army,* March 1962.

PARET, PETER, AND SHY, JOHN W. "Guerilla Warfare and U.S. Military Policy." In Lt. Col. T. N. Greene (ed.), *The Guerilla: And How to Fight Him* (q.v.).

ROSTOW, W. W. "Guerilla Warfare in Underdeveloped Areas." In Lt. Col. T. N. Greene (ed.), *The Guerilla: And How to Fight Him* (q.v.).

TANHAM, GEORGE K. "Some Insurgency Lessons From Southeast Asia." *Orbis,* Fall 1972.

———, AND DUNCANSON, DENNIS J. "Some Dilemmas of Counterinsurgency." *Foreign Affairs,* October 1969.

WOLF, CHARLES, JR. "Insurgency and Counterinsurgency: Old Myths and New Realities." Santa Monica, Calif.: The Rand Corporation Collection, P-3132-1, July 1965.

ZORTHIAN, BARRY, "Where Do We Go From Here?" *The Foreign Service Journal,* February 1970.

VIETNAM
Books and Office Documents

ARMBRUSTER, FRANK E., KAHN, HERMAN, ET. AL. *Can We Win in Vietnam?* New York: Praeger, 1968.

Central Intelligence Agency. *The Highlanders of South Vietnam, 1954–1965.* June 15, 1966. (Secret; declassified August 1974.)

CONLEY, MICHAEL JAMES. *The Communist Insurgent Structure in Vietnam: A Study of Organization and Strategy.* Washington. D.C.: Center for Research in Social Systems, American University, July 1967.

COOPER, CHESTER L. *The Lost Crusade: America in Vietnam.* New York: Dodd, Mead, 1970.

COOPER, CHESTER L., ET. AL. *The American Experience With Pacification in Vietnam.* Vol. 1: *An Overview of Pacification.* Arlington, Va.: Institute for Defense Analysis, Report R-185, 1972.

DEPARTMENT OF DEFENSE. *U.S.-Vietnam Relations.* Washington, D.C.: U.S. Government Printing Office, 1971.

DONNELL, JOHN C. "Politics in South Vietnam: Doctrines of Authority in Conflict." Doctoral dissertation, University of California at Berkeley, 1964.

DUNCANSON, DENNIS J. *Government and Revolution in Vietnam.* New York: Oxford University Press, 1968.

FALL, BERNARD. *The Two Vietnams.* New York: Praeger, 1963.

ELLIOT, DAVID W. P., AND STEWART, W. A. *Pacification and the VC System in Dinh Tuong.* Santa Monica, Calif.: The Rand Corporation Collection, RM-5708 ISA/ARPA, January 1969.

FITZGERALD, FRANCES. *Fire in the Lake.* Boston: Little, Brown, 1972.

HALBERSTAM, DAVID. *The Best and the Brightest.* New York: Random House, 1972.

HAVRON, M. DOAN, ET. AL. *Constabulary Capabilities for Low-level Conflict.* MacLean, Va.: Human Sciences Research, Inc., HSR-RR-69/1-Se, April 1969.

HOSMER, STEPHEN T. *Viet Cong Repression and its Implications for the Future.* Santa Monica Calif.: The Rand Corporation Collection, R-475/1-ARPA, May 1970.

KOCH, JEANNETTE A. *The Chieu Hoi Program in South Vietnam,* Santa Monica, Calif.: The Rand Corporation Collection, R-1172/1-ARPA, May 1975.

KOMER, ROBERT W. *Bureaucracy Does its Thing: Institutional Constraints on U.S.-GVN Performance in Vietnam,* Santa Monica, Calif.: The Rand Corporation Collection, R-967-ARPA, August 1972.

LACOUTURE, JEAN. *Ho Chi Minh: A Political Biography.* New York: Random House, 1968.

MCALLISTER, JOHN T., AND MUS, PAUL. *The Vietnamese and Their Revolution,* New York: Harper & Row, 1970.

MECKLIN, JOHN. *Mission in Torment.* Garden City, N.Y.: Doubleday, 1965.

Ministry of Revolutionary Development, GVN. *11 Criteria.* Handbook No. 12017, Saigon, 1966.

Nighswonger, William A. *Rural Pacification in Vietnam.* New York: Praeger, 1966.

Oberdorfer, Don. *Tet!* Garden City, N.Y.: Doubleday, 1971.

The Pentagon Papers. Gravel Edition. Boston: Beacon, 1971.

Pfeffer, Richard M., ed. *No More Vietnams? The War and the Future of American Foreign Policy.* New York: Harper & Row, 1968.

Pike, Douglas. *Viet Cong.* Cambridge, Mass.: MIT Press, 1966.

Race, Jeffrey. *War Comes to Long An: Revolutionary Conflict in a Vietnamese Province.* Berkeley: University of California Press, 1972.

Sansom, Robert L. *The Economics of Insurgency in the Mekong Delta of Vietnam.* Cambridge, Mass.: MIT Press, 1970.

Scoville, Thomas W. "United States Organization for Pacification Advice and Support in Vietnam, 1954–1968." Doctoral dissertation, MIT, 1976.

Scigliano, Robert. *South Vietnam, Nation Under Stress.* Boston: Houghton Mifflin, 1964.

Shaplen, Robert. *The Lost Revolution.* New York: Harper & Row, 1965.

Tanham, George K. *Communist Revolutionary Warfare: The Viet Minh in Indochina.* New York: Praeger, 1961.

———. *War Without Guns.* New York: Praeger, 1966.

Thompson, Sir Robert. *No Exit From Vietnam.* New York: McKay, 1970.

USMACV (United States Military Assistance Command, Vietnam). *Phuong Hoang Advisors' Handbook.* Saigon: November 1970.

United States Congress, Hearings Before a Subcommittee on Government Operations, House of Representatives, 92nd Congress, First Session, July 15, 16, 19, 21, and August 1, 1971. *U.S. Assistance Programs in Vietnam.* Washington, D.C.: U.S. Government Printing Office, 1971.

———, Hearings Before the Senate Committee on Foreign Relations, 91st Congress, Second Session, February 17–20, 1970, *Civil Operations and Revolutionary Development Support.* Washington, D.C.: U.S. Government Printing Office, 1970.

Warner, Denis. *The Last Confucian.* New York: Macmillan, 1963.

West, F. J., Jr. *The Village.* New York: Harper & Row, 1972.

Westmoreland, Gen. William C. *Report on the War in Vietnam (as of 30 June, 1968), Section II, Report on Operations in South Vietnam.* Washington, D.C.: U.S. Government Printing Office, 1968.

Zasloff, Joseph J. *Rural Resettlement in Vietnam: An Agroville in Development.* Washington, D.C.: U.S. Department of State, AID, n.d.

Magazine Articles

Brodie, Bernard. "The Tet Offensive." In Noble Frankland and Christopher Dowling (eds.), *Decisive Battles of the Twentieth Century.* London: Sidgwick and Jackson, 1976.

Buchan, Alistair. "Questions About Vietnam." *Encounter,* January 1968.

Carver, George A. "The Faceless Viet Cong." *Foreign Affairs,* April 1966.

Donnell, John C. "The Long Haul from Villagism to Nationalism." *Asian Survey,* August 1970.

———. "Pacification Reassessed." *Asian Survey,* August 1967.

———. "The War, the Gap and the Cadre." *Asia Magazine,* Winter 1966.

Ellsberg, Daniel. "The Day Loc Tien Was Pacified." Santa Monica, Calif.: The Rand Corporation Collection, P-3793, February 1968.

Goodman, Allen E. "Political Implications of Rural Problems in South Vietnam: Creating Public Interest." *Asian Survey,* August 1970.

Grinter, Lawrence E. "How They Lost: Doctrines, Strategies and Outcomes of the Vietnam War." *Asian Survey,* December 1975.

———. "South Vietnam: Pacification Denied." *Southeast Asian Spectrum,* July 1975.

Jenkins, Brian M. "The Unchangeable War." Santa Monica, Calif.: The Rand Corporation Collection, RM-6278-1-ARPA, September 1972.

Komer, Robert W. "Clear, Hold and Rebuild." *Army,* May 1970.

———. "The Impact of Pacification on Insurgency in South Vietnam." In David S. Sullivan and Martin J. Sattler (eds.), *Revolutionary War: Western Response* (q.v.).

———. "The Other War in Vietnam: A Progress Report." *Department of State Bulletin,* October 10, 1966.

———. "Pacification: A Look Back . . . And Ahead." *Army,* June 1970.

Osborne, Milton E. "Strategic Hamlets in South Vietnam." Ithaca, N.Y.: Data paper, Southeast Asia Program, Cornell University, April 1965.

Popkin, Samuel L. "Pacification: Politics and the Village." *Asian Survey,* August 1970.

Race, Jeffrey. "The Origins of the Second Indochina War." *Asian Survey,* May 1970.

Salter, MacDonald. "Land Reform in South Vietnam." *Asian Survey,* August 1970.

Thayer, Thomas C. "How to Analyze a War Without Fronts: Vietnam 1965–72." Washington, D.C.: n.p., March 1976.

Thompson, Sir Robert. "Squaring the Error." *Foreign Affairs,* April 1968.

Laos
Books and Government Documents

Adams, Nina S., and McCoy, Alfred W., eds. *Laos: War and Revolution.* New York: Harper & Row, 1970.

Dommen, Arthur J. *Conflict in Laos.* New York: Praeger, 1971.

Goldstein, Martin E. *American Policy Toward Laos.* Rutherford, N.J.: Fairleigh Dickinson University Press, 1973.

Langer, Paul F., and Zasloff, Joseph J. *North Vietnam and the Pathet Lao.* Cambridge, Mass.: Harvard University Press, 1970.

Schanche, Don A. *Mister Pop.* New York: McKay, 1970.

STEVENSON, CHARLES A. *The End of Nowhere: American Policy Toward Laos Since 1954.* Boston: Beacon, 1972.

U.S. Congress, Hearings Before the Committee on Armed Service, United States Senate, 92nd Congress, First Session, July 14 and 22, 1971. *Fiscal Year 1972 Authorization for Military Procurement, etc.* Washington, D.C.: U.S. Government Printing Office, 1971.

———, Hearings Before the Subcommittee to Investigate Problems Connected With Refugees and Escapees of the Committee on the Judiciary, United States Senate, 91st Congress, Second Session, May 7, 1970. *Refugee and Civilian War Casualty Problems in Laos and Cambodia.* Washington, D.C.: U.S. Government Printing Office, 1970.

———, Hearings Before the Subcommittee on United States Security Agreements and Commitments Abroad of the Committee on Foreign Relations, United States Senate, 91st Congress, First Session, October 20, 21, 22, and 28, 1969. *United States Security Agreements and Commitments Abroad, Kingdom of Laos.* Washington, D.C.: U.S. Government Printing Office, 1970.

———, Hearings before the Subcommittee to Investigate Problems Connected With Refugees and Escapees of the Committee on the Judiciary, United States Senate, 92nd Congress, First Session, April 21 and 22, 1971. *War-Related Civilian Problems in Indochina, Part II: Laos and Cambodia.* Washington, D.C.: U.S. Government Printing Office, 1971.

U.S. Senate, Staff Report Prepared for the Use of the Subcommittee U.S. Security Agreements and Commitments Abroad of the Committee on Foreign Relations. *Laos: April, 1971.* Washington, D.C.: U.S. Government Printing Office, 1971.

ZASLOFF, JOSEPH J. *Pathet Lao, Leadership and Organization.* Lexington, Mass.: Heath, 1973.

Magazine Articles

BARNEY, G. LINWOOD. "The Meo of Xieng Khouang Province." In Peter Kunstadter (ed.), *Southeast Asian Tribes, Minorities and Nations* (q.v.).

PAUL, ROLAND A. "Laos: Anatomy of An American Involvement." *Foreign Affairs,* April 1971.

WARD, JAMES THOMAS. "U.S. Aid to Hill-tribe Refugees in Laos." In Peter Kunstadter (ed.), *Southeast Asian Tribes, Minorities and Nations* (q.v.).

THAILAND
Books and Government Documents

KERDPOL, LT. GEN SAIYUD. *The Struggle for Thailand.* N.p., n.d.

LOVELACE, DANIEL D. *China and People's War in Thailand.* Berkeley: Center for Chinese Studies, China Research Monographs, no. 8, University of California, 1971.

RIGGS, FRED W. *Thailand, A Bureaucratic Polity.* Honolulu: East-West Center Publishers, 1966.

TANHAM, GEORGE K. *Trial in Thailand.* New York: Crane, Russak, 1974.

U.S. Congress, Hearings Before the Subcommittee on United States Security Agreements and Commitments Abroad of the Committee on Foreign Relations, United States Senate, 91st Congress, First Session, November 10–14 and 17, 1969. *United States Security Agreements and Commitments Abroad, Kingdom of Thailand.* Washington, D.C.: U.S. Government Printing Office, 1970.

U.S. Operations Mission, Thailand. *A Brief History of USOM Support to the Office of Accelerated Development.* USOM/Thailand, September 1969.

———. *A Brief History of USOM Support to the Thai National Police Department.* USOM/Thailand, August 1969.

Wilson, David A. *Politics in Thailand.* Ithaca, N.Y.: Cornell University Press, 1962.

Magazine Articles

Bennett, Alan. "Thailand: The Ambiguous Domino." *Conflict Studies* 1. London: Current Affairs Research Service Center, 1969.

Casella, Alessandro. "Communist Insurrection in Thailand." *The World Today,* May 1970.

Morell, David. "Thailand: Military Checkmate." *Asian Survey,* February 1972.

———. "Thailand." *Asian Survey,* February 1973.

Neher, Clark D. "Stability and Instability in Contemporary Thailand." *Asian Survey,* December 1975.

China (See also Communist Documents, below)

Girling, J. L. S. *People's War: Conditions and Consequences in China and Southeast Asia.* New York: Praeger, 1969.

Ho, Ping-ti, and Tsou, Tang, eds. *China in Crisis.* Chicago: University of Chicago Press, 1968.

Johnson, Chalmers. *Peasant Nationalism and Communist Power.* Stanford, Calif.: Stanford University Press, 1962.

———. "Chinese Communist Leadership and Mass Response." In Ping-ti Ho and Tang Tsou (eds.), *China in Crisis,* vol. 1 (q.v.).

Rice, Edward. *Mao's Way.* Berkeley: University of California Press, 1972.

Taylor, Jay. *China and Southeast Asia.* New York: Praeger, 1974.

Latin America

Davis, Jack. "Political Violence in Latin America." *Adelphi Papers,* no. 85. London: International Institute for Strategic Studies, 1972.

Einaudi, Luigi R. "Peruvian Military Relations with the U.S." Santa Monica, Calif.: The Rand Corporation Collection, P-4389, June 1970.

———. and Stepan, Alfred C., III. *Latin American Institutional Development: Changing Military Perspectives in Peru and Brazil.* Santa Monica, Calif.: The Rand Corporation Collection, R-586-DOS, April 1971.

Gall, Norman. "Peru's Misfired Guerilla Campaign." *The Reporter,* January 26, 1967.

GEORGETOWN RESEARCH PROJECT. *Castro-Communist Insurgency in Venezuela.* Alexandria, Va.: Atlantic Research Corp., 1965.

GOTT, RICHARD. *Guerilla Movements in Latin America.* Garden City, N.Y.: Doubleday, 1971.

JAMES, DANIEL, ED. *The Complete Bolivian Diaries of Che Guevara and Other Captured Documents,* New York: Stein & Day, 1968.

MAULLIN, RICHARD L. *Soldiers, Guerillas and Politics in Colombia.* Santa Monica, Calif.: The Rand Corporation Collection, R-630-ARPA, December 1971.

RONFELDT, DAVID F., AND EINAUDI, LUIGI R. *Internal Security and Military Assistance to Latin America in the 1970's.* Santa Monica, Calif.: The Rand Corporation Collection, R-924-ISA, December 1971.

THOMAS, HUGH. *Cuba or The Pursuit of Freedom.* London: Eyre & Spottiswoode, 1971.

U.S. Congress, Hearings Before the Subcommittee on Western Hemisphere Affairs of the Committee on Foreign Relations, United States Senate, 91st Congress, First Session, June 24, 1969. *U.S. Military Policies and Programs in Latin America.* Washington, D.C.: U.S. Government Printing Office, 1969.

VEGA, LUIS MERCIER. *Guerillas in Latin America: The Technique of the Counterstate,* New York: Praeger, 1969.

OTHER AREAS OF INTEREST

BASHORE, MAJOR BOYD T. "Dual Strategy for Limited War." In Franklin Mark Osanka (ed.), *Modern Guerilla Warfare* (q.v.).

CHANDLER, GEOFFREY. *The Divided Land: An Anglo-Greek Tragedy.* New York: St. Martin's, 1959.

CLUTTERBUCK, BRIG. RICHARD L. *The Long, Long War.* New York: Praeger, 1966.

KOMER, ROBERT W. *The Malayan Emergency in Retrospect: Organization of the Successful Counterinsurgency Effort.* Santa Monica, Calif.: The Rand Corporation Collection, R-957-ARPA, February 1972.

LANSDALE, MAJ. GEN. EDWARD G. *In the Midst of Wars.* New York: Harper & Row, 1972.

MURRAY, J. C. "The Anti-Bandit War in Greece." In Lt. Col. T. N. Greene, (ed.) *The Guerilla and How to Fight Him* (q.v.).

O'BALLANCE, EDGAR. *Malaya: The Communist Insurgent War, 1940–1960,* London: Faber and Faber, 1966.

PAPAGOS, FIELD MARSHALL ALEXANDER. "Guerilla Warfare." In Franklin Mark Osanka (ed.), *Modern Guerilla Warfare* (q.v.).

PARET, PETER. *French Revolutionary Warfare from Indochina to Algeria.* New York: Praeger, 1964.

PYE, LUCIEN W. *Guerilla Communism in Malaya.* Princeton, N.J.: Princeton University Press, 1957.

ROMULO, CARLOS P., AND GRAY, MARVIN M. *The Magsaysay Story.* New York: John Day, 1956.

SCAFF, ALVIN H. *The Philippine Answer to Communism.* Stanford, Calif.: Stanford University Press, 1955.

VALERIANO, COL. NAPOLEON D., AND BOHANNON, LT. COL. CHARLES T. R. *Counter-Guerilla Operations: The Philippine Experience.* New York: Praeger, 1962.

WAINHOUSE, LT. COL. EDWARD P. "Guerilla War in Greece, 1946–49: A Case Study." In Franklin Mark Osanka (ed.), *Modern Guerilla Warfare* (q.v.).

Communist Statements and Documents

DEBRAY, REGIS. *Revolution in the Revolution? Armed Struggle and Political Struggle in Latin America.* New York: Monthly Review Press, 1967.

Library of Congress, Legislative Reference Service. "Khruschchev's Speech of January 6, 1961, A Summary and Interpretive Analysis." 87th Congress, First Session, Document No. 14. Washington, D.C.: U.S. Government Printing Office, 1961.

LIN PIAO. "Long Live the Victory of People's War." *Peking Review,* September 3, 1965.

MALLIN, JAY, ED. *Che Guevara on Revolution—A Documentary Overview.* Coral Gables, Fla.: University of Miami Press, 1969.

MAO TSE-TUNG. *Mao Tse-tung: An Anthology of His Writings.* Edited by Ann Freemantle. New York: Mentor, 1971.

———. *Basic Tactics.* Edited and translated by Stuart R. Schram. New York: Praeger, 1966.

———. *Selected Works.* Vol. 1 and 2. Peking: Foreign Languages Press, 1965.

POMEROY, WILLIAM J., ED. *Guerilla Warfare and Marxism.* New York: International Publishers, 1968.

TRUONG CHINH. *The Resistance Will Win.* In Bernard Fall (ed.), *Primer for Revolt: The Communist Takeover in Vietnam.* New York: Praeger, 1963.

Two Communist Manifestos. Edited by Charles Burton Marshall. Washington, D.C.: The Washington Center of Policy Research, 1961.

VO NGUYEN GIAP. *The Banner of People's War: The Party's Military Line.* New York: Praeger, 1970.

———. *People's War, People's Army.* New York: Bantam, 1962.

Index

Index

★ ★ ★